# Beyond Post-Traumatic Stress

# Beyond Post-Traumatic Stress

## Homefront Struggles WITH THE Wars on Terror

**Sarah Hautzinger** AND **Jean Scandlyn**

Left
Coast
Press
inc.

WALNUT CREEK
CALIFORNIA

2084111

Left Coast Press, Inc. is committed to preserving ancient forests and natural resources. We elected to print this title on 30% post consumer recycled paper, processed chlorine free. As a result, for this printing, we have saved:

3 Trees (40' tall and 6-8" diameter)
1 Million BTUs of Total Energy
223 Pounds of Greenhouse Gases
1,211 Gallons of Wastewater
81 Pounds of Solid Waste

Left Coast Press, Inc. made this paper choice because our printer, Thomson-Shore, Inc., is a member of Green Press Initiative, a nonprofit program dedicated to supporting authors, publishers, and suppliers in their efforts to reduce their use of fiber obtained from endangered forests.

For more information, visit www.greenpressinitiative.org

Environmental impact estimates were made using the Environmental Defense Paper Calculator. For more information visit: www.papercalculator.org.

Left Coast Press, Inc.
1630 North Main Street, #400
Walnut Creek, CA 94596
www.LCoastPress.com

ISBN 978-1-61132-365-8 hardback
ISBN 978-1-61132-366-5 paperback
ISBN 978-1-61132-367-2 institutional eBook
ISBN 978-1-61132-733-5 consumer eBook


Library of Congress Cataloging-in-Publication Data:
Hautzinger, Sarah J., 1963-
Beyond post-traumatic stress: homefront struggles with the wars on terror / Sarah Hautzinger and Jean Scandlyn.
     pages cm
Includes bibliographical references and index.
ISBN 978-1-61132-365-8 hardback —
ISBN 978-1-61132-366-5 paperback —
ISBN 978-1-61132-367-2 institutional eBook —
ISBN 978-1-61132-733-5 consumer eBook —
1. Post-traumatic stress disorder. 2. Post-traumatic stress disorder—Patients—United States. 3. Veterans—Mental health—United States. 4. Iraq War, 2003-2011—Psychological aspects. 5. Afghan War, 2001—Psychological aspects. 6. War on Terrorism, 2001-2009—Psychological aspects. I. Scandlyn, Jean. II. Title.
RC552.P67H38 2013
616.85ʹ21—dc23
                         2013036337

Printed in the United States of America

∞ ™ The paper used in this publication meets the minimum requirements of American National Standard for Information Sciences—Permanence of Paper for Printed Library Materials, ANSI/NISO Z39.48—1992.

Cover Image: *Glory Girl* by Laura BenAmots,
           from Battle Portraits Series (battleportraits.com).
Cover design by Lisa Devenish
Text design by Margery Cantor

# CONTENTS

# LIST OF ILLUSTRATIONS

# PREFACE

hen soldiers return to the United States from the wars in Iraq and Afghanistan, they bring more than medals, battle stories, and visible wounds with them. The unseen effects from their experiences—combat stress and moral injuries, depression and suicide, substance abuse, and higher propensities for violence—ripple through the lives of combat veterans, their families, friends, and wider communities for years to come. Ideally, as part of processing all this, conversations and stories ripple outward as well. Stories, yes, about patrols and hits and battles in "theater," as soldiers call the places to which they deploy. But just as important to hear are stories about what happened relatively "off-stage," at home, about sacrifices made, about discovering new breaking points, and about mustering new strengths. This book chases those ripples, following the journey of a team of anthropologists over four years of fieldwork.

As ethnographers, we undertake writing a kind of "history in the making," a local story of soldiers coming home from war zones, and therefore inflected by regional, national, and global forces. We ask how those struggling after deployments are understood, both institutionally and in community, and give special attention to frameworks like "combat stress" and post-traumatic stress disorder (PTSD). In turn, we follow ways in which these effects radiate outward, drawing the community into their complexities.

We cannot stress enough how early it feels to attempt a written, collective accounting of how these wars play out at home. They are, after all, wars that in some sense are still unnamed, meaning that they probably still do not hold the names that history will eventually bestow as we settle into consistent usage (as with WWI and WWII settling long afterward). In this book's subtitle we refer to the Wars on Terror, a slight alteration of the military's GWOT—the Global War on Terror. For many Americans, the wars' official title appears to sit uncomfortably; it is not used in everyday speech. Naming a war "GWOT" may encapsulate some of the problematic open-endedness of fighting against terror, which is both a tactic and an emotion. The subtitle "Collective Struggles with the Wars on Terror," in the plural, captures some of the instability surrounding the very naming of the wars. In the rest of the volume we opt for a more neutral, perhaps place-holding term, calling them the "post-9/11 wars." Military personnel use OEF/OIF to refer to the Afghanistan and Iraq wars jointly (OEF refers to Operation Enduring Freedom in

Afghanistan, OIF to Operation Iraqi Freedom in Iraq). Writing in and about the present and recent past, we recognize, places inevitable blinders on our vision. How will history look back on the United States during the period of the post-9/11 wars? Will we be narrated as a martial force that took stands for the "freedom" that most American service members say they fight for? And what will be meant by freedom? Freedom to civil liberties, rule of law, and democracy? Freedom from terrorism, at any cost? Will we be narrated as championing greater global security and global freedoms? As enforcing the prerogatives of global empire?

After a decade of deeply controversial conventional warfare, the United States currently exercises more "surgical" (drone-driven) means of taking out adversaries believed to be terrorists. Many see surgical strikes as an alternative that should have been pursued in the first place, but they raise their own problems, not least that they are now increasingly used across multiple international borders. In the past decade, military, security, and intelligence sectors have easily tripled. Most tellingly, we write from a time and place where, while endless reporting and official diplomatic discussions are ongoing, much of this is not talked about directly, in American communities. Instead, in 2013, while the wars stretch in diffuse ways into the future and even as the United States is out of Iraq and drawing down in Afghanistan, most of the local stories we tell are about how we cope with the challenges war has brought to us and ours. How veterans come home, then, is at the heart of civilians' experience of war itself.

At the beginning of this project, we half-jokingly declared that we didn't want to venture into this research "without a clear exit strategy" (the military metaphors were rife from the beginning). But as can happen, the work expanded, both because of what occurred through our relationship with the army, and because of the nature of ethnography itself. Team members volunteered at Army Community Services and the USO (United Service Organization) facility at Fort Carson, interviewed spouses in their living rooms, volunteered on art projects designed to build community, and attended support groups for spouses and town hall meetings. Those opposed to these wars and to processes of militarization have had their hearing, as well, as we have attended meetings and protests against the war and the army's new helicopter brigade and its proposed expansion of training grounds in southeastern Colorado. Ethnography, the writing of in-depth interpretations of people or cultures—or in this case, a large social institution—is expansive in nature. It is the opposite of sound-biting; instead, it is thickening the description, complicating the questions we ask. The stories in this book move across many sites and contexts, drawing upon interactions circling from homes to battlefields to returning back home again. They unfold in the wake of repeated deployments, as families and communities welcome back profoundly changed individuals. By actively pluralizing the voices in the conversation, our hope is to offer a new framework with which to reckon war's impact.

We write well aware of all the uncertainties and limitations implied by the "fog of the present," compounded by "the fog of war," whether apprehended from near or afar. As with many ethnographic projects, this one has taken us in unexpected directions, on paths that at first appeared to be false turns but later turned out to be central to how individuals and the community were dealing with the effects of war. We have frequently asked ourselves what contribution ethnographers could make as journalists, psychologists, and others rapidly build a body of material of soldiers' and families' experiences and challenges. We have also come to value the time ethnography requires, how it enables us to recognize patterns and to reflect on and interpret experiences with a group of people or individuals over time.

Such questions fill us with trepidation and humility. We enter the labyrinth that is war's making well aware of the limits of any knowledge we can have gained; what we have learned is inevitably incomplete. And while we have tried to avoid polemics and ideology, this book contends with matters that are inherently political and emotionally laden. Our work is based in neither a clinical nor an empiricist framework; we make no claim to offer recommendations for treating PTSD, or for evaluating the effectiveness of varying treatment modalities or policy protocols: these are tasks for our colleagues in other fields. Rather than testing hypotheses, our approach is interpretivist, which in anthropology we understand as illuminating a specific time and place in all its complexity, with a humanistic orientation to varied, lived experiences. Our hope is that even readers at odds with particular depictions or interpretations we offer will nonetheless recognize our efforts to respect and honor those mostly deeply touched by war.

As semi-native (US citizens but nonmilitary) coauthors, the "we" voice in which this book is written has various facets. At times "we" narrate fieldwork encounters that may have been recorded by just one or some combination of us—Jean, Sarah, or any of the numerous student researchers on the project—simply to avoid belaboring the text with unnecessary detail. Elsewhere we may speak simultaneously as authors and citizens addressing our fellows; we hope any tension between these roles serves both honest and productive ends.

Names in this book are mostly pseudonyms, and we have often altered identifying information. We retain the names of most public figures and of those community members who requested it.

# ACKNOWLEDGMENTS

We gratefully acknowledge the dozens of enlisted and commissioned soldiers, family members, local service providers, and community activists who have been our collaborators in so many facets of this work. We refrain thanking many of you by name with some reluctance, but do so to protect your privacy and uphold confidentiality agreements. Our gratitude and admiration could not be more heartfelt.

Immeasurable thanks go to our students, for a profound aspect of this work has been watching them engage, as junior fieldworkers, with their often same-age counterparts who are service- or military-family members (and a few straddled both categories). We have learned shoulder to shoulder with them, watching them charter paths into "homefront struggles," each of us equally impressed at how intensely and urgently we were absorbed, discovering "military issues" to also be our own communities' issues. University of Colorado (UC) Denver graduates on the team were David Bayendor, Mike Brown, Jill McCormick, Tara Smith, and Kate Um; Colorado College thesis/research paper writers and/or interns were Giulio Brandi, Trevor Cobb, Andrew Conarroe, Julia DeWitt, Emily Faxon, Ben Felson, Victoria Frecentese, Joseph Glick, Angela Komar, Hana Low, Tara Milliken, Luke Parkhurst, and Stephanie Tancer. Additional student interviewers from the fall 2008 Community-Based Research Course (Army Microcultures and Combat Stress) were Sarah Andrews, Emily Havens, Anna Jackson, Molly Jankovsky, Elijah King, Caroline McKenna, and Megan Poole.

Works of scholarship bear the names of their authors, but they are the product of communities of scholars in dialog with each other. We thank the following individuals whose work and conversation inspired us: Evelyn Baleria, Andrew Bickford, Marilyn Cunningham, Cynthia Enloe, Max Forte, Gillian Feeley-Harnik, Roberto Gonzalez, David Havlick, Alison Lighthall, Catherine Lutz, Erik Mueggler, Sarah Mahler, Sidney Mintz, Katherine Newman, Carolyn Nordstrom, Dave Philipps, David Price, TG Taylor, and Heidi Terrio. Special thanks go to the four members of our manuscript review workshop, whose careful reading and critical insights made this a better book: Erin Finley, Kenneth MacLeish, Monica Schoch-Spana, and Anne Hyde, who also made the workshop happen. Chris Frakes's editing of an early draft of the manuscript was indispensable.

At Colorado College, Tess Powers guided our funding search with competent hands. The Anthropology, Collaborative for Community Engagement, and Feminist and Gender Studies programs provided home berths in important ways. Both at the college and in the wider Colorado Springs community, many brought support for our work, humor, and conversations that mattered: Joe Barrera, Laura BenAmots, Jessica Copeland, Bruce Coriell, Connie Dudgeon, John Gould, Jennifer Hampton, Steve Handen, Bill Hockman, Kate Holbrook, Mark Lewis, Jay Maloney, Amber Nicodemus, Jim Parco, Tomi-Ann Roberts, Nori Rost, Tamara Sherwood, Bill Sulzman, Jill Tiefenthaler, Virginia Visconti, Kathy Wade, Debbie Warner, and Tricia Waters each deserve our gratitude.

At UC Denver, we thank Carol Achziger and JoAnn Porter for their valuable assistance and guidance in preparing and managing the National Endowment for the Humanities (NEH) grant, and Laura Argys and David Tracer for institutional support for the project. Special thanks go to Debbi Main in Health and Behavioral Sciences, who provided constant support and encouragement. We also thank John Brett, Sharon Devine, and Sarah Horton for encouragement, valuable conversations, and reading of early drafts and conference papers.

As always, we would be lost without the assistance of Abby Fitch, Connie Turner (both at UC Denver), and Suzanne Ridings (at CC).

The project was funded with a collaborative research grant from the National Endowment for the Humanities, where we thank Lydia Medici at NEH in particular for her guidance. (Any views, findings, conclusions or recommendations expressed in this publication do not necessarily represent those of the NEH.)

Colorado College and the College of Liberal Arts and Sciences and the Department of Health and Behavioral Sciences at UC Denver provided matching funds. Additional funding came from Colorado College's Jackson Fund of the Southwest Studies Program, the Social Science Executive Committee, Faculty-Student Collaborative Grants, the Crown Center, and the Cultural Diversities Fund.

Jennifer Collier at Left Coast Press has shepherded this book to press with belief, humanity, and wit; we also thank Mitch Allen, Jennifer de Garmo, Michelle Treviño, and Jane Henderson.

Sarah treasures the love and support of Tim Ferguson, Jim Hautzinger, Marley, Alair, Andrew, Roxi, and Dorothy. She also holds close the memory of her grandparents, Jean Schadel O'Brien and Brigadier General John Gordon O'Brien, as well as that of their daughter.

Jean would like to thank Naomi Scandlyn; Thomas Scandlyn, a WWII veteran and Tennessee volunteer; Ann Scandlyn; and Andrew, Alex, and Randy Eppler for their love and faith in her and in the project.

Finally, the coauthors thank each other: for partnership, company, and wonderful walks and talks together.

# INTRODUCTION

## Sharing War: A View from Home

*A labyrinth is a symbolic journey or a map of the route to salvation, but it is a*
*map we can really walk on, blurring the difference between map and world.*

—Rebecca Solnit, *Wanderlust: A History of Walking*

"I'm seeing things like wives going to shrinks to get psychiatric meds that are *really* for their soldiers!" Jody Newsome, an army wife who also worked at Fort Carson with families of deployed soldiers, found such facts alarming and had sought us out in response. The soldiers, she thought, were wary of seeking help on record at Fort Carson for fear of what it would mean for their careers and their relationships with their "battle buddies." That it was more socially acceptable for nondeploying army wives to seek such medications in response to the stresses of holding down the home front was itself remarkable, something worthy of effort to be better understood.

Jody was one of Jean's social acquaintances. Because she had decided the problem was cultural—that "soldiers' *culture* makes it shameful to struggle"—she turned to us as cultural anthropologists, hoping we might work together with them to better understand stigma's role in creating barriers to seeking care. She introduced us to a battalion commander back from heavy combat in Iraq, that unit's second of two closely spaced deployments. He, in turn, invited us to interview a random sample of his infantrymen to explore how stigma or fear of reprisals in the "microcultures" of smaller units might prevent soldiers from even admitting difficulties, let alone seeking help.

Long-time colleagues who had taught and researched together, we (Jean and Sarah) had frequently discussed starting a project on the wars' impact on the military circles and wider community in the Pikes Peak region of southern Colorado. We decided to create a three-week, intensive course on combat stress and reintegration issues with 10 advanced anthropology students. In October of 2008, the group spent time at places ranging from lockdown psychiatric wards in Colorado Springs to a yurt in the mountains west of the city, ceremonializing with the shamanic-based healers who helped veterans retrieve lost soul fragments from yesterday's battlefields. The center of the project, though, involved three days of interviewing at Fort Carson, during which we spoke with 43 soldiers from a battalion of nearly 400. Little did we know on those days of interviewing that "our" very same battalion was already fast on its way to becoming *the* battalion locally distinguished for producing a disproportionate number of soldiers wreaking postdeployment havoc at home, including numerous murders. What happened next forms the unusual beginning of the four-year, team fieldwork endeavor upon which we base this book.

## The Interviews That "Never Happened"

The blinking answering-machine light announced six new messages. Five of them, it turned out, were virtually identical messages from the battalion's XO (executive officer), who had served as our principal contact with the unit, working with us to produce academic[1] and command authorization documents and arranging logistics for our meeting with soldiers. The messages implored that we get back to him immediately, and Sarah quickly dialed the major's cell. It was the evening following the third and final day of interviewing soldiers.

"Ma'am, where are you right now?" were the first words out of the major's mouth after Sarah identified herself. She said she'd just arrived home, and even explained where her house was, before asking, "So, what's up?" Her awareness of the privilege we had been accorded, and how tenuous our continued access to the post and its soldiers could be, left her cautious.

"Well," he paused. "We might need to get those surveys back, and all the copies. So, um, can you tell me where are they, right now?"

This was not what we had expected. Where to begin? Sarah affirmed our willingness and active interest in sharing the content of the interviews; it was part of our shared plan. She reminded the officer, though, that there were no written surveys to hand over: the research so far consisted of semistructured interviews, and sharing the resulting audio recordings was complicated. The agreement the battalion had signed on to, she noted, promised soldiers who consented to interviews that their identities would be protected, that commanders wouldn't know who had and had not been interviewed. So while we were pleased to share any useful content from this material, we could not do so ethically until the interviews were completely de-identified—a time-consuming, labor-intensive process involving at a minimum transcription and assigning pseudonyms.

What had happened to cause the battalion command to go from authorizing and effectively partnering with us in our interviews with active-duty soldiers to attempting to revoke permission and recall the data, all within just a few hours? In the days that followed, we were assured that battalion command had included their plans, in a brief for the higher-ups in the brigade, to allow anthropologists to interview soldiers. Perhaps it had not been read thoroughly, for the news somehow went unnoticed by officers preoccupied with next year's looming deployment to Afghanistan.[2] Though it is unclear what triggered the raising of alarm, it seems one colonel across Fort Carson got wind of the project, called the brigade commander, and asked if he knew what was going on in his own brigade. As soon as the brigade commander heard about the interviewing, he issued an order to immediately end the research. That the order came on precisely the day the interviews had been completed was as awkward for the battalion as it was fortuitous for us. Why the sudden caution? Pieces of a picture were starting to fall in place: ultimately, it would show that "our battalion" had produced a disproportionate share of the soldiers charged eventually with 14 local murders between 2006 and 2008.

It was still some time before we understood this. At the time, we began talking with brigade command: first with the brigade's PAO (public affairs officer), and later with the brigade commander.[3] The battalion commander was present at the first of these meetings, his recent admonishment for allowing the interviews hanging heavily in his boss's office. These were new assignments for all three officers, having had nothing to do with whatever baggage past units within the brigade brought with them, except to be held accountable, and respond as needed. The colonel never contested that our signed agreements to uphold soldier confidentiality meant we could not surrender the data. He did request that we submit a new proposal directly to him, requesting his authorization for "the research," but now with a focus on possibilities for future collaboration—and leaving in no-man's-land that the research that had already occurred had been officially authorized (even as a number of other officers across the post who had earlier provided support in writing for the research now retreated into a vague deniability we chose not to question). He also asked us to put in writing some of the assurances we offered about not publishing soon. Though the unit would deploy again without ever signing onto the new proposal, the series of conversations that ensued in the months and years to come would lay the foundation for a complex, sometimes uneasy, but also productive continuing relationship between this fieldwork and Fort Carson officialdom. But at that moment in 2008 only one thing was clear: behind the fences of the fort, it appeared, word had hit to batten down for a legal and media storm rising from soldiers' postdeployment behavior, and we had unknowingly slid in the gate just as it was slamming closed.[4]

Despite the brigade's collaboration with us creating vulnerability for the officers—"I told him we'll have to grow thicker skins," the PAO advised the commander on what working with us would ask—they shared our belief that this work could heighten their attentiveness to combat stress and reintegration issues, and continued to respect our autonomy. In return for refraining from publishing until command changed, which occurred in August 2010, we would later be permitted unparalleled access to shadow soldiers before and after deployments to Afghanistan, through "Battlemind" trainings, medical and psychological screenings, "Reintegration University" (with sessions designed to prevent, or educate soldiers about suicide, substance abuse, domestic violence, and depression), and later, at Family-Readiness Group meetings and welcoming home, memorial, and change-of-command ceremonies.

Part I of this book, "Soldiers Coming Home," eventually details the "media shitstorm" that engulfed the unit, but we work our way there slowly. First we listen closely to soldiers' talk from the interviews with the randomly selected group of infantrymen, before we knew the storm would break. Chapter 1 explores army responses to the stigma soldiers often attach to post-traumatic stress disorder (PTSD). Chapter 2 delves into the significance of soldiers' association with death, drawing on terror management theory to show how death pollution is managed. Chapter 3 details the local murders tied to soldiers in the unit; in chapter 4 we turn our attention to why and how PTSD has become the predominant expression of the suffering of military personnel and their families at this particular historical moment.

## Why PTSD?

For the first time, in the post-9/11 wars psychological injuries have taken center stage in the ways we talk about, digest, and engage with war and its consequences. In 2008, the RAND Corporation published *The Invisible Wounds of War*, a comprehensive report that named PTSD, traumatic brain injury (TBI), and depression as the three "signature injuries" of the post-9/11 wars, taking a toll on soldiers equal to or greater than physical injuries incurred in combat. The study estimated that one-third of previously deployed military personnel experienced PTSD, TBI, or major depression, with 5 percent suffering from all three.[5] Based on incidence alone, any of these three conditions could have become emblematic of soldier's postdeployment suffering. But TBI, an injury that is less amenable to treatment and has worse outcomes than PTSD or depression, received relatively little coverage in the media, especially in the wars' early years.

Instead, PTSD captured the public's attention. In most any conversation where the topic of returning soldiers came up, PTSD was mentioned in the first few minutes, serving as shorthand and explanation for the many difficulties they faced in these wars and on coming home. Martin Nunez, a peer mentor for veterans participating in trouble with the law, believes that "anybody that has been deployed more than one time has PTSD whether or not they have sought treatment or they believe they do." Journalists invoked untreated PTSD to explain domestic violence, reckless driving, and other distress veterans displayed following deployments. Stories about PTSD and its effects have filled radio, television, and newspapers throughout the wars. Building on Erin Finley's analysis of contemporary cultural influences on PTSD, which she calls "one shining fragment of the wrongs that veterans have been done by the military" (2011:9), we offer a new perspective on the contemporary history of the current conflicts by asking "*Why* has PTSD become the predominant symbol of the suffering of military personnel and their families at this particular historical moment?"

The American Psychiatric Association's (APA 2013) most recent definition of PTSD is long and complex, but its essential feature is specific symptoms or behaviors following exposure to a traumatic event or events that last for more than one month and cause difficulty in the person's ability to function in important areas of their life. The APA defines a traumatic event as "actual or threatened death, serious injury, or sexual violence" (APA 2013:309.81 [F43.10]). The person can experience the event directly themselves, witness it happening to others in person, learn about it occurring to a close family member or friend, or be exposed to extreme or repeated details about it; for example, "first responders collecting human remains; police officers exposed to details of child abuse." Symptoms include recurrent, involuntary, and intrusive memories of the traumatic event, recurrent nightmares, flashbacks in which it appears that the trauma is happening again, or psychological distress or physical reactions such as rapid heart rate. One soldier told us about coming home to Colorado Springs and realizing he was driving down the middle of the highway to avoid possible bombs along the shoulders. Another soldier, on temporary leave in Florida during a deployment to Iraq, dove off a rising escalator in a crowded shopping mall when fireworks went off outside, thinking that he was under attack. Persons with PTSD may avoid things that remind them of the event, withdraw from social interaction, have decreased interest in activities, or have exaggerated negative beliefs about themselves or the world. They may be hyper-vigilant, quick to anger or become aggressive, be reckless or self-destructive, startle easily, and have difficulty concentrating and sleeping.[6]

Although many view the symptoms of PTSD as universal biological responses to traumatic events in war, how those responses are interpreted, explained, diagnosed, and treated varies significantly across cultures and through time. The official diagnosis of PTSD, first adopted by the APA in 1980, represents the convergence of psychiatric conceptions of the mind and memory, historical responses to increasing mechanization of industrial society, and political activism in the United States following the Vietnam conflict. One indication of the cultural and historical aspects of PTSD in the United States is the fact that soldiers from the United Kingdom who fought in Iraq experience consistently lower rates of PTSD. While some of this can be explained by UK soldiers having shorter deployments and less combat exposure in Iraq, UK soldiers in Afghanistan had similar levels of combat but the prevalence of PTSD remained comparatively low. Lebanese anthropologist Lamia Moghnieh cites an American psychiatrist studying the effects of the Lebanese civil war who found little evidence of "psychic traumatization." This is not to suggest that the Lebanese did not suffer from the civil war, but that how they expressed their suffering did not necessarily fit the constellation of symptoms defined as PTSD. Instead, Moghnieh (2011) finds Lebanese engagement with collective, activist processes central to healing suffering after war, often directly related to rebuilding communities. In working with health professionals in Bolivia, Jean found that PTSD was something they had heard about in US media, but it was not commonly referred to even in emerging public discussions of violence against women. Numerous medical anthropologists have questioned the validity of applying PTSD cross-culturally.[7]

Thus to understand why PTSD has become such a prominent symbol of the post-9/11 wars in the United States requires a culturally informed analysis that takes into account how it has changed in the nearly three decades since its adoption. PTSD has gained broad public recognition and dominated discussions about distress from multiple kinds of trauma even as trauma itself now dominates the way we talk about and understand human suffering. We argue that PTSD serves as an "idiom of distress" that mediates and expresses indirectly social conflicts and problems that, because of differences in power and access to resources, cannot be fully expressed more directly. A key characteristic of idioms of distress is their inherent ambiguity: they comprise a variety of vague symptoms that can arise from multiple causes. Thus, as anthropologist Susie Kilshaw argues, PTSD may be best understood in the context of other war-related diagnoses characterized by unexplained medical syndromes such as Gulf War Syndrome and Desert Storm Syndrome.[8]

PTSD has also become the primary way for soldiers and their families to access mental health and supportive services. But successful treatment of PTSD demands compliance and standardization of treatment that may not adequately deal with all the issues of reintegration that soldiers returning from deployments face. As we discuss in this book, soldiers leaving military service—younger, lower-ranked, male service members in particular—return to a civilian economy as part of a group with the highest unemployment rates in good times and bad. Many young enlisted soldiers have only a high school diploma and limited work histories. Many joined the military because they didn't like or do well in school, so higher education, though paid for under the GI bill, may be an ill-fitting option for them.[9]

We recognize that depression, TBI, and substance use are each as fraught with tensions and complications as PTSD; we could have analyzed any one of them in the same way. But because of its dominance in discussions of the post-9/11 wars, we were invited by our army contacts to look at PTSD. We also realize that in focusing attention on PTSD, even with the objective of also "moving beyond" it, we run the risk of keeping it at the center of discussions of the effects of war. Many veterans object to the notion of PTSD or the presumption that post-traumatic stress is a disordered, rather than normal, response to experiences in war. This book's title acknowledges that tension; we do, however, refer to PTSD throughout the text, as this is how the term used in the public discourses we analyze.

However, we also offer an alternative way to view PTSD as embedded in the history of wars past and in the politics and economics of contemporary military organizations. In separating PTSD and treatment of trauma from issues of reintegration we hope to widen the spotlight from the soldier to bring out of the shadows the families and communities that have also suffered and endured and participated in these wars. In addition to the many myths of the hero returning from war captured in *The Odyssey* and *The Aeneid*, below we offer the myth of the labyrinth.

## Beyond PTSD

The soldier responding to a talk about how war was being understood from home, said, "Problem with PTSD is that it lets everyone put everything about the wars onto the individual soldier." From a society-wide standpoint, PTSD lets the rest of the nation off the hook.

We argue that recognizing and treating PTSD is a necessary, but not sufficient, response to soldiers' and communities' efforts to "come back" and heal from war. The reductive focus on PTSD in both popular and scholarly literature needs decentering. A narrow focus on PTSD too often sidelines attention to other injuries (TBIs in particular, in addition to depression and substance abuse); to soldiers' resistance to medical diagnoses as the sole pathway to reintegration and recovery; to the stress or distress that all those living closest to the wars experience; and to the healing of social fields, both domestically and internationally, damaged through the exposure to combat's inherent stresses and horrors. It is critical to separate PTSD and the treatment of trauma from issues related to reintegration that soldiers might experience whether or not they have PTSD. Neither should a narrow focus upon

PTSD stand in place of tracing the myriad home-based odysseys, which often only grow harder when veterans come back to stay.

This book's title, *Beyond Post-Traumatic Stress*, is therefore not meant to minimize the importance of combat stress injuries as an important reflection of the costs of war. Nor do we want to minimize the historical significance of PTSD in recognizing and legitimizing soldiers' suffering. Attention to PTSD in the media and from the public has spurred valuable research that has established effective, evidence-based treatments. Soldiers and veterans diagnosed with PTSD can access a wide array of services and may qualify for long-term disability benefits. Public acceptance of PTSD may have helped pave the way for increased attention to TBIs. As a medical diagnosis made by a health professional, PTSD has the potential to "end suspicion" that victims of violence and trauma, especially those suffering invisible psychological wounds, are not genuinely suffering, but malingering.[10] Rather, the title indicates the "both/and" strategy of the book: PTSD is one critical measure of war's effects on soldiers and their surrounding community, but this constellation of symptoms serves best as a starting place for inquiring about the effects of these wars, rather than the culmination of that search.

As our work proceeded, we found more and more people frustrated with the single-pointed focus on PTSD. A wife whose husband's TBI was so bad he was declared "terminal" feared PTSD was an easier, and more cost-effective, focal point for the army because prognoses and outcomes were better for PTSD than TBIs, most of which are essentially untreatable. Infantrymen expressed wild variability in their views of PTSD, from finding it an inevitable result of their degree of combat exposure to thinking most diagnosed soldiers were "faking it"; it clearly contradicted aspects of the warrior ethos that underlined individual will and discipline: "Never give up." Veterans increasingly suspected that journalists, other researchers, and activists emphasizing PTSD were using it as proxy for criticism of the war itself, implying that anything with these effects is best prevented.

The book "decenters" or moves beyond PTSD in other ways. We decenter the idea that the injuries of war are primarily individual, primarily medical issues, and instead insist on their social and collective dimensions, which are crucial to recovery, reintegration, and reconciliation with war's impact. We "decenter" the experience of war away from a single-pointed focus on the masculinized warrior-protagonist. We do so by introducing how war's effects play out in a broad range of settings, which here range from private, family-based sites to a broad array of public settings and media-based accounts. In invoking such a chorus of voices, those of soldiers' fellow citizens who are intimately caught up in being at war also become part of the story.

Part II of the book moves beyond not just PTSD, but also soldiers themselves by shifting the spotlight away from the battlefield to issues of reintegration. As our fieldwork engulfed sites all over the Colorado Springs region, we increasingly described the project as about "Deployment Stress," broadly conceived.[11] The army has expanded its programs to support the families of deployed soldiers, but we still know very little about how multiple deployments affect individuals and families who often stand outside the spotlight focused on veterans and soldiers. In chapter 5 we explore the limitations in human abilities to codeswitch, which in this context means the way soldiers and families must move between often radically different sets or "codes" of norms and behaviors as they undergo multiple deployments. Instead, we offer the labyrinth as better reflecting the complex paths that soldiers and families and community must trace in bringing soldiers "all the way home." In chapter 6 we examine how spouses' volunteer work, predominantly women's work, has been brought under the chain of command, becoming more imperative to military missions even as spouses have lost autonomy over this work. Chapter 7 paints the landscape of the proliferating number of providers of health, social, and pastoral services as well as community organizations who are seeking to meet the ever-expanding needs of returning soldiers and their families.

## The Post-9/11 Wars in Comparative Perspective

All wars have their singularities and distinctions, and the engagements the United States and its allies[12] undertook in Afghanistan and Iraq are no exceptions. Training "to fight the last war" may be a perennial problem, but from military perspectives, the Global War on Terror presents unique territory by any measure. Three particularities of *this* decade of American warfare stand out: the profile of surviving-but-wounded service members; the singular nature of the wars themselves; and the significance of the all-volunteer force (AVF).

The post-9/11 wars are set apart from prior conflicts through both the high survival rate of wounded and the unique profile of the injuries sustained. Colorado falls in the quartile with the second-lowest casualty rates nationally; nonetheless, standing at the entrance to Fort Carson, on the border between the military world of the post and the civilian world of Colorado Springs, looking at the eight sandstone tablets carved with the names of the 357 fallen soldiers who were stationed there, we sense the magnitude of war's costs and what it might mean for their home communities.[13] For these wars in particular, however, the impact is as much about the wounded as the dead. Due to advances in emergency medicine and field treatment of trauma, far more soldiers are surviving multiple injuries, which frequently include severe damage to the head, face, and extremities. In these wars there are 9.2 wounded service members for every service member who dies (compared with 2.2 to 1 for all other US wars from 1775 to 1991).[14] As a consequence, there are numerous survivors who face learning to recover or cope with injuries at the same time they confront reintegrating with family and friends. In addition, those able to work must retool their skillsets to find new employment. Contending with the legions of wounded service members promises to be expensive. According to the Associated Press, a record 45 percent of the 1.6 million veterans who served in Iraq and Afghanistan are seeking compensation for service-related injuries: well over twice the rate of Gulf War veterans (at 21 percent; Kane 2012).

We know that explosive blasts, largely from improvised explosive devices (IEDs), result in concussive events, any single one of which would take weeks to return to baseline rates. But as one wife of a soldier told us, "our military do not have the option" to recover from an initial insult to the cranium. "They get blown up, they go down the road and they get blown up again. I know guys that have been blown up two or three times in one day. On *one mission*. They come in, they're messed up, they know they're hurt and they get called out on another mission four days later."

The psychological and behavioral problems of the current conflicts are being treated with any number of psychotropic medications, and prescription drug use—and abuse—in theater and afterward have reached startling levels. The title of one article on the issue speaks volumes: "The Prozac, Paxil, Zoloft, Wellbutrin, Celexa, Effexor, Valium, Klonopin, Ativan, Restoril, Xanax, Adderall, Ritalin, Haldol, Risperdal, Seroquel, Ambien, Lunesta, Elavil, Trazodone War" (Senior 2011; see also Bray et al. 2010, Larson et al. 2012, and Levine 2010). The in-theater use of these medications is often "off-label" at the prescribers' discretion and based on the needs of the moment.[15]

The open-ended, uncertain nature of the post-9/11 wars poses a second area of distinction. Again, the inherent ambiguity of declaring a war on terror (an emotion) or on terrorism (a political tactic and practice) has obscured what mission accomplished, or ultimate success in either Iraq or Afghanistan would look like (short of removing all risk of terrorism, an impossible goal). What began in 1991 with President George H. W. Bush's call for a "new world order" in which "enduring peace must be our mission" took on a more sobering tone in 1999 with what many called a military "humanitarian intervention" in the former Yugoslavia under President Clinton. This shifting landscape of appropriate use of military force modulated yet again when, after September 11, 2001, President George W. Bush declared a War on Terror, and that those "not with us are with the enemy" (Douzinas 2007:3).

For many American citizens, haunting doubts spring from the stories emanating from places like Abu Ghraib and Guantanamo prisons, from Winter Soldier depositions, or NATO meetings where veterans return Operation Enduring Freedom (OEF)/Operation Iraqi Freedom (OIF) medals in shame and disgust, events that have themselves been profoundly distressing. The absence of weapons of mass destruction in Iraq alone, after an invasion based upon "proof" of their existence, configures the contexts through which Americans reckon with these wars. There is a sharp and conspicuous lack of consensus that we went to war only after exploring all other choices. The convergence of a professionalized, committed, and careerist all-volunteer force coupled with unprecedented growth in contracting, security, and intelligence sectors, creates a very different kind of nation than one committed to standing down after wars that were unavoidable. This alteration in American foreign policy renders many Americans tormented by the idea that we turned to lethal force when it was not necessary to defend and ensure our very existence. Many of the questions explored in this book relate to shame and guilt, or to anger and betrayal. How all of these feelings influence PTSD and postwar struggles at home cannot be understood without acknowledging the wider context of the contestable legitimacy and cost-benefit analysis of the wars.

For service members on the ground, the diffuse geographical nature of the wars finds them battling in low-intensity, urban- and village-based exchanges of fire, in which civilians can be indistinguishable from the enemy and where counterinsurgent combatants are typically not uniformed or aligned with a localized nation-state. When there are no clear battle lines, there can be no truly safe zones either. While only one in seven deployed service members in Iraq and Afghanistan are technically frontline combatants (the "teeth" in the tooth-to-tail ratio, where the other seven are "tail," providing support and services) the absence of clear battle lines means that supposed noncombatants, including women,[16] may find themselves in the line of fire or subject to blasts from IEDs (Bruno 2009).[17]

Since the Civil War, US home fronts have been physically distant from the sites of conflict. Global warfare takes on new meaning when families can often communicate with their soldiers via phone or Internet nearly daily. In the current conflicts, electronic communication has transformed the separation of deployment, bringing the conflicts closer to the families of deployed military personnel. This may overload families back home and create "a false sense of connection between the soldier and family; in reality, the longer the time away, the more frequent the tours, the farther apart they grow" (Arella and Rooney 2009). At the same time the general public is kept at greater distance, with coffins of dead service members not shown, news like the torture at Abu Ghraib prison only reaching the public through leaks, and Iraqi and Afghan civilian death tolls shielded from the average citizen. Soldiers and their families speak of "compartmentalization" as a necessary coping skill, to keep battle and home hearths in their places, and of building careful barriers, withholding news when necessary to keep worry and stress at bay.

The third characteristic of the post-9/11 wars is that they are the first large-scale, protracted engagements[18] fought and serviced exclusively by the professionalized AVF. Debates rage on about whether the AVF has disrupted or severed the social contract between the citizenry and the state (Fleming 2010; Krebs 2009), widening a cultural and social divide between civilians and military personnel. In a 2010 lecture at Duke University, then Secretary of State Robert Gates observed:

> *Indeed, no major war in our history has been fought with a smaller percentage of this country's citizens in uniform full-time—roughly 2.4 million active and reserve service members out of a country of over 300 million, less than 1 percent.*
>
> *This tiny sliver of America has achieved extraordinary things under the most trying circumstances. It is the most professional, the best educated, the most capable force this country has ever sent into battle. Yet even as we appreciate, and sometimes marvel at, the performance of this all-volunteer force, I think it important at this time—before this audience—to recognize that this success has come at significant cost. Above all, the human cost, for the troops and their families. But also cultural, social, and financial costs in terms of the relationship between those in uniform and the wider society they have sworn to protect.[19]*

Greater consensus exists around the idea that the AVF has enabled a more efficient and effective force (Rostker 2006), bringing a higher level of professionalism, combat-readiness and mission-flexibility, and discipline than in the largely conscripted forces from previous wars, as reflected in significantly lower rates of desertion, mutiny, and fragging (violence against superiors) than in Vietnam and in earlier conflicts (Cancian 2011).

As Gates notes, the costs have come mostly in the form of overstretching and overstressing existing forces. The Department of Defense created the AVF during a time of relative peace[20] in which the US military "downsized, outsourced, and privatized" (C. Lutz 2001:217). Thus, when the quick victory of overcoming Hussein's forces in Iraq led to a long and violent conflict, the AVF faced shortages of manpower leading to repeated tours of unprecedented number (Yingling 2010)—up to five yearlong tours for regular army.

Maintaining the needed numbers of troops in combat has also meant that the tempo of deployments has accelerated and dwell time (time at home in between deployments) has shrunk accordingly, often broken up with numerous trips away from home for training. Army officials acknowledge that shortened dwell time is associated with low morale and other problems.[21]

The army has also relied heavily on National Guard and reserve units both in support and in place of active-duty service members. These units make up 28 percent of the service members deployed to Iraq and Afghanistan, with 37 percent deploying more than once (O'Neil 2012). The fact that reservists deploy and return home in greater isolation, without the support and solidarity of active-duty service members, may contribute to their greater susceptibility to PTSD, which they contract at twice the rates (42 percent for reservists) of active-duty troops (20 percent) (Milliken et al. 2007).

In his speech at Duke, Gates also noted that skeptics' predictions that only "the poorest, the worst educated, the least able to get any other job" would join the military did not come to pass. However, his subsequent statement that "in broad demographic terms, the Armed Forces continue to be largely representative of the country as a whole—drawing from America's working and middle classes," doesn't tell the whole story either.[22]

To fill its need for new soldiers, the army must compete with civilian employers and colleges. When unemployment is low, the military is less competitive and the number of eligible, highly qualified young people willing to enlist drops (Warner 2012).[23] But the pool of less-qualified but willing recruits is relatively constant. In the early years of the war the US economy was booming, making recruitment harder,[24] so to fill their quotas for new recruits the army increased the number of low quality (LQ) recruits they could accept by lowering standards for education and aptitude scores (Kaplan 2008) and issuing more waivers for criminal history, drug and alcohol involvement, and personality disorders, among others.[25] This lowering of standards may have contributed to mental health problems and violence during reintegration. Thus the AVF relies disproportionately on poor and working class "young men of at least modest ability" who come from "disadvantaged circumstances, experience minimal connectedness to others, and report a history of adolescent fighting" (Elder et al. 2010:455).

By framing the AVF not only as a professional force, but a force made up of *volunteers* who choose to enlist, public rhetoric is directed, or even *mis*-directed, from recognizing the underlying economic forces that contribute to an individual young person's decision to enlist. Military service can and often does provide young men and women with a host of tangible benefits such as travel, education, training, and opportunities to "mature, learn how to work with others and gain self-confidence" (Pew Research Center 2011:1). Although young African American men and women have seen the military as a means of upward mobility (Kelty et al. 2010), the unpopularity of the wars in Iraq and Afghanistan may be changing this. However, these benefits are a powerful motivation for enlistment for white youth from working class families hardest hit by a changing economy, increased costs of higher education, and residence in small rural communities with few opportunities.

Young men who enlist in their late teens quickly surpass their civilian peers in income, enabling many to marry at younger ages and aid them in the transition to independence.[26] In 2009, wages for enlisted personnel corresponded to the 90th percentile of wages for civilians with a high school diploma, some college, and associate's degrees, and wages for officers corresponded to the 83rd percentile for civilians with bachelor's or graduate degrees (Department of Defense 2012:xvii).

Beyond class, enlisted service members may be viewed as regional, ethnic, racial, or rural draftees, as southern, nonwhite, and nonurban Americans have enlisted in the military in numbers disproportionate to other groups. This has meant the post-9/11 wars have created a different distribution, by class and geography, of the places deeply affected—and increased the places relatively unaffected—by being a nation at war.

## Terror Management and Stigma

What the military calls GWOT ("Gee-Watt"; the Global War on Terror) is clearly its own, very specific version of what anthropologists and psychologists have called terror management: it is a socially organized, culturally based response to a threat that triggers fears connected to death, and to one's own mortality. Our examination of war as opening up labyrinthine corridors at home is inflected by numerous other forms of terror, and its management. Fear for one's own safety, or that of a battle-buddy or deployed loved one, each implies its own dreads and horrors, as do events in combat, or agonies about the use of lethal force and its costs, particularly to innocents. Each form of terror is tied to its own deaths, real or imagined.

At home, we argue that these mortality-related terrors are often managed through stigmatization, or the branding of something that feels dangerous, as different or other. This branding serves to define, and to help contain and manage, the threat represented by the affliction. The forms of stigmatization tied to combat veterans—links with death, combat-based PTSD—are paradoxical in that, unlike most forms of stigma, the associated work and its performers are simultaneously lionized and sanctified. These processes are historically underwritten by militarized hypermasculinity (whether for male or female soldiers), misogyny, and homophobia.

Part III of this book extends questions about stigma and terror management at home into public and community settings cleaved by sharp social and political divisions. Chapter 8 explores ways that Colorado Springs is idealized by soldiers while also being a place where the impact of the military presence is controversial for many residents. How has the area's history of actively seeking military investment affected regional enterprises, schools, nonprofit organizations, and law enforcement? Chapter 9 inverts the angle on stigmatization, exploring military representations of civilians and civilian life as "flabby," unchallenging, and undisciplined. The exceptionalism and contempt in such depictions help further muzzle and disengage civilians, who are admonished that veterans' deployment experiences are incomprehensible, incomparable, and incommensurable with other experiences. We also present civilians who contradict these pernicious stereotypes, who are actively engaged in being a nation at war and with reaching across the divide to help veterans navigate the labyrinth. This section concludes in chapter 10, with accounts of public gatherings convened to promote military-civilian communication, from town hall–style meetings to informal dialogs. In these later chapters, we argue that the anxieties and fears intrinsic to warmaking fuel polarizing dynamics, enforcing walls between intimates, and rendering those once familiar as strangers. Facing wars' costs includes understanding the labyrinth at home as a project of social terror management.

## Coming Home, *Reintegration*, and "New Normals"

Homecomings are at the heart of soldiers' relationships to family and community. These include hopes that what happened over there can be left over there, that war does not have to be brought back home. However, it's clear that for many, at the very least, memories do come home to roost; combat-based PTSD is about nothing if not memory and memories.

Endless representations of *home*coming and *re*integration, however, are not without irony, when we speak largely of very young adults who often went directly from parents' homes into the most paternalistically supervised occupation imaginable. Soldiers stationed at Fort Carson are rarely native to the Rocky Mountain West, and many if not most will not have spent much time here as civilians, due to the deployment tempo over the preceding decade. "Home," then, for many is felt more in a nationalist vein, and "re-" integration misleadingly suggests reestablishing something that existed before, their integration, when that last looked quite different, largely in the form of adolescents for whom adulthood and separation from parents, family, and home coincided with joining the army.

A counterpoint to home and reintegration imagery is the way that, during the period of our fieldwork, 2008 to 2013, some in the military community used the phrase "the new normal" to sum up how many at home attempt to cope with the effects of war brought home. For a pacifist-leaning young woman falling in love with her soon-to-be soldier husband, this meant grappling with fears around loving someone who will be absent across multiple deployments, in danger, fighting, and at risk both of being killed or hurt, and of killing or hurting others in ways that may haunt him later. For army spouses, parents, siblings, and children, all of whom are their own kinds of "veterans" of multiple deployments, the new normal signals their struggles to accept a loved one returning from theater "a completely different person," as one wife we met concisely put it. For officers attempting to intervene in aspects of "warrior ethos" or army culture that prevent soldiers from seeking help for combat stress, a new normal communicates that old attitudes must change. How to do this, when the "never give up" element of soldier ethos may mean that succumbing to PTSD looks so much like giving up? How to return to a normal that these young people may never have had chances to establish? For soldiers and their families, then, the phrase "the new normal" captures their sense that what is considered abnormal for most has become typical for them.

## A Particular Place, Representing Many

Though this account digs into one American setting, it does so with awareness that any military site counts with manifold global and national interconnections to other places. Folks and the stories they carry in the Pikes Peak region have linkages across the United States and sweepingly beyond: to Afghanistan and Iraq, of course, but also to Germany, South Korea, Bosnia, Somalia, and the countless other places that due to duty tours and international conflicts they have been sent in recent decades.

Southern Colorado is but one of numerous American landscapes where sizable cities host sizable bases: the Virginia Beach area, San Diego, El Paso, Tacoma/Seattle (Figure 1). That said, there is nowhere better to explore reintegration challenges than in the city of Colorado Springs, dubbed the "Best Hometown in the Army." Fort Carson, the army's fast-expanding post on the city's southern border (and just one of five military installations surrounding the city), is now one of the country's largest army posts, and one of the named "Centers of Excellence" for addressing PTSD. Famous for "America's Mountain" Pikes Peak, the Garden of the Gods, and numerous other tourist destinations, Colorado Springs pilgrimages may include visits to the extraordinary chapel at the Air Force Academy, on the town's northwest side, or to Focus on the Family's immense "parachurch," just off the highway. Beyond "Focus," more than 50 additional evangelical organizations are headquartered here, making it a key focus for the conservative religious right. Regard-

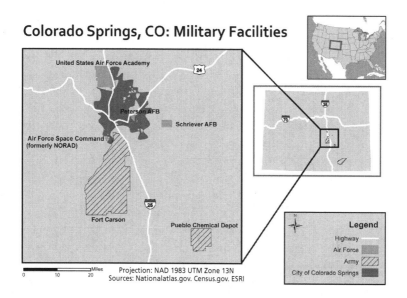

**FIGURE 1.** Colorado Springs area and military installations (map by Michael D. Brown).

ing partisan politics, with Colorado considered a quintessentially "purple" state (which can vote either Democratic Party "blue" or Republican "red"), much of the red in the mix emanates out of the Pikes Peak region, with Colorado Springs at its center.

The global presence of the US military and the deeply cleaved international relationships of the wars stand in tension with trying to ground part of a post-9/11 story in a particular place like Colorado Springs. We train our gaze on a specific location not to produce a regional or parochial account, but by way of underlining that these stories have counterparts across the United States, and on or near this nation's more than 700 military installations abroad (Johnson 2004; C. Lutz 2009). One goal, then, is to ask how local experiences align with the transnational "global" that typifies approaches to US military culture. This orientation refuses assertions that the army can be taken only as a whole, insisting that local actors—soldiers, family, and community members—experience its existence in situated, piecemeal encounters set in specific places and times.

### Spoken and Unspoken

In listening in across many sites, we attend both to what is said and also to what has remained unspoken, to silences and omissions. Most obviously absent in the conversations that inform this book is any semblance of balanced attention to the effects of the wars on Iraqi and Afghan lives, not to mention Pakistani, Yemeni, Somali, and so on, the other countries where this war unfolds. This imbalance, because it reflects what we heard, admittedly shapes this book. In community settings an unspoken orthodoxy around this appears to reign: we are at war, and embrace an unapologetic, single-minded attention on our own. It is not that the presence of the hundreds of thousands of Iraqis and Afghans affected by the wars is, or could be, wholly absent here. Rather, their collective presence is notably, significantly muted; it is both close at hand and walled off, seemingly inaccessible. Those who migrate between deployments and home are painfully aware of how small the world is, and in this sense the millions of lives battered by the wars are inextricably present in the complicated passages of all who survive them, combatants, uniformed and otherwise, and civilians alike. And, while the words of our subjects do occasionally wind around to witnessing or participating in the maiming or killing of children and other innocents, these stories emerge slowly, from memories ever present, threatening in the background shadows, as in therapy sessions whose content professionals later share with us (in broad strokes, without identifying details). In most exchanges, though, people avoid going there, having learned to do so as they learn the conventions of how we are admonished to talk about war.

Direct questions about what a combat veteran has seen or caused regarding killing are taboo, and soldiers anticipate them with fear. We rarely heard them, however, except as examples offered of crass and intrusive blunders. It is as if to speak openly of the symmetrical—or far greater suffering—on the other side of the elusive lines of these battles were forbidden territory, the epitome of civilian insensitivity that would simply dig into the wounds of veterans. Keeping such territory off-limits upholds a central assertion forwarded by veterans and military communities in many contexts: that deployment/combat/war creates experiences that are incomprehensible to civilians and both incomparable and incommensurable with other forms of experience. Because this book studies how this de facto censuring operates, it also reflects that prejudicial concern with us-and-ours, of avoiding talk of those we have injured, which itself is a testament to the mental and emotional predispositions of war.

## Story Lines and Myth

Embracing a humanistic anthropology brings readers into others' lives, through circulating their stories and thoughts, and then providing interpretive tools, for example, liminality and codeswitching (elaborated in this introduction), through which to better understand them. Writing in this way points us toward those aspects of anthropology, not surprisingly, most shaped by our sister disciplines in the humanities. For example, history, performance studies, and religious studies mutually inform our symbolic anthropological approach to both army ceremony and the ritualistic performances of grieving and reconciliations (Carden-Coyne 2009; O'Brien 1990; Paulsen 2005; Schechner 1985, 1993). Turner's notion of liminality—a state of being "betwixt and between" in time and space—provides a way of understanding complex PTSD as acute and transitional, even when it (paradoxically) becomes a chronic state or "liminoid" (Szakolczai 2009; V. Turner 1967, 1972, 1974), as in the soldier who knows he or she will deploy again and therefore does not "ramp down" from the hypervigilance necessary for survival in theater.

Liminal between-ness resulting from multiple deployments helps explain soldiers hitting the limits of "codeswitching." Linguistic approaches celebrate the ability of human beings to move rapidly and easily, or switch, between different languages and linguistic codes (Molinsky 2007), such as between professional jargon to informal slang, or from English to Spanish. Culture itself may constitute the process of developing and integrating multiple repertoires of behavior: for example, behaviors expected in the workplace, among friends at a neighborhood gathering, at a formal ceremony, or in a classroom (Mahler, personal communication, 2010). We began to use codeswitching metaphorically, and found that commanders readily latched onto it as shorthand for soldiers' having to switch between behavioral codes, such as between being a lethal soldier in combat and a loving husband and father on leave or between deployments. Soldiers also compared moving between "battle mode" and being home to turning a switch off and on. We argue, however, that the concept, though appealing in its simplicity, does not reflect the complexity of environments and social contexts where theater commingles with home through email and Skype, or soldiers alternating door-to-door searches with playing soccer with Iraqi or Afghan children. We also argue that many who deploy repeatedly in the current conflicts slam up against the limits of human flexibility and resilience in moving between such extreme and contradictory settings.

What kinds of stories did soldiers, their family members, and others in the community living closest to the wars tell us? Those of deployment veterans struggling to come "all the way home" certainly resonated, both for us and for our veteran consultants, with Jonathan Shay's compelling book *Odysseus in America* (2002), and others (Glantz 2009; Scurfield 2006; Tick 2005). Focusing primarily on the postwar struggles of Vietnam veterans, Shay draws upon Homer's epic *The Odyssey* as an analogy for the journey home from war often being longer and equally "embattled" as the literal battles themselves. Shay emphasizes how Odysseus possessed qualities that were fearsome on the battlefield, but could also "sow trouble" at home, even posing danger to his family and community (2002:2,143). Psychotherapist Edward Tick's *War and the Soul: Healing Our Nation's Veterans from Post-Traumatic Stress Disorder* (2005) shares similar concerns, but ranges more widely for "archetypal" story lines, touching broadly upon the practices of "traditional peoples'" (including Lakota and other Plains Indians, New Guinean societies, as well as Buddhist and Jewish communities) and their use of cleansing, ritual, and storytelling to take the stain of war off the warriors' shoulders, owning the burdens collectively by the wider culture, and thus readmitting returning combatants. These popular works speak so forcefully to those working with recovery and reintegration issues that counselors, community activists, and veterans themselves refer to them spontaneously, thus meriting inclusion in our account.

On the other hand, the epic journey storyline does not seem as useful for capturing and elucidating the experiences of the wider community: the family members, service providers, or activists so integral to reintegrating veterans and leading efforts to understand the wars' impact. Many who shared their experiences with us instead understood themselves as deeply entangled from home in the web of faraway wars, and this entanglement was largely vicarious, through soldiers bearing battles within themselves, unwittingly bringing them home. The sticky strands of war and its scars had, through highly varied means, penetrated from afar into domestic public settings, work spaces, and homes, gradually drawing them in. We started to wonder what new analogy might better capture the collective, community aspects of these wars. Were they, *en masse*, better likened to a web, a maze, a labyrinth?[27]

We easily discovered numerous preexisting associations between war and the maze. Just as the labyrinth in Ovid's *Metamorphoses* was built to contain the monstrous and hybrid Minotaur (Doob 1992:36), the image may apply to processes aimed at containing and managing the broken soldier who has turned dangerous to himself or others. Mazes are also easily likened to bureaucratic structures, as when journalist Aaron Glantz forcefully argues that veterans move from navigating battlefields to "navigating the maze" of red tape in the Veterans Administration and beyond (2009:37) and thus "trade one hell for another" (Glantz 2008). And game author Volko Ruhnke chose to name his board game "Labyrinth: The War on Terror, 2001–?" because the "term has come to mean a situation where there is no clear way out and no sense of where one is in terms of progress toward that goal."[28]

Labyrinths bring structure and definition to the notion of "the fog of war" itself, where endless uncertainties and obscurities override any ability to determine what is going on, who is "winning," or whether the war is "working." And just as veterans consistently affirm that those who were not there have no way to grasp war, labyrinths famously resist interpretation or facile "meaning-making" (Bemong 2003; Borges 1962a, 1962b; Danielewski 2000). Mazes and the beasts lurking within invoke fear, terror, and madness; they call up "incessant echoes of the past" and feelings of being hopelessly lost (Barrett 2011). Labyrinths invoke the uncanny, the etymology of which literally means "not at home"; being ensnared may feel perpetually "off" or not right, unable to find, or to feel, "at home" (Bemong 2003).

Further, labyrinths provide ways to talk about the wrinkles in space and time that our subjects face. Doorways and passages open up and close at unexpected turns, twisting back upon themselves and defying linear organization. Proper compartmentalization, keeping like with like, leaving what's over there over there—something given explicitly positive value as a coping tool during separations and thereafter—becomes impossible. Our subjects talk about daily contact via phone, Facebook, or Skype as both helpful and not, depending. One Iraq veteran spoke about the daily Skype calls to her husband who stayed home as agonizing: "Talking to him and having to pretend everything was great when I was scared *shitless*: it's like you have to build a wall *because* you have the means to communicate!"

PTSD itself represents a clear break in the linearity of time where past intrudes upon present, seeming equally immediate and real. The Argentine writer Jorge Luis Borges's notion of "a labyrinth that folds back upon itself in infinite regression" (1962a), inviting the wanderer to revisit, again and again, choices made and their repercussions, echoes the soldier reliving a moment in which he or she could have done something, or not done something, differently (see also Borges 1962b; Murray 2003).

Alternatively, the labyrinth may be a place of solidarity, a place where service members and civilians can share their engagement about war and its maddening, metastasizing passages. Labyrinths may have important roles for civilians with "clews" (clues) or skeins of golden thread, which they may offer to veterans as the mythical Ariadne offered Theseus, to help show them exits toward home. Here the "thread" may stand for willingness to listen and bear witness, with the idea that civilian presence as "audience" provides veterans with the opportunity to narrate, and make sense and meaning of, their own experiences and stories. Inviting the readers into the labyrinth, then, asserts an alternative to "going to the mall," whether out of protest, frustration, or simple disengagement, and to participate in collectively reckoning with the legacies of the post-9/11 wars.

If the labyrinth serves as a powerful, inclusive metaphor for these wars, a sprawling structure capable of encompassing radically plural viewpoints, what, exactly, is the labyrinth-as-metaphor saying or representing *ethnographically*? Simple binaries of home and theater; friend and enemy; teeth (combatant) and tail (support); civilian and military service member; appeal to our desire to find order and meaning, to explain and interpret. This is where we often begin talking about war. But ethnographic research allows for longer conversations in different settings. In these, a more complex picture emerges. Some enlisted soldiers wish the division between home and theater were simple, that they could just be soldiers instead of having to be husbands or parents when their spouses call them on Skype. Wives find themselves having to decide if their husband's outburst came from a flashback or from simply "being a jerk." Some soldiers find civilian counselors more sympathetic and helpful than military therapists. Thus applications of the labyrinth inform and complicate our approach, bringing in voices and experiences that contradict and erode simplistic oppositions and bring coherence—though of an intentionally chaotic sort—to the whole.

We view the labyrinth as a charter myth for reckoning with war as a fundamentally feminist intervention, decentering the Odyssean "mono-myth" of the masculinized warrior as the sole protagonist worth telling a story about.[29] A structure with innumerable, ever-shifting passageways presents us with something of such mindboggling complexity that it defies simple truths, or any individual's knowing or experience. In war-as-labyrinth we can imagine many stories winding together and apart, some of them on far-flung battlefields, but many too where the maze twists closer to home. The labyrinth insistently pluralizes: all who navigate it discover their own, unique pathways, and face varied challenges, stresses, and sufferings. For those truly ensnared, those living intimately with the unpredictability and terror war opens the door to, each faces his or her own minotaurs, or sources of fear and trauma, lurking around corners in the dark. When one veteran's wife says the most important thing she has learned across deployments is that "I have my own trauma, too, here at home," we offer the labyrinth as an inclusive framework, with space to accommodate the stories of so-called "secondary," supporting cast members as also central.

# PART I: SOLDIERS COMING HOME

## Chapter 1

# "PTSD = Pulling the Stigma Down"

*No one ever really gets used to nightmares.*
—Mark Z. Danielewski, *House of Leaves*

*I am not a fool. I am wise. I will run from my fear, I will outdistance my fear, then I will hide from my fear, I will wait for my fear, I will let my fear run past me, then I will follow my fear, I will track my fear until I can approach my fear in complete silence, then I will strike at my fear, I will charge my fear, I will grab hold of my fear, I will sink my fingers into my fear, then I will bite my fear, I will tear the throat of my fear, I will break the neck of my fear, I will drink the blood of my fear, I will gulp the flesh of my fear, I will crush the bones of my fear, and I will savor my fear, I will swallow my fear, all of it, and then I will digest my fear until I can do nothing else but shit out my fear. In this way I will be made stronger.*
—Mark Z. Danielewski, *House of Leaves*

On a bright, sunny April morning, we sat in an auditorium in the newly completed battalion headquarters at Fort Carson among rows of seated enlisted men and women dressed in pixilated camouflage army combat uniforms, sitting silently or chatting quietly among themselves as they waited for a predeployment training program. When the lead trainer concluded the introductory slide presentation, a man in his mid-thirties, who had a buzz cut and was dressed in khakis and a button-down shirt, strode to the front of the room. Soldiers sat up straighter or leaned forward, focusing on this man as he energetically paced back and forth before us, declaring, "The media tells you, 'War is going to fuck you up. You will come back harmed.' Well, I am here to tell you that war is the most adverse environment you will ever encounter, but you can come back stronger and wiser."

This statement opened the exercise segment of a training experiment for this combat brigade that would deploy to Afghanistan in a few weeks. The commanding colonel had embraced this new program, which promised to increase soldiers' performance, strength, and resilience during deployment. A professional athlete turned sports psychologist designed the training, which his for-profit company provided under contract to the army. The program combined a basic explanation of neurophysiology with meditation, visualization, breath-control exercises, and techniques from sports psychology. Enhancing their credibility and identification with active-duty soldiers, five members of the training team were ex-military personnel who had deployed to Iraq or Afghanistan. The program's creator emphasized the importance of stress and adversity, "We need stress in our lives—we cannot learn new skills without stress." He explained that the training would provide stress and adversity in a controlled setting so that they would be ready for "the real shit." "You must metabolize it [stress] so that it feeds you versus breaking you down. It's bad when you don't have resilience and it breaks you down."

The unit's commander had invited journalists and other public affairs contacts to the training, to show that they were taking active measures to address combat stress injuries. After receiving negative media attention for criminal violence committed by soldiers from this brigade, the commanding officer was understandably concerned that his brigade would return with as few mental health casualties as possible.

We begin our discussion of the army's effort to attend to post-traumatic stress disorder (PTSD) with this episode from our fieldwork because it took place prior to the brigade's deployment to Afghanistan. We have come to associate its emphasis on neurophysiological responses to combat on the one hand, and resilience, strength, and self-discipline in response to its stressors on the other hand, with the shifting terrain of discourse around these issues. Although military clinicians still provided trainings on recognition and treatment of PTSD, traumatic brain injury (TBI), and suicidal ideation, discussions increasingly included statements about soldiers' "normal" responses to war. Beginning with the brigade combat team's (BCT's) deployment to Afghanistan and expanded to seven additional posts in 2011, the army deployed combat stress and mobile behavioral health teams with combat units, teams designed to head off short-term difficulties during combat to prevent them from becoming long-term problems when soldiers returned home (Carabajal 2011).

This story illustrates one of the central dilemmas the army faces as it deals with mental health issues. The therapeutic and civilian communities widely accept the diagnosis of PTSD as a risk and consequence of exposure to combat. The fact that it is so widely accepted represents a significant achievement of Vietnam War veterans and their advocates to recognize, treat, and compensate veterans for the suffering they experienced. Yet, despite the army's concerted efforts to change the social meaning associated with PTSD, it remains stigmatized and problematic in the military. For Brigadier General Loree Sutton, who founded the Defense Centers of Excellence for Psychological Health and Traumatic Brain Injury (DCoE), it is stigma itself that is the major problem. The title for this chapter, "PTSD = Pulling the Stigma Down," comes from Battlemind, a program of the DCoE designed to reduce stigma associated with soldiers' seeking help for mental and emotional problems.[1] In our interviews, we found that many active-duty soldiers and officers resisted and challenged the diagnosis of PTSD even if they accepted it as a valid explanation for responses to the trauma of war. Instead, army personnel prefer to focus on "combat stress," a condition that has developed in parallel with the psychodynamic concepts that underlie PTSD, but that is more consonant with military institutions and culture.

## Warrior Ethos

A formative moment in this fieldwork came while sitting with the brigade's commander Scott Holmes. "We'll figure out how to deal with PTSD," he told us. "We figured out racial integration; we figured out integrating women— we're the army, figuring things out is what we do. And we WILL figure this out, guaranteed. You watch." One of the most interesting aspects of working in army settings with army personnel, particularly its leaders, is how frequently they invoke the concept of culture. Officers and mental health providers explicitly reference "army culture" and "creating cultural shifts." Whereas anthropologists view culture as difficult to define, multifaceted, and only one factor of many that determines human behavior, military leaders, like the commander cited here, generally take a more mechanistic or technocratic approach. Desperate to solve the problem of PTSD, they grabbed onto culture as something they might "operationalize" to solve it.

Like culture itself, the military is a dynamic social institution. During our fieldwork we have been struck by how experimental, even innovative, the army can be in some practices while simultaneously being very conservative in terms of values and norms. Because of its hierarchical structure and legitimated authority, the army can effect sweeping organizational changes quickly. In 1948, President Harry S. Truman issued an executive order that established equal treatment and opportunity for all individuals regardless of race, religion, or national origin in all branches of military service, and the first enlisted women entered the regular army. This order preceded the Civil Rights Act (1964) by 16 years (MacGregor 1981).

However, the military also shares US cultural ideas; for example, those that divide gender into dichotomous categories of male and female, men and women. In everyday life and social interactions, gender may be less rigidly divided today, with people accepting a greater mix of qualities and characteristics once identified as stereotypically masculine and feminine. Army personnel are trained to be very careful in speaking of "males" and "females."[2]

But the categories and stereotypes persist, and the military remains a highly gendered institution. The use of force and physical strength and the suppression of fear and emotional toughness are associated with men and masculinity and are highly valorized. Military occupations that require these qualities carry more prestige. So although infantry soldiers have the least status in rank and organizational prestige, their role in combat is more highly valued than those who serve to support them in clerical and housekeeping roles. Mutual stereotypes abound of the soldier with a desk job afraid to leave the protection of the base and the infantry soldier too dumb to stay out of harm's way. Soldiers also draw on public discourses about sexuality, gender, and power to enact and enforce this hypermasculine ideal, and this valuation persists regardless of whether a man or a woman occupies that role. One Iraq War veteran told us of several women soldiers who volunteered to carry the bodies of dead Iraqis, proud of their bloodied uniforms because they were visible signs that they had been near "real action."

The army's core values, "loyalty, duty, respect, selfless service, honor, integrity, and personal courage,"[3] which constitute a key element of army culture, remain relatively constant over time, but the expression and emphasis on those core values and how they are woven together at any given historical moment reflect political, economic, and social forces in the larger society. Recruiting ads are one reflection of changing public conceptions of military service. In 2006, well into the Iraq War, as the army struggled to meet its quotas for new recruits and the all-volunteer force (AVF) was stretched thin fighting on two fronts, the army launched its new advertising campaign, "Army Strong."[4] In the first Army Strong ad from October 2006, a movie-score theme that signals an impending battle builds in intensity as references to Webster's definition of "strong" and allusions to biblical passages from Ecclesiastes emerge on a black screen. Technology is ever present in the background, while soldiers, diverse in gender, race, and ethnicity, populate the foreground. In contrast to the earlier ads, the Army Strong campaign transforms soldiers from civilians to warriors. Several of the ads feature recitation of the army's core values as stated in the Warrior Ethos, the army's official statement of the principles a soldier should uphold. "I will always place the mission first. I will never accept defeat. I will never quit. I will never leave a fallen comrade."[5]

As part of its definition of strength, the new campaign incorporated the phrase "the strength to get *yourself over*," voiced over the image of a soldier climbing over a wall on an obstacle course, and "the strength to get *over yourself*," voiced over an image of a soldier reaching down to help another soldier over the same wall [emphasis ours]. From the first day of basic training through discharge, the military fosters team spirit or *esprit de corps*, camaraderie, and strong bonds among soldiers. Commitment to the group and its mission over individual needs, even when a soldier is injured, and accepting responsibility for others—"I will never leave a fallen comrade behind"—are actively fostered in military drills and training.

Whereas officers and politicians may invoke freedom and democracy to motivate their citizens to war, soldiers say that in the midst of a battle they fight for their fellow soldiers, their buddies. Soldier Wilson Lemmons said, "Whatever the American government's agenda is, I don't care, but when we get there it's about taking care of each other and our mission to protect the people."[6] For the infantrymen we interviewed, this bonding was explicitly about heterosexual brotherhood, as their battalion's previous nickname, "The Band of Brothers," shows. These bonds are essential to getting soldiers to willingly face death, to be effective in achieving their military goals, and to minimize injuries and deaths. As Kelsoe Fitzgerald said:

> *I really do feel sorry for all of these new soldiers that we get . . . that didn't deploy with us, because . . . yeah, they're part of the unit, but they're not necessarily part of the group. . . . But us guys that just got off this deployment, we're real tight knit. . . . We're like brothers.*

As the commander stated, the army is all about solving problems, and its leaders recognize that merely setting out a statement of values will not necessarily instill them in its personnel. The warrior ethos is a core feature of basic training: it is implemented in tasks, drills, and after action reviews (AARs), and it is reinforced through the recounting of "historical deeds and vignettes" of soldiers who have lived and died by its principles (Riccio et al. 2004:12). Upon completing the initial values class in basic training, soldiers receive cards and a set of dog tags printed with the army values and warrior ethos (Rogers 2004). At Fort Carson, reminders of army values abound. At the first traffic circle past the main gate to Fort Carson, a large sign notifies military personnel, residents, and visitors that army values are enforced. A series of signs, each one listing one of the seven army values, lines the winding road leading to Evans Hospital.

## PTSD versus TBI and the Mind-Body Dichotomy

For military personnel serving in Iraq, and to a lesser degree in Afghanistan, exposure to blasts from improvised explosive devices (IEDs) accounts for 40 percent of deaths and 40 percent of traumatic brain injuries (Elder and Cristian 2009). An IED creates an "overpressure blast wave" that can reach a considerable distance from the site of the explosion to shear and tear brain tissue even when the skull remains intact. Among civilians, a TBI diagnosis is often made by correlating a careful history of the event and assessment of the physical forces involved with observed symptoms. This task is made more difficult among soldiers in combat, as they often experience co-occurring injuries related to the blast; for example, motor vehicle accidents, wounds from shrapnel or other flying objects, or blunt force trauma from being thrown against solid objects.

Many soldiers fail to report episodes when they lose consciousness briefly. In the confusion following a blast, soldiers may not realize that they have lost consciousness momentarily or may not realize they are confused or disoriented as they concentrate on securing the area and taking action. They may be shocked to realize that they are okay or only mildly affected by the blast, often feeling guilty that they survived while others did not. So they focus on their buddies who were injured or killed, minimizing their own possible exposure and injuries. Some clinicians advocate retaining the term "concussion" over "mild TBI" because they expect full recovery from brain injuries at that level. One of the difficulties with mild TBI or concussions is that full recovery depends on adequate rest following injury. Officers may be reluctant to keep a soldier off duty for the recommended month, and soldiers may not want to be removed from activity duty for that long. So even when a mild brain injury is recognized, soldiers, especially those in frontline positions, may not receive adequate rest for full recovery.[7]

**FIGURE 2.** The Hello Dorothy Art Collective created alternative versions of these common children's toys (photo used with permission).

The soldiers we interviewed considered both PTSD and TBI medical diagnoses that require professional assessment and treatment. They also differentiated TBI from PTSD. They defined TBI as a physical injury to the brain resulting from exposure to physical force, such as an IED blast, in contrast to PTSD, which they defined as a mental or psychological condition. Their definitions and statements about TBI describe both the source of the trauma and its effects on the brain in specific and often vivid terms and, in general, match medical definitions of the injury. In comparison, soldiers' descriptions of PTSD are generalized and vague. Reinforcing the contrasting physical and mental sources of these conditions, soldiers see TBI as something for which reliable medical tests exist, as soldier Winston Wells commented: "TBI is actual physical trauma to your brain. PTSD is more of a mental thing, still in your head but you can't really do an MRI to see PTSD." Or as Scott Roberts explained it, "TBI is where your brain actually completely gets jarred in your skull, or your nervous system detaches from your brain and you start losing mobility. So it's more of a physical thing. PTSD is more of a mental condition." Clearly these soldiers use the mind-body dichotomy to understand and explain TBI and PTSD.[8]

The dichotomy between mind and body is significant because it affects how Americans attach social meaning to illnesses and their diagnosis and treatment. Biomedicine[9] privileges the physical body as the site of illness and the focus of treatment. We understand the body through science, and science is based on understanding the material world, which includes our physical bodies. Thus, illnesses or trauma with a direct and observable or identifiable physical and material source or cause are "real" in a way that mental and cognitive illnesses and trauma may not, or cannot, be. As neuroscience advances our understanding of the physical nature and functions of the brain and nervous system, mind and body converge and disorders previously considered "in the mind" or in a person's behavior become based in the body as well. This is the case with TBI. Whereas physicians and lay people have long recognized the physical effects of major trauma to the head, the association of milder and repeated head trauma with behavioral, emotional, and cognitive changes is relatively new. Although the public has been aware of cases such as boxer Mohammad Ali's trauma-induced Parkinson's disease for decades, only recently has attention to repeated mild TBI emerged as a major concern to the public and health care professionals, first in the area of contact sports and subsequently in relationship to the vast number of repeated blast injuries soldiers have suffered in Iraq and Afghanistan (Nocera 2012).

Although the effects of mild TBI can be deeply distressing and stigmatizing in civilian settings, many soldiers view it as an inevitable and natural consequence of head injury and therefore as less stigmatizing than PTSD. Moreover, because TBI is a very common injury among soldiers deployed to Iraq and Afghanistan, many of the soldiers we interviewed had direct experience with it. So despite advances in neuroscience, the mind-body dichotomy persists, and for the meaning PTSD holds for many soldiers, those conditions defined as primarily mental or cognitive remain somehow less "real" than those located in the body.

As Tucker Watson said, "There is a *huge* difference between TBI and PTSD. . . . Oh, I have a mental disorder. *You don't want to hear that.* That puts a stigma on it." Or as Bradley Kay, whose wife urged him to talk to someone about his anger, said, "Well, I went to go talk to somebody, and I kind of got ridiculed for that by my whole company." Ironically, PTSD is one of the few mental health conditions that is not heavily stigmatized in the general US population, perhaps because for civilians it confers individual distinction; that is, the person has been the victim of a singular, extreme event. Just as work in the military is highly gendered, injuries are similarly gendered. Physical injuries, which result from engaging in the masculine behaviors of a warrior, are valorized and counted as casualties in contrast to mental, emotional, and spiritual injuries, which, if even acknowledged as injuries, are feminized, dismissed, uncounted, and rendered invisible.[10]

## PTSD: Is There a There, There?

Anthropologist Allan Young (1995), in *The Harmony of Illusions*, argues that framing the cluster or symptoms—nightmares; flashbacks; feeling revved up or irritable, numb, or anxious; avoiding reminders of the traumatic event or situation; and intrusive memories—as PTSD is a culturally constructed diagnosis, "glued together by the practices, technologies, and narratives with which it is diagnosed, studied, treated, and represented by the various interests, institutions and moral arguments that mobilized these efforts and resources" (Young 1995:5). Young does not deny the reality of the symptoms or the suffering of PTSD; rather, he seeks to understand the social, historical, and cultural dynamics that shape the experience for soldiers and the clinicians who treat them. Most clinicians, though this is changing, consider PTSD a chronic condition, one that a person can learn to live with and manage, but that might not ever disappear entirely. As philosopher Ian Hacking (1995) has observed, a diagnosis, especially of a chronic illness, is a way of classifying people and affects how we think of ourselves, value ourselves, and remember our past. "This in turn generates a looping effect, because people of the kind [to have an illness] behave differently and so are different" (Hacking 1995:369).

Before analyzing the institutional processes that define PTSD and its treatment, it is critical to understand how those most affected by PTSD—soldiers of all ranks and in all areas of the military—experience it. Our interviews with soldiers provide ample material for understanding why PTSD is more stigmatized than TBI, particularly for active-duty soldiers. Contrasting views on PTSD demonstrate how, for so many soldiers, there's a great deal of uncertainty about whether "there's a there, there" when it comes to combat-based PTSD.

Bradley Kay was at a breaking point when he returned home from Iraq for a two-week leave. He remembers: "They'd shoot at us and then run away. Or we'd get blown up and no one would be around. So I got to the point where I was like, next time I get blown up or shot at, I'm just gonna shoot anybody that's near to me."

Kay had an earlier record of drug abuse: mostly cocaine and ecstasy. He'd turned himself in after redeploying from Iraq the first time and was demoted as a result. That record may have helped the army pick up on his state of mind during his leave on his second tour. As a result, instead of spending two weeks in Colorado resting, he spent three months in treatment for PTSD. During the time he was kept back, a truck that he would have been riding in was attacked. Five of the guys from his platoon were killed instantly and 11 more were injured. "So when I did get back after three months, they kind of blamed me," he told us. "'Cause I wasn't there . . . . When I got back I was like, 'Hey, how's it going,' and they didn't even look at me. They just walked on by."

Kay's story offers just one, rather extreme example of why therapeutic responses to combat PTSD create numerous contradictions and irreconcilables from the standpoint of active-duty infantrymen. Treatment literally pulled him away from "being there for the guys," and he was viewed as succumbing to pressure when others persisted. As a result, Kay, in contrast to many soldiers, readily gave validity to PTSD as a way of labeling the constellation of symptoms he experienced.

Tucker Watson, an infantry sergeant still mourning the fact that three of the nine men on his squad came home in caskets, voiced a contrasting view.

*God, I don't think PTSD really exists, to tell you the truth . . . . It is the fault of internal weakness—90 percent of it is dudes trying to get out, to not do deployments, and that is ridiculous. You have weak people in any part of the society. You have people who have psychological imbalances. That is not combat's fault.*

Tucker saw the behaviors associated with PTSD—sleeplessness, jumpiness, volatility—as normal, considering the territory. "It's REALITY stress, not combat stress." The first time he redeployed from Iraq to Colorado, "They tried to tell me I had PTSD because I was angry. I thought we were going nowhere in my first deployment—and we were! But it doesn't mean that I have PTSD, because I'm assessing a situation realistically." He felt that the emphasis needed to be on "get[ting] yourself recovered," to "overcome, overcome, overcome," as he repeated. In his view, framing PTSD as a disorder and a dysfunction prevents soldiers from calling on their own greatest strength to overcome hardship, to refuse to let down those counting on them, and to stay focused on accomplishing one's mission.

Kay's and Watson's perspectives illustrate contrasting perspectives on PTSD. We hasten to add, however, that the gulf between their relative positions is not actually all that wide. Both acknowledge the persistent association, for infantrymen, between PTSD and personal failure. At the same time, both recognize that in some cases soldiers might need help dealing with the effects of combat trauma and assert that the better the army attends to this, the stronger and more effective the institution is overall. Finally, both soldiers cite the specific circumstances—in these cases, anger and frustration over the effort in Iraq going badly—as critical factors in understanding their own combat stress.

The decision to seek or not seek treatment and the initial diagnosis are made in the context of social interactions (Hahn 1995). This is particularly true in the military, where a soldier must secure his or her superior officer's permission for time off for medical appointments, where a field officer can override the confidentiality between health care provider and patient if she or he needs to determine if the soldier is a risk to the unit. Medical officers, in turn, can override a field officer's need to deploy a soldier and declare them unfit for duty. All of these decisions can affect a soldier's retention and promotion. In addition, soldiers spend long periods of time with the other members of their unit, especially during deployment, so it can be very difficult to keep health care concerns private. Although stigma is only one of the barriers to soldiers' seeking care for PTSD, it is a significant one.

To this point we have taken for granted the concept of stigma as it is commonly used by soldiers, their families, and the broader society in public and private discussions surrounding the invisible injuries of war. People often qualify stigma as "social stigma," a characteristic or condition viewed negatively by society that is likely to discredit a person and adversely affect their relationships with strangers, friends, and family members. But what does it mean to be discredited, and what is it about a condition or characteristic that renders it discrediting?

"Guys will hide a lot of injuries and a lot of bad things. Just not to go there [talk about injuries or trauma]. You don't want to be a sissy, and you don't want to be the freak."Tucker Watson's statement here is typical. As Steve Sanders said:

> But if there was that guy that couldn't handle it he might be like laughed at by his peers, saying "Oh you pussy." That would probably play a factor. People would be afraid to do anything about it because they get criticized because it's true, not necessarily right, but true.

The diagnosis of PTSD, even the suspicion of it, though not necessarily its symptoms, mark a soldier as abnormal, as violating the highly masculinized military code of toughness, readiness for action, aggression, camaraderie, and attention to mission above all else. Soldier Dave Barry talked about how soldiers associate PTSD with "not being able to handle" combat on the one hand, and letting down fellow soldiers, on the other.

> It's true, especially in the combat arms. A lot of people don't want to admit that they have a problem because they see it as weakness and they don't want to seem weak in front of other people; kind of a bravado type thing. . . . If they do have PTSD, and they get separated from the army, they'll feel like they let down their friends and the people in their unit. Loyalty has a lot to do with it. . . . The way I see it is, they just don't want to let people down.

Soldiers emphasized how weakness affects one's own sense of self as well as the respect of equals and superiors. "You don't want anybody below you in rank not respecting you because it's getting around that you can't handle what happened over there and somebody else could," as soldier Sam Adams put it. (Soldiers were invited to create their own pseudonyms, hence the playfulness of many.) A soldier who admits difficulty coping could be told to "Suck it up!" or "Drink some water," or be castigated with more gendered expressions such as "Take some Motrin," or "Don't be a pussy," a "brokedick," or a "wuss."

For many of the soldiers we interviewed, PTSD meant failing the test of personal competence, of being able to do a tough job, a job few people are willing to take on or are able to do well. As Felix Sprout said:

> Pride. Pride is a big thing, you know. If I'm really messed up in the head, I don't want to lose my job; I want to stay in the army. So I'm going to play it cool the whole time . . . . With the army, if you've got PTSD, it's like you're not mentally fit.

Or David Jenson, who said "Most soldiers won't seek treatment. 'I'll just tough it out,' that's how most people are in the army. It's mostly the way we're trained, really."

## Combat Stress

Until PTSD emerged as a diagnosis after the Vietnam War (Young 1995), combat stress was the dominant model for understanding mental health issues in active-duty military personnel. Like PTSD, combat stress is also a culturally constructed category or way of thinking about what happens to people during combat. Its symptoms are almost indistinguishable from those of PTSD: hypervigilance, insomnia and nightmares, anger, social withdrawal, and difficulty concentrating (US Marine Corps 2000). Combat stress is defined as a biological and psychological response to the conditions of war: physical stresses such as exposure to heat and cold, sleep deprivation, noise and blasts, and malnutrition; cognitive stresses such as changing rules of engagement, boredom, and monotony; and emotional stresses such as loss of friends to death or injury, shame and guilt, fear and helplessness (Nash 2007a, 2007b). The major distinguishing feature of these two conditions is time. Combat stress is viewed as an acute reaction to stress; its symptoms appear when the soldier is in theater, they are temporary, and the symptoms can be eased through supportive treatments. In contrast, the symptoms of PTSD appear after a traumatic event, sometimes months or years later, and last at least one month. Soldier Dave Barry recognized this difference when asked to compare the two conditions. "Combat stress is something that you go through while you're in combat, whereas PTSD is after the fact, you know—*post*-traumatic."

William Nash, a navy psychiatrist who served in Iraq in 2004 and 2005, lists four key military attitudes toward combat stress that "form a lens through which combat and operational stressors can be either filtered or magnified for individual warriors" (2007b:11). Combat stress is viewed in a few ways:

**1.** As a weapon: "Combat stress is what *we* inflict on the *enemy!*" (Nash 2007b:13);

**2.** As friction to be ignored, just as soldiers might ignore incoming bullets, as they focus on their mission to take out the enemy;

**3.** As a leadership challenge to be handled through the personal relationship between leaders and their personnel. Here officers must learn to sense when to push, when to counsel and when to refer a struggling soldier;

**4.** As a test of personal competence to be endured and overcome just as one overcomes enemy fire.

Beginning in WWI, the army adopted a program for treating combat stress reactions called "PIE": Proximity (treatment near the front lines); Immediacy (immediate initiation of short-term treatment once the problem was identified); and Expectancy (treatment with the expectancy of a prompt return to duty) (Mandel 2007), which included placing psychiatrists, psychologists, and auxiliary mental health professionals at psychiatric aid stations and hospitals near the front and training medical personnel to recognize and treat combat stress. Short-term treatment consisted of temporary removal from combat, provision of food, and encouragement and medication as needed to ensure rest and to calm anxiety. At the beginning of WWII the army had viewed combat stress as the reaction of "weak neurotic men" and at the war's outset instituted a screening program to exclude individuals they assessed as susceptible to breaking down under the stress of combat from military service. The program failed to significantly reduce mental health casualties and kept individuals who might prove competent soldiers out of the army. As a consequence, the army subsequently adopted the view that "every man [sic] has a breaking point during combat exposure" and evaluated recruits' mental fitness on an individual basis (Mandel 2007:4). Rates of return to combat varied in the range of 70 to 80 percent (Mandel 2007) in Korea and Vietnam.

Whereas soldiers frequently mentioned that there was stigma attached to having PTSD, there was almost no mention of stigma in reference to combat stress. Instead, soldiers emphasized the normal aspects of combat stress and its universality. As Victor Herrera said, "Everybody has combat stress." Or as Kevin Watkins said, "Combat stress is the natural effect that [combat] experiences have." Dale Johnson viewed combat stress as critical to survival. "Combat stress keeps you alive, keeps you from getting complacent." So although soldiers acknowledge that combat stress can interfere with their ability to fight, they also draw from conceptions of stress as a positive force that can create strength and resilience that can make them better and more effective soldiers.

Although we did not ask specifically about seeking help or treatment for combat stress, several soldiers mentioned things they could do to help relieve its symptoms. "I got friends who smoke cigarettes; that's basically combat stress. Play games; read a book; talk on the phone with friends back home. That's combat stress you can deal with." Clinicians emphasized that normalizing frameworks, such as combat stress, encourage soldiers to seek help while in theater and therefore to recover more quickly. Rejoining their unit is desired both for tactical reasons—that is, to keep soldiers in the field—but also is viewed as treatment. Since soldiers' primary motivation for fighting during combat is to support and protect their fellow soldiers (Grossman 2009 [1995]), separating them from their unit may increase stress as they fail to "support their buddies." As soldier Danny Cottonwood told us, "Here in the army, you're with these guys all the time, going on patrols with them every day, going through what they're going through. So it really builds the bond together between soldiers. You don't want to let that guy down."

Reporting on combat stress among US soldiers in Afghanistan, Michael M. Phillips of *The Wall Street Journal* (2011) told the story of Corporal Seth Voie, a young Marine whose best friend, Corporal Chad Wade, was killed by an IED while their unit was on patrol. His squad leader, Sergeant Albert Tippett, recognized the signs of impending/potential combat stress. Based on the idea that the best treatment was to have Voie face his fears and traumatic memories immediately and directly, Sergeant Tippett assigned him to serve as "point," the soldier who leads the squad carrying a metal detector to search for mines and other explosive devices, for the next patrol on the same route where his friend was killed the previous day.

Behavioral health teams embedded with combat units provide continual assessment, monitoring, and treatment in theater with high rates of return to combat (Carabajal 2011). Although these teams provide professional, trained mental health services, both commissioned officers, but especially front line NCOs (noncommissioned officers) who have the most direct contact with and responsibility for front line troops, receive training in the signs and symptoms of combat stress and are involved in its treatment by rotating duties and providing soldiers with periods of rest from combat when possible.

As in the training described in the opening of this chapter, clinicians spoke about "inoculating" soldiers against combat stress, increasing their "mental, emotional, and spiritual fitness" as an adjunct to physical fitness in being able to handle the stresses of combat. Anthropologist Emily Martin demonstrates how military metaphors infuse scientific and popular cultural explanations of the immune system (1990). Mass media accounts compare the cells of the body's immune system to defenders against "foreign invaders"—bacteria and viruses—in the environment. In turn, army clinicians invoke these popular images of the immune system, with their allusion to protection from external enemies, to help soldiers understand the army's efforts to protect them from the harmful effects of combat stress as a tactical weapon of war. Consequently, soldiers view combat stress as a normal response to combat to be dealt with like any other aspect of combat and not as a medical condition to be treated by professionals. Ironically, it is the medical concept of inoculation that helps remove combat stress from the realm of pathology and medicine.

### "Faking It"

Almost half of the soldiers we interviewed spontaneously brought up the idea that many, if not most soldiers who claimed PTSD were "faking it." Soldier David Ellingboe's assessment is typical of this group: "I would say that 80 percent of PTSD, combat stress cases are exaggerated or not true at all." Soldiers questioned the legitimacy and reality of PTSD in their fellow soldiers who had not seen combat or who claimed they could not do their work but could function outside of work. "I think 90 percent of it is bullshit . . . . I know three of them that are all messed up during the week. You get 'em on the weekend: perfectly fine."

Fassin and Rechtman (2009) argue that once psychiatry accepted the event as "the sole cause of the pathology," suspicion that people were using symptoms for sympathy, to gain compensation, or to avoid work or combat disappeared. On the contrary, active-duty soldiers, spouses, and mental health professionals voiced numerous ways in which suspicion has not "definitely disappeared" (Fassin and Rechtman 2009:87) for combat veterans, but remains a strong undercurrent in some soldiers' conceptions of PTSD and contributes to stigma and barriers to getting help.

Underlying their statements of how frequently they believe soldiers fake PTSD is the idea that it is possible to fake it, to create a believable narrative and set of symptoms that will result in the diagnosis. As one soldier said, "[they] pull the crazy card. They know what to say." Kevin Watkins, an officer, explained:

> *I think PTSD is misdiagnosed a lot because people go in and they downright exaggerate or lie in order to get the PTSD diagnosis from somebody who doesn't know what happened. And it's not their fault because if I go in, and I tell you "I've been blown up forty times and I saw three of my best friends die," a psychologist or a psychiatrist is gonna be like "Wow, he does have PTSD, he's been through horrible experiences . . . ." So I think it gets misdiagnosed because they just don't really know what happened over there. They come up with some traumatic story and then of course they're gonna think they're going to have PTSD.*

Don Haskins remembers his officers reinforcing the idea that soldiers' symptoms might not be real. "My first deployment [it was] 'Quit making it up.' It was only a year in and they were telling you to quit making it up."

Soldiers gave three major reasons why others might fake PTSD: to excuse bad behavior, to obtain compensation, or to get out of work or the military. Getting out of the military and seeking compensation are identical to the suspicions placed on soldiers and injured workers in previous eras. Using

PTSD to excuse bad behavior may be distinctive of the post-9/11 wars and the AVF. Infantryman Brendan Truman thinks soldiers use PTSD to justify or cover up behavior that they should be held accountable for. "I think these days a lot of people are using PTSD as a crutch to get out of the army, or to cover up their problems. Some people drink and drink, get into trouble and say, 'Oh, I got PTSD, that's why I did it, that's why I drank so much.'" Marvin Smith is reluctant to attribute most soldiers' issues to military experience. "They don't have combat-related issues. They have issues. Period." Danny Cottonwood explains it this way: "It's pretty much just people being crazy before the army and deployment." David Ellingboe told the story of a kid who got into a lot of trouble even before enlisting, then "claims PTSD after getting into more trouble after Iraq. Gets to leave with an honorable discharge."

As an officer responsible for maintaining his troops' health and readiness for deployment or combat, Watkins has a different point of view than boots-on-the-ground enlisted soldiers. He had a soldier in his unit who had a record of trouble: "He had been in trouble a bunch of times before the Army, before he deployed, got in trouble while he deployed, and then got in a ton of trouble afterwards." After his deployment he denied any complaints on the PTSD screening, but later "said he had PTSD and got out of the trouble and just got let out of the Army, and that's why I have such a negative view on it. That's just one example of an experience I know happens all the time." Watkins thinks that a soldier's history of discipline or behavior issues should be considered in evaluating them for PTSD, to make faking it more difficult. While to Watkins and some other soldiers this personal history replaces PTSD as a possible explanation for a soldier's difficulties, researchers have found that "the *accumulation* of stressful events over the course of a lifetime increases an individual's risk of developing PTSD" (Finley 2011:68).

Several soldiers cited "working the system" to gain compensation or disability as a motivation for faking PTSD. According to soldier Brendan Truman, "A lot of people get out and claim PTSD to get that check. You can get $700 to $800 a month for the rest of your life if you get out and claim PTSD. You got a lot of people lying about stuff out there." Kelsoe Fitzgerald views them as looking for "unwarranted benefits," and Steve Sanders equates them with those who abuse other kinds of government services. "There's a lot of people that abuse a lot of things, welfare, all sorts of stuff. You're always going to have those bad apples that make something look bad." Seeking compensation was usually linked with wanting to leave the military. As Brian Turner puts it:

> *You know, they get to Iraq, or they go through with it, come back, and they just don't want to be in the military any more. That's the number one card*

*people are pulled and getting paid for it. "Oh, I got PTSD. Give me a check and let me get on with my life."*

Or, as Eric Nelson observed, faking PTSD might be linked to resistance to changing perceptions of military work: a form of conscientious objection, for example, without having to confront practices or institutions. "There are a lot of soldiers who will cheat the system because they hate their jobs at this point . . . . There is a lot of wasted money on it; if someone wants to go, I say let them go, there is always someone else who wants to do this." Quincy Stevenson, a 24-year-old who served in the reserves before going to active-duty status said, "There are people in my platoon who are faking injuries or PTSD, and when I ask them about it they say, 'I'm over it, I'm done, dude. I just don't want to do this anymore.'" When we asked him what are the factors behind their statements, he replied:

> *Some of them are just so lazy they don't want to wake up at 5, 6 in the morning to do PT [physical training], which is sad, but that is some of the problem . . . . Some guys are just so homesick they want to go home and be with their families. They can't handle it anymore. Most of them feel they served their country for 15 months, and they're done, they don't even think about the fact that they signed that dotted line for four-plus years.*

In these statements, honor hinges exclusively on the volunteer's fulfillment of his contract with the state. Competing versions of honor as tied to dissent or "breaking ranks" with post-9/11 campaigns as being just or necessary are absent here, or left unspoken.[11]

Sometimes soldiers say PTSD serves to get out of combat. Steve Sanders told the story of a soldier in his platoon that "cut his hand to get out of fighting" and then didn't see much combat. But when he returned to the United States, he claimed PTSD.

> *He said he was going to kill himself, kill everybody around him, and he's having mental issues. So they put him in the insane asylum for a while. He's been going about eight hours every day to the psychiatrist. And he's getting out of the army. That was his original goal to begin with; to get out of everything.*

Sometimes it was to avoid deployment. As Brian Tabor recounted:

> *So people are tired of going over there. Their wives are getting sick of it because they've seen them two years out of the last five. I think a lot of*

*people are just using it to get out of deployments. They're getting mental*
*discharge to get out of the army.*

For those soldiers who view the majority of cases of PTSD with suspicion, stigma arises less from the symptoms of PTSD than from using it to escape duty, combat, or service. It might seem that soldiers would embrace PTSD because it provides benefits such as medical services and compensation for disability that the military promises those who volunteer. But for active-duty soldiers still in the military, it is just this aspect of PTSD—obtaining honorable or medical discharge and benefits—to which many soldiers we interviewed objected most strongly. Steve Sanders said that the soldier who cut his hand "was frowned upon by everybody." Kevin Watkins had no tolerance with those claiming PTSD: "The people with PTSD there are a bunch of fakers." Faking PTSD challenged core values related to soldiering as work. It dishonored those who did the difficult work and fulfilled their tours of duty. Brian Tabor objects to soldiers who claim PTSD falsely because "they flood the offices of the TBI people and behavioral help people and they tie them all up with fake symptoms. It's the soldiers who are faking it who are ruining it for the guys that actually need help."

Watkins thinks that more enlisted soldiers claim PTSD than officers, and more lower-ranked enlisted soldiers than higher-ranked.

*You've got to ask yourself, "Why is that? They all see the same thing." And*
*it's because a lot of the lower enlisted that are claiming it, they don't have*
*commitment to the army, they don't want to be in the army anymore,*
*they're not thinking of making a career out of it, and it's an easy way out*
*and they know it.*

Whereas a diagnosis of PTSD confers legitimacy and makes it real for medical personnel and officers, for soldiers, the diagnosis or seeking help is conversely a sign that one doesn't have PTSD, that it is not real. As Mick Dean said, "There are more people that claim PTSD and don't actually have it than people who have it and don't seek treatment," or as Felix Sprout put it, "People that do have it don't say they have it." Brian Tabor pinpoints the issue when he says, "The good soldiers don't want to admit they have a problem. The soldiers who actually do their job in Iraq, they just suck it up. They might have it. They might actually not realize they have it. 'Oh, no, I'm fine.'"

Despite this group of soldiers' strong suspicion of those who claim or are diagnosed with PTSD, many others acknowledged that PTSD was real and that those who suffer from it should receive help. Kevin Windum told us,

*I see a lot of people with PTSD. I have this one buddy. His best friend was killed, basically right in front of us, and he was a good friend of mine, too. This dude was so close to him, he just snapped. Ever since then he's been totally different. He's had all sorts of run-ins with the law. He's lost like half of his pay because he's always getting in trouble for something. It's just ridiculous. He needs help, and he's starting to get it now, but it took him shooting a gun off in public for him to get the help.*[12]

## Barriers to Care

In the mid-2000s, research emerged indicating that stigma surrounding symptoms of mental illness and fear of being stigmatized by teammates and officers for seeking help were significant barriers to care. An article in *Military Medicine* reported that the attitudes of NCOs, those who work most closely with rank-and-file enlisted personnel, have a strong effect on perceived stigma associated with symptoms and seeking help. As a consequence, the authors suggest that contact with NCOs who are open about their own suffering from symptoms of PTSD or depression would decrease stigma.[13] Not surprisingly, many infantrymen echoed the findings of surveys on stigma as a barrier to care. As Bradley Kay remarked, "They tell you, 'If you have a problem, if you need help, come forward.' But then people are afraid . . . because they're like, 'Oh, well, 'scuse my language but, you're a pussy. Suck it up. Take some Motrin.' And so people are afraid to say anything."

Masculinized images of stoicism and the ability to act violently and be the target of violence without experiencing that violence as traumatic or upsetting, to "gut it out" as one officer put it, were dominant themes in these interviews. Since women predominate in counseling professions, these complex gendered dynamics may also affect seeking therapy, which may carry feminized connotations of the psychologized self (Kusserow 2004).

The initial point of entry for this project was how fearful soldiers were of seeking help for mental health issues. For those nearing separation from the military, treatment for combat-related mental conditions could jeopardize their future employment with the military as civilians. Persons who are being considered for positions in the military that involve access to classified information or that concern national security (and many positions do) must complete Standard Form 86 (SF-86). Question 21 on the form asks if the applicant has ever received mental health services. A positive response to this question could disqualify the soldier from obtaining a security clearance. Since many soldiers seek employment in the military after discharge, the army saw this question as a potential barrier to soldiers seeking care. In the summer of 2008, just as we were embarking on this project, the army amended the form so that the applicant could answer truthfully that they had not received mental health services if those services were "strictly related to adjustments from service in a military combat environment."[14] Thus, we began our interviews with active duty soldiers asking them about this change to SF-86. While the change may have been helpful to higher-ranked soldiers seeking security clearance as they prepared to leave the military, very few of the soldiers we interviewed were aware of the form or the change in regulations. As most of the soldiers we spoke with were relatively recent recruits occupying entry-level positions, concerns about how seeking mental health care might affect their future careers may not have been important to them at the time. The stigma they faced in seeking help was more immediate, coming from their unit and its leaders.

We also heard indications that army culture and attitudes surrounding seeking help were changing, particularly in small units below the battalion level: companies, platoons, squads, and teams. These smaller units, where soldiers spend most of their time when deployed and at home, are "micro-cultures" strongly influenced by the NCOs to whom they report. Several soldiers, like NCO Steve Sanders, told us of sergeants committed to ensuring that their soldiers availed themselves of mental health services. "They are receiving it [treatment]. If you ask for it they give it to you. About over three quarters of my old platoon was going to TBI clinic every day." He added, "It really affected our training 'cause we couldn't train at all because three-quarters of our people were either in the mental institution claiming they're crazy or in the TBI clinic." He also noted that in his unit there was no stigma associated with getting help.

> *It's not looked down upon. Any soldier of mine that needs it, I say, "Take it." If they say they need it, and they don't need it, I still say, "Take it." I'm not going to deny them anything because it's there for them. I'm not the doctor; I can't say who's got it.*

Because Sanders is an NCO, his attitude carries weight. Although his references to the "mental institution" and "claiming they're crazy" might indicate lingering stigma attached to symptoms defined as psychiatric, his use of humor might also be seen as a way to defuse conflict and tension so that the soldiers for whom he is responsible will seek help. Brian Tabor also described the shift in army culture.

> *All the ones that claim it in our unit, they go to counseling twice a week. If they need to go see a medic, they're authorized to go see a medic any time*

*of the day. We got all kinds of people to go talk to—chaplain, psychiatrist. Army pays for it all.*

The soldiers we interviewed had many critical things to say about the army's treatment of mental health issues—difficulty getting appointments, unsympathetic or overwhelmed providers, too many medications—but most still saw the source of the major obstacles to seeking care in soldiers' norms and values. Statements like those of Tabor and Sanders also indicate a shift in accepting help from health care professionals, in this case within the army. Nonetheless, change was uneven, and a significant number of young soldiers expressed suspicion about PTSD as a valid condition and seeking help as something carrying stigma.

### Fighting the "Real Enemy": The Real Warrior Campaign

Since we began our research in the fall of 2008, the army has taken multiple practical measures to better contend with mental health challenges connected to combat trauma, including the assignment in theater of mobile psychiatric, behavioral health teams and chaplains who specialize in trauma; the improvement of screening before and after deployment; stepped-up programming like the "reintegration university" to aid transitions from theater; education campaigns to raise awareness about suicide prevention; warrior transition units (now battalions) to smooth transitions out of the army; comprehensive soldier fitness, the army's focus on resiliency and placing psychological (plus social and spiritual) fitness on a par with physical fitness; and at Fort Carson in particular, the resilience training described in the opening passage of this chapter.

In addition to these practical measures, the army also initiated a campaign to change army culture in an effort to "Pull the Stigma Down" so that soldiers would seek help for combat-related mental health issues. This effort has two fronts: transforming "Army Strong" to include seeking help from mental health professionals and reinforcing the medicalization (discussed later in this chapter) of PTSD to reduce its stigma.

At the Warrior Care Summit in June 2009, General Loree Sutton introduces herself as General Graham's and his wife Carol Graham's "battle buddy over the last few years." Their shared battle is against stigma for seeking help with combat trauma, which she calls a "deadly, toxic hazard" and specifies that it is "not enough to minimize or reduce it, we have to eliminate it." She speaks with urgency, saying leaders must "have no patience" with persistent stigma and its costs for soldiers: "Time is not on our side." In 2008, under Sutton's direction, the DCoE initiated the Real Warrior campaign, which defines stigma as the primary obstacle to soldiers seeking help for PTSD.

As Sutton notes, it is not the behavioral manifestations of PTSD—pervasive anger, aggressive overreaction to stimuli, and numbness and disassociation from everyday life, friends, and family—that are dangerous. These behaviors are expected and normal survival responses to battle that can be treated if they persist outside of combat. Nor is it combat itself that is identified as lethal. Instead, the danger comes from the stigma associated with the diagnosis of PTSD that prevents soldiers from seeking treatment; as Sutton put it, "Stigma kills."

Army personnel who design these programs clearly recognize the conflicting symbols of Army Strong and invulnerability on the one hand, and PTSD and weak victims on the other. In response, a none-too-subtle effort has been made to extend the core metaphor of army strength to those seeking help. The clearest examples are straightforward. The Real Warriors campaign slogan reads "Real Warriors, Real Battles, Real Strength," and their website runs the headline "Reaching out is a sign of strength." It then elaborates reasons for seeking help that are consistent with soldiers' commitment to be "mission ready" for their "fellow warriors." The site emphasizes that combat stress reactions are common and will not hurt their careers. Suicide prevention materials specify that seeking help "is not a character flaw, but a sign of strength." Some studies suggest that personal contact with individuals with a given disability may be more effective than broad public campaigns in reducing stigma (Green 2009). In this vein, the campaign features written and videotaped personal narratives from a range of military personnel from enlisted men to NCOs who have experienced PTSD and sought help with positive results personally and professionally. The narratives provide contact, albeit indirect, with positive role models. In its recruiting materials, the newest version of the Army Strong commercial includes a visibly wounded soldier, standing with wife and child and so presumably back in the United States. The message here is, "You're still a warrior; you're still strong."

While extending the strength metaphor to invisible wounds is the army's primary rhetorical strategy, corollary metaphoric extensions accompany the move. One is the extension of the battlefield of theater to "battling" combat stress (although there are limits to this, as illustrated by the debate about whether PTSD qualifies as enough of a wound to be included in the criteria making soldiers eligible for the Purple Heart [Fata 2009; Schogol 2009]). Another plays on the mission-first, never-accept-defeat-or-quit warrior ethos shown earlier, but especially on its final line, "I will never leave a fallen comrade," emphasizing that a buddy struggling with PTSD or suicidal ideation must be included among the potential fallen comrades. Yet another is the journey home, invoked, for example, by the banner on the "hand2hand" contact website, which reads, "Bringing our soldiers all the way home."

For the army, the most efficient route to destigmatizing PTSD is to medicalize it: that is, to view it as primarily a physical condition as is TBI. "If we sent troops to sub-Saharan Africa," poses Sutton, "and one out of five came back with malaria, we wouldn't spend our time debating whether malaria was real, or asking why this soldier got it and not the other one." While lamenting what she calls "the Walter Reed tragedy," referring to the at-times scandalously inadequate care vets received there, the general views the associated negative press the army received as "a blessing, truly," because it served as their wake-up call and a public announcement of the challenge they face. It marked the beginning of what was "by necessity an era of proliferation." Soldiers' number-one complaint now is that there are too many programs, and they experience "choice anxiety," now giving way to the current moment, where programs are being synchronized and simplified.

Her narrative moves from merely optimistic to inspired and anticipatorily triumphant, as she speaks about the "changes in what we know about the brain in the last ten years . . .". "We're moving from gloom, doom and despair to now being able to build on what we now understand about nerve genesis in the hippocampus, about neuroplasticity and hyperbaric oxygen for regeneration, all coupled with exercise, diet, commitment." As an example of the application of this new knowledge, she presents the Integrative Reconditioning Program. In this program, troops can receive help in theater for a concussion from teams that may include a sports medicine practitioner, a chaplain, and a psychologist, "because it's about supplying interdisciplinary support." Her vision is "that when troops come back home from theater they can step right back into well-being." When Sutton shares the adage "We're putting the 'yes' back into yesterday," we wonder if she's referring to yesterday's insistent and unwelcome intrusions into today that is PTSD (Figure 3).

Sutton is consummately skilled in the arts of public presentation and generating hope to motivate recovery and healing. However, the apparent simplicity of her narrative is deceptive. Underlying her statements is a complex and often contradictory process that attempts to construct and build upon a shared social concept of PTSD in

**FIGURE 3.** "Putting the 'yes' back into yesterday": Brigadier General Loree Sutton, the Defense Centers of Excellence for Psychological Health and Traumatic Brain Injury (DCoE) (courtesy of DoD).

response to our contemporary conflicts in Iran and Afghanistan in the historical context of an AVF. "The campaign seeks to remove the barriers that often prevent service members from obtaining treatment for psychological health issues and traumatic brain injury *in the same way that they receive treatment for physical wounds and illnesses*" (US Army n.d.) [emphasis ours]. Campaign materials explain the clinical condition in biomedical terms, define its symptoms according to the standards identified by the American Psychiatric Association (APA 1994), and recommend that health care providers prescribe appropriate drugs or behavioral therapies or counseling. Just as Sutton compared PTSD to a physical ailment, in June 2009 the army issued a policy memorandum directing all personnel "in an effort to reduce the stigma associated with the provision of 'mental' health services" to use "'behavioral' health in lieu of 'mental' health."[15]

Part of defining PTSD as a medical problem is creating cultural consensus among health care providers and those at risk. Thus, the Real Warrior Campaign is more than anything an educational program that promotes a shared, medicalized version of PTSD by "disseminating information" and "sharing stories" of soldiers who were successfully treated. Because of its effects on how the army meets these challenges and the treatment soldiers will receive, it is important to unpack and analyze this process. Defining stigma as the enemy is a creative response, but one fraught with contradictions and conflict that may do little to help soldiers and leaders seeking definition and clarity.

## Chapter Two

# "It's Just a Job"

*. . . the Minotauros, as Euripides says, was "A mingled form and hybrid birth of monstrous shape," and that "Two different natures, man and bull, were joined in him . . . ."*

—Plutarch, *Life of Theseus*

In 2011, the Pew Research Center surveyed military veterans and American adults to compare their attitudes on war and sacrifice. In their preface, the authors state that the survey "presents what we believe is a vivid portrait—*albeit one painted exclusively in numbers*—of the rewards and burdens of serving in the all-volunteer military during the past decade" (2011; emphasis ours). Like Janus, this portrait has two faces, one regarding the wars and the other regarding the soldiers. Although 96 percent of veterans who served after 9/11 were proud of their service and 80 percent agreed that deployments made them feel they were doing something important for their country, only 34 percent said that the wars in Iraq and Afghanistan have been worth fighting and 33 percent said neither war has been worth the costs. Similarly, 45 percent of civilians said neither of the wars was worth the cost, but 90 percent expressed pride in service members. Despite the unpopularity of the post-9/11 wars, the survey suggests that civilians and soldiers distinguish their assessment of the wars from their support for the individuals doing the fighting in ways that differ significantly from attitudes toward soldiers coming home from Vietnam. Nonetheless, today's veterans fear negative reactions from civilians about their role in the wars. They also have the highest rates of mental distress of any previous group of veterans, distress based on experiences and losses, but that also may include feelings of shame and guilt for what they have witnessed and what they have been asked to do (Budden 2009; Finley 2011; Paulson and Krippner 2007).

The Pew survey provides valuable information on the demographic characteristics of recent veterans and shows the contrast in civilian and veteran attitudes and perceptions about the war and their respective roles in it. But the survey cannot go beyond the surface of the numbers. Nor does it go beyond the legacy of Vietnam—we can criticize the war and its mission, but not the soldiers we ask to fight it. Soldier Kevin Watkins rejected separating attitudes to the war from attitudes to soldiers.

> *I have a hard time buying it when you say you support the troops when you adamantly speak out against the war, and say everything is a failure over there. Because, yeah, maybe you're saying you support the troops because you want them to come home, but it's like saying (I can't take credit for this; I heard it on the news) "I'm a Vikings fan but I don't want them to win the Super Bowl" [Watkins laughs]. "I support the military but I want them to come back without success over there."*

The stories soldiers told us revealed the complexity, contradictions, and tension of their lived experience of war. Their stories also showed that within the labyrinth of war lurk minotaurs or monsters different from but related to PTSD, beasts that soldiers confront in the very nature of their work. PTSD is not the only, or perhaps the most important source of stigma that soldiers face, particularly when they return home and seek to reintegrate into civilian society.

### Doing Dirty Work

The infantry shares many of the same working conditions, though intensified, and skills as occupations in the civilian world: police, firefighters, and emergency medical technicians (EMTs). As soldier Connor Guiness said, "It's just another job. Like a teacher or a cop or a fireman." Not surprisingly, then, two of the soldiers we interviewed, David Quazar and Ronald Rheusenburg, saw the army as something they could do in preparation for their occupational goal of becoming policemen. As Ronald said, "I wanted to be in the police force, back home. But I was too young. I had four years to kill, so I joined the Army. And I just stayed in." These occupations, along with nursing or physician's assistant or EMT, are among the few areas in which skills gained in infantry positions can be fairly readily converted to civilian jobs.[1]

Like police and firefighters, infantry soldiers do "dirty work." Everett Hughes (1951) defines dirty work as tasks that society perceives as disgusting or polluting or degrading because they deal with dirt.[2] Much of the work of culture is establishing order through rules of behavior and categories of classification. As "matter out of place," dirt violates cultural rules. So while cleaning up is necessary and positive for society, workers who deal with dirt in its various forms are, at least in part, tainted and stigmatized. Stigma can arise from the work a person does and carries with it moral judgment about a person's character and social identity (Goffman 1986 [1963]). Occupations that require individuals to violate social norms about physical modesty and propriety—for example, seeing naked bodies or handling human waste—contaminate or taint the person who does them. Many aspects of infantry soldiers' work is dirty, from policing civilians, cleaning up after an IED explodes, digging ditches, to having contact with and using lethal force against people who are themselves stigmatized by being defined as the enemy. Work may be further stigmatized if it includes caretaking and everyday discipline (for example, guarding prisoners), tasks that society generally assigns to women and whose skills include emotional sensitivity and compassion that society characterizes as feminine (Tracy and Scott 2006).

Infantry soldiers' stigma is distinctively paradoxical, as it exists alongside their elevation and romanticization as heroes, selfless patriots, and ultimate "real men"; these idealizations may even mask and censor public acknowledgement of the pollution tied to their work. But infantry soldiers share with other dirty workers relatively high occupational esteem and pride. Work-group culture can provide alternative sources of value and norms to buffer against the stigma of dirty work. Soldiers can take pride in doing difficult work that few others can or will. They develop strong personal bonds through working, and sometimes suffering, side by side (Ashforth and Kreiner 1999). This camaraderie and the trust in "battle buddies" who have their backs also renders them vulnerable to grief and trauma when a fellow soldier dies. "Like last year I lost my best friend." Brian Turner told us.

> *The next day I had to go back on patrol. At first, I didn't understand. We had to go back out on patrol the next day . . . . I was like, dude, we just lost 5 people, 12 wounded. It sucks, and you're nervous as hell because you don't want the same thing to happen to you . . . . But you have to deal with it. It's part of the job.*

Those who survive may also be plagued with survivor's guilt and remorse. Sonny Diver, an NCO, explained his response to losing a soldier when their Humvee hit an IED. "There's nothing on earth that you could physically have done, but mentally you still feel guilty that you weren't able to help fix it."

Stigma is both imposed from the outside, or enacted, and internalized, or felt, by the stigmatized person. People who do dirty work may fear that stigma will be enacted, that they will be shamed or rejected publicly and visibly. Many of the active-duty soldiers and veterans we met repeated the story of veterans returning from Vietnam who were spat upon or called "baby killers." While these stories may have been relatively rare and isolated incidents,[3] they are potent social myths that convey today's veterans' fear of feeling ashamed or being shamed. Soldier Brian Turner thinks "most civilians don't really get it, they don't understand. And then they treat guys like crap when they come back."

## Terror Management and the "Things They Carry"

One aspect of soldiers' work that is fundamentally different from other occupations that include dirty work (with the exception of police) is the sanctioned use of lethal violence against other human beings. Combat soldiers are surrounded by death, its imminent threat, and evidence of the body's fragility. Anthropologist Ernest Becker (1973) theorized that one of the primary functions culture fulfills is "terror management." With its rules and norms, culture establishes order in the face of the arbitrariness of death. Through culture we create things—monuments, buildings, ideas, art—that endure beyond our lifetimes and transcend death. The Global War on Terror is explicitly a terror management project; we argue that managing terror is work that continues at home. Culture is also linked to self-esteem, which comes from seeing oneself as "a valuable participant in a meaningful and eternal reality," so "meeting the standards of value of one's culture" creates self-esteem, which further protects people from the terror of death (Goldenberg et al. 2000:201). In war, soldiers may offset the stigma and shame of violating norms about killing other human beings by believing that they are defending their nation and fighting a just cause. As solder Mick Dean said, "I know people don't like for us to be deployed, but if we don't do it, it's possible 9/11 could happen again. So we had to take a stand and do something about it." Indeed, one study found that soldiers' negative attitudes toward the wars in Iraq and Afghanistan increased their stress during deployment. Those who enlisted primarily or solely for the pay or education suffered higher rates of PTSD than those who were also motivated by the army's mission (Allen et al. 2011). A few soldiers told us they enjoyed being treated "like heroes" upon their return to the United States following deployment. Soldier Brendan Truman said "one of the best feelings when you get back is the ceremony. Everyone is so proud and appreciative. Most of the airlines will give you first class. People clapping, buying you beers . . . . You get treated like a rock star."

Societies create strong norms and rules surrounding death, and specifically around viewing and handling dead bodies. Because war disrupts the cultural practices that distance us from death, infantry soldiers, who are most closely associated with combat, risk censure from those who are more distant. Eric Nelson told us about the attitudes of those in support positions who never leave the base toward those who do.

*I can remember one day when two of our guys were wounded, pretty severely—and fortunately both survived. But all of us had been, you know, treating their wounds, and so we all had blood all over our uniforms. We get back onto our FOB [Forward Operating Base] . . . and we're like, we're gonna go eat; we're tired, everyone wants to take a shower. And we get into line, to go eat, and one of the support people comes out and yells at us because we've got blood on our uniforms. And our CEO, our Community Executive Officer, comes over and just chews this guy out. He's like, "Shut up. Look at them! Do you know where we just were? They're gonna go eat, and take a shower, and then clean their gear and go to sleep. So you can just shut up, turn around and go back to doing whatever you were doing."*

Societies also create rituals to cleanse and purify those who have been contaminated, whether by their association with death or other polluting acts or objects.[4] For example, in Judaism, dead bodies are a source of ritual impurity. Anyone who has been in the presence of a dead body, even if they have not touched it, must wash their hands before entering a home (Rich 2011).[5] During periods of heavy combat, a hot meal and a shower may serve as ritualized purification for soldiers contaminated by death.

That soldiers experience horror in the face of death, both the possibility of their own death and that of their fellow soldiers and the enemy, is inherent to war itself. As Sonny Diver, a sergeant with two Iraq deployments under his belt said, "How do you tell somebody who hasn't experienced a friend dying or a friend being dismembered that . . . you saw the person who was less than an arm's reach from you totally dismembered or dead." Horror, "an emotion so powerful as to overwhelm the individual's capacity for immediate sense-making or cognitive processing" (Finley 2012:272), is a key component of how psychiatrists define a traumatic event that can produce PTSD.

But what is less emphasized is the role that war plays in generating moral injuries that induce shame and guilt and can contribute to the development and severity of PTSD (Bracken 2002; Budden 2009). After returning from his last tour to Afghanistan, soldier William Busbee "began rubbing his hands over and over and constantly rinsing them under the tap. 'Mom, it won't wash off,' he said." When she asked what, he answered, "The blood." He also told his mother, "You would hate me if you knew what I've done out there." Two months after his discharge from the army, he shot and killed himself (Pilkington 2013).

Even though the use of lethal force is socially and culturally sanctioned in war, soldiers must overcome their most basic social training to kill another human being (Grossman 2009 [1995]). And the rules that sanction killing in war are rarely clear: the final decision rests with the individual and his or her conscience. Even soldiers who return from war relatively unscathed by physical or mental injury may yet be haunted by questions surrounding what they experienced (Paulson and Krippner 2007).

Dawn Weaver, an officer and psychiatric nurse, worked at Evans Hospital on Fort Carson in a new position as an emergency psychiatric response nurse in the emergency room. This taught Weaver things she believes too few people attempting to work with soldiers know or understand. Some were basic worries about clinicians "not getting it": "When a guy comes to a therapist's office with a Monster (caffeine-based energy drink), a giant Monster in his hand, and his leg is jiggling, and he's talking about not being able to sleep," clinicians need to pick up the thread by asking, "How much caffeine are you drinking?" But then there were the "dirty little secrets" she learned, in "back rooms with the doors closed in a moment of raw pain and anguish."[6]

> *I learned, for instance, that all of these guys are carrying weapons all the time. And I mean in their civilian life, while they're on post. Nobody is supposed to, but they're all carrying weapons. Combat veterans carry, period. In their boot, in their pocket. They're all carrying knives, and most of them are carrying guns. That's one thing I learned.*

She hastened to qualify that veterans carrying a weapon "have no intention of using it on the civilian world: they're carrying it for those 'bad guys' that they know are lurking out there, threatening them and those they love. It's a transitional object for some of them: helps them move from soldier to civilian."

The next secret Weaver finds "very difficult to talk to civilians about, because they are so repulsed." It is that "these guys become so primed to killing" in a way they directly connect to being constrained by the rules of engagement.[7]

> *They've been reined in on who they can shoot: there are all kinds of constraints, understandably, about who you can shoot and who you can't. But they are in situations where they can't defend themselves sometimes, and that makes them—and I use this word carefully—that makes them absolutely crazy. It makes them insane: where they are getting shot at, they are getting fired upon, and their lives are at risk, and they cannot shoot back.*

Becoming primed to kill in this way complicates many soldiers' attempts to reintegrate into civilian life after combat. "Now when they come home, they are so horrified by what their primal brain had them do, back here in the so-called civilized world, that they find themselves absolutely reviled, repugnant. They can't tolerate themselves." Weaver attributed the desecration of the bodies of dead insurgents to this "crazy-making," and warned against judging even desecration:

> No matter how repugnant these actions may seem to civilians, I am adamant that civilians cannot—must not—judge these actions because the context is lost in the telling. The only people who can possibly judge these actions are those who have lived, and nearly died, in combat. The rest of us have to accept that war has its own moral code about which we know nothing.

The most important secret, which she called the "*coup de grace*," soldiers work up to talking about only slowly.

> A lot of these guys have had to kill children. And by that I mean the insurgents have trained children to take weapons out on the street and point them at soldiers so that the soldiers will shoot them. Because they know that Americans will be forever damaged by that. These moral and spiritual injuries that that causes are exceedingly deep. And part of the reason that it is so bad is that they will not discuss that with their therapist. Because they don't trust their therapist to respond correctly to that.

## A Working Class War?

Although the military insists on retaining the rhetoric of the citizen-soldier volunteer, the reality is that the Department of Defense (DoD) is the nation's single largest employer. Soldier Felix Sprout, echoing the army's emphasis on the AVF as a professional force of highly trained soldiers said, "This is my job; this is my profession." It is also one of the few jobs that does not require higher education. Military wages and benefits are competitive in the labor market and enlistment as a private requires only a high school education and reasonable score on the army's aptitude test. As Daniel Quest told us, "I graduated high school, but it took me like five and a half years. It was northern Minnesota, so it was pretty hard up for jobs. The army is like the only job you don't have to work to get." Joining the army is perhaps the closest alternative to the high-paying manufacturing jobs that enabled many working-class families to move into the middle class after WWII (Scandlyn 1993). Consequently, many recruits, despite their assertions that no one forced them to sign up, are nevertheless under pressure of difficult economic situations. Unfortunately for many soldiers in the lower enlisted ranks, youth and financial inexperience, financial obligations of family, and businesses that prey on military personnel can quickly lead to serious financial problems and may contribute to high rates of suicide among returning veterans (US Army 2010).[8] And although the army's wages may be comparable to civilian wages, these are civilian wages that have declined by 4 percent in the last decade (Porter 2013).

Talking about class is difficult in a society where many people subscribe to the idea that everyone is middle class (DeMott 1990; Scandlyn 1993, 2009). In the United States, class has a "now-you-see-it, now-you-don't existence," with difference more often explained by race or ethnicity (Ortner 2003:12). The conversation is even more difficult in the military, where distinctions of rank, determined by merit and years of service, override distinctions of social class, race, and ethnicity. As a general stationed at Fort Carson told us, the army deliberately does not collect data that would clarify soldiers' socioeconomic status, in order to shield this information from public scrutiny. During the Vietnam War, protests over the unequal burden of casualties among low-income urban youth catalyzed around race, not class. Whereas since Vietnam blacks have generally been assigned to and elected support positions over combat positions, gays and women have fought to secure these positions and their badges of ability. Although the army, especially since the economic downturn of 2008, does not recruit from among the poorest and least well-educated Americans, it disproportionately draws white youth from working-class families in rural communities. Looking at casualty rates from WWII to the present, political scientists Douglas Kriner and Francis Shen found that "socioeconomically disadvantaged communities do bear disproportionately large shares of the casualty burden," and that this gap was highest during the post-9/11 wars (2010:15).[9]

Some of the soldiers we interviewed joined the military for personal reasons, to "turn my life around" or as a personal challenge, to see "if I got what it takes." But by far the most common motivations were economic. Mick Dean says he's a patriot, but joined to support his family. Don Haskins said, "I didn't really want to work in a factory the rest of my life." For Brian Tabor, the army was an escape "from a town of 500 people. If you don't get out you'll stay there forever and work minimum wage." We were struck by how often, even in a time of war, soldiers repeated the refrains "it's just a job" and "you just do your job" when talking about their life in the military.

These soldiers often resist being thanked for their *service*, preferring to characterize it as work done for pay and benefits. Connor Guinness said, "I don't see anybody going around shaking hands with police for doing their job. So when we come back we're not really looking to be honored. We're just doing our job." Or Don Haskins, who said, "If I didn't get honored I'd still do my job." Don Haskins denied enlisting from a sense of duty to nation or support for the military's objectives. "To us it's just a job. It's just how we survive, and a lot of people really aren't looking for recognition or honor. We don't want to be mistreated like the Vietnam era of course. It was horrible for them, but we're just doing this." By saying "we're just doing this," Haskins emphasized the pragmatic reasons behind his enlistment. Don Haskins and Connor Guinness, quoted here, reject military leaders', politicians', and civilians' portrayals of military service as exceptional, more heroic, and valorous than other kinds of work. As soldier Tucker Watson said, "Sometimes it is too much, sometimes they don't want to hear accolades and things, sometimes you do your job and there are really no thanks to be given."

Moreover, these soldiers will return to a civilian economy where jobs are increasingly scarce for those with a high school education and where military service may not readily translate into work experience. In 2012, 20.4 percent of new veterans ages 18 to 24 were unemployed compared with 14.6 percent for same-aged nonveterans. Of 4,000 Iraq and Afghanistan veterans surveyed, 16 percent were unemployed in January 2013. Of these, one-third (33.8 percent) had been unemployed more than one year and 17 percent more than two years (Tarantino 2013).[10] Teachman and Tedrow (2007) found that young men from disadvantaged backgrounds earned more than their civilian peers while on active duty, but this difference disappeared following discharge. Whereas the post-9/11 GI Bill passed in 2008 provides generous education benefits, most new recruits are "C" students with a high school diploma (Kelty, Kleykamp, and Segal 2010) or the first in their families to attend college, for whom college may pose considerable challenges.

Not only is dirty work stigmatized, it is often dangerous and physically taxing. Ken MacLeish, in his ethnography of soldiers at Fort Hood, describes the toll that heavy gear, designed to protect soldiers from bullets and shrapnel, takes on their bodies. "Advocates for the injured told me numerous times about what they saw as the absurdly high rate of degenerative disk diagnoses among soldiers no older than twenty-two" (2013:63). These conditions may not always be recognized as injuries that lead to disability status upon discharge, yet render stable employment difficult and contribute to substance use to handle pain. Ironically, disability is one of few safety nets available for workers (Joffe-Walt 2013).

## A Changing Social Compact

Jobs that involve handling physical dirt are usually of relatively low social status, as are the workers who do them. But some high-status jobs may also have tasks related to dirt. Surgeons, who have very high occupational status, handle body parts and fluids. But they minimize the time spent handling them by delegating their disposal to lower-status operating room technicians and nurses (Dick 2005). Similarly, infantry soldiers, who may be valorized as heroes in public ceremonies and in the media, are referred to pejoratively as "grunts" in comparison with special forces or the officer corps.

Anthropologists Catherine Lutz and Kathleen Millar argue that "war is a site of morality production," in which civilians and soldiers alike "search for moral grounding to justify the killing and to explain the suffering" (2012:497). Unlike the mercenary, the soldier is a volunteer who exercises his individual will and thus is a moral agent, calling not upon market exchange of labor for wages but on a moral exchange between himself and the state. In exchange for willing sacrifice, the state promises care in case of injury, and burial and support for spouse and children in case of death. Perhaps most important, the state asks for the sacrifice in a just cause and true need. Thus the soldier becomes a "moral exemplar" and a hero.

With its focus on professionalism and skill, benefits, and opportunities, in effect today's soldiers may share more with mercenaries than they did before the AVF. Mercenaries exchange their services, including risking their lives, for money in the labor market. As a fair and free exchange, no moral obligation is implied; the mercenary is free to come and go at will. When the draft ended, the military deliberately retained the concept of the "volunteer." Volunteer invokes the American tradition of the citizen-soldier. During peacetime the citizen-soldier exercises her right to pursue personal goals and agendas, but in times of war willingly *volunteers* to *sacrifice* her individual need and desires, and possibly her body and life, in *service* to the good of the nation and its citizens (Lutz and Millar 2012).

Some of the soldiers we interviewed expressed their decision to enlist in just those terms. Kevin Watkins said, "I think everyone should serve their country in some way at some point throughout their life. I'm not going to make a career out of it. It's just something I've always wanted to do. Plus there was a war going on." For Stuart Gallup it was 9/11 that inspired him to join. "I felt that I needed to do it to serve my country and help keep terrorists away from here." Wilson Lemmons, like a handful of other soldiers, came from families with a tradition of military service. "Most of the men in my family have been in the army pretty much since the Civil War, so it's just kinda like my turn. And I just always knew I was going to join the army when I was a little kid."

Andrew Bickford, an anthropologist and veteran who served in Germany, argues that the myth of the fallen soldier as hero denies soldiers' diverse class, racial, ethnic, gendered, and regional origins. Individual soldiers in life, identified by name on their uniforms, are in death alike in identical flag-draped coffins. Through the myth, soldiers' backgrounds disappear as something they have overcome through their military service and death, "transforming everyday citizens into something more than mere mortals." He adds that heroism is "the balm we use to soothe the suffering of family and friends" left behind, but it is a shallow remedy that many "heroes" and their families reject (Bickford 2010). When we asked Daniel Quest if being honored helps soldiers deal with PTSD he replied, "Probably not. I don't think it helped me. People just brought it up constantly, every day. I'd get pissed off. I'm a freaking hero because I was shooting 50-caliber rounds through families' living rooms and shit. How does that make me a hero?" At the memorial for Pat Tillman, an army Ranger and former professional football player killed in action in Afghanistan, as it turns out by "friendly fire,"[11] politicians and public figures lined up to say, "'Pat, you are home. You are safe.'" His brother Richard Tillman "refused that glory, standing up to say this: 'He's not with God. He's f----- dead. He's not religious. So thanks for your thoughts, but he's f---- dead'" (Bickford 2010). Not only might the myth fail to offer comfort, but it also shrouds the social forces leading less than 1 percent of the US population to join up. The myth also strongly affects how soldiers see and understand their own roles and their experiences in war. Front line "tooth" combatants are central to the fallen soldier myth, further obscuring those in the "tail" and those working from air-conditioned, domestic bases. Thus the myth of the soldier as hero, though it gives us a simple and coherent image of the costs and benefits of war, actually sends us directly into the labyrinth where the true costs are hidden around blind corners and dead end paths.

Fighting an unpopular war may make maintaining self-esteem more difficult, especially when veterans return home to a citizenry that has been largely distant from the wars' effects. Soldier Brian Turner said that after being in Iraq:

> . . . my old friends kind of stopped talking to me. "Why are you there? You shouldn't be there. You're risking your life for nothing." I tried to explain it to them, and they didn't even understand. I see it in small ways making you kind of depressed about the job you picked or what you've been doing.

Soldiers don't necessarily want to be treated like heroes, but they don't want to be just a cog in the military machine either. Soldier Eric Nelson put it like this:

> They [the VA] make sure you are physically whole and better. And really, those wounds, you can recover from them. But from what I've seen and been doing personally, the things psychologically that happen to you, I mean those are scars that don't heal. You basically adapt and learn to live

*with it. And I don't think there's enough done, not nearly enough. It really makes it tough, especially in the military. . . . They don't want someone to say, "I can't do it anymore. I'm used up, I can't take another day in combat." They will call you every name under the sun for wanting out. You do get to the breaking point where you can't take it any more. Your chain of command will look down upon you, your officers, things like that. They're not going to want to hear that. They want you to do your job, which is completely understandable. People don't really look at the human side of things. They don't realize that yes, like I said, we are not just an insert that fills this uniform. We are a person, just like everybody else. We may have been trained to do a job. Mentally, our processes, they could be very much different than, I would say, regular people, normal people [he chuckles]. Still, you can't escape the fact that you are what you are. We're all human. We're all going to interpret and deal with stresses differently. Especially stresses like that. I think for the most part our job, we do and see things that no human being should ever have to see.*

We argue that stigma tied to death and dirty work is foundational—both more basic and thus less visible—than the stigma attached to PTSD explored in the previous chapter, which is both more extreme and, in this war, more visible. Lutz and Millar (2012) decry the tendency to attend disproportionately to war as produced at its margins, and call upon us to address moral questions "produced at the center" (2012:485) of war. Moving beyond PTSD means recognizing that soldiers' normal, everyday dirty work includes managing terror and taint alike.

# Chapter 3

## Lethal Warriors at Home

*The blade itself incites to deeds of violence.*
—Homer, *The Odyssey*

After their second, harrowing tour in Iraq, the 2nd Battalion, 12th Army Regiment—better known as the 2–12th or the "Lethal Warriors"—simply didn't bother to do an "Uncasing of the Colors" ceremony.[1] Even more than the "Welcome Home" ceremonies that precede returning troops rushing into the arms of their waiting loved ones, the purposes of the more solemn uncasing ceremony are to celebrate a successful mission abroad, provide closure at the conclusion of a deployment, and to celebrate that the unit has arrived safely back at home.

It took us a while to understand the significance of failing to observe Uncasing ceremonies.[2] We first noticed the unit's colors while awaiting the beginning of a memorial ceremony at Fort Carson. A soldier stood holding a wooden staff, topped with a shiny metal spade and festooned with some 40 to 50 ribbons of every color, each inked with different sayings and symbols. When we asked about it, he said, "This baby is our pride. She goes everywhere with us," lifting his chin a bit. "Basically, it represents everything we have ever done. One streamer for each thing, each battle." Colors mounted in this way descend from the armies of ancient Rome, where they were used to identify allies on the battlefield in the confusion of combat. As one general put it, "The very soul of a military unit is symbolized in the colors under which it fights, for it records the glories of the past, stands guardian over the present, and ensures inspiration for its future." The colors chronicle the history of a unit, but also its collective identity, such that the soldier could refer to what "we" have done in a way that includes fellows-in-arms dead long before his birth.

Strict protocol governs the care of colors, including their casing—or covering them with a cloth case—when a battalion (typically about 500 soldiers) or the larger brigade to which it belongs (about 4,000 soldiers) is in transit, either deploying or redeploying (coming home). Uncasing colors when taking position on a new deployment signals that "we have arrived, ready to engage," and in continuing engagements, "we are taking over from the unit rotating out." Uncasing after a deployment, historically, has meant "mission accomplished; we can let up our guard, return to civilian life, stand down."

In the face of unprecedented tempo of rotations between home and theater, between peace and war, the once-sacred observation of the uncasing of the colors was observed with less regularity, and especially for war-weary units like the 2–12th. As the wars in Afghanistan and Iraq wore into their seventh, eighth, and ninth years, regular-army units "returned home" for the second or third time, only to immediately begin preparing for the next deployment. Such units simply might not have felt they had time for the observance, given the rush to prepare and train for ever-changing circumstances in the wars. But the difference is also expressive of a psychological and spiritual state that any soldier "home" between deployments knows only too well: to ceremonialize closure, safety, or "being back" only gives the lie to the notion of something being "over." As one combat veteran told us, "If you don't ever uncase [the colors], you never know when you're done. Without that ceremony of completion, you never know. You always have to be ready."

Perpetually cased colors became for us a chilling symbol of what protracted wars and multiple deployments had meant for soldiers, their families and communities, and the nations to which they deployed: open-endedness and uncertainty, relentless hypervigilance, and lives suspended in limbo or what anthropologists have called "liminality": a state betwixt and between, neither here nor there, and above all else, unsettled, unstable, and potentially dangerous.[3]

This chapter continues the story begun in this book's introduction, from the point at which the army sought to recall our interview material with 2–12th soldiers. In detailing the particular case of how this battalion's multiple deployments culminated in a disturbing cluster of murders and other criminality back home, we draw from our own ethnography as well as from journalists' and epidemiologists' contributions. We assess the dominant theories proffered to explain the violence brought home: that the spike in criminality (1) did not exceed rates of aggression in the general population; (2) was caused by a few bad or disturbed individuals; or (3) resulted from PTSD caused by extensive combat exposure. Ultimately, we reject each as in itself inadequate. Instead we advocate understanding the case in terms of a complex interplay between these factors, together with the pressures created by mission-first imperatives and a force stretched thin. The "microcultural" factors, or the experiences and conditioned practices cultivated in units at or below the battalion level, are equally key. It is important to view the more sensational stories that follow in the context of the voices of the more representative, random sampling of soldiers from the unit we presented in chapters 1 and 2.

These are exceptional cases, though they should not be viewed wholly as outliers, we argue. Most soldiers, even those deeply affected by what they have seen and done, do not return home to commit acts of violence.

## A Brewing Storm at Fort Carson

By 2008, when we stepped into the picture, commanders at Fort Carson had their hands full. Deployment readiness became increasingly challenging as units faced a third 12- to 15-month deployment; many, like the 2–12th, now faced serving in Afghanistan after two tours in Iraq. Thousands of soldiers still found their active-duty periods involuntarily extended through the "stoploss" program (even as this "involuntary draft" was seen as jeopardizing morale) (Henning 2009), and nearly half of reactivated reservists were simply not showing up for duty.[4] Soldiers from the 2–12th shared their fears about deploying "under force": at less than 50 percent in some platoons, yet they were even more worried about how to prevent the "bags" (whether "dirt-" or "shit-")—"that guy who's gonna get us all killed"—from deploying with them. While the speedy forms of chaptering problem soldiers out were not yet in frequent use (but see chapter 8), commanders were not above classing bad behavior as a psychological injury and sending soldiers to the Warrior Transition Unit to get them off their deployment rosters. Meanwhile, as previous chapters show, for those who sought to leave the army, the air was thick with accusation of malingering and betrayal, of cowardice and abandoning their brothers. On top of all this, commanders struggled to confront psychological and behavioral issues—increasing rates of PTSD, depression and other diagnoses, suicide (Blumenthal 2012), violence, and criminality—all of which represented relatively new territory for which they had little expertise. Little priority was accorded to such matters, therefore, until events forced the issue. It was clear that units like the 2–12th Battalion were in unprecedented terrain regarding what weathering multiple deployments would ask of service members and their communities, but also on what "blow back" they would bring home.

The murders began as a trickle: in 2005, a 2–12th soldier killed his wife and then himself while on block leave after an Iraq tour (Denver Channel 2005), and in 2006, a soldier from a sister battalion in the 4th Brigade was charged with murdering a teenage marijuana dealer in the course of attempting to rob him (Walsh 2009). Six months before the latter killing, the soldier's mother had called his sergeant to warn him that her son was a "walking time bomb," always packing a gun and given to violent outbursts while consuming alcohol and pain pills at alarming levels. The sergeant said there was nothing he could do, and then preceded to ridicule the 21-year-old with taunts like "Your mommy called. She says you are going crazy" (Philipps 2009a). This affirmed what soldiers told us about the critical roles their NCOs played in whether or not they felt they could seek help; whereas some units had NCOs who encouraged them to seek help and arranged their work so that they could make their appointments for counseling and treatment, others reported harassment and abuse from their NCOs, such as being called "shitbag" or "psycho," and in one case being shot with a pellet gun.

Colonel Howard West, a psychiatrist then serving at Evans Army Community Hospital, would later venture a hypothesis, after all 14 murders had come to light, to explain the number of murderers grouped into a single unit. "I think that there's a unique cluster of individuals," he told us. "I would not underestimate the toxic effect of one militant psychopath at the center of an epidemic. You know, one kid can cause a spike." The "kid" the psychiatrist likely had in mind was Kenneth Eastridge. Once the murders began, Eastridge emerged as the poster boy for modeling criminal behavior, and catalyzing it in others (De Yoanna and Benjamin 2009).

Eastridge had grown up in Kentucky with his father, abandoned by a drug-addicted mother at 10. He was playing with his father's gun at the age of 12 when it discharged and killed his best friend. He was convicted of reckless homicide, but did counseling in lieu of jail time; when he dropped out of school at 17 he was still only in ninth grade. He tried to join the army but learned he would need to be granted a waiver to override any juvenile felony offense and that historically a homicide offense would preclude a waiver. But, in 2003 when Eastridge began making calls to recruiters, the military was beginning to feel stretched by its two-front war. After dozens of calls, a recruiter in Nashville chose to be the "someone to give [him] a chance." Eastridge rode the beginning of a wave that rose to 80,403 waivers between 2004 and 2009 as the army sought to meet the need for personnel in the escalating conflict in Iraq (Philipps 2010:18).

His unit was first stationed in Korea. Then, in 2004 and 2005 they were sent directly (without returning to the United States) to Al Anbar, one of the bloodiest parts of Iraq, for 15 months. Back in Colorado Springs, Eastridge was arrested for pointing a gun in his girlfriend's face, and then went AWOL—Absent Without Leave—for six months. He resurfaced at Fort Carson just weeks before the unit was to leave for Iraq for a second tour. Once again, pressing need for deployment-ready boots on the ground overrode his criminal record, and he was off to yet another of the harshest assignments in Iraq, a neighborhood outside Bagdad called Al Dora.

Eastridge did not make it through the second Iraq tour, where he emerged as the antithesis of a soldier fit for winning Iraqi "hearts and minds"

after he unleashed 1,700 rounds on Iraqi civilians against orders. He estimated that "not that many, maybe a dozen" were killed (Philipps 2010:155).
He later told *Frontline*:

> *It doesn't really matter to me. They're all hadjis to me. If I see a dead hadji
> it doesn't make it better that it's a civilian or an armed guy trying to kill
> me. 'Cause to us they're all guilty. You disassociate; to you they're not even
> people. They're not humans; they're not like us; they're not the same as us.
> They're hadjis and we're not.*

He was confined to the FOB (Forward Operating Base), where he continued
his now-established practice of selling Valium and other drugs to his fellow soldiers. When he was caught passed out in bed with a female soldier
from a supply company, he lunged at his sergeant, yelling that he would kill
him, suck out his blood, and spit it at his children. This led to him being
court-marshaled on nine counts—none included the killing of civilians—but
for disobeying orders, drug possession, and assaulting an officer (Philipps
2010:155–56). When he was sent back to Fort Carson to be processed out
of the army, he escaped from custody, and holed up in a hotel. He relied on
two friends also sent back early from Iraq for transportation: Louis Bressler,
who had been medically discharged after punching his sergeant (as part of a
move to "get rid of dead wood" [Smith 2009]); and Bruce Bastien, who had
tried unsuccessfully to get out of the army by having Eastridge shoot him in
Iraq, then successfully by beating his wife back in the United States.

Just two nights after his dishonorable discharge from the army, Eastridge
was at wits' end, sleeping on Bressler's couch, broke, and scheming for ways
to pay for an apartment. With Bressler and Bastien, he began devising robbery schemes, targeting a sporting goods store and a nightclub. He wasn't
happy when Bressler brought along Bastien, whom Eastridge did not like,
but Bressler assured him that Bastien was "cool," and that they had "*done* shit
together" (Philipps 2010:163).

The "shit" had been done two months earlier, beginning when Bressler
and Bastien searched for men Bastien's wife reported had chased her home.
Stoned and drunk, they went hunting, and Bressler ended up shooting three
rounds at the first person they saw, a fellow soldier, and wounding him in the
shoulder. A week later, again drugged and intoxicated, they offered a ride to
Robert James, a drunken soldier who had lost his way trying to get back to
Fort Carson. When the ride turned into a robbery attempt, Bressler forced
James out of the car, shot him in the neck, and then three more times in the
face, leaving him dead in a bank parking lot. The next morning, police came

to Bastien's house on a domestic violence call. The following day, Bressler also assaulted his wife, commanded her to shoot him or he would shoot her, then attempted suicide by swallowing nearly one hundred Depakote and Remeron pills he had been prescribed for depression and insomnia. He was hospitalized and remained in a coma for over a week, and was then transferred to a lockdown psychiatric ward at Cedar Springs, a private hospital in Colorado Springs, which at the time was receiving problem veterans from Fort Carson at a rate seven hundred times the average for other army hospitals (Smith 2009). After just three days, Bastien, claiming to be Bressler's sergeant, managed to spring him to take him to Evans Hospital at Fort Carson.

One early morning in late October, while the three were laying plans for robberies, they headed to a pot dealer's house. On the way, they saw a young woman, 19-year-old Erica Ham, walking to a bus stop. Bastien suggested, "Let's rob that bitch." Bressler swerved the SUV and hit her. Bastien jumped out and stabbed her six times, puncturing a lung and slicing her deeply across the left eye.

A month later, the three spoke of robbery plans in the presence of a soldier from their unit, Specialist Kevin Shields, who had also been with Eastridge and Bressler in Korea and through both Iraq tours and was freshly returned to Colorado Springs. Shields, out celebrating his 24th birthday while his wife stayed home with their three-year-old, was driving around with the trio after the clubs closed, when Bressler began vomiting. They stopped the car so he could puke, while the other three ridiculed him. Being taunted by his two buddies was less of an issue than being taunted by Shields, who was not a buddy. Bressler was also concerned that Shields would give up their plans. He took a swing at Shields, who then "kicked Bressler's ass." What happened afterward is unclear, except that it ended when Bressler shot Shields twice in the head, "execution style." The three left his body sprawled on a sidewalk (Smith 2009).

Over the week that followed, Bressler, Eastridge, and Bastien were arrested by Colorado Springs police. Bastien, after admitting to police that he had seen Shields the night of his murder, later provided much of the information necessary for the arrests and criminal charges, thinking he could get himself off. However, Eastridge disclosed that Bastien had been the one to stab Erica Ham, and he too was taken into custody. Eastridge would ultimately exchange an agreement to testify against the other two for a 10-year sentence as an accessory to the murder of Kevin Shields. Bastien would plead guilty to accessory to the murder of Kevin Shields, conspiracy to murder Robert James, and conspiracy to commit aggravated murder in the stabbing of Erica Ham and received a 60-year sentence. When Bressler's trial began, after the other two had been sentenced, Bastien reneged on his agreement to testify. Without this testimony, prosecutors failed to convict Bressler of first-degree homicide. Despite all indications that he had pulled the trigger in both the James and Shields killings, he would be convicted solely for conspiracy to commit murder and, like Bastien, be sentenced to 60 years (Philipps 2010:178, 183).

## Out of the Frying Pan, and "Smoked"

Even as Fort Carson absorbed the blow of this trio's arrests, the bad news kept coming. Two marauding buddies from the 2–12th were arrested for cruising the streets of Colorado Springs and firing an AK-47 in an apparently random, drive-by fashion. First the pair shot an army captain in the leg; days later, they gunned down a couple who were posting garage sale signs (Frosch 2008; Mitchell 2008). These two arrests, however, puzzled their fellow soldiers; one told the *Gazette* that, unlike the trio arrested previously, these two were "just solid, average soldiers" (Roeder 2008a); they were what soldiers called "squared away."[5] The 2–12th's then-commander, Lieutenant Colonel Allan Sullivan, when asked to comment on the growing number of criminal counts leveled at his soldiers, argued that the "unit should be seen in a different light," and that he wanted "people to get to know the more than 99 percent of his soldiers who aren't under arrest" (Roeder 2008a). He added that the 2–12th's soldiers were proud to belong to a battalion that lost 32 men in combat since 2004. As the Colorado Springs *Gazette* reporter summed it up, just after the arrests in August 2008, "they're angry that as they're preparing to go to Afghanistan to battle the resurgent Taliban they have to again defend their reputation at home" (Roeder 2008a).

But the arrests kept coming: in the fall of 2008 there were two more. A soldier from a cavalry regiment also assigned to the 4th Brigade confessed to violently raping and then slitting the throat of a developmentally disabled 19-year-old woman, leaving her to die on a mountain road above Colorado Springs. Twenty-one years old and with a history of psychosis, he had revealed on his MySpace page that he saw himself as a human-born member of the Black Raptors race: "I'm becomeing [sic] a cold hearted killer and can kill without mercy or reason," he wrote in his MySpace profile days before the arrest (Benzel 2008).

Also arrested that fall was John Needham, "Surfer John," a former 2–12th soldier living back home with family in Orange County, California, and charged with beating his 19-year-old girlfriend to death. The accused veteran claimed no recollection of the event, but the tragedy followed numerous incidents of delusions and dementia, according to family. 2–12th Commander Sullivan pronounced a bad-apple reading on what had happened, as he had with the earlier homicides. "Anybody that does crimes of that nature, it goes deeper and farther back than anything in the US Army," he told the *Los Angeles Times* after Needham's arrest. "Nothing here has trained them to do what they are charged with" (Esqivel et al. 2008).

## Seeking Explanations

Until the pieces implicating the 2–12th and 4–4th Brigade began to connect, military brass and spokespersons had cleaved to what can be thought of as a "baseline thesis" for explaining service-member criminality: although rates of drug abuse, child neglect and abuse, domestic violence, and other forms of criminal violence by combat veterans might appear to be alarming, in fact they did not exceed rates in the broader population. In this line of thinking, service members like the soldiers at Fort Carson were simply thrust under unfair scrutiny, typically by sensationalizing journalists hungry for a story, or by critics of the wars and US militarism, who used pathologies among service members to further their political agendas about the fundamental waste, or wrongness, of war in general or these wars in particular. Like 2–12th commander Sullivan, they emphasized the majority of soldiers with clean records at home and honorable service while deployed.

As commanders began to recognize a problem of potentially epidemic proportions, Fort Carson officials began to rely more on the "bad apples" thesis, which focused on figures like Kenny Eastridge. With his juvenile felony record, admission to the military on a waiver, and reputation for atrocities in Iraq, he presented the perfect focal point for such a theory, as propounded by the psychiatrist looking to "one militant psychopath."

But it was becoming harder to fit the pieces together into neat versions of either the "baseline" or "few bad apples" explanations. First, though present during the two murders and one attempted murder for which the trio was ultimately deemed responsible, Kenny Eastridge had not been the one to pull the trigger, or wield the knife, in any of the three assaults. Nor did it explain John Needham, or the duo pulling drive-bys, or the earlier murders. Early 2009 would see still two more 2–12th soldiers charged: one discharged rounds into a party he had left, striking a young pregnant woman in the thigh (Philipps 2009b); the other shot and killed a young woman (her death was ultimately deemed accidental by a jury) during a card game (St. Louis-Sanchez and Philipps 2009a, 2009b).

Just days after we interviewed the 2–12th soldiers, then-Senator Ken Salazar wrote to a letter to Army Secretary Peter Geren and to Fort Carson's Garrison Commander, Major General Mark Graham.[6] He demanded a thorough review of the effects that waiving unqualified recruits into the army were having. "In the Army's effort to meet its target recruiting numbers, the service has been issuing an increasing number of waivers to recruits who may not meet educational or moral standards," Salazar wrote. Despite army claims of new programs and better screening for soldiers for PTSD and TBIs, Salazar emphasized more needed to be done, calling for improved tracking of problem soldiers once back home, and for the army to include more civilian providers to increase treatment options for soldiers. "Although the Army has taken steps to implement screenings and provide counseling after a deployment, the Army is clearly overwhelmed by the scope of the problem," he wrote (K. Mitchell 2008; *Colorado Springs Independent* 2008; Roeder 2008b).

Graham, one of the recipients of Salazar's letter, was just completing his first year overseeing Fort Carson. More than any other figure, he would become associated with Fort Carson emerging from a reputation of neglect and undertreatment of combat stress in the first half of the post-9/11wars, to being widely recognized as at the cutting edge of treating, and reducing the stigma associated with, combat stress. For Graham, the effort was deeply personal: he and his wife Carol lost their younger son, Kevin, a top ROTC cadet, to suicide in 2003. Kevin had a history of depression, which he had been successfully treating with medication. When he competed for selection to an elite leadership camp, however, he was faced with having to disclose his prescription use, which likely would have eliminated his chances of successful selection. So he discontinued the antidepressants. A month later, his younger sister found him hanging from a rope in his apartment (Philipps 2010:39–40).

Just eight months later, the Grahams lost their older son, Jeffery, a commissioned first lieutenant deployed in Iraq, to an IED blast. The Grahams later reflected that the differences between the ways they themselves, and the rest of the world, responded to the two deaths, were their personal initiation into the problematic stigma surrounding mental illness, especially in the military. When Kevin killed himself, people did not really know what to say, and many resorted to silence. The Grahams' own shame and confusion at what had gone wrong contributed to this silence. Jeffery's death in combat, by contrast, was something people knew how to recognize, allowing them to honor and grieve the loss. The Grahams' personal history is inevitably cited as part of what many, at least initially, viewed as Mark Graham's "breaking ranks." He stopped seeing violent crime and suicides committed by military personnel as dirty laundry to be minimized or normalized as inevitable costs of war, and consequently became willing to invite in civilian collaboration to understand and address the problem.

But all of this was just beginning when Graham received the senator's letter. In response, the general consulted with Fort Carson personnel in search of a strategy. Soon he was on the phone to the surgeon general and an epidemiological study was in the offing, to help them "get a fresh set of eyes on the problem" (Philipps 2010:236; Colonel Heidi Terrio, personal communication, November 2008). In November, a multidisciplinary team arrived at Fort Carson. They were charged with exploring the factors that may have contributed to the killings and were given free rein to go anywhere and talk to anyone they chose.

### The EPICON Report and the "Media Shit Storm"

On July 16, 2009, the epidemiological report, or EPICON, was released. At the press conference held that day, Graham summed up the findings: "This extremely in-depth study did not reveal any one single cause, but rather a comprehensive list of individual, predisposing factors such as criminal behaviors, drug and/or alcohol abuse, prior behavioral health issues, and barriers to seeking behavioral health care" (Edge 2010). An analysis of installation-wide trends at Fort Carson found that the murder rate doubled between 2003 and 2008; rape rates for 2008 were more than two times that of comparable installations.

One portion of the study analyzed the 14 soldiers arrested for murder, attempted murder, or manslaughter. Ten (71%) of these were from the 4th BCT and six of these were from the 2–12th Battalion. Nine of the 13 surviving perpetrators (one committed suicide) consented to be interviewed in custody. The report found that most of the 14 soldiers had experienced unusually intense combat in Iraq; six had returned early from the tour (three for misconduct, two for a suicide attempt or ideation) and did not receive full reintegration training. Eight had a documented history of all three major risk factors predisposing them to "negative behavioral outcomes": mental illness, criminal history or past history of violence, and substance abuse; all 14 had at least one of these factors. Six of them had criminal records before they joined the military, but only three had received conduct or alcohol waivers. Eleven of them had a history of substance abuse. Nine were taking prescription medications. The study concluded that leadership failures and barriers to seeking care, including stigma tied to mental health struggles, may have contributed to the killings (EPICON 2009). At the same time, the report emphasized that "these crimes remain very rare events in a large population of soldiers who, to varying degrees, share many of the same risk factors but did not participate in criminal activities" (EPICON 2009:17).

The study surveyed more than 2,700 soldiers, comparing the 4th BCT to a sister brigade, the 3rd BCT. Within the 4th BCT the research team conducted focus groups with more than 400 soldiers, with lower-level enlisted soldiers being oversampled, as the killings were all committed by "grunts" at these levels. While neither waivers nor other demographic factors were associated with criminality, aggressive behavior and other problems were strongly associated with combat intensity. The 4th BCT experienced a combat death rate of 8.9 per 1,000 soldiers during a first Iraq deployment and 9.6 per 1,000 on a second deployment. In comparison, the 3rd BCT had death rates of 0.4 and 2.1 per 1,000, respectively. In other words, the 4th BCT saw combat death rates more than 16 times higher in the first deployment and more than 100 times higher in the second deployment than in the comparison brigade (the 3rd BCT). The report's authors were careful not to equate the firm numbers of battle deaths with self-reports of combat intensity (subjective and therefore arguably less accurate or reliable). However, combat deaths are a reasonable index for combat intensity, and such significantly higher rates point to soldiers in the 4th BCT experiencing much more intense combat. Soldiers who reported being in high-intensity combat were at least twice as likely to report aggression, alcohol use, criminal convictions, and "self-reported behavioral health problems" as soldiers who reported being in moderate and low-intensity combat. Moreover, of those testing positive for illicit drugs, mostly cocaine and amphetamines, only 20 percent received the required drug screening within 30 days (EPICON 2009:17).

Factors called "amplifiers" that were found to increase aggression included distrust, access to weapons, and a "tolerant attitude toward the expression of aggression." The report added combat exposure and stigma tied to seeking help as additional factors. These would ideally be balanced by "attenuators," such as close social networks. However, this disregards the possibility that the nature of "unit closeness" could, under some circumstances, act as much as an amplifier as an attenuator. The authors speculate that the 4th Brigade and 2–12th Battalions experienced more amplifiers and fewer attenuators (EPICON 2009:17). The convergence of multiple risk factors might, the report suggests, compound the risk in the population as a whole, increasing the likelihood of the "clustering of negative outcomes" (EPICON 2009:20).

This was as close as the analysis came to exploring the possibility of patterns of belief and practice—what anthropologists call "culture"—taking root in specific units like the 2–12th. In a discussion of the EPICON report with *Frontline*, Brigadier General Stephen Xenakis (Ret.) ventures in a similar direction when he comments:

*Recently there's been some recognition of what's called "social contagion," a whole different area . . . . In the Army, for years we called that "command climate," and it's hard to measure, but we know that certain units who have had particular experiences, been in particular situations, seem to have either particular problems or for some reason they seem to be distinguished.*[7]

The report also registered important areas of change. Soldiers seeking behavioral health care had increased four-fold since 2004, attributable in part to higher "burden of disease," but also to better screening and efforts to diminish stigma attached to seeking care. At the same time, staff positions at Evans Army Hospital had 35 percent vacancy rates across psychiatrists, psychologists, and social workers (EPICON 2009:20). We address responses to these issues at greater length in chapter 4.

Critics of the EPICON report objected that the army was remiss in their interpretation of the investigation's findings. By arguing that the results are merely correlational and do not point to causation, army analysts skate over the degree to which repeated combat exposure and combat intensity appear to be at the base of the cluster of murders (Associated Press 2009; De Yoanna and Benjamin 2009b). Although it is important not to move directly from correlation or association to causation, many public health interventions are based on factors significantly associated with health outcomes that are plausibly related and match other sources of data such as observation; for example, smoking and lung cancer. Thus, the strong correlation between repeated combat exposure and combat intensity and self-reported behaviors of criminality, substance use, and aggression presented in the EPICON report are further supported in the RAND Corporation's national study of mental health injuries in US military personnel and studies of soldiers in the United Kingdom (MacManus et al. 2012; Rona et al. 2009; Tanelian and Jaycox 2008), provide strong evidence that these factors contributed to the cluster of murders. At the very least, given the destructive nature of the behaviors, they are cause for alarm and intervention.

The report did not address what Graham came to describe as a "crescendo" factor, based on the observation that few of the murders emerged without smaller offenses—warning signs—coming first: insubordination with officers, domestic violence and other assaults, rapes, suicide threats, and drug and alcohol abuse. Neither did it address such issues as soldiers carrying firearms back home, alleged war crimes by the unit, or the military deploying soldiers with pending civilian felonies (Philipps 2009b).

While the epidemiological team worked, the press did not lay idle. A mounting series of reports appeared spanning local and national media, and from print and live news sources, on what was increasingly referred to as "the murder brigade" or "the murder battalion": and thus fulfilling one veteran advocate's goal of creating "a media shit storm" (Philipps 2010:234).[8] This extensive reporting brought out an irony about attempts to tie the spate of murders to a particular "unit's" subculture or history, however.[9]

What was now the 2–12th Battalion of the 4th Brigade had simply not existed as such in either Iraq tour (2004–2005 or 2007–2008). Many of the longest-standing cohorts, including individuals now facing homicide charges, in their first Iraq tour had been part of a wholly different battalion, regiment, and division (the 1–506th of the 2nd Brigade, 2nd Infantry Division), better known as the "Band of Brothers" (whose WWII history was made famous by Steven Ambrose and later an HBO miniseries). After their first Iraq tour (2004–2005), they took the news they would be reflagged as the reactivated 2–12th battalion "like a sucker punch," one soldier's wife told us.[10] "It was like having their identity yanked out from under them." While routine army reorganization played some part, intervention was also an element: the new brigade commander vowed in 2005 that his "number 1 charter was to reset this brigade." A company commander decided to rename one of the battalion's companies, from "Charlie Company" to "Chosen Company," seeing a chance for the unit to break from what he called a "troubled past" (Philipps 2010:102–3).[11] The old Charlie Company's 3rd Platoon, a group of 40 that included Eastridge and Barco, would later form the focus of journalist Dan Edge's investigation for *Frontline*, titled "Wounded Platoon." After the cohorts' second Iraq tour, a similarly abrupt reflagging was again commanded when the battalion was moved from the 2–2 (2nd Brigade 2nd Infantry Division) to the 4–4 (Figure 4). The "unit" that was the focus of the EPICON analysis, then, was constituted as such mere months before the study was launched.

Anthropologists will not be surprised, then, how quickly attempts to characterize a unit's "microculture" is bedeviled by the same problems the culture concept confronts more generally: static, bounded, freeze-frame pictures cannot show the dynamic, complex, and overlapping actuality of

---

**FIGURE 4.** Combat patches for 2-2 "Indianhead" (A), the 506th's "Band of Brothers" (B), 2–12th's "Lethal Warriors" (C), and 4–4 Mountain Warriors (also 4th ID) (D). (Photos from www.usmilitariaforum.com, www.globalsecurity.org, Wikipedia, and www. militaryuniformsupply.com, respectively; used by permission from the Institute of Heraldry.)

A          B          C          D

individual and collective histories and practices. To get some idea of how for individual soldiers their previous, now residual unit identifications may trump their current assignments, consider the 2–12th, 4–4 soldiers' combat patches on their right shoulders. These patches—the ones they choose, unlike the command patches worn on the left shoulder that designate their current command and that they are required to wear—were as likely to be the 2–2 or the 1–506th's as the 2–12th or 4–4.

While these may seem fine or even trivial distinctions, they matter very much to individual soldiers, who again "fight for their unit colors,"[12] talk about them in terms of lineages and traditions, and in which they invest pride and identification.

Despite their different colors, lineages, histories, and traditions, the 1–506th[13] and 2–12th[14] battalions hold critical things in common: both are frontline, intrepid infantry units with histories of distinction on the battlefield. As Bradley Kay, who was a "Brother" before he served as a "Warrior," told us:

> If you look up the 1st of the 506, or the 2–12, since like WWII, we have the reputation of getting sent to the worst places, doing the best job, and winning the war overseas. And then when we get back, we have the reputation of getting in the most trouble. We do great over there, and kick ass over there, but when we get back, we get in trouble.

Particularly after each of the two duty tours in Iraq, with 33 of their soldiers lost (Esquivel et al. 2008), both units were known for visiting "home"—now the Pikes Peak region for both units—with problems.

### "Smoked": A Daunting Afterward

Leaders at Fort Carson worked on turning the tide on the worst effects of combat stress injuries, informed by the EPICON report's isolation of risk factors that had to be carefully managed and reduced. Even as it appeared that greater combat exposure was as close to an explanation for the murders as could be found, and that there was nothing singular in the "culture" of the 2–12th that led to the spike in criminality, the story continued to unfold, introducing sobering new details.

By 2010, "Surfer John" Needham, arrested in 2008 for beating his girlfriend to death, was out on a $1 million bail bond, living with his father in California, and undergoing a series of spinal surgeries, though still not receiving mental health care. Then suddenly he was dead, though whether from postsurgical infection, the presence of a tumor, or from an opiate overdose remained unclear. John's veteran father, Mike Needham, very much alive, continued to advocate for justice and his son's memory. A 2011 documentary revealed new angles on what Michael Needham, who had a background in military intelligence, learned from his son about his army experience that had yet to reach the public.[15]

First was the account on John's initiation into the 2–12th when he first arrived at Fort Carson:

> *Upon arrival to Fort Carson, John was taken down range, on the Fort, and the Lethal Warrior leadership, the NCOs and sergeants, took him to a small building, in which they initiated him with a kind of a Lethal Warriors welcome. It consisted of a cage fight. It was a bare knuckles, no holds barred, there was nothing . . . . Your job at that point in time was to beat the other soldier. And it was for a pecking order within the unit. So, the more successful you were in this fight, the better job you'd have gotten within the unit. And if you were at the bottom of it, you more than likely were going to get what they called "smoked." In the military, in the Army, "smoking" or to "smoke" someone means that you make them leave, quit. In some cases soldiers commit suicide.[16]*

John triumphed in his initiation, putting down five other soldiers, earning "a stripe" promotion, and getting assigned to the battalion's most aggressive platoon sergeant.

He deployed to Iraq in October of 2006, but was assigned to a unit separate from the 2–12th until March of 2007. When he got back to the 2–12th, he noticed immediately that "there was something wrong" with the unit; he "witnessed many killings of civilians that he thought was unjustified" and which did not follow the rules of engagement.

Once, when he questioned the killings, he was told in so many words, "Nobody that's on the street is good, so they all deserve to die," and to mind his own business. John became a soldier to be managed, according to his father. He was assigned to a squad where the NCOs would keep him away from such activities, but he still saw his share. Summing up what his son told him, Michael Needham said:

> *The 2–12th were basically street thugs, they were gangsters; they terrorized the neighborhoods. They would go on missions; they were kind of an "Apocalypse Now" type of existence where they were operating outside the known limits of the Army. They would bust down doors, go in houses, steal drugs, particularly pills they were looking for, any kind of opiates they were looking for Xanax and other types of anti-depressants. They looked for weapons. They were keeping weapons caches. In some cases they raped women.*

*In other cases they would brutalize the parents and put guns to heads of little children to make the parents give up information. And they were looking for money, too. There was a large amount of cash being pretty much given around town at that point in time. And these people were basically committing criminal acts.*

Other soldiers reported to Dave Philipps that 2–12th platoons would stockpile guns taken from Iraqis to use as "drop weapons," to be dropped next to anyone they killed who was unarmed to justify the kill. They would also shoot off these arms to initiate contact, so that the sounds of Iraqi AK-47s preceded "return" of US fire, and therefore was not subject to question.

John survived 14 explosions on the tour, and like other soldiers, received little or no care and went back out on patrol. Then in September, John and a lieutenant, another soldier who was not onboard with participating in war crimes, were sent alone on a "secret mission," deep in the middle of insurgent territory in the Al Dora neighborhood. As soon as they got to the appointed house, where they were to exchange cash for intelligence, they came under fire from three positions. John went through 16 magazines of ammunition holding off the assault; meanwhile, the two repeatedly called on the radio to the 2–12th for backup, and received no response. Finally, as they were running out of ammunition, a nearby cavalry unit came in and extracted them. When John returned to the 2–12th's FOB, he railed against his unit members, calling them out for setting him up and trying to get him killed. He received no response; no one came out or talked to him.

John grew increasingly despondent, started drinking heavily, and then became suicidal. He was with his bunkmate when he pulled out a pistol and put it to his head. His father reported, "He said, 'Goodbye, Chris, this is it for me.' And he started to pull the trigger and Chris leaped out and knocked the gun back behind his head, which fired into the wall."

Once the firearm discharged, John was taken into custody, but not before being beaten by members of his unit. Rather than getting help for being suicidal, he was charged with firing a weapon in the barracks, and held captive for 30 days with little food or water, much of which was snuck to him by friends. Only his father's involvement prevented him from being transferred long-term to a prison in Kuwait. Once he learned John was being held, Michael began making calls, finally reaching Fort Carson's inspector general.

John was taken for medical examination. His father summarized the findings: "He had a severe spinal neck and head trauma. Traumatic brain injury. Broken vertebrae in his neck, back, and lower back. Shrapnel throughout his body. And severe PTSD. He had TBI, PTSD, and physical wounds and was ordered back to the States immediately, medevac'd to Walter Reed Hospital through Germany."

The 2–12th's commander at the time, Lieutenant Colonel Steven Michael, did not want to give John up so easily, and ordered him to be taken back into custody at Fort Carson through the unit's rear detachment. Once there, the abuse from fellow soldiers began again, pounding on his door in the middle of the night, and putting John's name up on a board next to a photograph of a "pussy," or woman's genitalia, or placing a "Hurt Feelings Report" in his room, ridiculing his mental wounds. A doctor attached to the battalion examined him and declared him fit for duty; the unit prepared to return him to Iraq.

Meanwhile, Michael Needham had involved veterans' advocate Andrew Pogany and journalist Michael de Yoanna in the case.[17] Pogany went to General Graham, and John was given permission to be taken off-post by his father for several days, and later, back to California for four days. During this period, Michael became so alarmed by his son's state—both physical, with severe back pain requiring surgery, and mental, with numerous disturbing incidents of flashbacks and dementia—that he had him admitted to Balboa Naval Hospital in California. Michael Needham had also become fearful for his son's life under 2–12th control, and was determined to see that he not return to Fort Carson.

As John began receiving treatment in California, he started sharing his recollections of atrocities committed in Iraq. Pogany, the veterans' advocate, informed the family that John was obligated by international law and US law to inform the army, or be found complicit and potentially subject to prosecution. This resulted in John writing the following letter to the Inspector General, Secretary of the Army, Commanding General at Fort Carson:

December 18, 2007

**To:** Mr. Randy Waddle, Assistant Inspector General, Ft Carson, Colorado
**CC:** LTC John Shawkins, Inspector General, Ft Carson, Colorado, Major General Mark Graham, Commanding Officer, Ft Carson, Colorado, Major Haytham Faraj, USMC, Camp Pendleton, California, LT General Stanley Greene, US Army Inspector General
**Subject:** Formal Notification of War Atrocities and Crimes Committed by Personnel, B Company, 2–12, 2nd Brigade Combat Team, 2nd Infantry Division in Iraq

Dear Mr. Waddle:
My name is John Needham. I am a member of Bravo Company, 2nd Battalion, 2nd Infantry division, 2nd Brigade Combat Team, 2nd Infantry Division, (BCo, 2–12INF, 2BCT, 2ID). I deployed with my unit to Iraq from October 2006 until October 2007 when I was medically evacuated for physical and mental injuries that I suffered during my deployment. The purpose of my letter is to report what I believe to be

war crimes and violation of the laws of armed conflict that I personally witnessed while deployed in Iraq.

Upon arriving in Iraq in October of 2006 my unit was assigned to the 1-4 Cavalry unit at Camp Prosperity. In March of 2007 I was sent back to my unit, B Company 2-12 at Camp Falcon. It was at Camp Falcon that I observed and was forced to participate in ugly and inhumane acts against the Iraqi citizens in our area of responsibilities. Below I list some of the incidents that took place.

In March of 2007, I witnessed SSG Platt shoot and wound an Iraqi national without cause or provocation. The Staff Sergeant said that he suspected the Iraqi [to] be a "trigger" man. We had not been attacked and we found no evidence on the man to support the suspicion. As the Iraqi lay bleeding on the ground, PVT Smith requested to administer first aid to the Iraqi. SSG Platt said no and "let him bleed out." When SSG Platt walked away, PVT Smith and PVT Mullins went to the Iraqi, dragged him to an alley, and applied first aid. They then drove him to the cache for further treatment.

In June of 2007 1SG Spry caused an Iraqi male to be stopped, questioned, detained, and killed. We had no evidence that the Iraqi was an insurgent or terrorist. In any event when we stopped he did not pose a threat. Although I did not personally witness the killing, I did observe 1SGT Spry dismembering the body and parading it while it was tied to the hood of a Humvee around the Muhalla neighborhood while the interpreter blared out warnings in Arabic over the loud speaker. I have a photo that shows 1SGT Spry removing the victim's brains. On another occasion an Iraqi male was stopped by a team led by SGT Rogers as he walked down an alleyway. The Iraqi was detained and questioned then with his hands tied behind his back, SGT Rogers skinned his face.

1SGT Spry shot a young Iraqi teenager who was about 16 years old. The shooting was unprovoked and the Iraqi posed no threat to the unit. He was merely riding his bicycle past an ambush site. When I arrived on the scene I observed 1SGT Spry along with SSG Platt dismember the boy's body.

In August of 2007, I responded to radio call from SGT Rogers reporting that he had just shot an Iraqi who was trying to enter through a hole that the platoon had blown in a wall to allow them observation of the area during a security patrol. When I arrived, I saw a one-armed man who was still alive lying on a barricade. The man was about 30 years old. He had an old Ruger pistol hanging from his thumb. It was obvious to me that the pistol was placed there because of the way it hung from his thumb. The Iraqi was still alive when I arrived. I saw SGT Rogers shoot him twice in the back with hollow point bullets. The Iraqi was still moving. I was asking why they shot him again when I heard SGT Hoskins say "he's moving, he's still alive." SPEC Hoskins then moved to the Iraqi and shot him in the back of the head. SSG Platt and SGT Rogers were visibly excited about the kill. I saw them pull the Iraqi's brains out as they placed him in the body bag. CPT Kirsey must have learned something about this incident because he was very upset and admonished the NCOs involved.

I have seen and heard 1SGT Spry brag about killing dogs. He kept a running count. At last count I remember he was boasting of having killed 80 dogs.

On many occasions I observed SGT Temples, SSG Platt, and SGT Rogers beat and abuse Iraqi teenagers, some as young as 14, without cause. They would walk into a house near areas where they suspected we had received sniper fire, then detain and beat the kids.

I have photos that support my allegations. I also have numerous other photos on a laptop PC that the unit illegally seized from me. I have requested its return but they have refused.

My experiences have taken a terrible toll on me. I suffer from PTSD and depression. I had no way to stop the ugly actions of my unit. When I refused to participate they began to abuse and harass me. I am still in treatment at the Balboa Naval Hospital. I respectfully request that you investigate these matters, that you protect my safety by reassigning me to a different unit that is not located at Fort Carson, that you return my PC or, at least, seize it to protect the evidence on it, and that you issue a military protective order to prohibit the offending members of my unit from harassing, retaliating, or contacting me.

I have some photographs and some supporting documentation to these allegations.

Respectfully,

PFC John Needham, US Army[18]

One of the few tangible results of the letter is that John's pending dishonorable discharge was changed to a medical, honorable discharge. Though he then received surgeries and psychological care, it was not enough to stop his downward slide. Less than a year after penning the letter, he was arrested for beating his girlfriend to death, and 18 months later, he was dead.

On his son's ultimate fate, Michael Needham said:

*It's interesting to me that the Department of Defense, the Department of the Army, can spend unlimited amounts of money to invade a country, pay for any weapons, expend million dollar missiles without thinking, but they won't fund any type of recovery programs for the soldiers that come back.*

Author Dave Philipps, writing before John's letter or his apparent risk of life from his own battalion came to light, upholds the significance of the Needham case as contradicting any last validity a "bad-apple" thesis might hold:

*Needham's story, perhaps more than any other in the battalion, should offer pause for skeptics. He did not have a criminal past like Kenneth Eastridge. He was not a liar and aspiring gangster like Bruce Bastien. He did not have a history of violence in Iraq like Anthony Marquez. He did not drop out of high school and score poorly on aptitude tests like Louis Bressler. He came from a loving, supportive family. He was a smart, well-liked, and well-adjusted kid. He joined the infantry in a time of great need, driven by patriotic altruism. He was a model soldier with an instantly*

*endearing smile and a can-do attitude that made him a favorite of com-*
*manders. He fought bravely and resisted Iraq's tendency to turn soldiers*
*savage. It is very hard to look at the mug shot of John Needham and believe*
*he would have turned out that way even without Iraq (Philipps 2010:225).*

Philipps goes on to observe that though Needham availed himself of all the
psychiatric care the military had to offer and had the love and assistance of
family, in the end, they were

*not enough. They could not counter what Needham had experienced in*
*Iraq. They could not keep him from self-destructing . . . . The story of John*
*Needham is the story of how powerful the venom of war is for some soldiers*
*who saw the worst, and how poorly prepared society is to offer an antidote*
*(Philipps 2010:225–26).*

Yet, is it merely the "venom of war" in a generic sense that broke John
Needham? Newer aspects of his case in particular beg the question about the
degree to which *moral* wounds compound combat stress injuries. PTSD can
result, it is clear, from the rigors of "righteous" conflict, where horrific means
may still justify valid ends. But in cases like Needham's, was it merely seeing
and participating in bloodshed, or learning that it was often perpetrated, in
part, for the wrong reasons, and in defiance of international law? How much
did his disillusionment about leadership, enforced silences, betrayal by his
comrades, and finding himself at risk of all manner of harm within his unit,
factor in? Needham's case broaches unspoken, and often censured, territory
in discussions of the psychological ravages of combat stress injuries.

Whether John Needham's letter contributed to any investigations about
the 2–12th's activities in Iraq is unclear. An agent from Fort Carson's Criminal Investigations Division sent to interview Bruce Bastien, who while in
police custody began providing information about 2–12th war crimes, spent
just 39 minutes listening to Bastien. The investigator quickly became frustrated about the lack of exact dates and corroborating records. The army
asked at least one 2–12th NCO about the allegations. He simply denied
them: "That never happened." Police judged that the army "dropped the ball"
(Philipps 2010:186–90). It is equally unclear whether allegations of NCO
leadership in atrocities resulted in a housecleaning later, as reported in 2011
by the 4th BCT's outgoing Command Sergeant Major Charles Sasser, cred-
ited with helping to turn around "the murder brigade." When he moved up
to become the brigade's sergeant major in 2009, he focused on company first
sergeants, taking a hard look at those leaders. "Some didn't make the cut,"
Sasser told the *Gazette.* "I had to make sure we had the right people in the

right place." Whether this referred to operational inefficacy or disregard for rules of engagement, however, was left unspecified (Roeder 2011).

## Conclusion: Mission First

When Major General Mark Graham left Fort Carson after the typical three-year assignment, it was to become the Army's deputy chief of staff for operations, coordinating training and deployment for all troops, a position "instrumental in making sure no unit is sent to the worst places over and over, as the Lethal Warriors were" (Philipps 2010:243). The influence of one of the officers most identified with concern about the effects of combat exposure on soldiers, however, was not enough to prevent a unit like the 2–12th Battalion from twice more being deployed to the most heated battlegrounds: both of the battalion's tours to Afghanistan, from 2009 to 2010 and 2012 to 2013, were to Kunar Province in Afghanistan, the site of some of that war's most brutal engagements. The 4th Brigade as a whole lost 45 of the 49 Fort Carson soldiers killed in Afghanistan by the time they returned to Fort Carson in June of 2010.[19] The combination of institutional reorganization and the extended wars in Iraq and Afghanistan meant that the Lethal Warriors experienced multiple, long deployments with heavy fighting and casualties and short dwell time. Despite the army's promises of greater cohesion, less turbulence for soldiers and their families, and sufficient rest between deployments, the 2–12th was a battalion stretched in all directions, at home and abroad.

This chapter has presented varied explanations for the level of violence unleashed on home turf when a battle-weary unit returned to Colorado Springs—baseline, bad-apple theses, and combat stress injuries (PTSD) resulting from combat exposure. The EPICON report refutes the first two, and the soldiers we interviewed forcefully reject the third: "There's just no way they have PTSD so bad it causes them to do all these criminal things," as one said. In a case like John Needham's, we would want to understand the moral and historical dimensions at play: an idealistic young man confronted in Iraq with betrayal, horror, and trauma resulting in physical injury, depriving him of any sense of justice or rightness in the world. PTSD is certainly a factor, but to ask it to encapsulate what happened, much less explain why Needham killed his girlfriend, falls short. Like the bad-apple thesis, treating PTSD itself as explanatory is too simplistic and reductive, cordoning off the effects of combat on troops to something that is medically diagnosable. Instead, the interplay between multiple factors requires attention: yes, consider combat/violence exposure, but also conditioned perpetration of violence (do we expect refugees exposed to violence to import it into new settings?). Yes, do comprehensive individual assessments encompassing physical, psychological health, but also consider the pressures and imperatives created by "mission-first," boots-on-the-ground priorities trumping all under an AVF that deploys with unprecedented tempo.

Considering this interplay invites consideration of ways that war, rather than being "a thing to be explained," may be "an explanation in itself" for effects such as violence back home (Ferguson 2008:39). War may, moreover, ideologically "convert practical self-interests into the highest applicable moral values" (Ferguson 2008:38), elevating the willingness to use force to something that appears imperative, inevitable, and morally correct. Far from cordoning off local actors—families, institutions, and communities—from this complex dynamic, we wish to explore how these actors become "entangled in the circumstances of its production, just as the monstrous ethnic killer is lost not in his own pathological political fantasy, but in our collective one" (Ferguson and Whitehead 2000:xxviii).

We tell the story of the 2–12th Battalion in full recognition that it offers perhaps the most extreme case on record for the violence of the post-9/11 wars brought home, by a particular unit, to a domestic community. That we happened to already be working with the unit as the cluster went viral in the media made it central to this fieldwork, but also begs questions about how representative all-male infantry units, where some soldiers self-select based on willingness and ability to perform violence, are in the first place. We also need comparative research on other units with similar combat and violence exposure to advance assertions about microcultural factors. At the same time, this case should not be dismissed too quickly as a complete outlier, but be considered in the context of ever-multiplying other cases of US military microcultures that cultivate the practice of, and internal tolerance for, morally reprehensible violence. The spate of spousal murders at Fort Bragg in 2004, the abuse of detainees at Abu Ghraib prison in Iraq in 2002, the 2009 massacre at Fort Hood, the Fort Lewis-McCord scandals: each of these are deplorable occurrences with their own particularities, each soundly repudiated by the US military, which regularly asserts that they are far from representative of service members' actions. In early 2012 alone, we must add Marine videos of urinating on Taliban corpses;[20] the collection of "trophy photos" of American paratroopers posing with suicide bombers' body parts (Farmer and Allen 2012); the massacre of 16 Afghan villagers, 9 of them children, by an American staff sergeant (BBC News 2012); and, by mid-May, 15 "Blue-on-Green" attacks,[21] where Afghan army or police turn fire on American troops, usually in response to offenses to their honor (Shah 2012). Nonetheless, like the spate of soldier-perpetrated murders in Colorado Springs, they must enter into our reckoning with the post–9/11 wars, and be weighed as part of our accounting as we assess how effectively these wars have served to make Americans safer or more secure.

They also point toward the complexity of issues that soldiers returning from combat and from deployments in general face, issues that go far beyond PTSD and TBI. Focus on invisible wounds, while important, deflects attention from issues of leadership and accountability at all levels. As John Needham's case illustrates, in contemporary warfare soldiers are held accountable and may hold themselves accountable for making moral decisions when the rules of engagement are constantly changing and the very soldiers they rely on for their own safety and for accomplishing their mission punish them for doing so.[22]

Just weeks after our initial interviews with 2–12th soldiers, Colonel Holmes argued that those exchanges provided a mere snapshot into a particular window in time. "So many things have already changed," he told us. Now, with significantly more time having passed, from the perspective of many soldiers, the cluster of murders between 2004 and 2008 constitute ancient history. They "drive on," as the oft-used army expression goes, and these crimes rapidly recede in their rearview mirrors. The murderers themselves, we repeat, are less representative of the 2–12th Battalion than the voices of the 43 soldiers heard in previous chapters. While this chapter dwells at length on the story that opened up before us, of the unit whose story went viral, this book's remaining chapters explore how the imperatives of protracted war, multiple deployments, and accompanying mission-first thinking play out in multiple sites in the surrounding community.

## Chapter 4

# Decentering PTSD: A War Outgrows a Diagnosis

*Trauma is not just the result of major disasters. It does not happen only to some people. An undercurrent of trauma runs through ordinary life, shot through as it is with impermanence. I like to say that if we are not suffering from post-traumatic stress disorder, we are suffering from pre-traumatic stress disorder. There is no way to be alive without being conscious of the potential for disaster. One way or another, death (and its cousins: old age, illness, accidents, separation and loss) hangs over all of us. Nobody is immune. Our world is unstable and unpredictable, and operates, to a large degree and despite incredible scientific advancement, outside our ability to control it.*

—Mark Epstein, *New York Times*

*Ah how shameless—the way these mortals blame the gods. From us alone, they say, come all their miseries, yes, but they themselves, with their own reckless ways, compound their pains beyond their proper share.*

—Homer, *The Odyssey*

Infantryman John Needham certainly suffered from PTSD, but PTSD was only one of the many issues he faced, amid TBI, spinal injuries, and profound betrayal and disillusion. His case may be extreme; nonetheless, it points to the array of war's effects soldiers bring home with them and the limits of PTSD to express, explain, and respond to them. Early in our project we shared a grant proposal with Beryl Makris, whose husband was dying from a debilitating TBI following exposure to multiple blasts from IEDs and other weapons. The proposal explored PTSD as a focal expression of the damages, challenges, and contradictions posed by the post-9/11 wars. Placing so much attention on PTSD concerned Beryl. "I'm just worried," she told us, "that your project runs the risk of repeating the same error of reducing all the injuries needing attention to PTSD." Beryl's concern with making PTSD too much the center of our work resonated with our own growing concern about the problems with a single-pointed focus on PTSD.

First off, let us be clear that it would be difficult to deny the importance, and benefits to so many, that the emergence of PTSD as a diagnosis has brought. It would also be hard to refute that something like PTSD has manifested across war zones since time immemorial, or question understanding PTSD as a form of both individual and collective suffering. Medical anthropology shows us how medicalization can neutralize combat stress injuries and, optimally, destigmatize such injuries: this alone is invaluable. This ethnography, however, compels us to also consider some of the unforeseen consequences of PTSD's centrality for the current wars. To *re*contextualize the scenes through which PTSD plays out, we suggest crucial considerations and reasons to be cautious about attributing all or most of soldiers' difficulties with reintegration to PTSD. Though each war has its signature condition, no single diagnosis can hold all the challenges and distress of war. We focus on PTSD because it has been so prominent in discussions surrounding deployment and reintegration issues in the post-9/11 wars. But any of the alternative diagnoses or explanatory concepts we discuss—TBI, depression, moral injury, codeswitching, or combat stress—could be analyzed in the same way.

Beryl worries that overemphasis on PTSD is being intentionally used to cloak far less treatable (and more highly rated; that is, requiring more benefits) conditions like mild TBIs. This chapter explores numerous other, quite different concerns about the diagnosis and syndrome. Chapter 1 demonstrated how many soldiers are convinced that those who want out of the military are faking PTSD. Here we explore additional issues: some mental health providers worry about "bracket creep" (the standards of diagnosis growing ever looser), such that "secondary" or "vicarious" PTSD is increasingly being claimed and diagnosed. Military personnel grow suspicious of media, blogger, and activist attention to PTSD because they feel it is being used as proxy for critique about the wars, or of the military itself. Soldier Mick Dean explained his view:

> *They're probably back in the States using it as an excuse, you know, like saying, "This war was bad. Look at all these people that have PTSD." The activists that are against it [the war] will latch on to the whole PTSD situation and use it as a weapon for their cause.*

Family members worry that showcasing impressive new PTSD programs may distract from a dearth of other equally needed services. And local peace activists worry that sympathetic media attention to PTSD among combat veterans ennobles "our own" injured while pushing the far larger number of Iraqi and Afghan wounded, disabled, and killed even further into the background.

As a medical diagnosis, PTSD has its problematic aspects; foremost among them is its ambiguity. The diagnosis brings together a mixture of vague symptoms that overlap with other diagnoses such as TBI, anxiety disorders, and depression. The 2013 revision of the Diagnostic and Statistical Manual (DSM; APA 2013) has stimulated extensive debate among mental health practitioners over the definition of PTSD and to which category of disorders it should belong (Dobbs 2009; McNally 2003; Spitzer et al. 2007.).[1] Because a diagnosis of PTSD can qualify veterans for compensation, disability status, and benefits, it has also been highly controversial politically (Satel and Freuh 2009; Stein et al. 2007; and Vedantam 2005).

The RAND Corporation's study of psychological and cognitive injuries in post-9/11 veterans showed equal percentages of veterans screening positive for PTSD (14%) and depression (14%), with a higher proportion (19%) reporting a probable TBI (Tanielian and Jaycox 2008). Yet only very recently has TBI among veterans received equal attention in the media, in part from increasing awareness of TBI in professional football and hockey players. Depression, though it can be equally as debilitating as PTSD, is rarely mentioned or discussed in much depth unless it contributes to suicide.

As a consequence, our focus has shifted from asking "*What* is PTSD?" to asking "*Why* PTSD?"[2] Why has PTSD become not only one of the "signature injuries" of the post-9/11 conflicts, but perhaps *the* "signature injury"? We argue it functions as a potent "idiom of distress," a screen onto which many different individuals and groups, military and civilian alike, project their own ideas about service members and veterans, about the deployments and the campaigns, and about violence and trauma more generally. In this chapter we discuss the relationship among the invisible wounds of PTSD, TBI, and depression. We offer a recent history of PTSD, explaining many soldiers' resistance to its legitimacy as a valid diagnosis while serving as the dominant idiom of distress for veterans and their families. We conclude that PTSD is a medical diagnosis that is a necessary, but not sufficient, response to soldiers' suffering related to their service and participation in the post-9/11 wars—we must move beyond PTSD to recognize and effectively respond to the issues facing families, communities, and the nation.

## PTSD as a Diagnostic Category

Microbiologist Ludwik Fleck, writing about syphilis in the 1930s, observed that medical diagnoses and how we understand what causes them change and develop over time in response to a variety of factors, including new techniques for learning about disease processes, new knowledge, changes in social values and practices, and the coming together of ideas in new ways. Thus diagnoses are a product of their history or genealogy: they are socially or culturally constructed. This does not mean that they are not "real" or do not produce changes in the body that are distressful, debilitating, and sometimes fatal, but they cannot be understood apart from their social and intellectual history (Fleck 1979). Yet once a group of practitioners accepts the diagnosis and the explanation of its causes into medical knowledge as scientific fact, it is easy to forget that it was once new, that someone or some group of people at a particular time in history and a particular place identified it, described it, and named it. The diagnosis also becomes the way that lay persons understand bodily signs and symptoms and present these to their health care provider.[3] How many people know why Lyme disease bears the name of a small town in Connecticut, or that the human immunodeficiency virus (HIV) was first isolated in Paris in 1983? Both Lyme disease and HIV are now part of our medical nosology, or list of diseases, and are assumed to be universal; that is, to apply to all human beings. They are perceived as having always existed even if we did not always recognize them or name them in the same way. Similarly, researchers, clinicians, and the general public in the United States now accept PTSD as an established medical fact that is both universal and timeless. But it, too, has a genealogy or history that dates not to ancient Persia (*Gilgamesh*) or Greece (*The Iliad*), but to the mid-1800s during the Industrial Revolution in Europe and North America, when changes in the concept of trauma converged with research on the physiology of shock and new ideas about psychological disorders of memory (Hacking 1995; Young 1995). Its history carries important implications for treatment and recovery of individual soldiers. It shapes how we perceive the effects of war, what constitutes trauma, and who is and is not affected.

In 1866 John Erichsen coined the term "railway spine," which extended the definition of trauma beyond physical injuries or wounds to include mental injuries. He recognized that forces experienced during a railroad accident, common during the early decades of rail travel, that did not produce visible physical damage could nonetheless affect the brain and nervous system to produce symptoms of shock followed by anxiety, paralysis, weak pulse, difficulty concentrating, amnesia, and irritability. Many clinicians wondered if recently passed laws enabling victims of railway accidents to claim compensation for their injuries might affect their symptoms either consciously or unconsciously (Young 1995). Others observed that injuries that were eligible for compensation took longer to heal than those that were not, a condition defined as "sinistrosis." Thus the symptoms of mental trauma were linked with possible compensation for injury, and clinicians often viewed those who presented with railway spine with suspicion (Fassin and Rechtman 2009).

At the same time, research on the physiology of shock showed that intense states of emotion—fear and anger—could not only be mechanisms for survival by leading to fight or flight, but could also be pathological, arousing the nervous system to the point that a person could go into shock. An important development was the recognition that the mental processes of expectation and imagination play a role in generating pathological fear. Thus the expectation of death or serious injury, even following a wound that was physically trivial, could produce profound shock and even death. Fear thus becomes a conditioned response to a threatening, traumatic experience that remains in the individual's memory and can be re-evoked by situations similar to those that produced the original pain, a "pathogenic secret." By 1914, asserts Young, psychiatrists had incorporated the concept of the pathogenic secret into the concept of "traumatic memory." In contrast to traumatic memories, memories of usual, nontraumatic events do not evoke strong or disturbing memories, causing their capacity to evoke strong emotions and vivid images to diminish over time. But because traumatic memories are associated with pain and threat of injury or death, they remain powerful, able to evoke intense fear and anger. So we repress them or, if they occur suddenly and overload the nervous system, we "remember" them nonverbally, through bodily actions or behaviors. They remain in the mind, like a piece of shrapnel that can cut its way in, intruding upon the present, and generating the symptom clusters of re-experiencing, avoidance, and hyperarousal that are characteristic of PTSD. PTSD is a "disorder of time" in which the traumatic memory allows an event from the past to continue to produce symptoms in the present.[4]

The Industrial Revolution not only created new types of trauma that brought new ways of understanding the relationship between the mind and the body in the civilian sector, it also changed the nature of warfare and characterizations of its effects on soldiers. Whereas accounts and depictions of warriors' distress exist in ancient texts such as *The Iliad* and *The Odyssey*, it is only beginning with the Civil War that physicians began to observe and define it in terms of disease. Jacob Mendes da Costa, an American physician and surgeon, described a condition in which soldiers who had no physical abnormalities of the heart or circulatory system complained of cardiac symptoms including shortness of breath, fatigue on exertion, sweating, chest pain, and palpitations. The condition commonly known at the time as "soldier's heart" also bears his name (Da Costa 1871). Da Costa called it "irritable heart," and he attributed it to soldiers carrying heavy packs, exerting themselves physically, or suffering from homesickness, lack of sleep, bad food, or illnesses such as fever and diarrhea. In this case, explaining the cause of the distress of war as a physiological response to the physical demands of combat provided a less stigmatized "honorable solution" for the soldier and the military (IOM and National Research Council 2007:35). Da Costa's syndrome is now viewed as an anxiety disorder and one of a cluster of postwar syndromes (Engel 2004).

Contemporary clinicians equate soldier's heart with PTSD, but there are important differences. Civil War soldiers experienced disturbances of the heart explained physiologically, whereas today's soldiers experience disturbances of behavior explained by psychological processes.

During WWI, soldiers' distress manifested in several conditions: the most well known and the one most closely related to what would become PTSD is commonly known as "shell shock," which clinicians believed resulted from exposure to blasts. Although the symptoms occurred following a physical event, psychiatrists defined shell shock as a "neurosis," arising from psychological processes active within an individual's psyche. In other words, the traumatic event by itself was not sufficient to produce distress; in fact, the injury was often trivial. For shell shock to develop there had to be psychiatric "weakness" in the individual soldier or the motivation to obtain compensation or relief from work. This casts doubt on the "truth" of the event and contributed to the "culture of suspicion," where combat stress is seen as evidence of malingering or consciously or unconsciously adopting traumatic memories through suggestion (Young 1995). Fassin and Rechtman (2009) noted that during WWI, physicians recognized two other conditions: "combat madness" and "trauma insanity." A soldier suffering from combat madness, a combination of panic and exhaustion, might jump into action "sowing death and terror among the enemy ranks." Though recognized as suicidal and abnormal, it nonetheless "excited admiration, renewed hope, and reignited ardor in the troops" (Fassin and Rechtman 2009:42). In contrast, those suffering from trauma insanity were incapable of taking action and served as a source of demoralization and threatened the safety of the group. They were classed with those who deliberately injured themselves to escape combat and were scorned as selfish malingerers who lacked sufficient patriotism. Consistent with this view, treatments for trauma insanity were harsh, often involving electric shock, yelling, and other means to "shock" the patients back into service (Fassin and Rechtman 2009; Young 1995).

At this time the association of psychiatric war casualties with malingering and cowardice was gradually replaced by the normalized ideas of "combat fatigue," "battle stress," and "combat stress" described in chapter 1 (McHugh and Treisman 2007; Moore and Reger 2007). A more debilitating form of distress, especially common among older soldiers who had seen more days in combat, was "old sergeant's syndrome." The recognition that psychiatric injuries were related to the intensity and duration of combat "led to the military psychiatry principle of 'ultimate vulnerability'—in other words, 'everyone has a breaking point'" (Jones in Nash 2007a:49). This remained the dominant way of viewing combat stress through the war in Vietnam. This more normalized view created a perspective that would subsequently serve to bring together research on the neurobiology of stress responses, learning theory (especially the conditioning and extinction of fear in anxiety disorders), and psychological theories of memory.

In the post-Vietnam era, social and historical forces within and outside psychiatry converged to create the diagnosis of PTSD in 1980 (Fassin and Rechtman 2009; Young 1995).[5] Within the realm of mental health, psychiatrists were eager to gain legitimacy and respect for their discipline by placing it on a more solid scientific footing with clear, consistent, and measurable descriptions and criteria for each diagnosis. Not long after the Vietnam War, mental health professionals working with veterans recognized a cluster of symptoms they named "post-Vietnam syndrome," and lobbied to have it included in the DSM. As psychologist Richard McNally notes:

> *Members of the DSM-III task force were reluctant to endorse a diagnosis tied specifically to an historic event [the war in Vietnam]. Yet they eventually relented when veterans' advocates persuaded them that the same stress syndrome occurred in survivors of other traumatic events, such as rape, natural disaster, or confinement to a concentration camp (McNally 2003:230).*

In the version proposed to the task force charged with revising the DSM in 1980, the etiology or cause of PTSD was clearly and strongly stated: it arose from direct exposure to a traumatic event that "would evoke significant symptoms of distress in almost everyone" (APA 1980:238).

Fassin and Rechtman argue that these developments transformed how we view suffering and authenticity. Trauma emerges "as a commonplace of the contemporary world, a shared truth."[6] Psychological injuries related to traumatic events are no longer defined as merely neurotic, but as disordered. More than a simple renaming, this represents a significant shift in the relationship between symptoms and events. Instead of an abnormal person responding to a normal event, "trauma thus appears solely attributable to an unfortunate encounter between an ordinary person and an extraordinary event" (Fassin and Rechtman 2009:87). Because soldiers "see and do things no human being should have to," the event itself is abnormal and, in the case of war or genocide, horrific.

### The Medicalization of Suffering

By 1980, though it remained controversial within psychiatry, PTSD was fully medicalized. Medicalization refers to defining a behavior or a condition as something that falls outside the range of what is considered normal.

Society then views the condition as belonging to the realm or domain of medicine and considers it best understood and treated by medical experts, including scientists, physicians, and allied health professionals. On the positive side, defining something as a medical condition gives it a name or label and a coherent explanation for why it exists, even if the cause is presently unknown, and a recommended course of treatment. It thus reduces social anxiety over the meaning of an individual's behavior or symptoms. In most cases, the individual is viewed as a largely passive victim of a disease agent such as a bacteria or virus, or in the case of PTSD, of a traumatic event that produces an injury. As a result, the patient is generally not held responsible for contracting his or her illness or traumatic injury. Exceptions would include cases where people did not take reasonable care of their health or avoid a dangerous situation. When conditions or behaviors are medicalized, people may experience less stigma. For example, defining alcoholism as a psychiatric disorder is potentially less stigmatizing than defining it as a failure of will, self-control, or moral fiber. Seeking treatment is then viewed as taking responsibility for one's health, or as "doing the right thing." Thus the stigma may shift to how well a person manages their condition. Medicalization can also mobilize significant resources for research, diagnosis, and treatment and may be actively sought by advocates for groups suffering from a particular condition.

Like most social processes, medicalization is complex and often contradictory. Although some medical conditions may not be harmful, such as a heart murmur that does not limit physical activity, most are defined as pathological; that is, they cause disease and interfere with a person's ability to function. Focus on pathology and disability may create barriers to recognizing the role of resilience and the possibility of recovery and health both for individuals and for society (Rousseau and Measham 2007). To access resources ranging from expensive diagnostic procedures, surgery, and medications to disability payments or workmen's compensation, persons with a medicalized condition must also accept that they are sick and comply with medical treatment. Many social scientists therefore emphasize the role that medicine plays in social control as it assumes power and authority over ever-expanding areas of social life such as birth and breastfeeding, diet and exercise. In reaction to this control, individuals may resist diagnoses that define them as sick or abnormal and the loss of autonomy demanded by medical treatment (Foucault 1994 [1973]; Jordan 1992; Singer and Baer 2007). At the same time, in the past decade, more and more conditions are now viewed as the product of individual choices in diet and lifestyle so that individuals are once again seen as responsible for their own health. In the United States, medicalization focuses attention on the individual as the place where disease resides and where healing occurs, thus removing illness from its social, political, and economic context. If medicalization provides a primary perspective for understanding PTSD as a necessary response to the distress of combat, why, then, do many soldiers find it so problematic?

Although defining symptoms or behaviors as diseases may bring them within the auspices of medical authority, people do not submit to medical regimens passively or uncritically. Attitudes toward a particular disease may vary by context, as we see in soldier statements about PTSD. Even within the military framework, where war is accepted as "hell," getting help means accepting the social status of being ill and having a disorder. Soldiers with PTSD may be declared unfit for duty and removed from their unit, a source of shame and failure that may outweigh symptoms of PTSD. Claiming the diagnosis may bring suspicion of malingering. Perhaps most important for soldiers, PTSD negates a core principle of the warrior ethos and of soldier identity: free will and moral agency. Soldiers act in peace and in war, but PTSD is an involuntary response to trauma. In his ethnographic study of Vietnam veterans receiving care at a Veteran's Administration (VA) center for the treatment of PTSD, Young found soldiers' loss of agency was a significant source of resistance in therapy (Young 1995). But soldiers' attitudes often change when they leave the military. PTSD becomes the explanation for all kinds of reintegration issues and thus something that anyone who has deployed to a war zone might suffer and for which he or she deserves treatment and compensation.

### The Trouble with PTSD

Despite efforts of mental health professionals to maintain the integrity of PTSD as a diagnostic category, in the decades since its inclusion in the DSM, it has taken on a life of its own, undergoing significant "conceptual bracket creep." In the DSM-III (published in 1980), symptoms had to persist for at least six months; in the next edition (published in 1994), they only needed to persist for one month. In the DSM-III, a person had to directly experience or witness the traumatic event. In the next edition, a person could develop PTSD after learning about, but not directly witnessing, serious trauma affecting a family member or close friend (APA 1980, 1994). Although changing the criteria opened the door to more frequent diagnosis of PTSD and made it difficult to measure the incidence and prevalence of PTSD consistently and reliably, it was not necessarily problematic outside academic psychiatry. For practicing clinicians, diagnoses are often merely a starting point to provide a label that reassures the patient, provides an initial treatment plan, and secures insurance coverage. Treatment then proceeds according to the individual needs of the patient. This can put academic psychiatrists and clinicians in opposing positions about the strictness versus open-endedness of diagnostic practices.

Although controversial within academic psychiatry, in the past three decades, PTSD has become a widely accepted way to understand trauma in the United States. The acronym is often not spelled out, and most Americans take its existence and meaning largely for granted. This was brought home to Jean when she taught workshops on research in Bolivia. In discussing this research and post-traumatic stress disorder to health care professionals, she had to explain what PTSD was and how it applied to victims of trauma. PTSD's "popularity" in the United States arises from two converging cultural trends. Beginning in the late 1800s and accelerating after WWI and again in the 1950s and 1960s is the trend to explain human behavior in individual, psychological terms. The second is the establishment of "a commonplace of the contemporary world, a shared truth," that painful events generate stress and leave scars on the mind as well as the body (Fassin and Rechtman 2009:4). Following the attacks on the World Trade Center in 2001, a team of mental health professionals surveyed a random sample of adults, finding that 44 percent reported symptoms of stress. By expanding the diagnosis to include anyone who experienced a significant traumatic event, the diagnosis became more universally applicable even as it became more general and vague. Relief organizations are increasingly incorporating mental health teams at disaster sites.[7] "Vicarious trauma," "secondary trauma," and "secondary PTSD" have gradually superseded older terms like "burnout" and "compassion fatigue" to describe the cumulative effect of working with victims of violence or disasters experienced by mental health professionals, disaster relief and humanitarian workers, police, firefighters, first responders, and most recently military chaplains (Greer 2009; Hesse 2008).[8] Although secondary PTSD is not recognized in the DSM, we heard it mentioned frequently in our discussions with spouses and mental health providers, as with a clinician we meet in chapter 8, who suffered what she referred to as "secondary PTSD" when Fort Carson removed all soldiers under her, and other civilian providers', care. There are a host of websites offering definitions and advice on dealing with secondary PTSD.

Yet many academic psychiatrists and psychologists continue to debate the utility of PTSD as a diagnostic category (Dobbs 2009; McHugh and Treisman 2007; McNally 2003; Summerfield 2001). The current definition of PTSD, with its variability in onset of symptoms (from months to years after an event), overlaps in symptoms with other mental disorders, and association of symptoms with a memory of a traumatic event, make it difficult to reliably measure and study. Some psychiatrists advocate for viewing PTSD as one of a spectrum of responses to trauma that includes milder forms of PTSD that can develop into full-blown PTSD. Complicated PTSD, which occurs with other conditions such as TBI, depression, or substance abuse, may render it chronic or episodic, with periods of better and worse functioning (Moreau and Zisook 2002). Because screening is based on reviewing a checklist of symptoms, it is easy for patients and clinicians to identify symptoms on the list that fit how they are feeling or behaving instead of starting from their symptoms and behavior to identify an appropriate diagnosis (Young 1995). Since the range of symptoms on the checklist is smaller than what any individual might experience or report during a psychiatric history, it is likely that they will screen positive, resulting in overdiagnosis of PTSD (McHugh and Treisman 2007).

Some specialists argue that the meaning and significance attributed to past events is often colored by recent life circumstances. For instance, an individual for whom life is going well in the present might minimize a past trauma or discuss how it helped them grow stronger, whereas someone whose present life is problematic might find PTSD a compelling framework to explain their current distress. McNally argues that this better explains the onset of PTSD years after a traumatic event or in individuals who experienced no distress at the time of the event (Breslau 2004; Marlowe 2001; McNally 2007).

The National Vietnam Veterans Readjustment Study (NVVRS), commissioned by Congress and published in 1983, on which much subsequent work on PTSD was based, found that 15.4 percent of Vietnam veterans had PTSD at the time of the study, with 30.9 percent experiencing it at some point after the war even though "only about 15 percent of male Vietnam veterans had served in combat units" (McNally 2007:194).[9] Recent reviews of the data have revised these figures downward to 9 percent at the time of the study and 18 percent over a veteran's lifetime (Dohrenwend et al. 2006). When the criterion added in DSM-IV (APA 1994) that a person with PTSD must experience clinically significant impairment is taken into consideration, the range drops to 5.4 percent at one time and an 11 percent lifetime occurrence (McNally 2003). A comprehensive review of estimates of the number of cases (point prevalence) of combat-related PTSD in US military veterans since the Vietnam War found a range of 4 to 17 percent among US Iraq War veterans but only 3 to 6 percent among UK Iraq War veterans. The authors attribute the discrepancy to differences in techniques of measurement and screening, but also to "sociopolitical and cultural factors that may vary over time and by nation" (Richardson et al. 2010:4).

## Idioms of Distress

And so we return to our original question. Why has PTSD become the signature injury of post-9/11 wars? An "idiom of distress" is a concept from medical anthropology that is particularly useful for answering this question. Anthropologist Mark Nichter, who coined the term in 1977, submits that "idioms of distress are socially and culturally resonant means of experiencing and expressing distress in local worlds" (Nichter 2010:405). They necessarily vary across cultures and through history. In other words, individuals express painful feelings in culturally accepted ways using culturally accepted terms. They bring together a set of physical symptoms, behaviors, and emotional states into a syndrome that might, if severe enough, also be symptoms of recognized and legitimated medical or psychiatric diseases or disorders. Once established, much like a medical diagnosis, they are taken for granted, "so embedded in everyday interactions that they are considered 'common sense'" (Hinton and Lewis-Fernández 2010:210–11). Thus it is much easier to recognize them in another society or culture because they don't translate into a comparable condition in one's own society. Because we accept our own idioms of distress as natural and "real," it is hard to recognize that people everywhere may not experience them. The underlying cause of the pain expressed through idioms of distress is social, though the name of the syndrome and the way people explain it may not refer to those social causes directly or at all. This may be especially true if the painful feelings arise from situations involving conflict with powerful authorities, from key interpersonal relationships, or from work where the risks of speaking about the source of distress directly are high. As a result, identifying the underlying cause requires analysis, as the name of the syndrome may deflect attention from it.

An important characteristic of idioms of distress is that they are ambiguous and can have multiple meanings, so that individuals with a variety of distinct but related complaints can include them under the same label. Craig Janes (1999) classified *rlung* as an idiom of distress for Tibetans living in urban areas of the country under Chinese rule. *Rlung* itself means "wind" or "air" and is related to the life force in Tibetan medicine. When *rlung* is out of balance, it produces symptoms that can include dizziness, high blood pressure, heart palpitations, anxiety, depression, or unease. An imbalance may arise when a person's desire to attain culturally valued goals or aims are thwarted. In the 1990s, Tibetan physicians saw an increasing number of well-educated young men and women with *rlung,* many of whom worked directly with or under Chinese and were thus caught between Chinese and Tibetan values and agendas. Treatment consists of various means to restore balance such as herbal medicines, dietary changes, acupuncture, and rest, often in a hospital. Thus, *rlung* imbalance expresses social and political distress in a form that is legitimate within Tibetan society and provides a break from a difficult work situation yet does not threaten the relatively more powerful Chinese.

Lower back pain, which afflicts as many as one-quarter of US adults, is an example from our own culture (Strine and Hootman 2007). It brings together multiple cultural metaphors for the physical distress of work (for example, "back-breaking labor") and for work-based relationships that are conflicted or unsupported; for example, a manager who is a "monkey on my back" (Hinton and Lewis-Fernández 2010:211). Lower back pain may express changes in society, including lack of access to health care, the erosion of middle-class incomes, and the consequences of medicalization; that is, expressing socially generated suffering in individual, physical symptoms that are often viewed as chronically debilitating and deserving of disability compensation. None of this suggests that back pain is not real pain. It is a person's pain that generates the initial assessment of "lower back pain," and its physical expression, such as walking hunched over or spending long periods in bed, may contribute to muscle damage.

More directly related to PTSD is Gulf War syndrome (GWS), a condition of Gulf War veterans consisting of fatigue, diarrhea, hair loss, "vomit that glowed in the dark, and semen that burned" (Kilshaw 2009:1). Anthropologist Susie Kilshaw reports that soldiers were relieved to "have a name for what ailed them," even though the biomedical community views GWS as a medically unexplained syndrome for which no physical cause has yet been identified. Kilshaw argues that, like PTSD, GWS serves as an idiom of distress, bringing together a variety of anxieties and concerns to give them meaning and make them understandable (Kilshaw 2009:11).

Because these syndromes create relatively more socially accepted ways of expressing pain and distress, individuals often present themselves as bearing their specific symptomologies to health care practitioners. Thus, idioms of distress may serve as valuable markers for conditions like PTSD. More important, treating the symptoms of the idiom of distress often provides significant improvement in the psychiatric diagnoses, something increasingly evident with veterans suffering from PTSD. Medical anthropologists Devon Hinton and Roberto Lewis-Fernández identify "acting-out behaviors such as drinking alcohol and getting in disputes" as an idiom of distress in the United States (2010:210). We would add the need to carry arms/weapons and being primed for anger and violence to the list of symptoms of "acting out" among veterans. These are all behaviors that veterans themselves recognize as problematic, associated with deployments. Soldier Ronald Rhuesenburg described the way many veterans returning from a deployment behave.

*My heart starts beating really fast. If someone just shuts the door really quick, you know, that gets me. My patience has gone down a lot for a lot of stupid stuff. But to me, it is not noticeable. Some guys have a lot more issues with it, with their attitude. They're always angry and have drinking problems.*

These behaviors are also often the first and only way that veterans obtain professional help. Soldier Daniel Quest described a "buddy" who saw his best friend "killed right in front him." The soldier snapped and since that time

*He's had all sorts of run-ins with the law. Since he's been back, he's lost like half of his pay because he's always getting in trouble for something. It's just ridiculous. He needs help and he's starting to get it now, but it took him shooting a gun off in public for him to get the help. He was downtown at the club. He took the gun away from somebody else and held him at gunpoint and discharged the weapon in the air.*

The Veterans Trauma Court in Colorado Springs, discussed in chapter 8, is a direct response to veterans appearing in court on charges related to alcohol or drug use and violence, public and domestic. Recognizing that many of these veterans suffer from PTSD, TBI, and depression, they use a restorative justice model to mandate actions that directly address the symptoms of acting out as well as their psychiatric illness. PTSD in this context may function much as other idioms of distress by offering a framework for the expression of veterans' responses to soldiering without forcing confrontation with broader social and political processes that are implicated.

Post-Vietnam syndrome bore all the characteristics of an idiom of distress. It was an expression of pain and impairment of a particular group at a particular point in history that drew on emerging cultural ideas about the trauma of war, particularly of a war that was viewed as historically exceptional in US history. It enabled US society to minimize or avoid issues of American soldiers' complicity in atrocities (Breslau 2004; Fassin and Rechtman 2009). It provided a mechanism through which veterans could obtain benefits and assistance to address the problems with alcohol and substance use, unemployment, and homelessness they often faced. But as post-Vietnam syndrome was redefined as PTSD and the criteria for PTSD expanded, it became, as Lindsay French argues, " . . . a key symbol for Americans, with all the murkiness that implies, in part because of the way it plays upon notions of legitimate (even righteous) victimhood, and on a peculiarly American notion of moral responsibility to provide compensation to victims" (2004:211).

Although a current of suspicion still runs through soldiers' perceptions that "faking it" is rampant, and some critics of PTSD share this concern, for the American public PTSD is largely beyond suspicion. Critics of PTSD diagnoses' legitimacy are often charged with supporting the wrongful denial of benefits to veterans (Glantz 2009; McHugh and Treisman 2007).

## "A Name Drained of Both Poetry and Blame"

Though each war has its signature condition, no single diagnosis can hold all the challenges and distress of war.[10] One of the problems with PTSD as a catchall is the confusion that arises between symptoms directly attributable to PTSD and issues related to reintegration. From the post-Vietnam era until the middle of the post-9/11 wars, clinicians and patients viewed PTSD as a chronic illness. Medications helped control symptoms of anxiety and agitation, sleeplessness, nightmares, and suicidal thoughts, but did not eliminate them. Nor did various kinds of psychodynamic or talk therapy. As a result, clinicians "offered individual and group therapy sessions aimed at helping the veteran to develop better skills for functioning in the world" (Finley 2011:121). As Erin Finley observed in her study of PTSD treatment in the VA, by 2006 or 2007 " . . . a revolution was brewing" (Finley 2011:121). Younger clinicians with training in cognitive-based therapies, coming into a VA system overwhelmed by the needs of veterans returning from Iraq and Afghanistan, were dissatisfied with backlogs of veterans who needed assessment and treatment and the failure of an older generation of veterans to get better. They countered the prevailing bracket creep that lumped everything under the rubric of PTSD and began rigorously implementing and testing evidence-supported protocols (Finley 2011:121).[11] As these treatments proved effective in not just controlling but eliminating symptoms of PTSD and improving functioning, clinicians cautiously spoke of "cure" and began to shift the model of PTSD from a chronic, persistent illness to a more acute, treatable one.

But many veterans who do not meet the diagnostic criteria for PTSD nonetheless suffer, presenting at clinicians' and chaplains' and clergy's offices. In addition to fear and horror, guilt, shame, and anger are equally, if not more prominent feelings that veterans discuss in connection with their war experiences.[12] Soldier David Ellingboe told us about the survivor's guilt a soldier might feel when a friend is killed "and you feel that there is something you could have still done even though physically you couldn't. There's nothing on earth that you could physically have done, but mentally you still feel guilty that you weren't able to help fix it."

Shame and guilt are emotions based in our social relationships and the values and norms of our culture and society. Thus, they are inherently moral, or concerned with what is right and good or conversely unjust and bad. Events or actions that threaten the integrity of the self or our image of ourselves generate shame; for example, being caught in a lie, being naked in public, or failing a test. Other people can shame us through their judgments, or we can feel ashamed based on our own negative judgment of our behavior or feelings. Trauma can generate shame because it threatens our personal boundaries, damages our sense of control and autonomy, and challenges our sense that the social world is ordered and predictable. Torture relies explicitly on shame through the infliction of pain and humiliation (Scarry 1985). Americans are more likely to discuss these feelings in terms of guilt rather than shame, but Ellingboe's statement here could just as accurately be labeled shame at having failed to live up to his sense of himself as someone who can protect his buddy from harm even as he acknowledges that this expectation is unrealistic. When soldiers witness or engage in actions that violate their moral codes, they may experience intense distress, shame, and guilt that they somehow benefited from the event; they survived. Killing itself, a central aspect of the work of war, is not only dirty, but can feel shameful, given that US society prohibits willfully taking the life of another human being, even though most killing in war is sanctioned by the higher authority of the state.

War experiences may also provoke soldiers to raise existential questions about what they have done and what war has done to them, blurring the line between victim and perpetrator. Veterans express this when they say that "war changes you." As soldier Wilson Lemmons said, "When you've had two or three tours in Iraq or Afghanistan, it's expected you're not going to be the same person. Nobody comes back from that place unaffected." Edward Tick, a clinical psychotherapist who has worked with Vietnam veterans for more than 25 years, rejects the idea that PTSD is a stress disorder. "Rather, it is best understood as an identity disorder and soul wound, affecting the personality at the deepest level" (Tick 2005:5). Anger is a response to an assault on the self and is related to the loss of autonomy and the inability to determine one's actions and take responsibility for them.

Clinicians at the VA argue that these are "moral injuries" and should be distinguished from PTSD. A moral injury is "perpetrating, failing to prevent, bearing witness to, or learning about acts that transgress deeply held moral beliefs and expectations" (Litz et al. 2009:697). Unlike PTSD, which requires a diagnosis, "moral injury is a dimensional problem" that may be present at different times in a veterans' life. But like PTSD, moral injuries are indeed injuries whose effects are characterized by "shame, guilt, and self-handicapping behaviors" (Maguen and Litz 2012:1). War-related events associated with moral injury include betrayal, disproportionate violence, incidents involving civilians, and within-rank violence. For John Needham, who experienced betrayal by his peers and his superior officers, who witnessed the use of disproportionate violence, and who saw Iraqi civilians mistreated and killed, the moral injuries he sustained were fatal. Moral injuries are associated with risk-taking behaviors and suicide following deployment (Selby et al. 2010). Health care and religious professionals who work with soldiers and veterans suggest that repair of moral injuries require interventions that are spiritually, socially, and individually directed and involve collaborative, cross-disciplinary approaches.

As PTSD has expanded to include all kinds of trauma, it has lost some of its historical specificity in the individual and collective actions of the Vietnam War. By focusing on the individual, it deflects attention for the social character of distress that demands a communal response. Psychiatrist Jonathan Shay draws from Greek mythology, particularly Homer's epic *The Odyssey*, to understand and explain difficulties many soldiers and veterans face in reintegrating into civilian society. He defines simple PTSD as the result of physiological changes wrought by combat. Veterans can learn to adapt to these as they would any other disability and reintegrate into civilian life. He distinguishes this from complex PTSD, an injury to character in which social functions are disrupted (Shay 2002:150–51). Like Odysseus and his men, returning soldiers who suffer from complex PTSD are fearful and mistrustful of the civilian society that sent them into combat, requiring them to commit and witness acts that have injured their sense of self, separated them morally from the community, and forced them, as veteran Bob Kavanagh said, to "capitulate," to wear a mask of normality that hides anger, shame, and guilt. Shay outlines a three-step process, based on the work of Judith Herman, for reintegration from complex PTSD: (1) stop self-destructive and dangerous behaviors such as substance use and carrying weapons; (2) create a narrative that will help them to grieve losses of fellow soldiers and their own innocence; and (3) reconnect "with people, communities, ideals, and ambitions" (Shay 2002:168). Reaching out to other veterans and soldiers for authentic sharing of their stories is one way to create narratives and social connections. However, this often leaves family members, friends, and the larger community—the many Penelopes waiting to welcome soldiers all the way home—relegated to the role of appreciative audience. More active engagement between veterans, family, and community takes this process further. We recall, for example, how positively veterans viewed officers who made soldiers with psychological injuries work with children at Fort Carson; while at first the soldiers resisted, they ended up valuing it as an important part of recovery. Unlike many psychiatrists, therapists like Shay say that acknowledging and embracing the social and political aspects of PTSD is essential to healing. As we discuss in chapter 7, veterans charter many highly variable paths to heal their wounded souls and create supportive communities.

## Decentering PTSD

In the same way that PTSD cannot adequately capture the complexity of soldiers' postwar difficulties, such a focus also leaves many individuals and groups to suffer in the shadows because it focuses attention almost exclusively on those who engage in combat. As a result, the concerns and distress of these shadow people are often unrecognized, ignored, or minimized. In *Maneuvers*, feminist Cynthia Enloe's study of the militarization of women's lives, she shows a photograph of British male soldiers gathering for a meal on a battlefield in Turkey in 1855. In the background, on the periphery of the circle of men, stands a small figure. Enloe's caption identifies her as a "camp follower," who is "integral to the cook crew, yet scarcely of interest to the photographer. What would we learn about the Crimean War if we knew her full story?" (Enloe 2000:41). Indeed, women are largely invisible and certainly marginalized in accounts of war and its costs. We look at the effects of war on Iraqi women through collective figures of civilian dead and wounded or Afghan women as passive objects of patriarchal oppression by the Taliban.[13]

In the United States we may read accounts of female soldiers, and the television series *Army Wives* has brought some attention to the spouses and families of active duty military personnel, but what about the increasing number of ex-wives, caregivers, sex workers, women working for the military or civilian contractors to the military, veterans' advocates, and peace activists? How many military spouses express the demands they face through their spouses' multiple deployments and invisible wounds through idioms of distress like lower back pain, chronic fatigue syndrome, or generalized "stress," only to find their complaints dismissed as psychosomatic, or being told that they just need to "set aside some time for themselves every day"? Secondary PTSD may be an emerging idiom of distress that claims some of the legitimacy of PTSD and calls attention to the intensity of what they feel. But it comes at the price of being "secondary" and "less than" their spouses' distress. The effects of multiple deployments on children are receiving increased attention, but given pending cuts to military budgets, this is likely to fade into the background even as the needs of military children increase in the coming years.

The news media have begun to focus some attention on the effects of multiple deployments on communities as more veterans return home and leave military service. But there have been few studies of how multiple deployments and changes in the makeup of military personnel as a result of the AVF have affected community resources, institutions, health care, and other supportive services. Like spouses, many caregivers report what they call secondary PTSD from their work with veterans. With significant shortages in mental health care providers throughout the country, but particularly in rural areas where many national guard and reservists live, we need to pay careful attention to how caring for veterans affects health care providers in order to support and sustain their efforts.

Recognition of the invisible wounds of war has brought considerable benefits to soldiers and veterans by laying the groundwork to reduce stigma and suspicion and provide treatment and compensation. But the medicalization of trauma in PTSD often fails to take full accounting of contexts for psychological and moral injuries, or for the resilience, growth, and ability to endure and recover that might aid veterans in recovery and readjustment. Given the wide range of people and institutions, military and civilian, that are affected by the post-9/11 wars and the complexity of issues involved in veteran reintegration into civilian life, focusing too narrowly on these injuries, and PTSD in particular, leaves many of those affected in the shadows of our awareness.

PTSD is in some ways easy (except, of course, for those suffering its effects). It gives us a name, a label for what hurts and suggests ways to relieve that hurt. It also provides civilians with distance from the labyrinth of war, from coming face to face with our own moral injuries; such distancing may serve as one way to manage terror. Vietnam veteran John Nash, who runs a program in which veterans work with horses (described in Chapter 7), describes the fear of entering the labyrinth.

> So now we are trying to go down this road of recovery, and in order to move down this road to recovery we are going into the unknown. It's a fearful thing. Its like going into battle. Because it is the unknown we don't know what to expect; we don't know if we can do it. So getting them [veterans] to have the willingness to open that door is the key to everything.

In Part II we move into this homefront terrain, away from the focus on war's effects on soldiers to examine the effects of multiple deployments on spouses and families, caregivers, peace activists, ranchers, and community institutions.

# PART II: WAR'S LABYRINTH AT HOME

## Chapter 5

# Codeswitching and Sticky Switches: Navigating Absence and Presence

*My policy was to build up the estates of Odysseus so he'd have even more wealth when he came back than when he'd left—more sheep, more cows, more pigs, more fields of grain, more slaves. I had such a clear picture in my mind—Odysseus returning, and me—with womanly modesty—revealing to him how well I had done at what was usually considered a man's business. On his behalf, of course. Always for him.*

—Margaret Atwood, *The Penelopiad*

The sky is the deep saturated blue of a late June afternoon at high altitude as we approach the main gate of Fort Carson. Banners, large enough to be easily read from the highway, cover the security fence. A few are professionally printed signs welcoming the troops home or expressing thanks for their service, but most are bed sheets, with hand-painted drawings of houses, cars, pets, trees, and flowers surrounding hand-lettered messages in neon or primary colors that shout out, "Welcome Home, Daddy," "We missed you!" or "Welcome Home Pfc Moore." Though the ceremony welcoming home members of the 4th Brigade Combat Team from their first tour in Afghanistan won't start for at least another hour, a steady line of cars, vans, and pickup trucks streams into the dirt parking lot of the Special Events Center. Amid the many vehicles sporting bumper stickers claiming support for their father, son, or husband soldier, on the side window of an SUV, yellow-painted script says, "Wife, mother, soldier," and on the rear window, "My wife is my hero." Farther down the row, a pickup truck sports a bumper sticker with "Army wife" stenciled in bubblegum pink letters on a green camouflage background.[1]

Inside the event center, the polished wooden gym floor bears Fort Carson's insignia, "The Mountain Post." An American flag fills one wall. Lining the other three walls, banners represent "The 2–12 Lethal Warriors," the "1–12 Red Warriors," and "The Mountain Warriors," while others thank soldiers for their "dedication to freedom" and the Veterans of Foreign Wars praises them for a "job well done." Another says, "They are the chosen ones."

Families of three generations, women and men with small children, groups of teenagers, and groups of young women and men occupy two-thirds of the bleachers. A mix of anticipation and boredom fills the room. Children of all ages scamper up and down the bleachers or twirl and tumble on the floorboards or bounce in the inflated Spiderman house. Pop music blares from loudspeakers, making conversation difficult. A group of young women starts a line dance to a country song and entertains us for 20 minutes. A man sitting next to us explains that he and his wife drove up from Texas to meet their son.

Finally, a soldier announces that the ceremony will soon begin. "I'm Proud to be an American" blares as people settle into the bleachers, necks craning forward watching the double doors where their soldiers will enter. When the doors open, the crowd stands, applauding enthusiastically as soldiers march into the room in four parallel rows, bright sunshine silhouetting them and dust swirling around their feet. When all the soldiers are in the gym, the commanding officer—whom we only gradually realize is Major RJ Collins, the public affairs officer and person we knew best from the 4th Brigade, so changed was his lean and weary appearance—calls out orders to the troops. The soldier serving as emcee asks us to observe a moment of silence for those who will not be returning. The chaplain offers a prayer thanking the unit for their service and their safe return. After playing the national anthem, the emcee asks us to join in singing "The Army Song," whose words are conveniently printed on two banners hung on the opposite wall. The garrison chaplain welcomes the soldiers to the base and acknowledges their service. Suddenly, it seems, the ceremony is officially over and the soldiers are "released from duty."

At these words, friends and families flow down from the bleachers as soldiers zoom across the floor looking for their loved ones. A young woman leaps up and wraps her arms and legs around a soldier; a man in uniform embraces a woman in uniform who holds a toddler in her arms. A colonel in his late 30s or early 40s stands next to his wife, who wears a crisply ironed sundress and heels, along with his three children ranging from 7 or 8 to early teens. A couple in their 50s, holding a banner, finds their son and hugs him tentatively. After releasing their embrace, the father takes off his glasses and wipes away tears with his sleeve.

For many soldiers and their families homecoming is just what the images say it is: a happy ending to a story that started over a year ago when the soldier received orders to deploy. In the best cases, perhaps most cases, the welcome home ceremony signals to families and the community that the deployment has officially ended, and the soldier has safely returned to US soil. Yet for soldiers who are leaving the military, Jonathan Shay (2002) would remind them that whereas their physical journey from Iraq or Afghanistan took less than 48 hours, their emotional and spiritual journey to come "all the way home," like Odysseus, may take months or years, filled with many detours and challenges.

For others this is neither a coming "home" nor, as psychiatric nurse Captain Dawn Weaver observes, necessarily good or happy. Not everyone has someone waiting in the bleachers, searching the ranks to find their face. Many families must travel long distances at their own expense to attend the homecoming. Other soldiers come back to empty apartments. As we looked on, a male soldier scanned the bleachers over and over and then walked around the gym increasingly agitated, as if he expected someone to be there to meet him who wasn't there. One staff sergeant's wife said that at the welcome home ceremony her husband barely greeted his own family because "he was trying to take care of other soldiers. He had soldiers that didn't have family members that were going to meet them there. He had a couple of soldiers that were coming home to—well, basically they already knew their spouses had cleared out the house."[2] Other soldiers return to peer groups involved in criminal or gang activity that they joined the army to escape.

Welcome home ceremonies provide structure to soldiers' return and generate Kodak moments for the community, the press, and the military, but how beneficial are they for soldiers and their families? Weaver thinks they should be optional, with maybe a "separate party where you guys can all say goodbye to each other and then you can all get released from there. Then that way, guys aren't feeling humiliated and crushed by this welcome home ceremony."

Even for those soldiers whose families wait with open arms and for whom "reunion and reintegration" go smoothly, this time can be fraught with apprehension and anxiety. It might be easy to appreciate that a soldier who has been separated from his family and living in a foreign, war-torn country might find it tough coming home to a nation distant from battle to families occupied with the mundane details of school and work. But it might be surprising to learn that it is often spouses and children who are most anxious as homecoming nears and who find the adjustment most difficult (Booth et al. 2007:42).

In this chapter we examine the transitions that soldiers, wives, and their children face. We consider the major life transitions from citizen to soldier, from civilian family to military family, and back. The particular challenges created by the repeated transitions of multiple deployments in the post-9/11 wars merit attention. These challenges are situated in the context of the rapid moment-to-moment shifts that soldiers are trained to make in combat. As anthropologists we draw from our understanding of how societies use myth, ritual, and ceremony to guide individuals through major transitions; in addition, we examine how these ceremonies are frequently omitted or fail to adequately respond to the reality of repeated deployments, over the course of which feeling fully at home can become ever more elusive. On a more intimate scale, families find their own ways to accommodate changes in roles and responsibilities, and to communicate across the physical distances between Iraq or Afghanistan and Colorado Springs. Often the greater cultural distances are between being a soldier in war to being a family member in relative peace, as communication technology brings theater and home ever closer together. As Neil Shea says, the very skills and routines that are adaptive during deployments often become problematic when the family is reunited.

> *Of course, we require our fighters to be ready hurricanes, on-call combat machines. We want them held easily in check, and we expect light-switch control over their aggression. . . . Soldiers . . . so barely restrained, their switches unreliable after years of war, undermine this. But we have no good method for dealing with men who grow too dangerous. We vaguely hope their anger does not spill over, or come home (Shea 2012:6).*

Soldiers, like Shea, explained the change in behaviors and attitudes between deployment and home in binary terms, as switches they could turn off or on. When we initially applied the concept of "codeswitching," drawn from linguistics, as a powerful way to talk about these transitions, we found that officers seized upon it as a potentially useful framework for conceptualizing and planning interventions. Ultimately, however, we concluded perhaps "sticky switches" better characterized what we observed: that even when soldiers and family members claimed they could codeswitch easily, close examination revealed that the transitions were far more complex and multifaceted than they acknowledged at first. The compressed tempo of multiple deployments during the post-9/11 wars made it increasingly difficult for soldiers and families to adapt to continuous oscillations between war and home, absence and presence.

### Two Mindsets

Quincy Stevenson, 24, in combat uniform with his hair cut in a military "high and tight," sits across from Luke Parkhurst, a Colorado College undergraduate student a few years younger, who is an economics major with a passion for anthropology. Stevenson has served back-to-back tours in Korea and Iraq and is in training for an upcoming deployment to Afghanistan. He hails from the Southeast and joined the army rather than the air force, navy, or Marines because he could choose being in the infantry. Stevenson speaks with an in-your-face edge, perhaps aimed at the college student interviewer. "Personally, I just did it to shoot people; that's why I joined the infantry; I like this kind of work. It's fun. It's a good time."

"Has it had any effect on your day-to-day life?" Luke asks.

"No, not really. That's like the whole mentality thing. It's like a switch. You know I was over there and had the mindset I needed to have to do my job, get it done. Came back here and totally turned it off." He adds that he had "no need to worry about what happened over there, because, you know, it's done. So it hasn't really affected me. I mean, I can't remember anything. But I don't have nightmares." He explains that "It's two totally different things. You don't have anything like that," referring to roadside bombs or insurgents shooting at him, "going on over here. So there's no need to stay in that mindset and worry about stuff like that, because the odds of it happening are much slimmer to none than over in Iraq so it's not a big deal." And he can turn it back on when he needs to, as when his unit is training. "I kind of go back in the same mindset when we go back in the field, searching, because they want us to pretend like it's a real combat situation and stuff like that so we can get trained up for Afghanistan." Stevenson adds with pride that he and his buddies in the unit, "we're all pretty good at having that mindset you know, switched on and off."

Stevenson's depiction of the soldier-in-combat and the soldier-at-home as two distinct mindsets associated with distinct actions, responses, and responsibilities fits the model that our society holds of the soldier and civilian as two distinct and contrasting social roles or positions. The Go Army website describes basic combat training as a 10-week "journey from civilian to soldier," in which recruits learn the "Seven Core Army Values, how to work together as a team and what it takes to succeed as a Soldier in the US Army."[3] A Marine Corps recruiting ad posted on YouTube calls joining the Marines a "rite of passage," the phrase anthropologists use for rituals that mark transitions between major and relatively permanent life stages or statuses.[4]

Anthropologists also note that transitions are dangerous times. As Becker (1973) says with regard to terror management, social structure—the system of institutions, roles, and positions that human groups create—provide us with a sense of order, predictability, and safety. Societies divide life into stages with corresponding roles of infant, child, spouse, worker, retiree. While the roles associated with each life stage are relatively stable, the transition between them threatens the group's cohesion and stability. In the case of the military, leaders might wonder: will new recruits handle their weapon responsibly, follow orders, put aside their own needs for those of the mission, master military protocol; in short, be good soldiers? Thus they mark, regulate, and control the passage from civilian recruit to soldier through elaborate, costly, and time-consuming sets of rituals and instruction.

Rites of passage also invoke myths to convey information about the recruit's new role and their rights and responsibilities. Speaking of basic training as a "journey" evokes the archetypical myth of the hero's journey that begins with a period of initiation in which the hero receives, in person or through dreams or visions, instruction and training from seasoned leaders or warriors (Campbell 2008 [1949]). In basic training, recruits or initiates are removed from their everyday routines, stripped of their former roles and responsibilities, and given the uniforms, haircuts, and equipment for their new roles. With the physical transformation comes the personal transformation from civilian to soldier. One of the soldiers we interviewed, Brendan Truman, told us, "Army's culture, especially in the infantry . . . it's all guys. Steely-eyed killers, that's who you're supposed to be. Hard as nails. They beat it into your brain that when you go over there you're indestructible. I don't wanna say brainwash, but they kinda do it." As the Marine recruiting ad concludes, "You will be changed forever."

Although the military's ultimate purpose is to defend the civilian population, the government and businesses that sustain it and the families that reproduce it, the military demands, especially in war, opposing sets of actions and values as expressed in the warrior ethos discussed in chapter 1. Unlike a civilian, a soldier's mission must come before their individual goals and needs. Unlike a civilian, the soldier must be loyal above all to the group—to their battle buddies—before their family or even their own survival. Unlike a civilian, the soldier must be willing and able to wound, kill, and destroy without mercy in addition to protecting, or building and otherwise serving, local populations. Unlike civilians, especially the women and children that he or she protects and defends, a soldier must show strength and control or suppress fear, grief, anxiety, and tenderness. Like civilians, soldiers retain the right and obligation to challenge orders that violate military codes of conduct or the Geneva Convention, but this is the exception, because unlike a civilian, a soldier must demonstrate unquestioned obedience to orders and respect and honor the chain of command. For the military, it is crucial that the contrasting codes between civilian and soldier be opposed and separate (Douglas 1966). As Shay notes of these conflicting codes of behavior, "Ancient Greek heroes were men of pain who were both needed by their people and *dangerous* to them" (2002:2).

This code of behavior, which contrasts strongly with so many principles of American democratic society, suggests that return to civilian status will require another rite of passage that will once again mark, with considerable social investment of time and resources, this transition.[5] Another factor that complicates the transition between military and civilian life is that during deployments to combat zones, soldiers live within the confines of what sociologist Erving Goffman (1961) called a "total institution."[6] To accomplish its mission, the army controls and regulates most aspects of a soldier's life. Whereas a civilian sleeps and eats at home, works at an office or job site, and goes to a bar or movie or park to recreate, many soldiers do these activities on the military base or under military command. The army tells soldiers what to wear, how to cut their hair, where they can have tattoos, and when and what to eat, with rewards for compliance and punishment for infractions. Several soldiers commented that when you live in the barracks you lack privacy, not only from your fellow soldiers (although at Fort Carson soldiers living in barracks have their own rooms), but from officers who do regular inspections and random searches. As soldier Edward Wallace noted, "It's not the Hyatt, you know?"

Heroes' myths conclude or resolve with the hero's return home, transformed, bringing his "life-transmuting trophy" (Campbell 2008 [1949]:167). Joseph Campbell, in his analysis of hero myths around the world, identifies the challenge of the return as the final recognition and acknowledgment that these two worlds are not in fact distinct but are aspects of the same world. "The realm of the gods is a forgotten dimension of the world we know" (Campbell 2008 [1949]:188). The hero's task is to give up her everyday concerns of "normal" life to explore this opposing, forgotten dimension, getting close to the "dark side" portrayed in our own *Star Wars* myths. In some myths, heroes, weary and exhausted by their journey and still seeing the two dimensions as completely separate, refuse to return, while in other myths other agents, supernatural or human, must rescue the hero to bring them back across the threshold to normal life.

*The Odyssey*, the story of Odysseus' 10-year journey home from the Trojan War, is one of the few heroic myths that describe the challenges homecoming presents. In *Odysseus in America* (2002), psychiatrist Jonathan Shay takes each chapter of the epic, and drawing from his work with Vietnam veterans, uses it as a metaphor to help soldiers and civilians understand what today's soldiers face when they return from war. These include difficulty turning off the switch from "combat mode," fleeing pain and boredom, adjusting to civilian work, searching for safety, re-establishing intimate relationships with women (Shay focuses on male, heterosexual veterans), keeping faith with memories of dead comrades, and facing the truth of what they did and experienced in war. But at the end of the epic, Odysseus leaves home once again: what can this myth tell us about fully reintegrating into civilian life?

For many soldiers and families weathering multiple deployments, home-coming is not an end but a way station, one of a series of departures and returns, another corner in the labyrinth. Normally, the unit follows the wel-come home ceremony with uncasing of the colors, described in chapter 1, but this is the "new normal" where the colors may not be uncased as the unit acknowledges that they are only home temporarily.

### "Resetting" and "Flipping the Switch"

"What's it like in the days right when you get back? As you're trying to make that transition?" Luke asked.

> *Coming right back? It's uh, it's weird. The day I got back, I had to carry my M4 with me everywhere I went. You get so used to that over there, you always have your weapon on you. You don't go anywhere without it. And uh, so, the day I came back here and had to turn it in, I went to go sit down, and I was freaking out. Sitting down, looking around for my weapon.*

Stevenson says he quickly realized:

> *But you know it's just habit, you always have certain things on you at all times, no matter what. And it just weird coming back and not having to carry your weapon. Just freaking out. A lot of us did that because it was over 15 months we had to keep our weapons on us, so coming back was defi-nitely weird.*

He was insistent: "But we adjusted really quick, we're like, 'We don't have to carry that any more? Awesome!' So it wasn't that bad."

Though Stevenson minimizes the distress of "freaking out" at loud noises or not carrying his weapon—and most soldiers do readjust fairly quickly (Faber et al. 2008)—others find that the switch from soldier to civilian or from different facets of the soldier's role may not be easy to flip: some switches grow sticky. Brian Turner said that even in theater it can be difficult to return to active combat, patrols, or engaging the enemy if an event has jarred him out of the warrior mindset. "Getting back in the fight, that's the hardest part. If they see someone get hurt, wounded or die." He says that if a soldier is not ready to see it:

> *it messes with his head. He'd hesitate on pulling the trigger, or he'd hesitate on going to hold his friend that was wounded and pulling him to a safe spot. He'd hesitate on anything, and that's a danger to us. So the hardest part is getting them back in.*

Nor are these shifts in mindset restricted to infantry soldiers, who have more direct contact with the enemy. Because the wars in Iraq and Afghanistan are waged by insurgents in the midst of civilian society, those providing support to infantry troops also come under attack and fire. Kevin Vasquez, who joined the army to find work closer to where his daughter lived with his ex-wife, drove trucks in Iraq. He talked about traveling between two forward operating bases (FOBs) in a remote area near the Jordanian border where a father and son team created a device for automatically setting off mortars at the base. Because convoys were targets, and given their large fuel tanks were also highly explosive, drivers had to be constantly vigilant and ready to switch from driving to shooting in seconds.

By contrast, several soldiers told us that life is simpler when they are deployed because they don't have to move between different roles. Kevin Windum said that civilians "expect you to turn it off like a switch," but added, "You can't just turn it off like a switch. You're going over there every day, getting shot at, shooting at other people and then you come back, and it's all calm and nice." Bradley Kay told us, "You don't got to worry about the day-to-day things over there that you have to worry about over here, like your regular life, and then the military life." He described military life as clear and ordered. "You wake up in the morning and I'm going to go on mission from here to here, and this is my job, this is what I gotta do." But in Colorado Springs, "I think a lot of people get into trouble in my opinion because they've got bills, cars, they can drink, drugs are easily available. All this stuff. It's just, a lot more on people here compared to over there, is what I think." Kay himself, like several other soldiers we spoke with, had done well and been promoted during deployments only to be demoted when they got into trouble with drugs or fighting when they got home.

Felix Sprout explained that after deployment, "most people get aggressive: that's how we are over there. When you're over there it's normal, like at the beginning it's kind of bothering you because you've got to keep pushing yourself. But then when you've got a routine down you just stay aggressive." In Sprout's opinion, this is the source of problems when soldiers return. "Then people come back with those thoughts, back over here, and that's how everybody becomes all crazy, soldiers killing other people, stuff like that."

Early in our project, searching for concepts to help us explain what soldiers were telling us about the shifts between soldier-in-combat to soldier-at-home, we explored the concept of "codeswitching" borrowed from linguistics. Codeswitching occurs when someone uses two or more languages or "codes" in a conversation or interaction (Woolard 2006:73–4). For example, a native Spanish speaker might insert a Spanish phrase into a sentence in English, "*Vaya a la bodega* ["go to the store"] and buy me some soap." For many years, linguists and nonlinguists viewed mixing elements from different languages as evidence that the speaker was not fully fluent in one of the languages and so had to resort to using their native language to communicate their ideas. In most cases codeswitching carried a negative connotation. But in other situations, a speaker might use a word or phrase from another language because it provided *le mot juste* ("the right word") that best expressed the idea they wanted to get across. By the 1970s, however, linguists viewed codeswitching as "systematic, skilled, and socially meaningful" (Woolard 2006:74). The ability to switch between languages was a resource that people could use not only to express their ideas or share information about the world, but to convey many kinds of social information.

The military is known for its distinct code filled with acronyms that recruits and even their families, as we discuss later, are required to study and master. These range from the obscure renaming of common objects like a pencil ("portable handheld communications inscriber") that appear in written documents but are rarely used in speech (Lutz 1990) to phrases that have become so incorporated into nonmilitary speech registers that we no longer recognize their origin; for example, the use of "campaign" for everything from selling a new brand of soap to "fighting the battle against infectious disease." The military uses its code to convey specialized and specific information, but just as importantly to mark its boundaries, to signal who is a member and who is not, to "close the ranks" when needed, or open them to those outsiders and service members it wishes to welcome in. Soldiers may use military language to show that they are part of the team and to build solidarity or to form and express their social identity as a soldier (Bucholtz and Hall 2006).

In reality, codes are not clearly bounded. The character of fighting in the post-9/11 wars illustrates how difficult it can be for soldiers to follow rules of engagement that constantly change or distinguish an enemy combatant from a civilian going about her daily life. An officer told us that when he was in Afghanistan he relied on his enlisted soldiers to have their eyes open, scanning the surroundings, their fingers on the trigger ready to fire so that he could focus on building relationships with village leaders. In fact, one of the things soldiers told us most frequently was how fuzzy and unclear the lines were between combatant and civilian, situations where de-escalation of violence was warranted and those where violence was necessary. Moreover, behavioral responses were largely unconscious and embodied, the result of experience and training. Like firefighters and first responders, soldiers develop the capacity to quickly compare a new situation to those they have experienced in the past and to take appropriate action (Klein 1995). These decisions occur "intuitively," below the level of conscious intention and awareness and are communicated to other members of the team rapidly and often nonverbally.

Thus we came to see codeswitching as more accurately reflected in the way soldiers *talked* about their experience of moving back and forth between theater and home, battle and nation-building. It was their "folk theory" that explained what they did and made it comprehensible rather than their actual experience, which was messy, complicated, and far from clear.

## Comprehensive Soldier Fitness

And so we found ourselves in the role of "inadvertent applied anthropologists." Officers liked the concept of codeswitching, in part because it reflected their shared way of talking about the experience of moving among different roles, and in part because it offered an effective way to represent interventions to help soldiers. Soldiers, like firefighters, can and do become adept at moving between different kinds of action in the field. Indeed, anthropologists have long noted and celebrated the human capacity to create and master multiple languages and complex symbolic systems of behavior. But our myths tell us that shifting between some codes is not that easy and may come at a high price to the individual, especially when the behaviors are as extreme as those demanded of infantry soldiers in battle.

In an effort to maintain soldiers' fitness and effectiveness and to prevent the mounting numbers of psychological casualties, leaders at Fort Carson experimented with programs designed to increase soldiers' psychological fitness and resilience. One such program is being run by the Magis group, which bases its training on current research on how traumatic stress affects brain function.[7] Animal studies confirm that fear and avoidance are learned responses to traumatic stressors in the environment, but to survive, animals must also be able to recover from fear and avoidance, to extinguish fear and "reset" and resume normal behavior. Recent studies support the idea that extinguishing fear is a separate learned response that does not erase previous learned responses of fear and avoidance. More important, "[l]earned fears generalize more readily and widely than does learned security" (Kirmayer et al. 2007:14). Thus a new or novel threat may trigger the old fear response. This is especially likely to happen to people with prior histories of trauma, particularly during childhood, or who have not had a chance to fully recover or reset from a traumatic event. Thus, psychiatrist Arieh Shalev concludes that PTSD is "a disturbance of recovery from the early and normal response to traumatic events" (2007:219). Mental health professionals hoped that these trainings would improve soldiers' ability to recover from traumatic events more quickly and fully in theater to prevent combat stress from developing into PTSD later on.

In response to continued and rising levels of psychological injuries and particularly of suicides among soldiers, the army invested $125 million in the Comprehensive Soldier Fitness (CSF) program in 2009 "to enhance the resilience, readiness and potential of Soldiers, Army Civilians and Family members. The goal of the CSF strategy is to help prevent potential problems due to stress by shifting the focus from intervention to prevention, from illness to wellness."[8] Comprehensive fitness is based on five "pillars" of strength: physical, emotional, social, family, and spiritual; as a result, the army relegates its historical focus on physical strength to but one facet of overall fitness. Although the army's evaluation of the CSF program in 2011 showed improvement in scores on resilience and psychological health (Lester et al. 2011), critics of the program questioned whether "the positive psychology strategies that characterize the CSF program" were adequate for the task.[9] By focusing on individual soldiers' resilience or strength, they argued, this approach deflected attention from other sources of distress and suffering: the horrors of war and the added demands of repeated deployments.

## Army Families

Perhaps the most important aspect of CSF is its inclusion of the family as a base for soldier fitness. Part of what this signals is a historic shift in the composition of today's army, in which a higher proportion of junior enlisted military personnel is married and has children. Further, there is an extension of the role of spouses and families as sources of stability and unremunerated support and care, which officers' spouses have played in the past, and an increasingly explicit acknowledgment of the demands that multiple deployments place on spouses and families. We explore these changes in depth in chapter 6, but mention them here to provide context for understanding the transitions that families must make when soldiers deploy.

The AVF has significantly changed military policies toward marriage and the family, particularly for junior enlisted men and women. From WWII until the institution of the AVF, marriage was the purview of officers. Older officers were expected to marry, as the wife's (at this time older officers were almost exclusively heterosexual males) role was to support his career through managing their social life (Goldman 1976). Military policies discouraged marriage among enlisted personnel, requiring that they get approval from their commanding officer to marry.

With the institution of the AVF, military leaders had to appeal to their members' lifestyles to compete with civilian employers to attract and retain personnel, and a significant aspect of lifestyle was marriage and family life (Janofsky 1989; Karney and Crown 2007). The biggest change has been in the number of junior enlisted personnel who are married. In 1953, 38 percent of all active duty servicemen were married (Segal 1986:24). By 2005, 54.6 percent were married, including 51.6 percent of enlisted members (Hogan and Seifert 2010:425). Today's enlisted personnel in the junior grades (E1–E4) are more likely to be married than their civilian peers aged 18 to 24. The relative economic stability offered by the military—full-time work for a specified, contracted period of time with benefits—makes marriage possible for many young people, in particular men who are not college bound, at younger ages than in the civilian workforce. Because the military links housing and medical benefits to marriage, active-duty military personnel are more likely to marry their partners than are civilians (Lemmon et al. 2009). This is not only a matter of financial incentives. As a family readiness group specialist told us, the military officially recognizes blood relations and legally married spouses, but not partners who live together. A cohabiting partner, even in a relationship of many years, cannot receive official notification of their partner's injury or death.[10]

Several factors contribute to the army's large proportion of young families with young children. The bulk of the active-duty army (85%) consists of enlisted personnel who are generally 29 years old or younger. Their spouses are also young; in 2004, just over half (53%) of army spouses were 30 years old or younger. Just under half (47%) of army personnel have children, with an average of two children per parent. And their children are young, too: in 2005, half of army children were 7 years old or younger. Since the institution of the AVF, the American family has also changed, and these changes are reflected in the variety of families that soldiers belong to. Seven percent of soldiers are single parents (Booth et al. 2007:20), and with the repeal of "Don't Ask, Don't Tell" in 2012, the army can at least acknowledge gay and lesbian couples and include them in family and counseling services even if federal law prohibits them from being legally recognized as married and being eligible for spousal benefits.[11] Many soldiers are members of blended families, and it is important to remember that single soldiers have families, too.

All of this means that family members outnumber service members and that a significant number of civilians are thus directly affected by multiple deployments and the absence of family members for military duty for periods of days to years at a time.[12] Here it is important to return to consider the army as a social institution. Sociologist Mady Segal proposes that the army is less a total institution than a "greedy institution" (1986). A greedy institution does not control every aspect of its members' lives, but it does ask much of them in terms of loyalty, time, commitment, and energy. Although many civilian occupations make considerable demands on workers and their families, Segal argues that the way these demands combine in military work creates a "unique constellation" of requirements. This pattern includes risk of injury or death, geographic mobility, separations, residence in foreign countries, and normative constraints. By normative constraints, Segal means that spouses' and children's behavior reflects on their military family member. This kind of social control is most apparent when families live in military housing, where how they maintain their yards and houses is subject to inspection. Spouses, especially officers' spouses, may feel pressured to participate in military social networks (discussed further in chapter 6).[13]

The combination of demands on military families and aspects of military culture—its use of acronyms, ritualized behaviors signaling rank and authority, its emphasis on hierarchy—that separate it from civilian culture means that spouses and children also undergo rites of passage into their roles as members of military families. As the National Military Family Association states on their website: "some people have compared military culture to a foreign country without a guidebook."[14] The need to learn military culture was brought home to Zena Bailey, who, although she had been married to a soldier for many years, had not been "military minded" until her husband's first deployment to Iraq in 2003. With him overseas, she realized she needed to know more. So, she enrolled in the army's family team-building classes "to learn about the military, from the simplest level one class of learning how to read his LES, which is his pay stub, to learning military acronyms and rank, the basics, to leadership, how to be an FRG (Family Readiness Group) leader."

Initiation into military life may also coincide with initiation into marriage, as many couples are newly wed and may have had little time to establish their own patterns of intimacy, communication, and roles prior to deployment. Tracey Hall is an elementary school teacher married to a senior NCO. "Just last week we celebrated our fourth anniversary, and we have been together for 20 months of that. So not even two years." The challenges of establishing a new relationship with a spouse who is absent for long periods of time are compounded for spouses who are also immigrants and who may not speak English.[15]

Greedy institutions like the military must compete with other institutions, such as hobbies, clubs, service organizations, and religion, for their members' time and energy. The institution in most direct competition for most military personnel is the family.

While competition and conflict between the demands of family and work also exist in civilian life, they can be even greater for military families in time of war, and in particular in the post-9/11 wars in which the military has depended on ground troops on two fronts for over a decade. Almost every brigade has served multiple deployments, some as long as 15 months, with extensive mobilization of army national guard and army reserve with a significant increase in the regularity, number, and length of family separations (Booth et al. 2007; Faber et al. 2008; Karney and Crown 2007).

To retain personnel and to increase soldier readiness for deployments, the army has devoted considerable resources to supporting families. Health care benefits, signing bonuses, increased pay during deployments, child care, support for disabled children, housing benefits for married couples and couples with children, and multiple programs to assist soldiers and families to prepare for and manage deployments and reintegration may all contribute to military couples staying married despite the separations and challenges of multiple deployments. A study by the RAND Corporation to explore the effects of multiple deployments on military marriages found that increased length of deployments actually reduced the risk that a marriage would dissolve;[16] this effect was strongest for young couples who married after 2002. The authors conclude that structural factors outside the marriage, such as those listed here, may outweigh the emotional and other stresses of multiple deployments in terms of whether or not a couple stays together. The authors caution that they did not assess how well marriages functioned or whether partners were satisfied with their marriages (Karney and Crown 2007). When learning to adjust to deployments coincides with developing patterns of responsibility, problem-solving, intimacy, and communication in a new marriage, the two may reinforce one another. In other words, these newly married couples learn to be military couples. Karney and Crown compare it to becoming a parent. Couples who married in 2002 or later knew that their soldier would be deployed. They expected that deployment would be difficult but had norms and support to aid them in adjusting to this new situation. Through its extensive programs on marriage and family life, preparing for deployments, the work of the FRGs during deployments, and the preparation for reintegration, these young couples, if they chose to participate, had access to a wealth of free resources and support.

While families have always been affected when soldiers go to war, the space–time compression of contemporary life has brought the living room to the battlefield and the battlefield into the living room. Each deployment incorporates a cycle that moves soldiers and their families through different patterns of routines, communication, and interaction. The "deployment cycles" consist of three phases: notification and preparation, separation, and reunion (Karney and Crown 2007:xix).[17] So there are big transitions and little transitions, epic transitions and those that happen every day.

## In Deployment Mode

*It's so much harder when they come home than when they leave. It's so much harder.*

—Theresa Thayer

In *The Odyssey*, Odysseus's wife Penelope must endure what may be the longest deployment in history. Her husband wages war in Troy for 10 years only to take another 10 years returning to Ithaca and the embrace of his wife and now adult son, Telemachus. Although Odysseus's journey is the focus of the epic, we do learn of the many challenges Penelope faces during his absence.[18] How do today's army spouses manage the transitions surrounding multiple deployments for their families? Perhaps not surprisingly, several of the spouses who agreed to interviews or that we met in a variety of community settings were coping well, even thriving, and were eager to share their experiences with us. While they acknowledged that deployments are stressful and may have long-term consequences for themselves, their marriages, and their families, they manage, viewing the challenges as a source of growth and strength. Looking at how these families cope well reveals how many different factors must come together positively to make a "successful" adjustment.

Faber et al. (2008), in a study of families in the reserves, use the concept of ambiguous absence to describe families' experiences during deployments. "Ambiguous absence occurs when a person is perceived by his or her family members as physically absent but psychologically present" (Faber et al. 2008:223). Families may be preoccupied with the absent members' safety or feel uncertain about what kinds of information to share or what role they should take in the family. The stories that follow show how several spouses managed this ambiguity.

As we walk out of the Canyon Café after talking with JJ Thomas, a military spouse, her words echo in our minds: "We're just fine here—everything's great!" She finishes her statement with thumbs up, and a smiling, tilted pose to her head, as if she's taking a snapshot of herself in her mind. And indeed, we think later, if she's Skyping with her husband Derek in Afghanistan, she would be watching herself have those conversations on a smaller, inset window next to his image. "I'm safe, nobody's shooting at me. I'm not sitting out there in 130-degree weather with no air conditioning, you know, sand and those big crab things that look like spiders." For JJ,[19] the deployment is not about her, but about her husband. Taking care of things at home, finding fun things for the kids to do, and setting goals for herself is how she supports him in his work. "He would call every so often, and he'd say, 'Great! I hear the kids are fine.' You know, I don't want him worrying about that. Because it's not about me."

Despite her strong self-assurance, JJ acknowledges that handling deployments wasn't always easy. "The first deployment to Iraq was hard. The kids were little, two and five. We had just moved back here. I really didn't know a whole lot of people at first, and it was scary because it was right after 9/11 . . .

everybody was just afraid." But his second deployment to Iraq was the most dangerous, "that was when he was in the middle of all kinds of things."

*It was fresh; it was new. But you know, I just had my pity party for a few days and just said, "Ok, I got to move on. I've got these kids. We gotta to do this and that." So I got them involved in music and in gymnastics and I keep them really busy. And that's just what I do.*

She notes that anybody's first deployment is going to be difficult. "But you've just got to 'Buckle up, buttercup' and move on. You have to be independent, you have to be resourceful, you have to have goals. You have to want to progress and move on and well, be able to handle it."

For Theresa Thayer, the key to handling deployments is to maintain a stable home routine, especially for her two young children. Theresa met her husband when they were both enrolled at the Defense Language Institute in Monterey. They've been married seven years and started their family right away. While Theresa admires women with children who remain on active duty, she says, "I know a lot of moms who are active duty, and yay on them, but I saw what it was like when my next door neighbor had to turn over her six-year-old and deploy." So Theresa left the military and takes care of her children and household full-time. She keeps track of when the car's registration will expire, when the children need checkups, and insists that her soldier-husband respects this. "Because they're gone for so long, you have to pick up the pieces. You put together a very specific life as to how and when things get done." Like JJ, Theresa attributes her ability to cope to her independence. "I think we were very lucky because we were raised by a family of fiercely independent women. My grandmother raised five children in the military and my grandpa was never around. There's pictures of her flying back from Paris with my two uncles on leashes. It's chaos."

Husbands and wives also develop ways of protecting each other from distressing news or events. Several of the wives labeled this "compartmentalization." Theresa Thayer says that she and her husband are lucky because "neither one of us are people who need large amounts of emoting." When he is deployed and they need to emote, they "have other people that we go and talk to so we don't blur those lines." They have "some very clear lines" about what kinds of information they share. "If it's not important, he doesn't need to know. When my one-year-old broke her leg, I told him that. At the end of the lice adventure [head lice in school], I told him that." But she doesn't tell him about things he cannot fix.

Both JJ and Theresa emphasized the importance of maintaining daily routines. JJ plans fun things for her kids around the holidays that give them something to look forward to. "We have good times for Christmas and New Years and birthdays, make a big deal of that, but we don't go," she adds, imitating a sobbing voice, "'Ohh, Daddy's not home.' Let's plan some fun things. . . . We got Halloween coming up, we got Thanksgiving coming up. We have Christmas—what are we going to do?"

Despite parents' best efforts, deployment can be a time of marked stress for the children. Young children with deployed parents see pediatricians more frequently for mental and behavioral health issues than those whose parents are not deployed (Chartrand et al. 2008; Gorman et al. 2010). Older children and girls of all ages have more problems with school, family, and peer relationships (Chandra et al. 2009), with younger children and boys at higher risk for depressive and behavioral symptoms (Cozza et al. 2005). Other researchers caution against pathologizing children of military families, and some recent studies show that military children have similar or somewhat better adjustments than their civilian peers (Ender 2005; Kelley et al. 2003; Watanabe and Jensen 2000).

Mary Estrada, a mental health consultant with the Community Partnership for Child Development in Colorado Springs, reports that she is observing behavior in preschool age children with deployed parents that is "very, very explosive and aggressive." Estrada says that children of deployed parents show decreased scores on measures of resiliency, and some are being kicked out of preschools for aggressive behavior. A Head Start teacher spoke at a public event about preschoolers' aggression that she thought was depression-based; she even worried about suicidality in her young charges. Noreen Landis-Tyson, who heads the Community Partnership, says the children experience very high levels of stress related to continued cycles of deployment (Lane 2009).

Laurie Wilson is the principal of Milton High School, an alternative high school for at-risk students. About half of her students come from military families. "How do I handle the kiddos who are drawing machine guns and war . . . tell them, 'You can't do that' when that's their life, reality, that's what Dad is doing. That's what is in their house. Camo . . . it's just their culture." She attributes this to military culture rather than problems with aggression and anger. "I do struggle with that. Because the majority of it comes from a military kiddo, drawing that type of thing. And, just, *boys* in general . . . . How do you teach them how to handle that appropriately, instead of just . . . cutting it all out?"

Wilson says that adolescents learning new roles in the family when a family member deploys experience high levels of stress. "Whether they're stepping in as Dad or whether they're stepping in as Mom . . . having to get a job, or having to become babysitters to the brothers and sisters. Or they're taking on extra responsibilities at home. And that cuts into their school time, whether it's attending school or doing their [home] work." Students often miss school to spend time with a parent who is about to deploy, who is home on mid-tour leave, or to prepare for their homecoming. Stress often manifests in bad behavior. "Kiddos will snap more often. They'll get in trouble more often. Not serious trouble, necessarily, but you can just tell that that stress level is higher." She says that although some students will use their parent's deployment to excuse absences or bad behavior, for the most part they are honest in reporting when a deployment affects their schoolwork. "Definitely, you could tie anxiety to deployments. I think a lot of depression . . . too, and lack of motivation. Just not caring, not doing their schoolwork, not doing their homework." She adds that at times this can be severe. "We've had a couple kiddos in the hospital for really severe depression. Not just with the thoughts, but also plans. There's a big range, but big time is the lack of motivation." While worrying about their deployed parent's safety can make concentrating on schoolwork difficult, focusing on school activities and peer relationships can provide distraction from fear and worry. When we asked her about romantic relationships, she replied, "Sometimes I love it when it motivates the kid. Because there's this girl they're interested in in the classroom and all of a sudden their grades go way up and they start participating . . . . I think that's fabulous. Whatever it takes to get them to school!"

Over the past few years the schools at Fort Carson have increased resources for mental health. One of the post's elementary schools has a counseling office by the front entrance to the school so that parents can drop by when picking up their children and have informal, unscheduled conversations with a mental health professional. Wilson says the MFLCs ("Em-Flacs"; marriage and family life counselors) have been a wonderful source of support for many of their families, although their relationships are limited by the temporary nature of their assignments. The school's family advocate, part of the Army Community Services program, is working to decrease the stigma that families associate with getting help. "Instead of her calling up just when there is something bad going on, she goes and visits every home proactively, so that they already have a relationship with her."

Kathy Edwards, the children's program manager at a Colorado Springs agency that provides services to victims of sexual abuse and assault, reports high levels of child abuse during deployments. "Children can't emotionally regulate so they're having significant behavior problems, they're having significant academic problems in school, they're having problems with their relationships with peers—they're fighting because they have this overwhelming fear." If the mother is not used to being a single parent and is overwhelmed herself, she is not able to "create the safety, stability, security they need. Mom's stressed, overburdened, can't emotionally regulate herself." Families often look to the returning spouse to establish stability, but if they are having difficulty regulating their emotions after returning from deployment, they end up escalating the children's distress and acting out, a setting for child abuse.

As JJ so astutely recognized, how well children do during deployments is "strongly determined" by the quality of their relationships with their parents and how well the nondeployed parent is coping.[20] Deployments of nine months or longer and more frequent deployments place female spouses at greater risk for depression, anxiety, and adjustment and sleep disorders (Mansfield et al. 2010; Sherman and Bowling 2011). As JJ put it, "You cry, you know, when you have to. And you try not to worry about it because my whole philosophy is you've got little kids, don't be cryin' every single minute of the day and freakin' them out, you know. It's all about how mommy handles it, and how the kids are going to handle it."

## Reintegration

If deployments put soldiers and families in the middle of the labyrinth, then redeployment or return and reintegration represent their journey out, back to a life more integrated with the civilian world of extended family and community. How do they negotiate this journey and what programs and services are there to assist them?

As the time of the soldier's homecoming nears, anxiety rises with anticipation (Allen et al. 2011). This is the time of greatest risk, and one that the army takes increasingly seriously. While family members and counselors describe the initial days and weeks following return as the "honeymoon" period in which family members enjoy seeing each other again and are eager to make the transition smooth and easy, the period 30 to 60 days following return is also often fraught with conflict and unease. Spouses and children have established routines and roles that have a certain efficiency of energy that resists change. Faber et al. (2008) characterize this as the time of "ambiguous presence," when the soldier is perceived as physically present but psychologically absent. As with ambiguous absence, family members also experience ambiguity about their roles, how to communicate, and how to fit the formerly absent member into the routines established while they were away.

Karen Levine, an army wife who provides training in parent nurturing at Fort Carson explains that "We were very well-functioning without him . . . became very self-sufficient. Do you want to really welcome that person and embrace them in? . . .[Y]ou know they are going to be leaving again for another 9 to 12 months. I think that's hard."

Theresa Thayer's husband is in special forces, which means that in addition to deployments, one of which lasted almost 18 months, he is often gone for several weeks to a month for training classes. "In February, he was gone for two weeks, came home for three weeks, left for a month, came home for 36 hours, and left for another month." So when he came home and wanted to take her and the children out to lunch, she said, "I understand you want to go out to lunch, but nap time starts at 12:30 and there's nothing that I can say or do to change that at this point. We have to be at this house and in this bed at 12:30." She acknowledges his need to reconnect ("I know how much you missed everybody"), though she adds, "but you can't come back and change everything in an afternoon."

Theresa says that her insistence on maintaining the routines that she establishes when her husband is gone when he returns has been a source of frustration for him and conflict between them. "Especially parenting kids. We disagree about that all the time. When he comes back after a year and a half he's like, 'I just want to be involved.' I'm like, 'That's cool. How about we do it this way?' He's like, 'Well, I don't feel included.'" For JJ, mid-tour breaks, when husbands would return for a few days, were the hardest. "Especially that two-week R&R [rest and relaxation] thing in the middle which eventually they're going to get rid of as soon as they go to nine-month deployments, it's going to go away. That is a big problem." Not only does it place major logistics demands on the army that must manage getting personnel back and forth from Iraq or Afghanistan, it creates problems at home. "And then all the problems that happen when the soldier comes home in that two weeks. You have a lot of domestic violence issues . . . and a lot of marital problems because they come home and nobody knows how to interact with each other . . . . So a lot of us don't even want them coming back for that two weeks because it's just not enough time to adjust, for them to fit into the family."

When Theresa's husband had a 36-hour leave, "we thought about not having him see the kids because he flew in on Friday night and left Sunday morning." Given the short period of time he would be home, they decided it would be better for him to see their children away from home. "He got home and we went out to dinner with the girls. They were with him that whole night and into the next morning. My sister is a godsend. We just dropped them off [at her house]." Her husband and the girls were able to see each other, but with less disruption. "It was so much easier just to be that short time period and almost none of it at our house than it would have been to have him come home and play with them and give them baths and get into that routine. That would have been horrible to reset."

One of the biggest difficulties that spouses related was the compression of these phases, particularly in the early years of the wars. In principal, dwell time—the time between deployments—is supposed to be a time for soldiers and families to readjust to being together and recover from the stresses of separation and the intensity of military missions (Doyle and Peterson 2005). But in the early phases of the post-9/11 wars, as the army faced rising insurgency in Iraq, the tempo of deployments increased along with the intensity of conflict. Frequently the reunion phase from one deployment was interrupted by the preparation for the next, so that although soldiers were in the United States, they were still absent for considerable periods of time. Soldiers spoke of "feeling deployment stress, including predeployment arguments," with one sergeant adding, "it's easier to leave if you are arguing." By 2007, the army shortened time at home still further, with some troops spending less than a year at Fort Carson between tours in Iraq. "We're getting mad over here and, yes, it's destroying morale," one soldier wrote in an email to the *Gazette* from Iraq (Roeder 2013). As Susan Wilson, who teaches classes on TBI at Fort Carson told us, this deployment tempo often means that families are never able to make the transition. "And it's a long time to be in a war where you are supposed to have down time between. . . . So they're always in that mindset," stuck long-term, as it were, betwixt and between.

But after a deployment, the family must readjust to one another and make that transition. For Theresa, the experiences her husband has during deployments mean that he returns a different person. "I've gotten a new husband three different times. So much changes. . . ." They renegotiate their marriage, and who will do what, each time. "It's like bearing a new person." She attributes some of this to changing phases in the family, but some to the different experiences they've had while they've been separated. And here the mechanisms, like compartmentalization, that couples develop to handle deployments, may make the process of reestablishing intimacy more difficult:

> If you're interrogating and working in the community trying to find people you have to learn how to completely compartmentalize everything, you can't have emotions. Coming home, you have to turn that off and sometimes it takes a while. Sometimes it's hard to remember his kids are his kids and you're allowed to have emotion.

Wives who have become more independent may not be willing to give up the control they have worked hard to achieve, and this can be a source of conflict as husbands return and try to find a role for themselves in the family. Adolescents often worry that their parent will not recognize or acknowledge how much they have changed and matured or the new responsibilities they have assumed while one of their parents has been deployed (Chartrand et al. 2008; Huebner and Mancini 2005; Richardson et al. 2011). She added that financial matters can be another source of stress as families must adjust to losing the $150 to $225 of monthly "combat pay."[21]

While many families negotiate this transition without too many bumps in the road, for others it brings serious and long-lasting problems. Doreen Brennan married John, an NCO in the infantry, and moved to Fort Carson a month prior to her husband's first deployment to Iraq. While preparing to deploy he spent little time with her, preferring to spend time with men from his unit. Though disappointed, she understood this as anxiety over the upcoming deployment. "The last . . . month before they leave their behavior might be a little more irrational just because their clock is ticking and they get nervous and scared." In contrast, his deployment was a time of greater intimacy because they communicated more. "When he was gone he would call me almost every day . . . . I liked that and our relationship actually grew a lot when he was gone because we had to communicate. John always had a problem with communication."

But after John had been home a month, Doreen noticed changes. "He was a different person every day. He didn't want to go out any more; he wanted to stay at home . . . . His spending habits went through the roof." She said that he bought a car without telling her, saying that he deserved it. "He had really bad mood swings, and he would throw stuff and kick things, which he never used to do. For instance, the little things, little tiny things would set him off, like Cheerios in the sink." It affected their physical intimacy as well. "Weird sounds in his ears reminded him of flesh and blood and body I guess. If I got close to his ears he would freak out." He no longer wanted her to touch him. "He never wanted me to do any form of massage, scratch, tickle . . . . The only thing he wanted was for me to just sit there with my arms around his waist, which was very weird." She stopped looking him in the eye, because he would look down at her and point, treating her like one of his privates. When she reminded him, "I am not one of your soldiers. I am your wife. Do not talk to me like that," he would apologize. "He would say, 'Oh, I'm really sorry.' But it is almost like he didn't know he was doing it." Doreen wanted to help him, to hear about his experiences in Iraq, but while he would show pictures from his deployment to his grandparents, he wouldn't share them with her. He began drinking heavily, got a DUI, and abandoned her at a downtown bar at two o'clock in the morning. "He just got drunk and went home and left me there."

John got treatment for PTSD and TBI at Fort Carson and from a civilian therapist off-post. But nothing seemed to help. Doreen acknowledges that some of John's behaviors presented before he joined the army, but "Iraq really, really heightened his negative aspects, made him so bad." Raised as a devout Baptist, John is tortured by the memory of shooting an Iraqi civilian who would not stop at a checkpoint. "He is tortured. Every single day he lives through the torture, and I think a part of him wants to try and be normal, but he can't." Feeling increasingly isolated, abandoned, and without her family to help keep John's behavior toward her in control, Doreen filed for divorce and moved back to be near her family.

Sarah Jones, who is a counselor at the agency that assists victims of domestic violence, noticed a distinctive pattern in domestic violence following deployments. "I was able to pull queries from this access database and find the numbers that were doubling" for domestic violence cases "in the units that had returned from Operation Iraqi Freedom, 90 days out. So in other words, when they returned, rates were pretty average, maybe even a little lower for the first 30 [days], normal at 60, and doubled at 90." She explained that symptoms of combat-related PTSD and depression may not appear immediately following return from a combat zone. "It takes two or three months before the depression sets in."

She added that many of these cases were different from those they usually see. "We see people who are arrested for domestic violence that we wouldn't consider a crime of power and control. So there are instances, for example, when a soldier has a flashback in the middle of the night and strangles his wife." But she cautions that in many of these cases, combat-related stress and the means soldiers use to self-medicate—alcohol and drug abuse—amplify relationship dynamics that existed prior to deployment (Bell et al. 2004). "The general excuse was it's PTSD. Then I talk to the wife and find out, he had done this before deployment, he had done this before he was in the army, but *now* it's being excused as PTSD." While PTSD can escalate domestic violence, they are separate issues that both demand treatment. "So you have to treat both of them. But you don't ignore one and treat the other and think that one is causal of the other, it's just not effective. We're not doing our service members any good by pretending that there aren't two issues when they're doing both."

Not only does PTSD contribute to domestic violence, it is associated with significant psychological distress in spouses, often defined as secondary traumatic stress or secondary traumatic stress disorder (STS/STSD) (Renshaw et al. 2011).[22] Children of veterans with PTSD may exhibit many of the same symptoms as their parent as a way to identify and connect with them or acting as a rescuer by assuming some of the parent's responsibilities or withdraw emotionally (Price 2009). Many soldiers and veterans who experience PTSD and depression self-medicate with alcohol or drugs (Brady et al. 2004). The combination of combat-related mental health issues, alcohol and drug use, and violence often land soldiers in jail, with felonies, debt, and other consequences that can contribute to long-term economic and social problems.

The army has responded to the potential dangers of reintegration with postdeployment sessions, known at Fort Carson as Reintegration University. The program is mandatory for all returning soldiers and includes classes for couples, singles, and couples getting divorced, as well as classes on drug and alcohol issues, financial matters, sexual assault, domestic violence, and child abuse. Spouses are invited and encouraged, but not required, to attend. The army has combined this with increased screening for PTSD, TBI, and depression at multiple points after deployment in the hope of detecting issues earlier and getting soldiers into treatment.

We attended a pre-reintegration training for spouses on the topics of domestic violence and communication with children led by a counselor from Army Community Services. He talked about patterns in relationships that were healthy and those likely to lead to conflict and domestic violence during reintegration. By recognizing these patterns, spouses would be able to understand the dynamics of the situation and be able to find alternative ways to resolve or diffuse conflict before it escalates to violence.

## Approaching the Limits of Human Flexibility

Although humans can adapt to a wide range of social settings and communicate across differences in language and culture, in settings as radically different as war and civilian peace we may be bumping up against serious limitations to our flexibility. JJ, Theresa, and many other wives of deployed soldiers are functioning well, by and large. Theirs are the success stories, and they might be quick to point out that despite the "problem wives" who "can't handle deployments," most spouses do handle them. Many even thrive, developing skills and a newfound independence and strength. Karen Davis is an army wife married to a senior NCO for many years. We asked her what advice she might give to her daughter. "Just be prepared for some tough times, mentally and physical, 'cause it's going to be exhausting. But the rewards . . . . You'll know how strong you are, that you can do it."

Kay Ogden, who leads training sessions on reintegration through Army Family Services, says that "there are a lot more families that are strong and figuring it out than aren't. But I think it impacts everybody." Nor does it necessarily get easier over time, with more deployments. Zora Bates, who has found a fulfilling career serving military families, nonetheless confesses, "The military families are just fractured. They are truly fractured. I personally, with three deployments, I didn't think we would make it. It's a challenge . . . . It's across the board; with multiple back-to-back deployments it has broken the family."

Although deployments may strengthen good marriages, they may hasten the dissolution of troubled marriages. Even in the time of relative peace prior to the post-9/11 wars, military personnel had higher rates of divorce than civilians (Lundquist 2007).[23] Active-duty infantry soldiers spoke repeatedly about marriages falling apart. For Don Haskins, it's a matter of families being able to sustain themselves while soldiers fully readjust.

*And I think they give up too fast, because they might think the help's [therapy] not working or whatever. It takes time. It takes a long time. I hear the shrink say it takes six months to a year and by that time you're deploying again. So by the time you're just getting over it, you're starting another one. You got to really have a patient family.*

Kelsoe Fitzgerald is single and wishes that his parents had access to programs to prepare them for the changes they see in him following his deployments. "Every time I come home they expect me to be like I was before I even left for the army. I keep telling them, 'Hey, I'm not that person anymore. I'm different.'"

And then there are the soldiers who never fully come home. Beryl Makris was leaving the next day for a family trip to the Caribbean with her injured veteran husband and daughter.

"This trip is about making family memories for our [14-year-old] daughter," she said. "Especially memories with her dad." She took a breath, her voice steady. "He's been declared terminal. He's deteriorated to the point where there's no hope of recovery. They're giving him a year, maybe." She shared details of their arrangements, adding, "We're not going to be able to go to Australia like we'd always planned; his health and our finances make it impossible. So three days in the US Virgin Islands will have to do."

Since her husband Charles had returned from Iraq in 2006 with a debilitating TBI following exposure to multiple blasts from IEDs and other weapons, his functioning steadily worsened. When we next saw her a few months later, his behavior was "out of control," and to protect herself and daughter, Beryl had committed him to institutional care.

Charles reached the limits of human flexibility; he will never recover from multiple head injuries to exit the labyrinth and be home. Beryl and her daughter will, but their journey has already been arduous, filled with unanticipated twists and turns, and they will likely face more detours in the coming years. Thousands more will live out their lives with chronic pain, illness, and disabilities resulting from their war experiences. Others will choose to end their distress with suicide. For such soldiers and those closest to them, neither comprehensive fitness nor compartmentalization may suffice to help them weather the back-and-forth of war and home, without devastating, permanent costs.

## Chapter 6

# "Under the Chain of Command": Spouses' Volunteer Work

*The shroud itself became a story almost instantly. "Penelope's web," it was called; people used to say that of any task that remained mysteriously unfinished. I did not appreciate the term web. If the shroud was a web, then I was the spider. But I had not been attempting to catch men like flies: on the contrary, I'd merely been trying to avoid entanglement myself.*

—Margaret Atwood, *The Penelopiad*

"But, these are *public* meetings," Chelsea Neel repeated, shaking her head. "*Any*one can go." Chelsea, the captain's wife and prominent Family Readiness Group (FRG) leader for the company, had been handed the unpleasant obligation to retract the invitation she herself had initially made to us, to attend an FRG event, and she vehemently disagreed with the reasoning that forced her to do so.[1] The "Reconnection Workshop" to be held that night was in anticipation of the brigade's imminent return around the winter holidays of 2012. One of our student interns couldn't attend, though, and asked us if we might tape it. She meant audio, but we unfortunately didn't specify when we asked Chelsea for permission; she consulted other FRG leaders: some, it turned out, for the first time. Laney Howard, the senior leader and wife of the battalion's commander, responded that she did not want "my ladies being observed"; she was understandably concerned they would not share as easily in the sessions with researchers present. For now, though, Chelsea was asked to make it clear that "tonight should be for spouses only."

FRGs are the primary means through which the army involves families in deployment and reintegration issues. In this chapter we approach FRGs as places for exploring how the centrality of the soldier affects everyone else: on the liminal periphery of the labyrinth, as it were, but in terrain where strict formality of protocol and tradition very much apply, and where power and authority can be intensely contested. The FRG mission is "to assist commanders in maintaining readiness of soldiers, families, and communities within the Army by promoting self-sufficiency, resiliency, and stability during peace and war" (Operation Ready 2010). Though various versions of volunteer-based spousal labor play roles throughout US military history, during the post-9/11 wars FRGs have taken an altogether new level of centrality. FRGs are key sites in which army spouses cope, and many in some ways thrive, across years of bimodality, as their spouses continually transmigrate between "downrange"—whether this is training or foreign theater—and home.

During this period, the chain of command has officially extended its control over spousal volunteer work. This has brought, we argue, greater officiality, visibility, and in many ways recognition to their labors. At the same time, more has been asked of them in terms of work that is often demanding and stressful, and which continues to be an overwhelmingly unpaid, feminized form of "volunTOLD"-ism (as their joking phrase has it), in stark contrast to the paid, masculinized work soldiers perform in an all-volunteer force.

In the US Army, where male soldiers comprise 86.5 percent of the ranks,[2] the overwhelming numbers of army spouses are women. Recognizing this, our subjects often refer to themselves as "army wives," and here we treat the term as virtually interchangeable with army spouses, except when we specify we are speaking of gender-mixed groups or individual MANspouses (to borrow a term a male-spouse blogger uses). Although the army may have "figured out how to incorporate women" into its ranks, as one senior officer put it, it remains a highly gendered organization in which the positions and roles most closely associated with action directed at achieving its mission are valorized, privileged, and masculinized, while positions that provide support or whose activities are more distant from the mission are less valued and feminized.

### Institutional Background

Wives have long histories of self-organizing, from the "camp followers" of the Revolutionary War through women's accompaniment of frontier and constabulary forces of the nineteenth century (Keller 2006 [1990]:xx). But, in part because only officers were allowed to marry until 1925, officers' wives have long anchored the "unique social system dedicated not only to common courtesy, but community building" (Keller 2006 [1990]:xxviii). Eventually, military ambivalence about wives as likely impediments to soldier mobility tipped toward valuing them as "force multipliers," who could greatly aid both mission readiness and retention. By the time WWII concluded, it became ever clearer that as long as wives help "make [the] military's men less indebted, more reliable, and less prone to disease," and don't interfere overly in "global effectiveness" or "dilute the male bonding that remains the preferred glue holding together military units," they were a net military asset (Enloe 2000:156). Officers' wives clubs, and their attendant official teas and coffee functions, were most longstanding and central, but by the 1960s, NCO and enlisted wives' clubs also flourished, often dubbed "Waiting Wives Clubs," and all with social, charitable, and community-building emphases. By the 1970s, with the women's movement and wives' greater pursuit of paid employment, wifely volunteerism rates diminished.

Enloe enumerates that part of the agreement women may make in service of the "Good Military Wife" may include prioritizing her husband's performance as the measure of her family's well-being; being a competent single parent managing household finances and chores; being "pleased to relinquish" head-of-household duties on his return, and tolerating the results of his deployment stress; "liking moving" (PCS-ing, or "permanent change of station") and viewing it as an exciting opportunity; enjoying unpaid work; and taking pride in her own children entering the military (Enloe 2000:162–64). Even before the 9/11 wars, "agencies once fully staffed by Army-wife volunteers and regarded as 'nice to have' were now recognized as critical to Army life" (Keller 2006 [1990]:xxix).

Such recognition led to a concerted effort by the army to formalize family support, most notably with the 1988 mandate that units create Family Support Groups (FSGs). As a pamphlet on the FSGs explained: "FSGs are not new. They are, quite simply, a formalization of activities spouses have been involved in since the beginning of Military service" (Gassmann 2010:108–9).

In 2000, the groups were reclassed as Family Readiness Groups (FRGs); for the first time, these were stipulated as command-sponsored,[3] or under the chain of command, "a straight line that runs from the president of the United States . . . down to the newest, lowest-ranking soldier. Every member of the Army is responsible for his or her actions to the person above" (Crossley and Keller 19930:354). Public duties, geared to families co-producing readiness rather than supporting one another, now officially took precedence over social aspects; the degree to which wives-as-leaders exercised autonomy was explicitly undercut. The titles of the handbooks and manuals that guide these shifting role assignments tell their own story: from *Army Wife Handbook* to *Family Readiness Leaders Handbook* to the current *Operation Ready Smartbook*, various editions of the *Battlebook* (I–IV), and even "family Battlemind." Battlebook IV explains:

> *In theory, making the FSG [and FRG] a "Green Suit," (i.e. military member),*
> *[sic] responsibility, would take the pressure off of the spouse volunteers, who*
> *were getting overextended due to the many duties asked of them during the*

*increasingly frequent deployments. However, because of the high opera-*
*tional tempo, military members were fully engaged in operational require-*
*ments and their tendency remained to de-emphasize the importance of*
*Family[4] readiness, leaving it to the spouses to sort out and execute the*
*functions of this still new organization. (US Army War College [USAWC]*
*2011:38–9)*

*Battlebook IV's* chapter on FRGs takes pains to distinguish them from the
"Coffee Groups" (and Wives' Clubs) that were their predecessors. Coffee
groups historically undertook many of the activities FRGs are now charged
with: fundraisers of all sorts, community social events, and sending care
packages to soldiers in the field. Because officer and NCO wives had pre-
dominated, however, they specifically "did not encompass junior enlisted
spouses, whose need for unit information was not being met" (USAWC
2009:32). Information sharing in support of mission readiness became
the primary charge, something that would take on unforeseen dimensions
with the unprecedented number of deployments of OEF/OIF. "Gossip," to
consider one highly gendered activity often considered overly personal for
professional/public work, is contrasted five times in the 2010 FRG Handbook with accurate, "timely information" and the "professional handling of
personal information"; gossip is "taboo" (USAWC 2009:34) and, along with
"Army bashing" and "personal and political agendas," has no place in FRG
work (Enroth et al. 2010:34,40).

Battlebook IV admonishes the senior spouse leading an FRG that it is
"[n]ot a democratic group but has to feel like one!!!" Coffee groups were not
actively disbanded, but "FRGs are the primary unit based, Family member,
group now . . . . [A]ttention goes there first; coffee groups are secondary"
(USAWC 2009:33). While "social cohesion *can* develop" [our emphasis] in
an FRG, its importance is ranked low-to-medium, whereas for those with
time to also organize coffee groups, socializing is ranked high (USAWC
2009:27). Similarly made plain is that coffee groups must remain *purely*
social: "No fundraising, no decisions made regarding unit Family issues or
FRG business activities" (USAWC 2009:27) is to occur. The guide recognizes
that this may mean "double-duty" for the senior spouse (USAWC 2009:32),
but does not probe the ironies of this reorganization resulting from diminished availability of time for volunteering.

## Public or Private?

How does bringing FRGs under command authority bear upon the awkward
"uninvitation" with which we open this chapter? The disagreement between
two wives, a captain's and a lieutenant colonel's, about the relative private or

public nature of an FRG event did not mark our first invitation to attend FRG functions, and neither was it the first time that we would be invited and then have the invitation retracted. In 2009, when the media attention had erupted over ties between "our" battalion and the spate of soldier-perpetrated murders, we found ourselves effectively frozen out of a number of "senior spouses" meetings we had earlier been invited to; when it was politely intimated that "now wasn't the best time to do this," we put plans aside. Our follow-up efforts to revisit the possibility of attending events resulted in strings of unanswered phone and email messages. Though we continued to connect well and conduct interviews with a number of individual wives (of enlisted, NCOs, and officer soldiers), until recently we had not sought to attend any FRG functions.

Three years and two deployments later, specific officers and spouses had moved on, tensions had diminished, and it appeared we were more welcome. A few weeks before, at Chelsea's invitation we had sat in on a "Kids Chat and Ice Cream Social" convened by one of the brigade's battalions. While the moms did a workshop on "Learning Your Gemstone" or communication style (which two dual-military marriage, soldier/male-spouses of deployed female soldiers abstained from), the kids were broken into groups of 8 to 12 each, according to age. Over craft projects or between games, depending on the age, social workers from Army Community Services gently raised issues regarding their fathers' impending re-entry into the lives of their families. The group of young teens entertained questions like "What do you want to discuss about your dad coming home—good parts, concerns?" and "What is something your dad might not know about you that you would like him to?" After the teen group broke up and its members dashed toward the ice cream, we asked Oscar Pierce, one of the social workers we'd come to know well over the years, about the nondeploying parent. "Do you ever ask the kids similar questions about the moms? Like, 'How do you think your mom is doing right now?'"

"Well," he responded, "some of the really deep stuff, we don't go for it directly; it's too hard. We just let it come out in its own time." Relationships with the nondeploying parent, then, were at once less salient and more sensitive: so much so that addressing them directly could aggravate tensions. Interestingly, this approach kept the soldiers on center stage, and their spouses, as secondary supporters, in the wings.

After the revoked invitation, Chelsea wrote that next time we would not inform anyone that an observer would be attending. Sarah replied that although "we've been hanging around 4th BCT events for years now, and don't always have to wear placards announcing ourselves as researchers in ways that are disruptive or obtrusive," we were still committed to openness and informed consent. "It is really up to FRG leaders, so one question I have for you is: who is the 'we' that won't be telling folks we're there as participant-observers?" This referred to Chelsea's preceding message, that next time we would not inform anyone that observers would be attending. "Do your other FRG leaders in the brigade know?" Sarah asked. This exchange led to the lunch, and Chelsea stressing the public nature of the meetings. She did not directly address whether other leaders had been informed prior to the taping request, explaining only that she preferred to not draw unnecessary attention. Far from giving up, she had simply invited us to a similar reconnection workshop being held for another unit the following week, which we attended. Meanwhile, introductory notes to Howard went unanswered. As with our revoked invitations of two years earlier, senior spouses exercised with impunity their prerogatives to engage or ignore communication with "public" outsiders.

The subsequent session we attended brought together, somewhat discordantly, intensive sessions on behavioral health challenges, violence prevention, and community service referrals on the one hand with sections dedicated to positive thinking, and models from marriage counseling including love languages and rekindling romance on the other. The organizer opened with some sobering GWOT (Global War on Terror) statistics: as many as 39 percent of postdeployment service members might expect PTSD diagnoses; 66 percent would experience primary relationship difficulties, with 35 percent of marriages ending in divorce; 59 percent experience problems controlling their anger, and 35 percent have thoughts about hurting others; 68 and 38 percent would abuse substances and alcohol, respectively. Most tellingly, postdeployment service members would experience a 400 percent increase in their committing of violent offences. With the formidability of what lay before wives (no male spouses were present) awaiting their husbands' return established, marriage and family therapist Keith Anderson rose to speak about relationships. He invited those present, as "relational creatures," into "community interdependence," "resiliency" (the central mantra in military coping with multiple deployments) and "learned happiness" skills. "Hunting out the good stuff" helps, because "focusing on the negative kills joy," he offered.

Then Keith challenged the wives, first invoking the Journey song "Faithfully," to "faithfully rediscover each other all over again. How many would like to?" A few tentative hands rose. Keith diagrammed the "Form and Flow of Reintegration," from a 60- to 90-day honeymoon, to potential struggles in adjustment, to a "new normal." Postdeployment dopamine deficits in the brain could be reinvigorated through "20-second kisses, twice a day . . . Make a time when it's not about the kids, or about the army," he encouraged. The collision of intimate and institutional substantiated Laney Howard's original sense: this was highly personal territory for an official public meeting.

In their disagreement about the openness of the meeting, both Laney Howard and Chelsea Neel had to go through the rear detachment commander to make their respective cases. That officer, meanwhile, was on an out-of-state, several-week training exercise and "wanted no part in this; he could not care less," Chelsea reported. We never asserted that fieldworkers had any right to carry out participant observation in such a setting when it felt invasive, but we were pleased to attend subsequent affairs, for which we took care to secure permission from public presenters we had known for years. The disagreement around this event, we submit, reveals how much the appropriation of spousal volunteer work as official, public, and command-controlled remains relative, contested, and highly ambiguous. Laney's desire to protect her "ladies" from public observation reflected how much of their now nominally public work involved concerns and relationships that remain markedly private, potentially revealing, and personal. Chelsea Brown's contrasting strategy illustrated a desire to actively characterize army spouses: She had become invested in opportunities for wives to represent themselves and to tell their own stories, and she saw fieldwork like ours as one way to do this. She asserted her own authority as a former-enlisted-wife (her husband had recently converted to officer rank), and as an FRG leader at the company level who was "more in touch with real families," of the rank and file. As such, she was quite comfortable taking a work-around, nonconfrontational approach to seeing her own agenda realized. The fact that she had to work through the chain of command both reflected her subordination in that chain, and enabled her to exercise a kind of authority that "skipped rank" between spouses.

In her study of FRGs, Jaime Gassmann argues that the loss of control of work that before was relatively private has high costs for many wives. While the institutionalization of FRGs "seeks to promote family members' integration into and acceptance of the ways of military life," it also allows "the Army [to] craft the mission and purview of FRGs (as opposed to [giving] unofficial support, over which it had less control)" (Gassmann 2010:24). When family well-being becomes conflated with soldier readiness and retention, this creates two dangers: first, wives' service as force multipliers can easily supersede actual self- and family caretaking, becoming the primary work of social repro-duction. Second, as Gassmann puts it, the army's taking control of FRGs "produced an arena in which it can control the public expression of private feelings" (Gassmann 2010:24). Borrowing from Hochschild (1979, 2003), Gassmann views this as a shift from private, emotional work to public, emotional *labor,* assigned exchange value that is actually measured in army accounting, though it remains unremunerated (Gassmann 2010:12).

## "I Don't Play FRG Anymore"

From numerous directions we heard folks bemoaning the low participation rates of spouses and other family or supporters in the FRGs. Many we spoke with had been highly involved in first, or earlier, deployments, but felt they knew how to stay informed on their own in subsequent deployments. Beyond that, as army spouse JJ Thomas put it, "I just don't really see the point. They raise money for very bizarre things that I don't understand like yearbooks and blankets and stuff like that." The intent is to be supportive, but "my husband told me that the guys out there don't care if you're sending everybody a lighted Christmas tree, they don't care about that, honestly. So why waste the time? 'Cause all they want the FRG to do, if it's run right, is to help their spouses at home." Some decline FRG involvement, rear detachment officer Cliff Hannigan speculated, because they are "off doing other things" such as paid work, "but most of them just don't care, or they don't want to be bothered, or they have some sort of negative perception that we want to be in their business. And, that I'm going to track them and their new boyfriend down during the deployment and take their money away and do something ridiculous. Right?" Then he recalled, "I did that a few times, actually: not on purpose, I just figured it out."

As this comment suggests, it is difficult to separate thinking about army wives' FRG involvement from the stories and stereotypes that surround them (Figures 5 and 6). We were told numerous accounts of young women

**FIGURE 5.** Terminal Lance #159 (copyright Maximillian Uriarte 2010–2013).

who had married opportunistically but quickly tired of their husbands' absence and transgressed in various ways. A cabbie told us of taking a soldier home "early," only to find his wife and boyfriend holding a garage sale of his stuff before intending to disappear together. Theresa Thayer, the formerly active-duty, now-reservist army wife, was scandalized when she heard a wife "who said, 'I'm only single for another week, my husband's getting home.' They wanted this soldier in uniform," said the driver of the bus provided from downtown nightclubs back to post, "to take them and their boyfriends back to their houses on post. How is that not wrong on so many levels in your head?" Theresa keeps her distance from most of her army-wife neighbors because she tries "to avoid the drama of them not being able to cope. We had one, her husband came home last week, and the week before that, she was out in the front yard in her booty shorts and bikini top trying to hit on her next-door neighbor's husband . . . . They're stereotypes for a reason; these things happen!"

Theresa remembers an FRG-produced formal ball for the unit where she was "outnumbered by strippers three to one at my table!" The guys in her husband's special forces unit have "either been married and their wives haven't been able to put up with it so they're not going to get married again: there's no point, they're never around." So when a ball comes around that they're required to go to, they ask "'Let's see who I can take?' The guy sitting next to me had flown his stripper from Wisconsin." Theresa's sister Wendy, who was engaged to a soldier, chimed in. "I've gotten calls from friends where their buddy just found their wife cheating and they're kicking her out: and she was a stripper! I'm like really, why are you marrying strippers?" But Theresa explains:

> I understand because I've talked to the guys and they're like, "She was eager to be in a relationship with me, she was more than willing. I was looking for that before I deployed." They get desperate. Those women are like, "Oh, free health care, a paycheck every month and I can just sit at home." It's not just a life where you are sitting at home; you're sitting at home alone.

Such depictions relate to why many, more senior spouses wearied of the expectations and demands of more junior wives. Harrell's pre-9/11 study contextualizes junior enlisted wives more sympathetically, and explores the degree to which junior enlisted wives conform to negative stereotypes as "young, immature, lower-class spouses . . . [or] 'big-haired, trailer park babes with too many children' who do not know how to manage their money" (Harrell 2000:11–12). While her profiles of actual wives vary considerably, Harrell stresses how these stereotypes are compounded by isolation, class barriers with officer spouses, and the "separation between the wife's private life and her husband's professional life" (Harrell 2000:107). The nature of soldiers' work makes it hard for wives to contribute to household income, or depend on soldiers to watch children, share family vehicles, and so on; Harrell recommends stabilizing the payment structure so household income does not dip during deployments or training (separate rations and allotment payment agreements are deducted) (Harrell 2000:108).

Chelsea Neel remembers that when she went to her first FRG meeting in the mid-1990s, "The company commander's wife—I remember she and her kids wore jeans overalls, which were in fashion then, but expensive—she didn't even look at me. I was nothing. I remember thinking, 'You don't know who I am. You think I am a 21 year-old, poor, ignorant person, but I'm not. I'm from a good family, and educated.'"

Eighteen years later, Chelsea strove to provide a very different welcome for Jeannette, a young wife her husband asked her to call on because she had just had a baby. The family was from Tennessee, Chelsea told us, and though

> *I'm not trying to be stereotypical here, but she has, well, her teeth are just rotted in the front. Probably not the best upbringing in the world, her and her husband. Very young when they joined the army, when he joined the army. You know, the smokers, the drinkers, I don't know what. But, she does everything. I mean she's a fabulous person! The first one I call.*

Jeannette's friends, she told Chelsea, asked her, "'I don't know why you go to the FRG. It's not going to do anything for your husband!' And she says, 'Well, I don't care.'" The friends say, "'Well, all the FRGs are, are a bunch of snotty women.' But she's like, 'No, not at all.'" Chelsea reflects on the FRG's value for someone like Jeannette:

> *Now she feels like she's something. She could go home and be nobody, but in the army she can be something, contributing, because she is a volunteer in the FRG. People know who she is, and she's appreciated . . . . Like, one time she got brigade volunteer of the quarter. And she was so excited. I mean, I think a lot of these women come from nothing, but they can be something. Not so much for their husbands, more for themselves.*

Still, Chelsea can also share disillusion about relations in the FRGs. "A lot has changed, and a lot of women feel entitled; there's less respect in the way women treat other wives," she said. "I've had calls [from wives]: 'Who's gonna take me to the commissary?' 'Who's gonna watch my kids?' It's like, 'The army took my husband away, now who's gonna do for me? What can the FRG do for me?'" She thought the very services provided to military families—"the best health care; the best dental plan; the best everything because their husbands are going to war"—promoted entitlement, and that most spouses didn't think about this comparatively. "I mean, my father-in-law was a steel worker for 30 years, and I guarantee my mother-in-law never called anybody and said, 'Ok, I see there's a meeting. Is there going to be childcare?'" For proudly independent military spouses and service members alike, such dependency triggers shared disdain. Remembering one woman who had left her soldier husband and kept calling the unit to see when childcare payments would arrive, Chelsea commented, "I don't think Walmart's going to make somebody that is separated from his wife pay her $800 a month for childcare. I mean, the army does these things." On a similar note, a sergeant working with us recalled that every time he pointed out to junior soldiers that the level of services they received was akin to a socialist utopia in miniature, they were invariably shocked; they had never thought about it in this manner (Bayendor, personal communication, March 2010; see also Kristoff 2011).

Demands and feelings of entitlement were only part, however, of why Thayer told us, "I don't play FRG anymore." At her previous post, she got into an argument with her FRG leader, who called Child Protective Services and tried to get them to take her kids away, "all because she didn't like me." Her experience reflects how the FRGs' ambiguous, yet de facto extensions of the chain of command insert divisions of rank, and conflict, into spouses' lives.

More recent versions of the "Ladies, please seat yourselves according to rank" depiction of the wives' clubs, coffees, and teas of yesteryear often revolve around the soldier's wife who wants to "wear his rank." A YouTube clip by "Dash" and her service-member husband offers a particularly acid take dedicated to the topic of this oft-reviled interloper (ironically titled, after the bumper sticker, "Don't Confuse Your Rank W/My AUTHORITY!"). They offer a revealing rant about women who "didn't do anything, just chased him down, married him, popped out some babies, and claims his accomplishments."

Every post has stories of "chasers" or military gold-diggers: compared with civilian life it's "times-50 in the military world," Dash opines. One who marries into rank and expects "the carpet rolled out for her," should "get the hatchet." Dash allows that if she is a higher-ranked (captain, major) officer's wife or a commanding NCO, she might have more genuine duties, but her husband chimes in that even for such a woman,

It's pretty much: drag her ass down to earth . . . . I don't care [if] "I'm a general's wife!" No, you're a spouse, you don't have rank. You didn't sign a contract, you don't deploy. You didn't go through basic. You don't work

**FIGURE 6.** Terminal Lance #183 (copyright Maximillian Uriarte 2010–2013).

*odd hours. Get down to earth. Woman, get a job! She needs to earn some-*
*thing . . . . That's one thing I hate about everybody that's been given stuff,*
*who don't work for a thing.*

"That's what I say," Dash concludes. "Get the hatchet."[5]

As many of our earlier examples show, there can be a degree of derision that attaches to stereotypes about military wives; here we see how even the general's wife shouldering formidable FRG activities may still be viewed as "jobless," as having achieved nothing on her own. Once again, cartoonist Uriarte captures the service member's contempt for any comparison of warrior work versus staying home, of wearing "boots" versus "flip-flops": Somewhere between Chelsea's conviction that FRGs are places that nobodies become somebodies and these dismissive and demeaning stereotypes, army wives negotiate their identities, roles, and power, however constrained by the gendering of volunteerism and work that power may be. Far too diverse to be reduced to "good wife" or "bad wife" stereotypes, the recirculation of these images play critical roles in boundary maintenance, gatekeeping, and forcing conformity to ideologies that keep soldiers and combat readiness at the center.

## One Wife's Lament

Of course, the relatively visible and public volunteer work performed through FRGs is far from the bulk of unpaid work undertaken by military spouses. Others have chronicled at length the "offloading" of the "burden of care" for multiple deployments and combat-based trauma on to service members themselves, their families, and their communities, including health care systems and schools. Less visible forms of this work include extensive "home nursing" of all manner of injuries, as well as managing increasing tendencies to violence, depression, suicidality, and substance abuse (Enloe 2010; Howell and Wool 2011).

In the previous chapter, we argued that multiple deployments challenge the limits of human flexibility in adapting to radically different codes of behavior. Spouses and children are increasingly enlisted to serve as Ariadnes to guide their soldiers home to some semblance of normal life in the civilian world at the same time that they, too, are caught in the labyrinth of war and its aftermath. Many devote years to this task, giving up jobs and dreams of their own to care for their wounded spouses.

At a recent panel discussion convened in Colorado Springs by Citizen Soldier,[6] Dolores Vargas, a young wife of an infantry sergeant, spoke to a room of veterans, family members, service providers, and activists. Dolores began her talk in a quiet, calm voice, thanking everyone for showing their support and giving her the opportunity to "bring up awareness of our real lives, behind closed doors." She paused, collecting herself. "Sorry, I'm trying not to get emotional." Her husband joined the army to fulfill his dream of becoming a command sergeant major. His first deployment was to Iraq, with a unit that, like the 2–12th Battalion, would stand out for postdeployment troubles. "You know, a lot of my husband's soldiers are in jail. . . . There's a lot of murders, a lot of domestic violence. A lot of them are part of his unit." After that first deployment he self-medicated with alcohol. During his second tour to Iraq in 2006 he suffered a TBI following an IED explosion. It was following this deployment that Dolores noticed significant changes in his behavior. She urged him to seek help at Fort Carson, only to be turned away by an army doctor who said, "'There's nothing wrong with you. You're faking it.' They said, 'You being the rank that you are, I have like two hours blacked out to see all these other low-ranking soldiers. And you're wasting my time.'" Dolores went to see the physician who agreed to diagnose her husband with PTSD and put through papers for a medical discharge. "How am I supposed to help him get to where he was before without any help, without any knowledge? You know the military didn't tell us about PTSD. They didn't tell us about traumatic brain injury. They didn't tell us that they were going to come back different." Dolores begins to cry. She says she doesn't know how to answer her children when they say "I want my old daddy back."

In the six years since her husband's return she has quit her job to provide and advocate for his care. Dolores' husband still feels responsible for helping out soldiers from his unit who are suffering from PTSD and other effects of the war. But Dolores is clear whose responsibility this is. As we leave the auditorium, Dolores' refrain, "It's not ok" echoes in the room.

## Both Secondary and Central

Military spouses are awkwardly positioned; they are at once explicitly secondary, but also often find themselves, like Dolores here, shouldered with leading their families and navigating bureaucratic mazes when injured spouses can no longer function. Mission first, plain and simple, puts everything—and everyone—else second, especially during wartime. For spouses, mission first becomes as nonnegotiable as it does for the soldiers themselves; their supportive roles, while ancillary, have become increasingly imperative.

"From the beginning," Kathleen Dougherty says of her life as a military wife, "they made it very, *very* clear: this is not about you. You are not the star of the show." Her second marriage, to a special forces operator, came well into motherhood, and also after earning an advanced degree; being a second-fiddle sidekick was new to her.

How was it made clear? When invited to promotion ceremonies and other rituals, she remembered:

> There's definitely a sense that the women and children are "allowed to come watch sometimes." Even at the beginning, when you have to get signed in and you're vouched for by your man such that you're granted access into this physical space, even starting there, you wear a tag that identifies you as attached to him. And, there are times when you're ushered out and it's just man-time. And again, it's an all male unit. There are no women in his career field so it's especially that way.

She found "the tone of emails and letters during deployment from higher command seeming to suggest that first and foremost we're wives, we're support, or we're families, but not really alluding to the fact that some of us may have other careers." Too, the whole family could be easily summoned for important memorials and reunions, "to pull the kids out of school, fly the kids across the country in the middle of the week because the guys want to have a family thing" even when the soldier himself was rarely summonable.

Doreen Brennan, who married a soldier just before intending to start college, spoke of giving away her coffee shop shifts and not filling out financial aid forms for school, "because I wanted to spend time with him before he was leaving." She

> . . . wouldn't go to orientations or I would push semesters off because in my head I was like, "It's okay, he's leaving in a month. I can spend this last

*month with him and if I was in school right now I wouldn't do good on my studies anyway . . . ." So I was just kind of making excuses and you really have to be careful not lose yourself.*

But lose herself she did.

*It's almost impossible when everything is about them: where you live, what phone number you have, what kind of house you can live in because they pay for it, what friends you can have, everything: their school, their money, when they go out to the field, when they come home. You are really like their personal assistant because you have to take care of everything when they are gone. It's very strange. It's weird cause I really did lose myself.*

This made it harder still when he got back from deployment early and was diagnosed with "personality disorder, severe anxiety, alcoholism, and they were going to run tests on bipolar disorder"; they divorced shortly thereafter, amid restraining orders and Doreen fearing for her safety.

Marianne Brighton, whose husband was completing 20 years and would retire as a top NCO, embraced an altogether different approach. "At the very beginning of this, we decided that this was going to be a 'we' thing, and that if he was going off to do all these strange and wonderful things for this country then I was going to know what he would be doing." She immersed and educated herself to "know the language," and "immediately jumped in and did the company newsletter," through what was then the FSG for her unit; 20 years later, she has led numerous FRGs. "I joke that it's OCD and controlling, but it may have actually started like that." In short, there was no passivity or reluctance in Marianne's own "enlistment"; she never resisted an amalgamated, "we" identity, and this laid the basis for her distinction as committed army spouse.

By the time her husband was retiring, after an early Gulf War tour and two in OIF/OEF, Marianne was launching her own professional career. She had brokered her extensive insider army knowledge, together with completing a self-paced master's degree in social work. But, she absolutely *hated* that he was retiring, explaining

*We got in this as an E-nothing, to be an E-9? If his last deployment was not so horrible, I would still be fighting him. But he's got a mild TBI, he's got PTSD he refused to deal with, and he's had soldiers die in his arms. Two of his drivers were blown up when he was in the Humvee. So what do you do with that? I can't say, you have to stay in. He's hit his limit, and I have to respect that. And I still get to work with soldiers at Fort Carson, so my connectivity to my community will still be there.*

She worried about what he would do, and described doing paid work as a social worker as a near demotion from doing work where she'd found her calling:

*Because I—we—have really enjoyed being in the army. I have loved being an army wife. I've loved taking care of soldiers, and you can't take care of soldiers and families like you can as First Sergeant's wife. That is a special privilege, honor. There are some bad things about it [laughs], but it's a job that cannot be replicated anywhere else in the civilian community. When you are First Sergeant you are the father, the counselor, you are the judge, the jury . . . .*

Soon, when seeing soldiers as clients, she imagined she would "have to find a different credibility with these guys." Nonetheless, Marianne was just one of numerous typically more senior spouses who established careers in paid work highly dependent upon knowledge gained during their unpaid careers as military spouses. Today many can be found working as advocates, provider educators, and service providers, often specifically connected to behavioral health issues, working on- and off-post.

Beryl Makris, whom we met in chapter 4, chafed at officer wives treating her as inferior, when she held a degree in neuropsychology and was more highly educated than many of them. She runs a family advocacy nonprofit for military families coping with brain injuries. She had divorced her former-NCO husband who was dying from multiple TBIs, whom she still loved but knew was unsafe to have around their daughter. In discussing what she faced in caring for her husband, she bemoaned that

*Most spouses don't even know where to start. They don't know what it is they're dealing with. When we tell them they're TBI or PTSD they say, "Okay, now what?" They still don't know. You have to kind of lead them to programs, to information, to going to the doctors' appointments, because a lot of information—because of memory impairment—does not make it home. So we strongly encourage the spouses to become personal advocates, or parents to become personal advocates of their injured service member so they can get a better picture and be educated along the way. The more education that they attain, the better the chance that they'll have a better direction to look for resources. It's kind of like getting an education!*

Like Marianne and numerous others, Beryl's practical and formal knowledge translated into a career niche, though she struggled with having the time and funding for her nonprofit organization.

Nora Jane Curtis moved in the other direction, from that of a paid soldier in an AVF to unpaid work as the unit's FRG leader. She left active duty as a captain, after eight years in, to raise their three girls while her husband continued deploying. One of several women in formerly dual-military marriages we spoke with,[7] Nora Jane's experience sheds light on wifely volunteer work. She told us of a 2–12 officer who never went out on patrol and later committed what she viewed as guilt-driven suicide because he "couldn't fight and defend his brothers, couldn't pick up a gun and help them out." Then, she likened his guilt to her own; because she "sat behind a desk" when she was on active duty and never deployed, "I have that guilt he had . . . . It's probably why I compensate and do all the stuff I do back here, and volunteer as much as I do."

Jacey Eckhart, in *The Homefront Club: The Hardheaded Woman's Guide to Raising a Military Family*, elaborates that the accepted style of coping in military communities includes such features as: you can complain if you end up with a plan of individual action to resolve your complaints; you don't question the ultimate value of what the military is doing as long as you or your family member is in active service; and you accept strong gender roles especially within marriage, despite changes with more women serving, privatization, and so on (Eckhart 2005). She also notes the relative importance, for military families, of social institutions in general: religious organizations, family, "what the soldiers are fighting to protect," and the customary weighing of personal sacrifice alongside collective benefit and duty.

These examples show varied responses to the many pressures for military wives' priorities to revolve, to greater or lesser extents, around their husbands' soldiering. Despite the drastic differences between paid "volunteering" for service members and unpaid, homefront "volunteering" for wives, they have more in common than the shared term. The ways female spouses talk about their lives with the army underline continuities between the spheres as well. Many military wives we met positively valued their selfless relationships to soldiers and the wider army community, and their sense that they could count on others and be counted upon. They took pride in their independence and competence, which was required to hold down their ends of the mission, in a mission-first, deployment-readiness driven world. Others, like the family therapist whose husband was also a therapist until he joined the army during a midlife crisis, deplored the Iraq war in particular and chafed at all that deployments meant for her and their four children. For the women on the inside of these experiences, critical cleavages between wives differently positioned, largely by their husband's rank and specialty, shape their experiences: officer versus NCO versus junior enlisted, lifers versus short-termers, those who live and/or work on post versus those who do not, and so on.

Given all the different ranks and roles that transmute from service member to families (for example, school districts on post in effect organized by rank),[8] the most adaptive and positively reinforced strategy for "successful" army wives often means embracing a fused identity, a "we," as central, even as their day-to-day lives so often do not include the soldier. This is on a par with the commitment soldiers make to one another, to battle buddy esprit de corps, but soldier-husbands do not make a similar commitment to their wives, and are not asked to, in the same way wives are asked to, and do, to them. For soldiers, the soldier-soldier bonds that comprise their commitment to the military often trump the soldier-family bonds, whereas for wives the latter are primary and central. Across all ranks, those most actively embracing a collectivized, de-individualized identity with their spouse are also among the most difficult to simply describe as subordinated; their agency, pride, and even territoriality around their "turf" are unmistakable.

### "Not Your Playground" versus Re-gendering FRGs

Spouses can be hailed, and found hailing themselves, as "the true heroes" of weathering multiple deployments;[9] self-assertions about their importance are not hard to find. Most living in American military towns during the post-9/11 wars will have seen bumper stickers reading, "Don't Confuse Your Rank with My Authority" (a motif also available in t-shirts, iPod covers, and even business cards, all with versions also for military moms and girlfriends, and tailored to individual services). Having kept the hearth over so many deployments, wives make explicit claims about themselves as a defined interest group.

The most recent print edition of *The Army Wife Handbook*, still actively circulated among officer and NCO wives, has a short section on military husbands stating that "husbands who have the time and interest to join wives' clubs are always real assets. They bring a fresh perspective to projects and activities, as well as strong arms and backs where they're needed." Reaching out to male spouses may mean changes in constitutions, but "it isn't even necessary to change the club's name from wives' club to spouses' club, though some clubs have done so and it does send the right message—that all Army spouses are welcome, regardless of gender" (Crossley and Keller 1993:202). Such a statement begs the question of why the authors elected to retain "Army Wives" in the name of the handbook itself, and why, 20 years later, "wives" persists as a much-used, gender-specific organizational category in army circles and in many FRGs.

Tracey Harris, an officer's wife, offers an answer as to why army wives might resist making all references to FRG work gender neutral. She spoke of her husband's pride at her volunteer work for the unit, as in planning a post-deployment, formal cocktail party when he was still in Afghanistan. "He felt pride from that, where I feel pride when I hear that he has done something great in the field. So we do hold very specific gender stereotypes still to this day. And it seems slightly archaic . . . but it's just kind of the way that it works best, honestly."

We recalled how the same cocktail party was referred to dismissively by an officer in the brigade; still weary and fresh off the plane from their deployment in Afghanistan, he thought most soldiers saw it as a burden, "just a chance for the wives to wear fancy dresses."

Like the veteran who told us that to "take a civilian and make him into a combat soldier, you have to train them hard, ride them like dogs—brutalize them," and that female soldiers undercut the army's ability to do this, Tracey supported her husband's view that women in combat would make him "certainly feel a little more protective of her than a man," and so felt that gendered separation of combat work to be important. "So I think it also expands into the spouses' world. To take somebody else who is completely different in many ways from us, and their needs into consideration, would be encroaching on our thing."

When asked if *The Army Wife Handbook* should be retitled for army spouses, Tracey reflects:

*Honestly, being very frank about it, again I'd feel like they were encroaching on our thing: this is our thing. But I know when I think about it that it's their [male spouses'] thing too. They're an army spouse; they're going through the same thing. However, I certainly would have that guttural instinct of: no, this isn't your playground. Go play somewhere else. Socially, that's unacceptable, I know . . . .*

Not wanting to share the homefront FRG "playground" here means several things: enjoyment of the ways in which the volunteer work is gendered feminine, and how it converges with feminized social networks. It also may indicate distinct possessiveness about the territory of social reproduction itself: claiming that part of the mission one's group may excel at, and then wanting credit for the work done and acknowledgment that they do it better than their husbands could. Nora Jane put it judiciously: "I know Chuck could do it. He could do it, he loves his kids," two of whom were playing around us as we talked. "He'd figure it out. But they probably wouldn't be in karate, soccer, making holidays special, so many things . . . . Yes, they all would have been fed, they all would have been dressed, they all would have made it to school. But, it probably would have stopped at about that."

Chelsea Neel, the FRG leader and captain's wife, had a very different reaction. She felt "a little bit offended" at the notion of books like *The Army Wife Handbook* retaining gender-specific titles, asking why a male spouse should have to be emasculated just to be informed. She remembered that, during the previous deployment, at brigade-wide reintegration seminars, "There was always one guy: the same one, at the time. And I just thought, 'Good for you!' Of course there were the other ladies that were like, 'What's he doing here?' What do you mean, what's he doing here? He has a wife. Who's deployed. He's home. He can come."

But Chelsea also revealed how she herself perceived the position of "waiting spouse" to be feminizing. She remembered one husband of a deployed soldier-wife, who was formerly active-duty himself, wondering if "there was anything going on over there?" after days of no communication from his wife. He wanted to call someone in the rear detachment or FRG to ask, but did not, perhaps worried that "maybe they'll tease him . . . 'What are you worried about? Just go home with your baby . . . . Don't worry. Your wife's in Afghanistan. She's working.'" Chelsea was impressed how even this former soldier was positioned, "[j]ust like a woman! Waiting in the dark, wondering . . . ."

Because the company whose FRG Chelsea now led was not active combat, but instead a support unit, they had more male spouses than other companies. So Chelsea amended emails, referring to "our spouses" rather than "our husbands," for inclusivity's sake. They made company t-shirts that on the reverse read, "'My soldier's got your back,' not 'My husband's got your back,'" and avoided highly feminine, "Let's all get mani-pedis!" (manicure-pedicure) FRG activities. Still, male spouses never came to educational or fundraising sessions, though they did appear at big events, like a winter cocktail party.

While the army can no longer officially mandate volunteer work or treat its absence as a career impediment to the soldier-spouse, the prevalence of humorous expressions like being "volunTOLD" to do something and "mandatory fun" give a sense of how for many wives, it can still feel de facto obligatory. Sociologist Margaret Harrell observes of military wives' volunteer work that "[f]irst male spouses are not expected to perform these roles (thus they are gendered), and second, there is no biological reason why men cannot perform these roles (and thus, they are culturally gendered)" (Harrell 2003:69–70). Fellow sociologist Jaime Gassmann plainly states, "[e]xpectations for Army husbands differ from those for their female counterparts in that there are simply no expectations of the male spouses" (Gassmann 2010:87).

Reasons for male spouses' reluctance for participating in FRG activities are complex. Christopher, a soldier who is gay, remembers attending a single FRG meeting when his partner deployed, before he joined the army himself. His partner put him on the family roster, passing him off as a roommate who "just wanted to know information about when he was coming home or whatever." When he attended, he "was the only male there and they were looking at me like, 'What the hell?' They were like, 'Are you married to one of the female soldiers?'" He explained he was a roommate, but "after that they just turned their backs on me and shunned me out of the little female group that they were in. I couldn't imagine being a male spouse in such a female-dominated support group." He never went again.

The blogger MANspouse offered a suggestion about how to get male spouses involved: creating some guy-guy affiliation that would cut through the feminized ether in FRG rooms. "Imagine," he writes, inviting us to picture an intimidated MANspouse at his first FRG activity,

> *if one of the guys in uniform, a rear detachment captain or first sergeant, came up to him and took him away from the conversations that were about spa trips, girls night out, menstrual cycles, lactating breasts, fashion styles, bikini waxes, and of course how* "Sally thinks Brenda is wrong for thinking that Judy shouldn't be angry at Melissa for unfriending Melanie because of what Veronica said about her" [italics in original]. *Now I know and most of you know that those things I just mentioned aren't really what happens, but hey . . . clue phone . . . it's for you; a lot of guys think that's all women talk about. So guys have this mental block that gives them the heevie jeevies about getting involved in these ever important information briefs. And I will say it, my wife is right,* "Boys are stupid."

Even as he confesses himself susceptible to these stereotypes, however "stupid," his urgency to gain access to this world in a way he feels comfortable with is genuine. He wants information, of various types:

> *As a man, we want to know who the guy she talks about ALL THE FREAKIN TIME is. We want to know who that fantastic leader that she admires is. We want to know who has our wife's back. We want to know that we can trust our wife with the people she is literally going to war with.*

But negotiating this position as a man was difficult.

Recognizing men *as* men, he argues, would facilitate including men in homefront, FRG work. Being approached by rear-detachment soldiers "talking to us about cars, sports, video games, hunting/fishing, beer and meat;

prior to and after the meeting" would "ease the tension that is there for us." But soldiers doing outreach to male spouses are warned to be prepared "for some of us to get overly excited like a puppy dog seeing his owner for the first time all day. Cuz some of us men have little to no interaction with other men." In his view, it is not merely company they crave, but same-sex camaraderie that female spouses cannot provide, or only provide at a cost of MANspouses feeling emasculated. "[W]e want to be the hero in the story instead of the damsel in distress . . . . We want action and adventure. We want to hunt, kill and eat something. We want to be giant boys."

MANspouse also conveys a vision of how male spouses, once invited as men, by men, into the club, might affect the broader climate. To get wives on board with his include-male-spouses-in-FRGs project, he writes,

> *Imagine what would happen if your husband befriends a MANspouse. Maybe some of our diaper changing, clothes washing, dinner making, house-cleaning way of life will rub off on him. Maybe we as MANspouses will give him a bit of insight into what your day looks like as we shoot the breeze. When he calls us up to ask us to go to the bar or out fishing and we say* "no . . . . I have 3 loads of laundry to do, a roast in the oven and a teething infant that is going to get up at 11pm, 2am, and then at 4am, for good" . . . *maybe your husband will stop and think about that for a second.*[10]

His vision, in other words, essentializes man-man affinity, while also underlining the need for the kind of information and support provided through FRGs, and the importance and challenge of what nondeploying spouses do as work, as social reproduction necessary for the family's continuation.

### Gendered Power, Separate Spheres, and FRG Work

Given the two senses of "volunteerism" in army communities—paid soldiers, mostly men; unpaid volunteers, mostly women—it is difficult to refute the argument that FRG work is critical, and now officially required, work offloaded onto wives and others. The weight grows especially acute amidst the shortfall of services created by 12 years of war. Work both private and public is shifted onto the backs of spouses and other family and community members, taking forms that include emotional, technical, administrative, and plain heavy lifting. The rising demand for readiness services are met by enlisted families, who contribute their lives as "labor" for a warring nation with multiplying burdens and costs for families. If soldiers' codeswitching fails to toggle with infinite flexibility between theater and home, spouses' bimodality comes delivered from afar and means shouldering total responsibility alternating with relinquishing ground to the all-central soldier. In the

margins and peripheries of the labyrinth the gatekeeping, boundary maintenance, and hierarchizing may be paradoxically intense. As three wives once
joked, where the stakes were lowest the "politics" could be the "meanest."[11]

Thirty years ago, feminist anthropologist Michelle Rosaldo worried that
separate, gendered spheres of social organization underpinned the most persistent forms of gendered inequality (Rosaldo 1980; Rosaldo and Lamphere
1974). She stressed that we should understand the divide between domestic, often-unpaid, private work (largely) by women and nondomestic, highly
rewarded work (largely) by men as an ideological rather than an objective
and necessary set of terms.[12] Considering together processes of domination
and resistance, of subordination and agency is how we "begin to explore the
differences in formulations which may appear initially to be 'more of the
same'" (Rosaldo 1980:402 n.20; see also Lugo and Maurer 2000:20–1). The
recent repeal of both "Don't Ask Don't Tell" (a policy officializing homophobia in the military) and bars against women in combat roles will continue to
reshape gender difference within the military. However, at the same time,
the impact of the last decade's multiple deployments brings new depths to
the gendering of cleavages between home and work.

First, military culture may select for a pronounced gender division of
labor from the outset. "To the extent that military work roles map closely
onto traditional gender roles," Karney and Crown write, "this suggests that
the military will select for men with highly traditional views of gender roles
and women with highly nontraditional views. These sex-role attitudes have
been directly linked with marital satisfaction" (Karney and Crown 2007:20).
Second, sex-role spillover theory, where "people endow a job with the sex-
role expectations of the numerically dominant sex" (Herbert 2000:28), combines powerfully with the masculinization of soldiering and the feminization
of homefront work; actors may become conditioned, and then actively subscribe to, divergent gendered spheres. Like no other work culture, in the military "we may expect the expression, 'men are men and women are women'
to be taken seriously" (Herbert 2000:10).

At the same time, a simple domination-based analysis does not suffice to
capture much of what this process means, or how it is experienced, by army
wives. For those "all-in" army wives best adapted to a fused soldier-wife
identification, the officialization of wifely volunteer work under the chain of
command provides wives with "a public arena in which to perform that support and be acknowledged for it," as Gassmann puts it (2010:27,81). As the
major's wife Tracey told us earlier, though the gender-stereotyped organization of this work may be "slightly archaic," it nonetheless "works best" and is
no one's "playground" but their own, even with respect to her feelings
toward her few male-spouse counterparts. She speaks for numerous women

who would resist complete degendering of FRG wife-work into spouse-work because for them, the turf represents hard-won accomplishments. Social reproduction on the homefront is work for which wives want credit and some portion of control. And to the degree that their experiences are grounded in a historical, persistent set of traditions and practices that are inextricable from their roles as wives, mothers (sisters, and so on) of service-men, many want *gendered* credit, as *women* shouldering the formidable labor remaking their domestic social worlds and, relatedly, to reproducing the US military itself. They claim that they do this work better than their husbands could, and want this to be part of the record.

Domination-based arguments tend to underline the ways in which women are hegemonized through such processes and structures. Agency-based arguments complicate the picture, including depictions of army wives resistant to the secondary cast-member role as well as of women who strongly identify with, and feel empowered by, their roles, and of course, all manner of intermediary positions across a spectrum. For many of the women in this chapter, it is clear they value and prioritize this work, and to varying extents chose it, regardless of whether it is recognized or remunerated. As unpaid support work becomes increasingly official and public, and with the attempted degendering of army wives' historical roles now officially falling to a supposedly neuter army spouse, the persistence of gendered markers is remarkable, even as it is shaped by new tensions and ambiguities. In communities surrounding Fort Carson, we find domestic, largely women's private, familial, and social work increasingly of a piece with the public, homefront labor required for deployment readiness.

## Chapter Seven

# Waiting to Serve

*They also serve who only stand and wait.*
—John Milton, "On His Blindness"

"The question we keep coming back to is, at what point does it stop being about PTSD—or depression or addiction or suicidality or whatever—and become about *war?* War itself?" The professor of a psychology of war class posed the question in response to our short presentation, in which we argued for going beyond PTSD in assessing reintegration challenges. This is a central question in meeting the rising tide of need of soldiers returning to home communities, needs that will not soon abate even as the wars wind down. How well are these needs being met by local resources, both on-post and off, in the wider community? And to what extent are the ways that these issues are framed and discussed in the media and public conversations help or hinder efforts to meet those needs?

This chapter appraises the local landscape for treatment and other kinds of programs that aid recovery and reintegration, beginning on-post at Fort Carson, and then travelling into the adjacent city and beyond. We argue that the conflation of medical conditions like PTSD with the challenges of reintegration poses dilemmas for military and civilian providers in how they market and fund their programs and services. PTSD has become a primary legitimation for helping soldiers with a host of reintegration issues, a component of veteran identity, and a means for veterans to connect with one another and create community. The public views soldiers and veterans suffering from PTSD as deserving of help in ways that soldiers struggling with financial difficulties or marital problems may not be, so linking services to PTSD may give providers access to funding and resources and aid appeals for donations. All of this inadvertently contributes to bracket creep and a profusion of mental health services that often do not meet the standards of evidence-supported therapies for PTSD.

But PTSD is only one of many issues that soldiers and families face during reintegration, and though this chapter focuses largely on health care services, many contests around legitimacy arise in the gray areas between treatment for conditions versus rebuilding lives and communities more generally. When soldiers are physically disabled they need help adapting their homes; when they have debts or trouble making ends meet on their salaries they need financial counseling and short-term assistance; when families need respite from the stresses of deployment or caring for a disabled soldier, or reconnecting after deployment, they need affordable recreation. With respect to mental health issues, soldiers and veterans may suffer distress from moral and spiritual injuries even in the absence of PTSD. So while it is essential to make standardized, evidence-based treatments for PTSD widely available to everyone, to assist soldiers and families with reintegration we need varied and multiple pathways out of the labyrinth of war. Though at first this project focused on barriers to seeking care within the military, we quickly realized that the military-civilian interface in mental health services was a key to understanding the lasting effects of the post-9/11 wars. So here we start with mental health care providers at Fort Carson, illustrating the tension between their desire to keep mental health services on-post and in-house and the reality that they were caught unprepared to handle the rapid rise in need as the wars continued and accelerated in the mid-2000s. This tension often led to uneasy collaborations between military and civilian providers and fluctuating policies regarding referrals of military personnel to civilian providers in Colorado Springs.

Our treatment here is necessarily selective, omitting much of relevance: providers and caseworkers at the VA or Disabled American Veterans (DAV); soldiers and family members' perspectives on services; and the complex issues surrounding the Warrior Transition Units or Battalions to help wounded soldiers. From the dozens of organizations offering services to soldiers, veterans, and families in the Colorado Springs area, here we highlight programs that complement clinical, evidence-based treatments and more traditional psychotherapy to address some of the many other issues, both practical but also social and spiritual, that veterans and families face during reintegration.

As our research moved out into the community of Colorado Springs we were continuously impressed by the number and range of creative and innovative programs and services directed to soldiers, veterans, and their families. A common refrain from providers is that the contemporary United States lacks rituals to help soldiers process their experiences and find meaningful ways to reconnect with their families and communities when they return from war. But what we found—and celebrate here—is that rituals and other meaning-making, healing practices are alive and vibrant in Colorado Springs. In character with US culture, rituals are often not labeled as such. And they are varied and individualistic, ranging from working with horses or creating giant figures from children's books to hang in the lobby of an elementary school to sitting in a sweat lodge or rafting down the Colorado River.

## The Contradictory Missions of Military Psychiatry

As documentary filmmaker and psychologist Jan Haaken notes, military psychologists and psychiatrists have "two conflicting missions. One is to prevent psychiatric casualties, and the other is to maintain the fighting forces."[1] On a warm, sunny fall afternoon, we sat in a local coffee shop with Colonel Howard West, a psychiatrist leading behavioral health services at Fort Carson. His description illustrates the paradox of being a military psychiatrist. On the one hand, he was concerned with gaining the trust and confidence of the officers who can promote or impede his work to heal soldiers stressed by multiple deployments. To that end, he must be seen as a "force multiplier," someone whose behavioral health teams return soldiers quickly to combat or to their next deployment. "We kept over 95 percent, if not even higher, of people that came to us for care; over 95 percent of our people completed their tour. . . . Once a company commander realizes I help him sustain his soldiers, I'm his best friend."

Part of West's task was getting officers to move beyond a simple assessment of a soldier, based on his or her ability to perform their duties, to recognize that some soldiers may not be performing in the present moment, but with treatment and support, could perform again. "And, when that soldier can't perform anymore, how do I communicate an effective metaphor to that commander? That he's bent, he's broke, or he's bad. . . . And those are three different things. . . . Bent means I can fix him. Broke means you can't use him. You know, he's done. He can't continue to contribute to the team, and we have to take him out." For West, the last category, "bad," would include soldiers like Kenneth Eastridge (discussed in Chapter 3), who had histories of violence or criminal behavior before they enlisted, or who have significant behavioral problems or mental illness and consistently violate military or civilian rules of conduct in combat or at home.

On the other hand, West's psychiatric training taught him to value each individual and what is best for her or him, not necessarily for the organization. West also saw this quality as the hallmark of a good military leader. "And having a deep personal conviction that care saves lives, and you don't just throw people away." It is also part of honoring soldiers and what is asked of them. "But on some level, that mother has to know that her soldier is valued anywhere in the world. That his life is treasured, that it will not be spent unwisely, you know. The goal is to win the war, not lose the sons." Thus West's clinical goal concerned each soldier's ability to function. "On some level I don't care if I send them back or not. If I optimize their functioning—we all win." For West, an important measure of optimal function is the ability to re-engage with one's family, to be vulnerable. Hence, the objective of treatment for traumatized combat soldiers is for them to be able to re-experience vulnerability, to work through the loss of a relationship on the battlefield or back home, or to develop a valued identity outside the military. Trust between therapist and soldier is key to achieving this goal. While he acknowledged that some soldiers may prefer to do this work "in private away from the military," he also said that civilian providers may have difficulty establishing "face validity" and trust with soldiers (though a number of soldiers told us that they would, in fact, prefer civilian therapists precisely because they are not part of the military and its culture). Civilians lack the "tribal identification" and shared experience of military service and combat on which to build a relationship of trust.

West spoke about the challenges he faced in meeting the mental health needs of soldiers at Fort Carson. "Part of what we're trying to do in garrison right now is get behavioral health on board, like that combat stress detachment.[2] Get early case identification; get my doctors referred by the company commander, the brigade commander." He prefers to bring these services more directly under his command, to have "more uniforms" and secure "real estate" on Fort Carson to house individual and group therapy, an outpatient clinic to treat PTSD, alcohol and substance abuse treatment, and family advocacy. To that purpose he will "more than double the size of the behavioral health organizations to accomplish that. I've already increased my staff by 40 percent."

So although many of his new staff members are army, he told us, "the vast majority of my workforce is civilian." Given the army's lack of anticipation of and preparation for the high rate of mental health casualties in Iraq and Afghanistan, it has scrambled to recruit and retain mental health providers. In 2009, 15 percent of the army's psychiatric positions were unfilled and 35 percent of Fort Carson's positions for psychiatrists, psychologists, and social workers were unfilled (US Army 2009). Heavy caseloads and insufficient staffing were cited as contributing factors to the army's retaining psychiatrist Major Nidal Hasan, who was accused of killing 13 people at Fort Hood, Texas, that year.[3] When we spoke with Colonel West in 2009, Evans Hospital did not have an inpatient psychiatric facility; all patients that required admission were referred to two local private facilities. But even if the army filled all of the mental health positions allotted to active-duty and reserve personnel, more than half the psychiatric staff (57 percent) would be civilians (Mount 2009).[4] So West will continue to "buy behavioral health" in the private sector as long as necessary to meet soldiers' needs.

## Uneasy Collaborations and the Fickle Spigot

On a cold, bright February day in 2009, we drove to the campus of Pikes Peak Community College, which sits on a hill overlooking Fort Carson, to attend a town hall meeting. In addition to providing updates on proposed expansions at the post and their economic impact on the community, this particular meeting focused on mental health care issues. In a breakout session that afternoon, civilian providers on the panel outlined the need for increased mental health services for active-duty soldiers and their families. Providers spoke of long waiting lists for therapeutic assessment and treatment, and of military families comprising 19 percent of domestic violence cases in civil courts.[5] The medical director of Peak Vista Community Health Centers, which provides primary care services to low-income and underserved populations in the region, stated that not only did the region as a whole suffer from a shortage of psychiatrists, but also of primary care physicians, who are the main providers of medical treatment for depression (mainly by providing medication).[6] During the discussion period, a Head Start teacher reported that they were seeing soldiers' preschool-aged children exhibiting behavioral issues at home and at school with emotional "acting out," violence, and even suicidality.

Several members of the audience identified themselves as child, adult, or family therapists or counselors who were willing and eager to offer their services to military personnel and their families. But they often were not sure whom to approach at Fort Carson, or how. Many were unfamiliar with Tricare (the military's health insurance program), with what services were covered, and how to become a preferred provider. Both the head of Evans Hospital and garrison commander General Graham, who were sitting in the audience, assured them that their offers of service were welcome, and that the army was working to better coordinate care through the newly created Warrior Family Community Partnership.

Four months later, we gathered under a massive white tent on a June morning for the Warrior Care Summit. This time General Graham was on stage, presiding. The summit was his parting contribution before he resigned garrison command of Fort Carson, designed to bring behavioral health care at the post to a whole new level. He showed the latest "Army Strong" video clip. When it ended, and he barked "hooah" (or "HUA," meaning "heard, understood, acknowledged") to the audience, they echoed it back, thunderously.

Unlike the town hall meeting, the summit was clearly sponsored and run by Fort Carson. Like the town hall meeting, it took place in civilian territory, in the Penrose House Pavilion of the El Pomar Foundation, an important philanthropic player in the Pikes Peak region.[7] It was a symbolically important setting for engaging civil society as Fort Carson launched the Warrior Family

Community Partnership Center Initiative, whose goal is to work with local organizations and the VA to extend services and integrate care, a response, in part, to the town hall meeting in February. "The community wants to help; it's very encouraging. This will make it easier to plug in," says General Graham.[8] It was clear that Graham saw the army as maintaining control; he asserts that for the Warrior Family Community Partnership to succeed in better coordinating access to care, provider networks, reintegration programs, and other services, many of them provided by civilians, need "to be brought under the chain of command." From a military standpoint this makes sense: the army is responsible for providing health care to its personnel, and it is responsible for ensuring that the care they receive is safe and effective.

While civilian providers do not have the same obligation to balance soldiers' deployment readiness with wellness, they quickly learn to be sensitive to how these dynamics affect army policy with regard to referrals and mental health practice both at the national level and locally as leaders at Fort Carson balance readiness and wellness with different mixes of military and civilian resources. When leaders move on, referral policies may change, resulting in an inconsistent flow of referrals. Whereas early in the war, civilian providers strained to keep up with the stream of soldiers coming to them for treatment, by the end of 2011, the tap had been all but turned off.

Frequent changes in Evans Hospital's referral policy sent Debra Carrera, a psychiatric nurse practitioner with a private group practice in Colorado Springs, into a tailspin. A petite woman with a radiant smile and soft voice, Carrera's energy is restless, as if sitting still requires effort. Until she retired, she was a military officer who had served as an active-duty psychiatric nurse on an inpatient unit at two military medical hospitals. As a nurse practitioner, Carrera could prescribe psychiatric medications and used a combination of talk therapy, cognitive behavioral therapy, and medications to treat PTSD. In addition to direct referrals from clinicians at Fort Carson, because of her reputation for her skill in working with soldiers, many soldiers and family members referred themselves to her practice.

In 2010, Fort Carson's behavioral health staff brought treatment of active-duty personnel back on post, all but ceasing referrals to nonmilitary providers. Though Carrera didn't challenge the change, its abrupt implementation created problems for her patients and her practice. "It's not a Tricare thing. It's a post issue. It's not just me; it's true of any medication provider. They're not letting anyone who prescribes see active-duty soldiers." She added that "the active-duty can still come in for therapy . . . . I've got providers in my practice who are seeing the soldiers. I can't see them for fear that I would hinder their current prescriptive regimen."

"But, if they're so backed up, why is that rational?" we wondered. "Are there soldiers getting multiple prescriptions from different providers?"

*That's part of it, and I caught them on that. I was more collaborative than they were with me; it was one sided. I was calling out there saying, Do you understand that this soldier is shopping and hopping?" I was alerting them many times for a soldier at risk. . . . I can't tell you how many instances I saw of soldiers being handed 90-pill packs of Percocet, like it was candy for crying out loud. You got a pain, here you go. It's like, "Get a grip, people!"*

More important than the issue of overmedication, what bothered Carrera was the abrupt change in her relationship with her patients. "But it became so abrupt that I wasn't given an opportunity to get closure with any of the individuals that I was working with. So I had heard a lot of horror stories and had developed a phenomenal trust that was transferred to and fro. I was made to say goodbye." All of this came to a crisis point in the summer of 2010, shortly after she retired from the military. "I found *myself* seeking therapy because now *I* was suffering from secondary PTSD for feeling I had abandoned *them*. Not real different than the survivor guilt that many of them expressed to me."

## Contracting Out In-house Mental Health

In 2004, the army's institutional drive to bring mental health services in-house, a response to public criticism and to meet the increased need to support deployed military personal and their families, combined with reliance on private contractors for a multitude of services (Howell and Wool 2011; Lutz 2002), led the Department of Defense (DoD) to pilot the Military Family Life Consultant program, or MFLC (pronounced "Em-flack"). The DoD subsequently expanded the program to serve all military branches in the United States and abroad. MFLC hires counselors—psychologists, social workers, professional counselors, and marriage family therapists—for short-term contracts of two to six months and assigns them to military bases where they deliver short-term counseling on stress, marital and family issues, alcohol and substance use, and financial matters.[9] Although MFLC counselors discuss substance and alcohol use and mental illness, they "do not diagnose or treat mental disorders," but refer any mental illness or addiction to army medical personnel (MHN 2012). While on post at Fort Carson, MFLC counselors wear identifying nametags to facilitate informal encounters with soldiers. Their goal is to increase soldiers' access to care by normalizing their presence on the post and thus reduce the stigma of seeking help.

MFLC counselors do not maintain written records of treatment. The stated purpose of this policy is again, to reduce stigma and soldiers' fears that seeking help may negatively affect their careers.

The MFLC program raises a number of questions about the balance between soldiers' needs and those of the army and private contractors. On the positive side, the program provides mental health services across army installations where local civilian mental health services may vary greatly, augments mental health resources that for much of the post-9/11 wars were stretched very thin, and creates centralized administration through the contracting agency, MHN Government Services. However, because counselors are not from the local community, their referrals are often limited to military programs and services. Given that some soldiers and family members prefer community-based services and that soldiers with severe or chronic mental health conditions are likely to receive medical discharges and may return to civilian life in Colorado Springs, hiring local counselors with knowledge of resources available locally might provide better long-term care and support. In addition, the program, like many contracted military services, is costly.[10] In a community like Colorado Springs, where approximately 600 counselors and therapists in Tricare's network are authorized to provide mental health services to military personnel, the MFLC program diverts resources from local providers who could deliver services at lower cost (Cotter 2011). As anthropologist Catherine Lutz, director of the Costs of War Project at Brown University, argues, "militarization is a *tense process*, that is it can create conflict between social sectors," between those who might benefit and those who might not (Lutz 2002:725–26). She notes that this happens on the local level and is most evident in communities like Colorado Springs that are home to large military installations.

### Veterans Serving Veterans

Eager that their younger fellow service members and veterans not feel abandoned or ignored as they felt they had been after Vietnam, veterans in Colorado Springs and other communities along the Front Range have joined with local residents to create an overwhelming range of service organizations for active-duty soldiers and veterans of the post-9/11 wars. To help coordinate services with the military, facilitate collaboration, and simply catalog what is available in the region, in 2006, Brian Norris and Oscar Pierce created Military Support Colorado (MSC), a network for organizations serving injured military personnel, veterans, and their families.

Norris, who retired from an active military career and then worked for various nonprofit organizations in the area, volunteers his time organizing the meetings, arranging for speakers, and working with some of the programs.

Pierce coordinates deployment programs at Fort Carson, which support readiness of enlisted and civilian military personnel and their families. Programs include relocation readiness, financial readiness, family advocacy (which includes victim advocacy, stress and anger management classes, emergency placement care, and family violence prevention briefings), Family Readiness Groups (FRGs), and employment services, among others. Like the support services the military outsources to spouses discussed in chapter 6, this program relies heavily on volunteers, especially when the garrison faces budget cuts (Emert 2010).

MSC comprises dozens of participating organizations and more than 600 people on its mailing list. The group meets monthly at a community center near Fort Carson; they celebrated their sixth anniversary in 2012, making it the longest-standing group of this nature in the United States of which many participants were aware. At each MSC meeting, representatives of three to four local programs or service organizations make a presentation to the entire group. Programs and organizations range from mental health providers, Paralympics, low-cost legal services, granting agencies that fund programs, and contractors who adapt houses for disabled soldiers, to Celebration of Honor Fly that provides hot-air balloon rides to service members at Fort Carson.

The Colorado Springs region boasts an extensive range of programs based on physical activity and outdoor recreation that capitalize on the state's climate and natural beauty; as the website for Forward Operating Base (FOB) Summit County Colorado proclaims, Colorado offers a "'personal and magical' healing spot." Tom Torres retired from the 82nd US Army Airborne Division after he "was deployed five times, wounded three times, and suffered two heart attacks." He knows firsthand the barriers that wounded veterans may face in navigating the VA system. In response he founded the nonprofit organization Forward Operating Base (FOB) Summit County Colorado "to be a support system for returning military personnel and to expose them to alternative possibilities for nurturing and guidance." Torres included FOB in the organization's name to represent "a safe zone or home base. It is known that if they can make it back to their FOB then they are 'home.'" He keeps his costs low by using volunteers to do administrative work. Since 2009, the organization has served more than 300 active-duty, wounded, and retired military personnel, taking them snowmobiling, fishing, hunting for deer and elk, biking, camping, whitewater rafting, and to Colorado Rockies baseball games, among other activities. All members of the board of directors receive training in PTSD, TBI, and suicide prevention and work with licensed massage therapists and holistic medicine specialists "to introduce our soldiers to Alternative Healing and support systems."[11]

Although commissioned officers generally fare well in the civilian economy, this is not always the case for young enlisted men and women who may face all kinds of problems when they leave military service. For WWII veterans, military service often led to upward social mobility, in large part through the generous benefits of the GI Bill. The bill not only paid for college education and vocational training; veterans could receive up to a year of unemployment compensation, zero-down payment home loans at low interest rates, and low-interest loans to start businesses. These benefits, used by 2.2 million veterans, helped fuel a national housing boom and move the nation out of the postwar recession (Scandlyn 1993). Today's young veterans who leave military service without college education and with financial obligations for young families enter a very different economy. Education benefits for veterans of the post-9/11 wars vastly improved with the passage of the Post-9/11 Veterans Educational Assistance Act of 2008. Veterans may still qualify for no-down payment mortgages if they can secure jobs whose salaries qualify and for guaranteed loans for businesses.[12] But many of the soldiers recruited during the early years of the war have poor educational histories that can make taking advantage of those benefits difficult. And leaving military service often means a cut in pay and benefits even if they find full-time work, and they re-enter the civilian economy in an age group with the highest levels of unemployment.

Some veterans recognize a niche they can fill that uses their knowledge of the military to connect with soldiers and other veterans. Others want to share the paths they found, largely on their own, as they struggled with PTSD and reintegration. But they may be caught between these personal motives and the military's obligation to provide safe, standardized, evidence-based care. If their programs fall outside established treatment guidelines and therefore outside Tricare's or the VA's funding mechanisms, they are often left ready, but waiting, to serve. Here we profile two such programs: a relaxation center and an equine assisted therapy program.

The Relaxation Center is tucked away around the corner from a large tattoo studio/parlor in an unremarkable strip mall, one of many that characterize development in the areas surrounding downtown Colorado Springs. Leaving the bright sunlight, we enter a reception area that is dimly lit, with sage green walls and generic prints hanging over small fountains with water spilling gently over rocks. A Mozart sonata plays softly, and there is the distinct smell of an aromatherapy blend. Antione Johnson, the center's founder and director, is tall and trim, and greets us with a warm, firm handshake. He explains that every aspect of the center was created to provide a relaxing atmosphere, "more like an Olive Garden than a Texas Ribhouse."

Johnson served 20 years in the army as a sergeant training soldiers. When he retired in 2000, he earned a master's degree in cognitive education. Although he never served in combat, based on his own military experience and combat soldiers' accounts, he identified the core issue soldiers face as "anhedonia," an inability to feel positive, joyful emotion. Although Johnson uses a term for a symptomatic disturbance, he denies that it's a disorder. "They cannot experience pleasure . . . . It's not a disease; it's not a diagnosis; it's not a condition. Which means that it could be fixed, you know, based on environmental factors." He attributes their lack of feeling to the hardness of combat and multiple deployments. He says some soldiers who come to the center are so numb they don't realize they aren't feeling anything. "And I used the example of him [the soldier] seeing the birth of his son. And I said, 'How did that feel, man? You were here from the war, delivery room, holding him in your hand.' And he couldn't even grasp that. He couldn't find the pleasure within it."

So Johnson provides veterans with pleasurable experiences. As he explains to a soldier, "Well, what we try to do is bring you as many pleasures as possible so that you can actually experience, you know, what it feels like to enjoy yourself now. You just came from H, E, double-L, and now we want to try to present the opposite." The core of the center's therapeutic program is the relaxation response, developed by Dr. Herbert Benson (1975; Benson with Proctor 1984). Following an initial evaluation by a social worker, clients go through a program that teaches them basic principles of neurophysiology related to stress and trauma and how the relaxation response can transform stressful patterns into healthier, more pleasurable, and relaxed ones. To practice and elicit the relaxation response, clients sit in massage chairs, listen to classical music, and focus on positive affirmations or prayers. Johnson acknowledges that some soldiers may not be able to let down their guard enough to benefit from his program.

Johnson and his wife invested $300,000—the bulk of their life savings— to open the center trusting in the "build it and they will come" maxim. But leaders from Fort Carson break meetings with him, blandly stating they will make no promises. "And that's the point where I noticed he [an army officer] started backing up. Not answering my emails, canceling meetings . . . . And then he had his major call me and said that he didn't want to have anything to do with the center. Yeah, that was after we went out and invested all of this money into this place, so I'm burning up with fire, you know." One of the barriers that Johnson faced was that Tricare does not cover programs based solely on relaxation techniques because they are not evidence-based. In July 2011 he hired two licensed clinical social workers to augment the relaxation response program and joined the Tricare network. Tricare covers the social workers' services, and Johnson hopes they can subsidize the relaxation services until they are approved by Tricare.

The majority of Johnson's clients are veterans or soldiers who are in the process of receiving medical discharges from the army, with referrals depending upon individual officers: "I mean you have those few that care, like Captain Hannigan. He's the first guy that actually came to me and said he's having a bunch of suicide issues, divorces, DUIs . . . . And he was really on it . . . . And these were the same kids who were faithful coming here." While the military must maintain standards of effectiveness and safety in the treatments that it funds through Tricare, officers like Captain Hannigan recognize that programs like the relaxation center can complement clinical treatment. But he also acknowledges that they are financially precarious. "Most of your nonprofits that work with military go under. They have a revenue source at first, but they're never really going to get any funding from the military." So the referrals are slow in coming, and Johnson is uncertain how long he can keep his center open.

John Nash is another veteran currently working outside the circle of evidence-based treatments (Figure 7). On a hot early summer Sunday in June 2011 we visited Nash and his wife Jackie at their home, Moon Fall Ranch, on the plains northeast of Colorado Springs where they run the nonprofit organization Combat Veterans Cowboy Up. Nash is a certified equine specialist, and his program is based in Equine Assisted Psychotherapy (EAP), which uses horses to assist therapists in treating veterans suffering from PTSD and TBI. He greets us in the drive and is dressed in jeans, a denim shirt, and cowboy boots, his skin tanned and wrinkled from a life spent mostly outdoors. He served two years in the army, with a one-year deployment to Vietnam.

Nash's work with veterans arose from his own struggle with PTSD. Like many Vietnam veterans, for many years he medicated his symptoms with overwork and alcohol. During the day he worked as a carpenter, returning to his ranch in the evening.

*I'd get home, and I'd be all drunked up or something, and instead of going in the house I would get some hay and go throw it*

**FIGURE 7.** John Nash of Cowboy Veterans Cowboy Up, Colorado (photo courtesy of Victoria Frecentese)

*in the corral, and Rainey, that horse I was pointing out over there, she would*
*come to me right away. I'd be sitting Indian style . . . sitting on the ground*
*or we had a big tractor tire out there, and I'd be sitting on the edge of that.*
*And she would come up to me and start nibbling the hay around me.*

Eventually he would pass out, but when he woke up, "She's got her head right over me and I can feel her breath going down my neck. And she had been there all that time. And she wouldn't leave until she felt I was okay and she would nudge me."

*And to tell you the truth, I didn't really care if she stepped on me or not.*
*I was at that point. That's what happens to us [veterans]. We don't really*
*ever care if we live or die, so we take all these unnecessary chances, and*
*many times it kills us. Go over a cliff, wreck our motorcycle at 180 miles an*
*hour. All that's suicide to me . . . . I credit my being alive to that horse.*

Nash subsequently sought care at the VA, where they diagnosed him with PTSD and severe depression and started him on a course of psychotherapy and medications.

Nash's experience with Rainey convinced him that working with horses could help other veterans. He sees horses as having a special affinity with veterans suffering from PTSD in their need to be with other members of their herd or group, their hypervigilance as prey animals, and their ability to "read" emotional signals expressed through body language, body odor, and heartbeats. Nash compares the transition from soldier to civilian to a transformation from predator to prey. The work is all done in the corral, with the veterans on the ground with the horses. It is through the client's interaction with the horse—for example, whether they are able to get the horse to come to them or if it shies away—that the client, Nash, and the therapist create metaphors to work through the veteran's issues. "The power of the team is to come back without a pause and start building a metaphor on what they said that relates to their life. That's the power in this, is the metaphors and the horse is what creates the metaphors. The dealing with the horse."

Nash is careful to define his program as "equine *assisted* therapy," because he combines the work with horses with therapy offered by his partner, who is a licensed therapist. One of the first questions veterans ask during orientation, he says, is "[a]m I going to have to talk about trauma?" I say, "Absolutely not, and if you start I'm gonna shut you down as soon as I hear it. I don't wanna hear about the trauma. . . . That's why you're in traditional therapy. That's their job to try and bring out that trauma." He tells them that at the ranch they deal "with the effects of that trauma and how it screws up your life": relationship issues, self-medication, depression, rage, and survivor's guilt.

Nash asks veterans to track their emotional state using a graph. "The bottom axis I call the choice line, that's the suicide line, do I want to live or die? That's the worst it gets, and I've been there and I am not proud of it, I never want to see that again . . . . The other side is the intensity of whatever the issue is, with 10 being the worst." He shows us dozens of completed graphs in which we can see the progress that veterans have made through their work at the ranch.

Like Carrera and West, Nash regards establishing trust as key to the program's success, facilitated by his being a veteran.

*We go to traditional therapy, and we get a therapist who's never been in the military and they're asking us all this stuff about combat and we're thinking, why should I waste my breath? . . . . How could you possibly understand what I'm talking about? You weren't there. It's kind of the same thing here, maybe that's why they start so fast here. Because I'm one of them. I have the same crap going on that they do, and still do, there's no cure. There's a maintenance program that's pretty heavy duty. I'd like to think of it as demons, demons that are always there. They're up here like this [indicates head level] and when these triggers happen, these demons start rearing their ugly heads and when we let them get up here they have control of us.*

For many clients, this is one in a long line of treatments and therapies they have tried, and often they have felt abandoned at the end of a program. Nash reassures them that they are always welcome at the ranch; that there does not have to be a definite endpoint. For some veterans in the program, working with horses becomes an avid interest that refocuses their lives and reinforces healing metaphors. "It seems as though those that are moving into the horsemanship side, that part locks the first part right into place, permanent. All the metaphors and all the stuff is just in there for good."

Nash is adamant that soldiers and veterans have "paid enough" and funds the program through donations or out of his pocket. "You will never pay a dime. I refuse to charge a veteran." He sees establishing the program's clinical efficacy as the key to sustaining it financially and expanding the model to other sites, and he wants to demonstrate scientifically what he believes his graphs show, so he has teamed up with researchers from a local university to do a systematic evaluation to move it toward being an evidenced-based program.

Healers are those who intentionally seek to restore health, and, in many healing systems, are those who themselves have been healed (Hahn 1995). Through their experience they can speak with authority about the healing journey and about what may or may not work. For John Nash, equine assisted therapy offered him the opportunity to "convert" from patient to healer and through this process find meaning and purpose in his struggle with reintegration (Finkler 1994).

For soldiers and veterans, healing, reintegration into civilian life, and adjustment to disability often require reorienting their daily activities and social relations, and the post-9/11 wars have stimulated many new programs targeted at healing social relations (Finley 2011). To achieve this, veterans need a wide variety of activities and service, from inside provider's offices to outside those offices, in the community. As they go rock climbing with Outward Bound or create murals with a local arts organization, veterans may find new interests that help them connect with others in their communities, veterans and civilians alike.

## Healing in the Hills

We now move further afield, not only from Fort Carson, but to healing practices that lie even further from conventional therapies to specifically speak to the social, spiritual, and moral aspects of soldiers' experiences and their need for community. In the past few decades, medical anthropologists have emphasized the role of meaning and narrative in the experience of sickness and healing.[13] In crafting the stories of our illness and suffering we draw from culturally shared metaphors, images, and story lines that make our stories understandable and accessible to family and friends. Thus activities such as working together to create a work of art can be healing even if this is not their stated purpose.

At the foot of Pikes Peak sits Manitou Springs, a place where Native Americans gathered to enjoy the healthful benefits of spring-fed mineral water and also known for its community of artists. Here we met Steve Woods, the director of Concrete Couch, a local arts organization. Woods is full of energy, with longish brown hair and beard sprinkled with bits of gray and a smile that is instantly warm and welcoming. He graduated with an art degree from a local college and has lived in the Colorado Springs area ever since, teaching at a local art school and working for more than 20 years with Outward Bound. These experiences convinced him of the power of art and outdoor recreation to create community.

In 2003, he worked with a group of Vietnam veterans through Outward Bound. The veterans became interested in the civil arts projects Woods' organization sponsored, and they joined together to build a sculptural fence in a local park using handmade tiles incorporating poetry and images. "They really liked connecting with the community and for some of them it was a little unusual. I know the first day on the Outward Bound course, at the end of the day getting to know people, it's always kind of stressful. They were like, 'You civilians are okay!'" Woods describes the event as "eye-opening," as he had not thought of himself as a "civilian," nor had he realized how much their military experience was a part of these veterans' identity. "And here these guys are, 30 years out, 'cause most of them just served in the war in Vietnam; they didn't make a career out of it. Conceiving of themselves, to this day, as military, as being essentially changed and different," was what most struck Woods. He realized that the art community had something valuable to offer: not only do veterans break down their stereotypes, but civilians, too, learn to see military personnel in a different light.

Woods and other artists at the center emphasize that they are not art therapists, that the intention of their work is not therapeutic, though occasionally, by climbing a rock wall or creating a tiled bench, catharsis occurs. For Woods, as much as military personnel and veterans might benefit from creating art, "they need job training; they need all kinds of things. But you know what they really need? They really need community. They need to make connections in this community that are important, that are vital, and that can sustain them. So that really is our mission in our work." He says that many veterans and active-duty soldiers are suspicious of programs that target them, so all of their programs are free.[14] "That takes the whole pressure off for a lot of people. They're like, 'Oh, you're not scamming us.' 'Cause I think the military community gets hit up all the time . . . . There's this whole section of society that really is trying to enrich themselves greatly through military contracting, not always with the military's best interest in mind." He is also respectful of the different place that many Vietnam veterans are now in. "They've been through it all. Marriage and divorce, and drugs and jail and primal scream therapy and Outward Bound, and now they are like hanging out with people and doing art and hiking through the woods and writing poetry. So I have to be careful that I'm not overwhelming those guys."

At the same time that the general public accepts PTSD as a valid diagnosis for combat stress injury, there is increasing recognition that the emphasis on individual treatment is insufficient in helping soldiers reintegrate. The military is filled with rituals to mark entry into combat and its return, but some practitioners and chaplains call for more collective action, for rituals and ceremonies based in civilian values and ideals to aid in healing and reintegration. Like Shay (2002) and Tick (2005), who looked to Greek mythology to better understand war-related trauma, many healers draw from nonwestern societies and cultures, for models to create rituals and ceremonies to aid healing and reintegration.

In the foothills 20 miles west of Colorado Springs, we drove several miles on a dirt road and pulled into a parking lot amid a stand of tall pines. Just up the hill we saw a yurt, a round, white, canvas-covered structure like the portable homes of nomadic peoples in Mongolia. Yurts dot Colorado's mountain areas, adopted as a popular form of shelter for backcountry expeditions. But Helen Stevens and John Devon specifically and intentionally chose to build a yurt when they established their ministry, Healing Circles, on this site. Its round shape symbolizes the wholeness that those who come here seek, and its origins in northern Asia reflect the shamanic practices used in their ceremonies.

Devon directed us to the yurt, where Stevens greeted us as we entered. She asked us to take off our shoes and find a seat. Hanging from the wooden frame that supports the yurt's canvas walls were several large, round, thin drums, gourd rattles, feathered dream catchers, and photographs of mountain scenery. The floor was covered with Southwestern Indian rugs, with piles of cushions around the perimeter. The light coming through the windows and canvas was soft and diffused, and we found ourselves speaking quietly. Stevens is in her early 40s and has a relaxed and easy manner. She explained that she has been studying shamanism for more than 17 years. The term "shaman" comes from nomadic groups living in Siberia and refers to individuals in the community who are recognized for their ability to enter trance states and communicate with spiritual beings to bring back knowledge and power (Balzer 1996). Most shamans use this power for healing and to benefit their community, for example, in times of war; however, like most supernatural powers, it may also be used for malevolent purposes. Stevens trained through the Foundation for Shamanic Studies established by anthropologist Michael Harner, who spent many years studying shamanism among hunter-gatherer societies in the Peruvian Amazon.[15] Stevens is clear that she is not a shaman, but that she uses shamanic practices for healing.

Neither Stevens nor Devon are veterans. Stevens came to her work with veterans through her career teaching massage therapy. Several of her students were Iraq war veterans who suffered from multiple physical ailments, PTSD, and TBI. One thing they told her was, "I feel like I left a part of my soul on the battlefield." Soul loss is a central diagnosis in shamanic healing traditions that can explain a wide variety of physical, emotional, and behavioral symptoms. In experiencing a life-threatening trauma, part or parts of a person's soul can be separated from their body, leading to a sense of unreality, loss of feeling, and sense that one is not fully connected to the present and to life. Stevens explained that psychiatric symptoms—dissociation,

depression, and gaps in memory—were signs of soul loss or soul fragmenta-
tion. " . . . [O]ur belief is that when you are in extreme trauma is that your
essence, your soul leaves your body. Your physical body is still there to function, but it [your soul] comes in and out, and it can get frightening." Because
Stevens sees the real source of their continued distress as soul fragmenta-
tion and loss, conventional psychotherapy cannot address the underlying
cause. "We've talked to and worked with a number of soldiers from Vietnam
who've talked to and gone to various therapists for 30 years and they can't
break through . . . . Talk therapy is great, but once again, if you're not whole
and present it's just not going to work." She added, "And this really explains
why so many guys went back to Korea; so many guys went back to Cambodia
and Vietnam so many years later. And they tell you, 'I don't know why I'm
going, but I know I have to go.' It's this feeling that they left part of their true
essence and spirit behind."

Thus the ultimate cause of soul loss is not psychological, but spiritual.
The shaman's or healer's task is to enter a trance state and seek the help of
spirits to retrieve that part or parts of the soul that have been lost. To perform soul retrieval, Stevens must become a "hollow bone" through which
compassionate spirits can work with living human beings. She is quick
to note that she does not do the work; the spirits do. So although Stevens
does not have combat experience, the spirits, who have been with the soldier throughout his life, have direct knowledge of their suffering and the
authority to restore wholeness. Restoring wholeness brings inner peace and
strength, so that clients can sleep, relax, and engage fully with the world and
the people around them.

Echoing a classic article by the anthropologist Claude Lévi-Strauss
(1963), Stevens emphasizes that community plays a key role in shamanic
healing. She encourages clients to bring someone with them to their sessions
to witness the ceremony and confirm that indeed something "real" occurred.
"So that when you're making that declaration . . . in the ceremony, you've
got community supporting you for it." She added, "We're shaking rattles,
drumming, making weird noises, burning things! Not everyone is comfortable with that, so we always encourage people to bring a support system so
people can watch." Although Stevens sees the value of the community of veterans in supporting each other, she believes strongly that healing must also
involve family, friends, and the larger civilian community.

Finally, both Stevens and Devon underlined that a soldier's identity as a
warrior must be honored and preserved. "To me it's just so important that
we understand that these guys are warriors. And I've seen so many people
that try to take that away from the soldier." She says that "The medicine man

would actually work with them and do ceremony and do ritual with them, would work with them on detoxing their bodies. Getting everything back into balance. And sometimes these soldiers would spend 30 days or more with the shaman before they ever went back to their families and into the culture." Stevens compares it to a spiritual debriefing that "was to enable them to once again become the peaceful warrior before they had to go back into their society. . . . "

For the same reasons that Johnson and Nash cited—frequent change of command, shamanic healing falling outside the range of standard therapies, and lack of reimbursement through insurance—Stevens and Devon have found it difficult to work with the military to serve active-duty soldiers. As Stevens said, "we have a lot of therapists that refer to us, but it [shamanic healing] is still kind of weird and out there!" An additional concern was that they would help soldiers reestablish wholeness and begin to feel better only to see them sent back to Iraq or Afghanistan. "And the last thing we want to do is put them in harm's way. I could not live with myself if I knew that somebody I worked with got redeployed [here meaning "deployed again"; sic] and because of the spiritual shift in his life got killed." Whereas shamanic healing may be too "New Age" and "out there" for many veterans, it can appeal to those who seek a spiritually based practice that is not based in any one religious tradition, is something that can benefit families and communities, and is compatible with the warrior ethos.

Norman Jackson, a veteran and Native American Sundance spiritual leader, leads purification sweat lodge ceremonies for soldiers every other weekend (Figure 8). Fort Carson's chaplain command provided a permanent site for the lodge, or *inipi*, on its Turkey Creek Ranch, a recreational facility just south of the installation. Jackson has been leading sweat lodge ceremonies at Turkey Creek for more than 15 years. "Culturally, we've always had our warrior society surround new warriors when they get out of the service . . . . When we do get done, the warrior society is there to greet us and the warrior society helps us readjust in the community." Jackson

FIGURE 8. Michael Hackwith outside the sweat lodge at Fort Carson's Turkey Creek Recreation Area (photo used with permission of Monica Mendoza, Michael Hackwith, and Wendy Chunn).

says that it is difficult to explain the effect of the sweat lodge in words; it is something you need to experience. Through physical hardship—extreme heat and dark—soldiers must confront themselves, but surrounded by a community that cares about them. "We give them an opportunity to face themselves. Put them in a dark spot. As a community we say, 'We're glad you're here. We're glad you're praying with us.'" Like Stevens, he emphasizes that neither he nor the community provide healing. "It's the creator's doing. I know lodge works, and I've seen soldiers turn around. That's not my doing, that's the creator's doing."

When a member of the research team, Giulio Brandi, attended several sweat lodges led by Jackson, he found that Lakota beliefs about trauma were particularly relevant for those suffering from PTSD.

> It is believed that individuals, out of sheer love, "sign a contract" with the creator before they are born and agree to go through various ordeals during their life. Wakan Tankan [the creator] may ask one to suffer traumatic ordeals, but there is always a purpose behind the suffering; for example, a survivor of domestic abuse may become a skilled social worker and alleviate the suffering of other victims of domestic abuse (Brandi, personal communication, October 2011). The first breath taken by a newborn baby is the "signing of the contract" and if one's trauma becomes too great, the creator is always available to help. The sweat lodge is one of the mechanisms of reaching for help. With this framework in mind, individuals suffering from PTSD can reclaim ownership of a seemingly meaningless traumatic event. They are also given a framework for how to live, and a framework to cope with stress, most notably the sweat lodge. An interesting characteristic of the lodge is that it is facilitated by one who "pours water," but the experience is ultimately one's own. It is a personal, inner journey where an inner-locus of control is emphasized; in short, one's traumas were agreed upon before birth and the onus is on the individual to understand their hardships (Brandi 2012:19–20).

## Seeking Credibility and Legitimacy

The Department of Defense has made significant efforts to increase mental health services through increased recruitment of mental health professionals, establishment of behavioral health teams in combat units during deployment and on military installations, and expanding services and facilities to support families. In April 2012, Fort Carson opened a new family resiliency campus that features a behavioral health center with plans to build an additional facility. In 2011, soldiers at Fort Carson made 108,000 visits to behavioral health specialists, a dramatic rise in the proportion of soldiers seeking

treatment. Colonel John McGrath attributes the rise in soldiers seeking care
to placing or "embedding" behavioral health teams in combat brigade facilities where soldiers live and work (Rodgers 2012).[16] But demand continues to
outstrip the military's mental health resources, and the most recent review
by the VA's Inspector General found that the Veterans Health Administration is facing similar issues in providing timely, quality care to veterans
(VHA 2012).

A key responsibility of the military is establishing treatment protocols
using safe, effective, and evidence-based treatments and warning against
those treatments that are ineffective or harmful. Research demonstrates that
early intervention following a traumatic event for those with symptoms of
acute distress can improve recovery and may prevent the development of
PTSD (VA/DoD 2010). But not all soldiers have symptoms immediately following trauma or are able or willing to report them if they do. Symptoms of
PTSD can appear six months or more after a traumatic event. Thus, many
veterans will receive treatment, if they ever do, in the civilian community.
Even within military and VA health care systems, evidence-based protocols
are relatively new, not widely available, nor consistently implemented. Many
civilian providers may not be aware of current recommendations or lack
training in using them. So they continue to rely on approaches used in the
past that have not always been effective (Finley 2012).

Many civilian providers face significant challenges acquiring credibility
and legitimacy with the military. We found that civilian providers, many of
whom had never been in uniform, especially those working directly with
active-duty personnel at Fort Carson, often adopted military language and
metaphors—what we call "battlespeak"—to describe their work. The best
examples come from several service-providing agencies that "embed" civilian counselors with particular units. In one we heard several referring to
their fellow counselors as "battle buddies." We were also struck when we
heard them talk of performing a "surge," referring to a relatively new practice
of saturating brigades (approximately 3,000 soldiers) just as a unit got back
from deployment so that every soldier would receive a 30-minute counseling appointment within the first 30 days. Among the most pervasive uses
of battlespeak is that of battle itself: from the battlefield theater to "battling"
combat stress. When we asked about the uses of such terms, one counselor
told us that while their agency does not deploy overseas with units—and
carefully added that their work "doesn't compare to being deployed to a war
zone"—that they do notice and talk about the parallels between the soldiers'
lives and their own.

Battle is a well-established trope or figure of speech not only throughout the military, unsurprisingly, but also in varied parts of the interstices

between military and civilian subcultures.[17] Why do nonmilitary service providers "sign up" for using battlespeak, and what are they expressing or achieving by using such expressions? In a domestic setting absent of gunfire and explosions, what or who are they battling against? As simple metaphor, the counselor's battlespeak may stand as an expression of solidarity—getting behind the war effort—and of empathy with soldiers. They may convey willingness to work hard, in what for civilians are relatively extreme conditions, or to sacrifice, by journeying from home and "normal life," to help those who have journeyed still farther and risked more. Emotionally, battlespeak may fortify them. Likening their work to that of the soldiers they work for may allow them to take courage and inspiration for their own work, which also calls for intimate dealings with death, injury, loss and grief, and struggles with conscience and morality.

By comparison, veterans like Antione Johnson and John Nash seek legitimacy within the realm of biomedicine, developing programs based on their own experiences of healing or education. For now, they collaborate with licensed providers, but as Nash's nascent collaboration with researchers shows, they hope for a day when they can present scientific evidence that their programs are efficacious.

## Transforming Practices

The psychiatric nurse Debra Carrera's crisis at having soldiers yanked from her care not only revealed conflicts and contradictions in military collaborations with civilian providers, but limitations in ensuring that soldiers and veterans receive consistently high-quality care using the latest evidence-based approaches to treating war-related trauma. At Fort Carson Carrera reinstituted case management to coordinate psychiatric services and improve continuity of care. "This was the missing link for the military" she says. "There are great services—Family Readiness Groups and family support services—but they are scattered," especially for family members. She said that a soldier might come to the emergency room in distress, but the spouse was sent elsewhere. "There were 'no' support services because she didn't know where to go."[18]

She also brought her experience to her group practice. Initially, she focused on talk therapy and medications, but notes that talk therapy was "a bust, let me tell you. They didn't come there to talk. They came to feel. And at the same time the inner contradiction, the inner conflict is such that they don't want to feel what they have to feel." So over time Carrera and her colleagues shifted the focus of their practice with soldiers and veterans to therapeutic modalities based in alternative systems of healing, such as Reiki, or more experientially based practices like drumming.

*And we all have a common beat, and it's our heartbeat. So we can start with that heartbeat, and then as trust develops I can say to this group, "Can you pound that out on the drum? Can you tell me what that felt like?" And their inhibitions are gone because they are not expected to explain, they're just feeling it.*

Incorporating bodywork in treating PTSD is an essential element of Eye Movement Desensitization and Reprocessing (EMDR), which combines experiential and body-centered therapies with cognitive and behavioral therapies. EMDR is an evidence-based treatment accepted by the DoD and the VA (EMDR Institute, Inc. 2011).[19] Hugh Trumbold, a psychologist in private practice who uses EMDR, explains, "We attempt a cognitive reframe— the left brain buys it, the right doesn't, to address negative self-concept and beliefs about the world." While being asked to remember a traumatic event, the client attends to an external stimulus, the most common being tracking moving light on a light bar (eye movement) or sounds or taps and to note the associations of thoughts, emotions, and sensations that come to mind. With repetition over a series of sessions, distress and negative beliefs about the incident diminish until they become "normal" memories. Trumbold adds that other therapies that "get" to the right side of the brain, for example, art, movement, yoga, thought-filled therapy, and acupressure, can be effective as well (Faxon 2013).

One theme in Carrera's practice that has not changed is that of acceptance. For soldiers who have been in combat, she says, the biggest fear they have is that what they have done and who they are is unacceptable. She talks about helping soldiers with the "face the mirror test," in which they can tolerate looking at themselves in a handheld mirror. She said that a soldier told her the most helpful thing she said to him was, "Given the same explanation, given the same intel [military intelligence], given the exact same situation, you would probably make the same decision today. And that's okay." She then related the soldier's story that prompted her statement. "Because for them, the reflective self-contempt came in that we had bad intel, and because of that bad intel this officer authorized them to attack," only to find out they hadn't hit a vehicle carrying insurgents, but a vehicle carrying children. "And you can imagine the horror stories. So loud and clear. They have to know that they are loved." Carrera may also ask a soldier to write down the narrative of his or her traumatic experience to externalize it. Afterward, they may tear it up or burn it as a symbolic recognition of putting it away, outside, taking away its power and making sense of it.

Carrera says that her work is not about morality, that she does not have the power to "put a moral code on it." Moreover, like West, Carrera is faced with the possibility that soldiers still on active duty may deploy again. In discussing the moral aspects of their actions, "we risk totally disempowering them and putting them at risk if they have to go back out. That's my fear. If I leave them with a sense of what they did was totally wrong, have I really handicapped them? God forbid they put a light on the situation. Who am I to say? I genuinely don't know." In recognizing her inability to assign meaning and moral judgment on a soldier's action, Carrera is not avoiding their moral character, but honoring their autonomy and moral agency (Young 1995).

With the advent of a narrow range of effective, evidence-based programs for PTSD emerging, that path may become more straightforward and easy for soldiers to navigate. But moral injury is a consequence of war that clinical psychologists are just beginning to study, and not a diagnosis. Moral injuries arise when a soldier transgresses the norms of her society; they are inherently social. As health and religious professionals who work with soldiers and veterans suggest, moral injuries cannot be "repaired" through individual psychotherapy alone, but must be accompanied by spiritually and socially directed interventions. This requires "multidisciplinary effort that also considers social systems in which the individual is based and can receive help and support" (Maguen and Litz 2012:3). So for the many other issues soldiers, families, and communities face during reintegration, they will continue to need multiple threads to guide them out of the labyrinth.

# PART III: DIALOG

## Chapter 8

# "Best Hometown in the Army"

*Before I got here, I thought for a long time that the way out of the labyrinth was to pretend that it did not exist, to build a small, self-sufficient world in a back corner of the endless maze and to pretend that I was not lost, but home.*
— John Green, *Looking for Alaska*

One after the other, soldiers and army family members told us what they liked about the Pikes Peak region. Fort Carson, Colorado Springs' "Mountain Post," could be considered the "Best Hometown in the Army"—and an assignment there so desirable and elusive it could even be called "the unicorn of the army" (see Figure 9).[1] The sunny, dry climate and athletic, outdoorsy culture contributed, but the military-friendly, yet not-too-military balance were also important. The army's Fort Carson is by far the biggest of the five military installations surrounding the city of Colorado Springs (total population 660,000); most of the others are air force. This makes for a total of 75,000 active-duty personnel, who are roughly split between soldiers and airmen,

**FIGURE 9.** Marker outside Fort Carson's main gate (photo courtesy of Victoria Frecentese).

meaning that sheer numbers of "green-suiters" and "blue-suiters" in uniform at shopping centers and restaurants near bases make for a visible presence.

What stood out for many who spoke with us was the fact that Colorado Springs is not *exclusively* a military city, unlike Killeen, Texas, or Fayetteville, North Carolina, where they had been stationed: "If the military were to pack up and leave, this place has enough tourism and other industry that it would still be a town," army wife and former active-duty soldier Theresa Thayer commented. Thayer appreciated the chance for her children to go to school with civilian kids, and drove them an hour each day to off-post schools to achieve this; otherwise, it was hard to have "any semblance of normalcy when every six months five of your friends leave," as was the case at military-majority schools.

Being the best hometown means that some 47,000 military retirees choose the area, and are prominent—and often predominant—in leadership of local governmental and nonprofit organizations.[2] Best hometown status may mean more families choose to come here when a soldier is transferred. "It's a compliment to Colorado Springs," a general stated, when 600 students show up for the first day at a new elementary school at Fort Carson, built for just 450 children, because families come in higher-than-average percentages. Deployment-weary soldiers may feel less likely to be subject to public hostility in southern Colorado, where "everyone makes military feel welcome and supported," soldier Chris Stimpert told us. By contrast, one of his buddies was doing recruiting in Washington State—"the worst place to be a soldier"—where people spit on him, and one even threw a drink on him. Another soldier recalled being called "baby-killer" in San Diego when she was quite visibly pregnant and in uniform; the memory made her snort with laughter, but also visibly angry.

As the wars have worn on, however, southern Colorado's reputation as a military-friendly place has acquired its blemishes as well. In 2011, when Sarah struck up a conversation with the rail-thin soldier standing in front of her in the Colorado Springs airport security line, it turned out they had met before: General Todd Pettigrew had served as the deputy commander at Fort Carson before moving to Washington, DC, to direct the Comprehensive Soldier Fitness program.

Returning to visit the region was bittersweet for the officer. "Lately, when I hear talk about Colorado in DC," the general told Sarah, "it is being seen as very unfriendly to the military—even hostile."

"Really?" Sarah responded, surprised. "What do you think that's about?" He did not respond right away, so she offered, "The opposition to expanding Piñon Canyon down south? Or to bringing the new Combat Aviation Brigade here in town?" She could have added the intense local and national media attention garnered by the spate of murders perpetrated by soldiers (chapter 3), but refrained.

"Both, I think." Then he added, "Just—the whole thing."

Later, we reported this exchange to long-time local activist John Champion, who was ever at the forefront of various antimilitarist efforts. After being drafted and serving in Vietnam, John became a Catholic priest; he was a vocal proponent urging the Vatican to develop greater critical thinking about "just war," and issues related to the separation of church and state (such as calling for an independent civilian chaplaincy that could remind service members that they have a right to refuse an order). As a result of creating "this kind of disturbance," he had been "basically fired" by the church hierarchy. Disillusioned with the Church's ineffectiveness in providing young people potentially headed into the armed forces with a "moral compass" to navigate "indoctrination centers" like the local Air Force Academy, of which he was a frequent critic and protestor, he left the priesthood and church altogether.

On hearing Colorado Springs painted as territory hostile to the military, John gave a thoughtful chuckle, adding, "All 10 of us—we're behind Colorado being seen as unfriendly? Well, I guess that's good news."

The small group of dedicated protestors to which Champion referred was perhaps closer to 20 stable activists in the city itself; they were at times joined by dozens more, depending on the issue and participating organizations. Several overlapping groups narrowed their efforts toward varied issues related to concerns about militarization: Citizens for Peace in Space, for example, focused on satellite, missile, and, increasingly, weaponized drone operations, where the local Commission for Justice and Peace focused on educational and international issues and the National War Tax Resisters Coordination Committee on eroding funding for war. Assorted members of these groups gathered every Friday at busy intersections around town, holding up banners whose messages varied over time, reflecting specific moments over the course of the wars. In addition to general messages like "Non-Violence Works: Find It, Study It, Use It" or simply "Peace. NOW," in 2013 one might see:

*"Ground the Drones—Remote Control Murder"*

*"BRING MORE WAR DOLLARS HOME"*[3]

*"We're Creating Enemies Faster Than We Can Kill Them"*

*"Main Street Pays for War, Wall Street Profits from War"*[4]

**FIGURE 10.** Activists "bannering" on a busy street corner (photo courtesy of Donna Johnson).

In earlier years, banners were more likely to include messages like:

*"Change must mean peace—Democrats please Stop Funding the War"*

*"Beware of the Military-Industrial Complex"*

*"Healthcare not Warfare"*

*"Iraq/Afghanistan/Palestine—Occupation is a Crime"*

*"No Blood for Oil"*

Even here, in a place as overwhelmingly promilitary as the Pikes Peak region, "a few vocal individuals" (as numerous media stories refer to the activists) can highlight resistance to accommodation of military goals and the ways they reshape the local landscape for large sectors of the public (Figure 10).

Examining what preparing for war demands of not only individuals, but also their communities and surrounding landscapes, demonstrates the diverse dimensions through which war is, inevitably, brought home. How do we think about "security," and how do we assess when, and which, sacrifices are necessary to ensure collective safety and security? This chapter explores differing perspectives among residents of "homefronts" like southern Colorado as they assess what challenges and costs their communities face in making, and recovering from, war. Are the costs of war "worth it," or necessary for securing a way of life?[5] Divergent answers to this question shape how a place can be simultaneously viewed as friendly or hostile to the military. Calculating the "costs" and "benefits" of military action depends on variable ways of conceiving security, the level of threats faced, and attempts to weigh intangibles: the value placed on conserving lifeways, environments, and peaceable law and order.

In response to these challenges, some call into question the national security paradigm itself, and offer "human security" as an alternative paradigm. Whereas national security centers on the state as its primary referent and military responses as the principal means of creating security, human security places individuals, communities, and environments as its central referents. Human security, broadly defined as encompassing "freedom from threat to the core values of human beings, including physical survival, welfare, and identity," offers a promising rejoinder to cost-benefit analyses that privilege militarist responses (MacFarlane and Khong 2006:14). While the freedom-from-threat standard can and often must include national security, a more holistic approach introduces imperatives that might challenge the effectiveness and priorities of militarist strategies, and contest the black-box secrecy that supports them.[6] Just as the labyrinth pluralizes the tangle of stories of lives wrapped up in war, a human security paradigm "opens new lines of analysis, gives voice to new actors" (Fakuda-Parr and Messineo 2012:3).[7]

## "This Land Is Not for Sale"

Two controversies Jean mentioned to the general, expanding the Piñon Canyon Maneuver Site in southeastern Colorado and adding a Combat Aviation Brigade (CAB) at Fort Carson, show how affairs at Fort Carson and Colorado Springs radiate outward across the broader region.

Diego Mendez, an octogenarian from southeastern Colorado, has driven long miles from his ranch to the town of Trinidad, on Colorado's southern border with New Mexico. He joins a small group of us who have come down from Colorado Springs to hear from members of the Piñon Canyon Expansion Opposition Coalition (PCEOC). This strange-bedfellow, grassroots movement is made up largely of folks from traditional, often sixth-generation Coloradan ranchers and farmers, mixed with activists, artists, preservationists, and archaeologists. The one thing that unites them is their opposition to the army enlarging the 238,000-acre training area that Fort Carson uses for large-scale, force-on-force mechanized brigade combat exercises, involving tanks and armored units.

The DoD obtained the current parcel of land known as the Piñon Canyon Maneuver Site through the largest condemnation of lands in US history. The effects of that seizure, in which residents of 41 ranches were relocated, 11 of them unwilling sellers, still rankled locally. The army's promises to replace lost tax revenue to schools and to bring a boom in new civilian jobs fell short. Original commitments not to fly so low as to stampede cattle were violated, and the ban on use of live fire was rescinded in 2004.

The biggest broken promise of all, though, was that the site would never be expanded. In 2004, a report titled "Piñon Vision" revealed plans to gradually increase military holdings to 6.9 million acres across five phases, serving not only Fort Carson but "Joint, Combined and Multi-National units" across branches.[8] This would make PCMS three times larger than any other military base in the United States, representing an area larger than countries like Israel, Rwanda, or El Salvador, and bigger than the states of Maryland, New Hampshire, and Massachusetts. Creating the "Pentagon's 51st state," as some call it,[9] would displace 17,000 residents. Troops require enhanced training and equipment for current and future engagements, commanders argued, and their land requirements spiral: acreage needed for full-scale tank and infantry maneuvers grew from 4,000 acres in World War II to a remarkable 80,000 acres by the early 1990s (Lanier-Graham 1993).

The DoD report circulated like wildfire locally; commonly considered a "leaked" document, today it is public record.[10] Residents of the area were still absorbing the full implications of the creation of the original site, but since 2006, when the news of the report spread, the region has been engaged in an ongoing struggle to resist army expansion (Figure 11).

**FIGURE 11.** Piñon Canyon Maneuver Site, with potential expansions (map by Michael D. Brown).

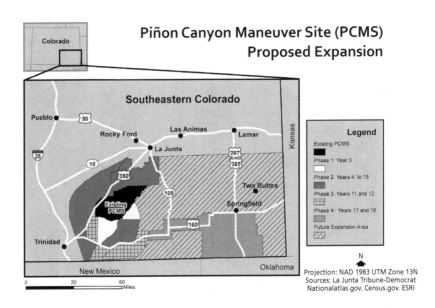

"Someone in my family has fought in every American war," Mendez tells the group. "I served, and so did my sister, my aunt, and my cousin. We are patriotic Americans; I salute the flag." He swore his family would give whatever was necessary for the nation's security. "If the Army could show me *exactly* why they need my family's land to defeat insurgents," Mendez assures us, "I would be the first to give it. But they just have not been able to do that."

Writer Trey Garrison (2009) characterized the impact of heavy weaponry on the fragile, historically significant terrain at Piñon Canyon in this way.

*Even today, the ruts made by wagons traveling the Santa Fe Trail more than a century ago are plainly visible in the flats. Imagine what a 67-ton Abrams tank or an 18-ton Stryker combat vehicle on maneuvers can do, not to mention the impact of live-fire exercises in a place where lightning sparks grassfires that burn hundreds of acres at a go.*[11]

Historic, prehistoric, and paleolithic sites are especially in evidence around Picketwire Canyon alongside the Purgatoire River. As John Champion once remarked about damage being done to the fragile microclimates around Piñon Canyon, " . . . if that's what they're doing here, where they're supposed to be careful, can you imagine the effects in Iraq and Afghanistan?"

Between 2006 and 2009, residents across the vast region organized quickly, alarmed at the 6.9-million-acre scale and speed of potential expansion. Across sizable distances, more than 1,000 regular participants mobilized to gather, talk, and plan in towns from Trinidad to La Junta, Walsenburg to Colorado Springs. Three early successes converged to provide breathing room. In the state capitol in Denver, Southeastern Colorado legislators shepherded bipartisan bills in 2006 and 2008, which the governor immediately signed into law. The first refused permission for state lands to be condemned under federal eminent domain claims, and the second barred state lands, checkered across the area for school funding purposes, from being sold or leased to the DoD. (Both raised new questions for state versus federal jurisdiction, and either could be overridden.) Meanwhile, in 2008 Colorado's congressional representatives in Washington passed a moratorium through both houses banning federal funding for condemnation, which was successively renewed, year by year, through 2013 (*The Colorado Observer* 2013). Together, these measures significantly lessened the likelihood of the army successfully invoking eminent domain. Finally, Not 1 More Acre brought a federal suit contesting the army's 2007 Environmental Impact Statement finding of no significant impacts; they won in 2009, when a federal judge deemed that the report insufficiently accounted for noise, pollution, and damage to historical and cultural artifacts (Woock 2011) (Figure 12).

**FIGURE 12.** Painted boxcars near roadsides in the Piñon Canyon area (photos courtesy of Doug Holdread).

These obstacles dampened army ambitions; they scaled back hopes for a phase one addition of 418,000 acres, based on a 2007 Pentagon-approved land acquisition waiver, stating it "would settle for as little as 80,000" new acres. Though the military hinted it had willing sellers in line for this smaller parcel, said sellers did not materialize. Meanwhile, activists learned they could not rest on earlier victories, but perpetually needed to gear up for the next round of strategizing from fresh reinforcements, corresponding with each change of command at Fort Carson. Their biggest fear was of eventually getting worn down, of losing their energy and vigilance. Meanwhile, they discovered how to navigate environmental impact statements, create the largest known ecological study conducted on private lands,[12] carefully document breaches to agreed-upon uses, pursue state and federal lawsuits, and craft state and federal legislation. Roberta Jordan, a local archaeologist and preservationist, told us, "I'll never forget when a Fort Carson spokesperson said to me, 'We didn't think you people would be smart enough to use a cultural landscape argument,'" referring to a then-novel tactic she had been part of enacting as part of the federal lawsuit. So far, opposition activists have stayed one step ahead of the army, albeit just barely.

Between 2006 and 2013, Piñon Canyon had become a focal site for adapting to new challenges in warfare; why the army needed this particular area mutated with successive phases of the post-9/11 wars. When the focus was on Iraq, PCMS's similarity to Iraqi topography led them to construct mock Iraqi villages, for which Iraqi refugees were recruited "to act as wartorn citizens in small Middle East villages."[13] Since 2009, Afghanistan moved to the fore at PCMS, with Afghan nationals from the Denver area now helping units rehearse for Afghanistan scenarios. The army now emphasized Colorado's high altitude and PCMS's proximity to the mountains, from which flight-based trainings could be run, that made it the best-suited training site for providing military readiness.

During this same period, Fort Carson emerged as a leading candidate to house a new Combat Aviation Brigade, which would bring 2,700 new soldiers and 137 Apache, Chinook, and Osprey helicopters. A group of concerned citizens back in Colorado Springs formed the group "Stop the Whop Whop," which opposed bringing the brigade on grounds that the noise and use of public Forest Service lands to the west would have negative impacts for noise, airspace traffic, and environmental sustainability in the mountains.

Opponents of the new helicopter brigade shared a particular concern with Piñon Canyon expansion opponents: that once the problems created by extensive helicopter training so close to Colorado Springs became clear and elite neighborhoods adjacent to Fort Carson complained, this would be used as yet another pretext to push through the expansion of PCMS, to provide greater buffers from high-density populations. A collective outcry arose as these groups' efforts converged, apparently vocal enough to tip promilitary southern Colorado toward being suddenly seen as distinctly military-unfriendly in Washington.

In spite of the region's newfound notoriety, the group opposing bringing the helicopter brigade failed: the army announced in the spring of 2011 that the unit was definitively coming to Fort Carson. Within six months of that announcement, 25 landing zones on federal lands were providing helicopter training to brigades from across the country from Fort Hood, Texas, to Fort Bragg, North Carolina.[14] In this same period, Air Force Special Operations announced plans to create a low-altitude training zone between PCMS and two air force bases in eastern New Mexico. Aerial maneuvers, involving both manned and unmanned robotic weapons systems (drones), would use as much as 60,700 square miles (nearly 39 million acres) of civil airspace.[15]

To continue tracing the intensifying military impact on the region, we return to Colorado Springs, the military epicenter of the Rocky Mountain West.

### "All Addition, No Subtraction"

In 1918, Randolph Bourne famously wrote that "War is the health of the State," in bringing unparalleled unity of spirit and effort. Nearly a century later, with so much of the civilian citizenry indifferent about the wars and their effects and less unified generally, Bourne's unity may no longer hold or be a desired means to achieve national agendas. Nonetheless, in locales like Colorado Springs in El Paso County, war can still be said to be the economic driver, and therefore also, by default, the primary local development strategy for a healthy economy. In 2012 DoD brought $5.93 billion to the state of Colorado, 85 percent of which came to El Paso County. The military represents 25 to 30 percent of the local economy, employing more than 70,000 people directly, and that number again, on average, in indirect employment of civilians on bases and through contracting (Binn 2010). The government sector is the largest and fastest growing sector in Colorado Springs, and Fort Carson alone is the largest non-state employer in Colorado. From the opening gesture of the City of Colorado Springs purchasing 5,533 acres and selling them to the federal government for $1 (Shackelford 1984:14 cited in Felson 2011:4), to a city councilman arguing in 2013 that "we have to do things to let the military know that we want them here, that they're appreciated," Colorado Springs has played a willing host to the military (Gillentine 2012).

Historian of religion and local Paul Harvey calls Colorado Springs a unique marriage between "activist grassroots religious conservatism, faith in (and reliance on) the military-industrial complex, and a historic western libertarian hatred of 'big government'—combined with an economic reliance on big government" (Harvey 2012). Indeed, how we view the military's presence and regional impact depends a lot on the angle we adopt and whose interests are at stake. The summer of 2010 brought the worst effects of the 2008 economic crisis, coupled with the drought, home to all residents of Colorado Springs. It became stunningly clear how close to the bone the local economy was running. Municipal jobs and programs were cut, already meager city bus service was halved, and plans to remain 70 percent dependent on a dirty, coal-burning power plant downtown stretched into the century's second decade. The city did not water or mow medians and parks or pick up trash; though some volunteer groups stepped in, most public areas deteriorated into litter-strewn, sunbaked lots of overgrown weeds.

Colorado College student Ben Felson interned that summer for the Deployment Stress Project; the following academic year he would write the senior thesis "Camouflaged Costs: The Military's Influence on the Cultural Geography of Colorado Springs."[16] Thinking hard about the city's economic situation compelled him to write a public response to the 2010 report of the Quality of Life Indicators for the Pikes Peak region.[17] By all accounts the outlook was grim; a local editor called it "the largest single serving of bad news that Colorado Springs and El Paso County have encountered in modern times" (Routon 2010). For example,

. Since 2000, real wages declined by 10 percent.

. The region's population increased by 90,000, yet the only new jobs belonged to 16,000 military service members, while 2,000 civilian jobs were lost.

. The county could boast methamphetamine use at a rate 40 to 50 percent higher than other large counties in Colorado.

. The area saw a 63 percent jump in the number of children living in poverty from 2000 to 2008: more than 9,000 kids in eight years.

. During 2009, El Paso County received the most child abuse and neglect referrals of any Colorado county, a number that had been trending upward for several years.

. The suicide rate for 15- to 19-year-olds was 80 percent higher than the national average, and the suicide rate among males 25 to 54 years old was higher than for the rest of Colorado. (The following year's Quality of Life Indicators [QLI] reported that the veterans' suicide rate was "alarmingly high" at 50.5 per 100,000, more than double the rate of the general population in El Paso County.)[18]

The report was alarming, but Ben found still more worrisome the way in which the military presence was nonetheless cast as a perpetual bright spot. In a letter to the editor he wrote:

Indeed, the report highlights the suffering local economy using red flags to high-light critical issues that need attention. But the report commends the military influence for providing "a stabilizing influence" as well as "business growth and employment growth for the region."

This may seem contradictory amid the dramatic increase in troops at Fort Carson. The military's multibillion-dollar economic impact figure, which the report cites, is all addition: it fails to subtract for school costs, lost property tax, lost sales tax from commerce on post, and jobs lost when companies move elsewhere. Soldiers living on post pay no property taxes but still use the roads, parks, police, and other city services.

Similarly, using estimates from the absence of sales tax at the commissary, PX, and other retail establishments on post, Colorado Springs loses about $1 million annually. Courts, police, mental health services, homeless shelters, and other social services face increased pressure without adequate compensation, which passes on the costs to the Colorado Springs community. Moreover, a fair amount of the $2 billion is lost when it goes straight to outside, private companies not based locally.

These costs should be taken into account as we consider the city's future. As Fort Carson prepares for a possible new combat aviation brigade—adding 2,000 more soldiers, their families, and 100-some roaring helicopters—we must rec-ognize the impact, both positives and negatives, this will have. It's time to start building a local economy that does not depend on a federally subsidized institu-tion. If we don't, to concur with [Independent Editor Ralph] Routon, "We also will have to pay for it."

— *Ben Felson*
*Colorado Springs*[19]

During this period, as Felson notes in his letter, Fort Carson doubled the number of active duty personnel stationed there, from 14,500 in 2005 to 26,000 in 2012, with dependent family members increasing from 19,500 to 42,000. One arena reflecting the demands this increase places on public ser-vices is in the consistently higher rate of domestic violence within military families.[20] In 2008, Colorado Springs' domestic violence shelter reported incidents at six times the rate for civilian families (PPACG 2010, Section VIII:10); among military families rates doubled, significantly, 90 days after combat brigades returned from deployments (PPACG 2010).[21]

Though civilian employees and contractors increased from 4,300 to 5,800 in the same period, Fort Carson's continued expansion did little to protect Colorado Springs from sharing in the distress of the national eco-nomic crisis of 2008 (DoD 2009). Because its cost of living and median household income have been stable during this period, Colorado Springs is now ranked as the second most affordable city by median household income (Felson 2011:22). Nevertheless, Colorado Springs has been slower to recover and has seen higher rates of unemployment than other cities in Colorado. In February 2011, the unemployment rate in Colorado Springs reached 10.5 percent, 1.6 percent higher than the national rate and 1.3 percent higher than the rate elsewhere in the state. Government plays a significant economic role in the Pikes Peak region. Although Fort Carson and the influx of federal dol-lars has grown steadily since 9/11, over the long term, dependence on mili-tary spending is comparably cyclic.[22] Through national recessions military cash infusions into the local economy have been heralded as the source of its relative health, habituating the Pikes Peak region to what Bourne called "the peacefulness of being at war." Meanwhile, as military conflicts recede along with federal dollars, business leaders wring hands about how to diver-sify, and puzzle over why Denver's "black hole" to the north draws high-tech business and young professionals away from Colorado Springs. Absent in these discussions is whether the military presence, and accompanying high rates of violence and related social pathologies, may repel diverse businesses from choosing the area. As then 4th Infantry Division commander General Perkins told a town hall gathering concerned with the growth of Fort Car-son, "we are not a benign neighbor."

## B Street: Strip Joints, Loan Sharks, and Tattoo Parlors

Army wife Theresa Thayer, who appreciates that Colorado Springs is not exclusively a military city, nonetheless acknowledges that "it becomes very *very* military-centric where most of town is B Street." B Street, the seediest of local commercial strips and that most closely linked to Fort Carson, borders the middle-class residential housing development of Stratmoor Hills at the southern end of Colorado Springs leading to the army post's north gate. While housesitting in the area one summer, Jean was awakened every morning at 6 a.m. by reveille blasted on loudspeakers at the post. Throughout the day she could hear the rumble of ordnance firing in the distance or the noises of construction. B Street's short section of strip malls is peppered with small businesses that cater to the young, mostly male, mostly single, military population with a steady supply of ready cash to spend: strip joints, massage and tattoo parlors, pawnshops, liquor stores, laundromats and dry cleaners, and predatory, high-interest payday loan services.[23] Between the strip malls and the entrance to Fort Carson, the road is lined on both sides with blocks of rundown one-story subsidized apartment buildings, many of them occupied by lower-ranked military personnel from Fort Carson.

In most military cities, these commercial strips are typical and prominent features of the landscape. Before the army closed Fitzsimons Army Medical Center in 1995, Denver had its own B Street, a large section of the eastern end of Colfax Avenue, State Highway 40, that tourists coming from the east traversed on their way into the city. In contrast, "although it would be difficult to find a soldier at Fort Carson who cannot find B Street," the area itself has become difficult to find, by design (Felson 2011:28). To improve public relations with local residents, Fort Carson's leaders moved the main gate for visitors from B Street to its present, highly visible location on the western side of the base, where a stone sign welcomes visitors to "The Best Hometown in the Army."

There is a visitors' center, a statue of Kit Carson, an array of retired Apache helicopters and tanks, a memorial to the Global War on Terror, and sandstone plaques arranged in a semicircle bearing an ever-lengthening list of the names of soldiers from Fort Carson killed in Iraq and Afghanistan.

Moving the gate left B Street as a side road little used by local residents not affiliated with Fort Carson. On the opposite side of B Street from the strip malls and housing projects is an infrequently used railroad spur, fenced and topped with barbed wire along the road, creating a barrier between Stratmoor Hills and B Street. On the Stratmoor Hills side of the rail spur sits Stratmoor Hills Elementary School, which serves students from the development and the housing projects across B Street. In 2010, the army proposed upgrading the railroad spur to support the base's expansion and increased tempo of deployments. Although blueprints included building an elevated pedestrian bridge to allow students at the elementary school to cross the tracks safely, the plan concerned Stratmoor Hills residents, who worried that increased rail traffic would contribute to the already considerable noise coming from Fort Carson, and that parked railcars would prove an attractive target for graffiti and vandalism (Felson 2011:29).

Stratmoor Hills residents may also be fearful of decreasing the physical barrier between them and B Street, which they view as dangerous, frequented by prostitutes and often armed drug dealers. Veteran Tim Vincent, who grew up in Colorado Springs, said that the housing projects off B Street, known as "the pinkies," were crack houses. "I got the shit kicked out of me every day. . . . When I was seven or eight years old I got to walk down the hallways and see people dead with needles hanging out of their arms . . . ." This was also his introduction to soldiers and the military. "It extends, the military culture, out there. You get soldiers, mostly E-1 to E-4,[24] living seven or eight to an apartment. So when I was 11 years old my favorite pastime was to go up the street and play dominos with the soldiers. My mom had no clue where I was; I was up there winning money, drinking beer; they're handing me cigarettes" (see also Felson 2011:28–9).

The growth of Fort Carson has also contributed to Colorado Springs's urban sprawl, particularly in the southern and eastern edges of the city, where housing developments and apartment complexes sprung up to house the 70 percent of soldiers who could not be accommodated on the post. Visitors to Colorado Springs's modest downtown are often shocked to learn that the area's population exceeds 660,000. The sprawling commercial arteries to the city's east, north, and south contribute to the decline of businesses in downtown Colorado Springs; filled with strip malls, big-box stores, and fast-food joints, these swaths are de facto downtowns for most residents, epitomizing car-dependent, anonymous America, and leading author Eric Schlosser to choose Colorado Springs as the site for his book *Fast Food Nation: The Dark Side of the All-American Meal* (2003).

But soldiers still venture downtown to frequent a two-block strip of bars and clubs known in the Vietnam era as "GI Corner." On any Friday or Saturday night, it might seem that little has changed, with soldiers arriving in groups, roving from bar to bar; prostitutes trolling for customers; and police waiting to stop brawls and maintain some semblance of public order. Captain Cliff Hannigan told us that most major bars downtown are periodically placed off limits by post command: "If I let myself, I'd have a heart attack sitting outside and watching soldier after soldier" stream into off-limits establishments on any given weekend night.

## Their Just Due

In 2008 a public defender, the district attorney, and a representative of the Colorado Department of Human Services met to create a special court to handle criminal cases involving veterans, based on the principles of therapeutic justice, which began hearing cases in December 2009 (Warner 2010). One of the first veterans to participate in the Veterans Trauma Court (VTC) was Nic Gray. In 2006 Gray deployed to Iraq, where his unit provided security for convoys and construction crews building outposts, going to areas so dangerous that "the security detail had a security detail." Yet, typical of many soldiers who have seen heavy combat, Gray said of his tour, " . . . people look at me and say, 'No, you were in the shit,' and I say, 'No, I had it pretty easy, they had it way worse.'" In 2007, Gray returned to the United States and was honorably discharged from the army. He moved to Colorado Springs, which he knew to be a military-friendly city, with the intention of achieving his lifelong goal of creating a Fortune 100 company. He was making good progress, had quit smoking, and was training for triathlons. Then, at 10 p.m. on October 21, 2009, Gray stood in his yard, shouting something incomprehensible. He rammed his elbow against the window of a neighbor's car and threw something at it, then scaled a chainlink fence into neighbor Edward Lynch's yard and, while, Lynch called 911, broke down Lynch's front door, "clearing the house" as he'd done in Iraq.

Once inside Lynch's house, "all aggression seemed drained from his demeanor," and he did not resist arrest when the police arrived. Gray doesn't remember the incident and awoke in jail facing two felony charges and a misdemeanor. He says the flashback-like incident in which he appeared to be "clearing" the house "just happened out of the blue." "[T]he only thing that really makes sense to me as to why it happened is that I was conversing with a friend about our experiences over there. And that's the last thing I really remember." Given Gray's history of combat duty in Iraq and PTSD, his case was transferred to the VTC. In Gray's first court appearance, Edward Lynch and his wife Caroline confronted him, saying "we don't want a pound of flesh from Mr. Gray," but they also emphasized that he had "scared the hell out of us" and asked the court for a no-contact order. Gray received a two-year deferred sentence dependent upon 30 hours of community service, attending a VA treatment program, paying to replace the Lynches' door, and writing them a letter of apology. If he completes his deferred sentence, he can have his court record sealed.[25]

The VTC is an institutional innovation that responds to unprecedented and unforeseen challenges returning veterans create for Colorado Springs's community and sense of place. Because they recognize how war has challenged struggling veterans, courts like these are understandably showcased by military communities. At the same time, we argue, even such measures provide too little, too late for many of the most damaged veterans. Moreover, this high-profile kind of support is disturbingly unrepresentative of the treatment a far greater proportion of the most vulnerable veterans receive. Because they serve a relatively small number of veterans, and not always those who are most dangerous, they do not necessarily enhance the community's human security.

To be eligible for the VTC, a defendant must be a soldier or veteran facing criminal charges who also has deployment-related PTSD or TBI and who has not received a dishonorable discharge. They must agree to plead guilty to the charges against them, and their crime cannot involve serious injury, assault with a deadly weapon, or threatening a child. Participants' crimes include, among others, possession of drugs, property crimes to obtain drugs, drunk driving, assault, domestic violence, and giving false information to a pawnbroker. The court focuses on providing participants with resources to take care of themselves, getting them into appropriate treatment, and mandating that they make restitution for their crimes.

The VTC meets at 3 p.m. every Thursday afternoon in the El Paso County courthouse downtown. When we arrived outside the courtroom at 2:30, men and a few women sat in the half-dozen chairs or leaned against the walls in the hall outside the designated courtroom. One young man, dressed in jeans and a t-shirt, his hair in a military cut and his arms heavily tattooed, conferred quietly with a peer mentor (a veteran employed by AspenPointe, a local nonprofit social services agency that provides support to participants in the VTC). A young woman, also in jeans and a t-shirt, sat across a table from the VTC's evaluator, filling out a form. Shortly before the session began the district attorney and public defender, readily identified by their suits and boxes of files, led participants into the courtroom.

Between the judge's bench, raised several feet above the main floor on a wide platform and a podium that faces the bench, stood an easel with a pad of paper listing 10 names under the heading "Strong Performers." Just after 3 p.m., the judge, dressed in a suit and tie, entered the courtroom, sat down, and immediately began shuffling through a stack of file folders. He opened the session by noting the long list of strong performers and reminding participants ordered to appear on that day's docket that they were free to go out into the hall to meet with their parole officer or the peer mentor. Other than the judge's reminder and the armed bailiff standing in the corner, there were few other signs that participants were only "free" to come and go at the will of the court.

The judge then called "Mr. Quincy" to the podium as he looked up from the file on his desk. "Well, I was real glad to see you were one that was identified as a solid performer. You get a 'HUA' [hooah].'" Everyone in the court-room applauded. "So, give me a sit rep [situation report]. What's happened since I last saw you?"

"Well, I went to a memorial for my grandmother in Montana. Saw the whole family. My mom and 13 brothers and sisters. First time in forever everyone was together," Quincy reported.

The judge, referring to the parole officer, said, "Mr. Donaldson was telling me that you've really made quick progress and you've gotten on things right away. . . . " They discussed moving Quincy to the final phase before graduating from the program. The judge commended him for "really fast-tracking it," and invited him to bring a letter to the next session that explains why he thinks he is ready to be promoted.

In the four sessions we observed, the judge reviewed on average 22 cases. Only three participants were handcuffed and taken into custody, and one was brought into the courtroom wearing an orange jumpsuit, handcuffed, and accompanied by an armed guard. Though the judge maintains a degree of formality in the courtroom, addressing participants as "Mr. Jones" or "Ms. Smith," he also makes marked efforts to connect with participants on a more personal level. He asks them about their family members and how school or work is going and listens to their responses without interrupting them. He might ask them about their occupational specialty in the military, where and when they served overseas, and share his own military background. While one of the judges we interviewed doesn't believe it is essential to be a veteran to serve in the court, he does think his having served helps him appreciate what veterans have experienced and create a bond of trust with them.

These stories highlight differences between the VTC and conventional criminal courts, which are based on an adversarial model in which judges are relatively passive while their lawyers battle for their clients' interests (Schroeder 2010). Defendants may plead in a variety of ways, including "no contest" or *nolo contendere*, which means that the defendant may "accept the consequences of a conviction without going to trial and without admitting guilt" (Wexler 1993). In contrast, the VTC is based on therapeutic and restorative models of justice that arose during the 1970s and 1980s as part of an emerging "therapeutic sensibility" in American culture (Nolan 2003:1551). Therapeutic sensibility assumes that untreated mental illness or trauma underlies many problematic behaviors such as substance use, domestic violence, and some victimless crimes. It follows that these crimes are best approached therapeutically through drug and alcohol treatment, anger management, and counseling. This shift led to the establishment of "problem-solving courts" for domestic violence, substance abuse, and persons caught driving under the influence (DUI), among others. By attempting to "get at the root of the individual and social problems motivating criminal behavior" (Mirchandani 2008:854), reformers hoped to reduce recidivism and increase defendants' abilities to function in society. One of the judges we spoke with explained that while sometimes being arrested helps a veteran recognize that they need treatment, "iron bar therapy" (putting them in jail) is rarely effective. Helping them find work and stable housing, resolve domestic conflicts, or receive treatment for PTSD or TBI can be.

Critics of therapeutic justice, like sociologist James Nolan, emphasize its unintended consequences.[26] Nolan has strongly criticized drug courts, the first problem-solving courts and one of the models for veterans' courts. Defendants in drug courts must have substance use *disorders*; veterans in the VTC must have trauma-related *illness*. As a result, authority for treatment shifts from legal personnel—judges, attorneys, and parole officers—to counselors and psychologists, and the effectiveness of treatment is judged by sentiment or feeling rather than rational judgment of punishment fitting the severity of the crime (Mirchandani 2008:865). Nolan adds that court-mandated therapeutic regimes are often more punitive and coercive. Participants in the VTC not only must attend therapy sessions, they are often required to submit to routine urinalysis screening for drugs and alcohol, meet more frequently with their parole officers and peer mentors, and perform community service, all of which may take longer than a jail sentence. One of the judges said that some defendants who qualify for the VTC choose regular courts for this very reason: they "do their time and are finished." This is especially true for misdemeanors.

The domestic violence community objects to the VTC's expunging of domestic violence felonies because doing so might not be a sufficient deterrent to repeat offenses or offer sufficient protection to victims. The judge countered that if domestic violence offenders go through the VTC, at least they get treatment and court supervision. However, many choose to stay in regular courts because 85 percent of domestic violence victims fail to show up in court to press charges, and the case never goes to trial.

In contrast to these critiques, scholars Rekha Mirchandi (2008) and Katie Wright (2008) argue that it is important to assess the intended and often positive consequences of problem-solving courts. Although by virtue of having an illness an offender is absolved of responsibility for their underlying condition, they are not absolved from responsibility for making restitutions and for complying with treatment to manage it. As Nic Gray explained, the VTC takes into account that these "crimes would not have been committed if they [offenders] had not served in a combat zone fighting for your country." But the crimes do have consequences. "So there are still repercussions that come from the actions taken, but the main focus is on helping that individual and finding out why it happened and prevent it from ever happening again."

Though they fall within the category of problem-solving courts, veterans' courts are more like juvenile courts that define their participants by their status. "You have to prove your veteran status or your active-duty status," explained peer mentor Martin Nunez, adding that participants must also have formal documentation of trauma-related PTSD (depression would come under the PTSD diagnosis) or TBI. But there is some leeway; for example, the diagnosis does not have to be in place prior to being accepted into the program. "I'm working with one [veteran] right now who was administratively discharged [from the military] prior to getting his psych evaluation; it happens way more often than it should. He got a psych evaluation today, a pro bono psych evaluation from a doctor I've been working with who is also very committed to veteran's causes." Nunez believes that "anybody that has been deployed more than one time has PTSD whether or not they have sought treatment or they believe they do." Another peer mentor, Stan Miller, said, "I don't like to call it special considerations; that might be what it is, but I don't see how anyone could ever say that these veterans don't deserve to be in a special court considering that PTSD and TBI, those are the signature injuries of these wars that are going on." Miller also sees the VTC as a "win-win situation" because veterans get the help they need, which they wouldn't get in jail, and society benefits because "these same people are gonna be in our neighborhood someday living there."

One of the prosecuting attorneys, who has never served in the military, commented, "I am sure them putting themselves in harm's way makes them a lot different from most people. In that regard I think yes, the sacrifices that soldiers make for the United States should entitle them to something more than just the run-of-the-mill prosecution." For this attorney, like the judge, one of the key benefits of the VTC is its pragmatic aspect, which enables the court to connect veterans with services.

> So that's the justification under basic law. . . . Prosecutors are obligated to seek similar sentences for similar crimes in similarly situated defendants. . . . So that's how we justify treating soldiers different, is we give them a more favorable disposition up front, but we ask more in the long run than we would of anybody else . . . because they have put themselves in harm's way, because the services are more available and they are entitled to services.

Persuasive though such reasoning is, this high-profile, showcased treatment remains far from representative or typical of the support the most troubled—and therefore potentially most dangerous—veterans receive.

Many more are ejected from the service and thrust upon their communities without even veterans' medical benefits. When leaving military service, a soldier receives one of five types of discharge: honorable, general, other-than-honorable, bad conduct, and dishonorable. Bad conduct and dishonorable discharges can only be given following a court martial. Soldiers may appeal their discharge status, but the process is lengthy and rarely successful. Misconduct is the most common reason for an other-than-honorable discharge, which precludes soldiers from receiving military and VA benefits. An investigative report by *The Gazette* in Colorado Springs documents the dramatic rise (67 percent) in discharges for misconduct in 2012 at the eight Army posts where most combat units are stationed. "And soldiers with the most combat exposure are the hardest hit" (Philipps 2013). These are the very soldiers most likely to have PTSD or TBI, and many of the charges of misconduct include behaviors related to PTSD and TBI: missing appointments, reporting late for work, or losing their temper. Whereas at the height of the conflicts in Iraq and Afghanistan, minor misconduct would have been treated within a unit or ignored, as the wars wind down, military budgets are cut, and the army downsizes, it increasingly suffices as cause for discharge. In addition to the pressure to discharge soldiers quickly, with multiple deployments troops are often actively fighting while wounded from previous deployments. So commanders are forced to decide which misconduct results from "bad behavior" and which results from invisible wounds. For officers who suspect that PTSD is faked malingering, discussed in chapter 1, the decision to treat problem behavior as misconduct may be less difficult. As *Gazette* reporter Dave Philipps notes, in many ways these soldiers have less legal protection than civilians (Philipps 2013).

Despite the deserved accolades of the VTC, the numbers of soldiers receiving what may be considered the most sympathetic and tailored treatment is small. In 2013, the Pikes Peak Area Council of Governments reported, "To date, more than 100 veterans have participated in the program; 35 have graduated; 5 have transferred to courts in other states; 12 have failed to complete the program; and 50 veterans are currently enrolled." By contrast, more than 76,000 soldiers have been kicked out of the army since 2006. In one increasingly common tactic, the civilian criminal system is enjoined in coercing soldiers to sign agreements to no benefits. To "Chapter 10" a soldier out of the army without a protracted process, he must be declared a violent threat (often for comparatively minor misconduct and often without a violent history), and be taken into custody and placed in the county jail. While behind bars, he is offered the option of signing a Chapter 10 (other-than-honorable discharge, in lieu of court martial) agreement, foregoing benefits to avoid a court martial and jail time. Most sign, assured they can try to contest the move, though in reality they are unlikely to succeed. This allows both the army and the VA to wash their hands of them; those who pose actual threats of violence or other dangers are unleashed upon communities.

As Alair MacLean and Glen Elder conclude based on a review of research on military service and the life course, "Across all eras, combat veterans have had worse health and were more likely to get divorced than noncombat veterans and nonveterans. In addition, preliminary findings suggest that combat veterans had lower socioeconomic attainment" (MacLean and Elder 2007:188). Even in the model VTC courtroom, we felt an air of heaviness as we watched veterans struggle against pain, frustration, and near futility. Each of the VTC program participants searched for a path out of their own particular labyrinth. They went from having had full-time (military) jobs with benefits and the camaraderie of military service to being caught in a relentless spiral of court hearings, indebtedness, unemployment, and often homelessness.

### Afternote: Home/Land/Security

In the bristling hot, drought-parched summers of 2012 and 2013, two fires erupted on the outskirts of Colorado Springs; tens of thousands were evacuated, and in all a shocking 842 homes were lost. Though numerous others fires burned across the American west simultaneously, these threatened a major urban area to unique degree, and quickly gained center stage in the media. References to the "firefight" and the importance of "mission" and "chain of command" filled the airwaves, but in this moment, the stakes in home, land, and security concerns were anything but distant campaigns, but murkily connected to the defense of community interests.

The fires afford an interesting comparison with the post-9/11 wars, raising critical questions about prioritization and resource allocation. As the post-fire headline "Does Colorado Springs have Post Traumatic Stress Syndrome?"[27] indicated, both war and a destructive wildfire are potentially traumatizing threats. From a holistic, human security standpoint, we might ask: what kind of monumental labor force and investment would it take to responsibly caretake Western forests damaged by drought, pine-beetle kill, climate change, and fire suppression? Even this colossal undertaking would likely constitute just a fraction of the human and other resources invested in managing terror through the wars in Iraq and Afghanistan. For a community like Colorado Springs, which would offer greater return on our investment, in terms of human security?

Chapter 9

# "Clueless Civilians" and Others

*The word "clue" derives from "clew," meaning a ball of thread or yarn. It had come to mean "that which points the way" because of the Greek myth in which Theseus uses a ball of yarn, given to him by Ariadne, to find his way out of the Minotaur's labyrinth.*

—Kate Summerscale, *The Suspicions of Mr. Whicher*

The man in the tailored suit was already stalking determinedly toward the exit. One of the organizers brought up the lights while another, with an eye to the fleeing man, hurriedly addressed the crowd in the small theater, "Can we . . . ? Well, I'd just like to hear what brought people here tonight." The man stopped by the door and turned abruptly to face the seated crowd, pausing to make sure he had the floor. "I just wanted to see who would show up for this, in a country where we think it's alright for one half of 1 percent to fight our wars, while everybody else goes to the mall."

We had just finished a screening of the film *The Dry Land*, about a soldier returning from combat theater to his hometown and struggling with PTSD. It was the first event in a three-day series at Colorado College around Veterans Day in 2011. The modest numbers appeared to confirm the man-in-the-suit's expectations, and his frustration about public disengagement with the effects of the wars in Iraq and Afghanistan. His name turned out to be Lionel, and for him the question was deeply personal. Taking care of his Afghanistan-veteran son who had severe PTSD and a TBI, and experiencing his son's struggles through the filter of his own tour in Vietnam 40 years before, aggravated his still-festering wounds at feeling deplored and rejected by his countrymen upon returning.

Veterans (including active-duty service members who have deployed), and frontline combatants in particular, tell us that their experiences "seeing and doing things no one should have to" create real difference. They come back "different," as "strangers" who "will never be the same," and parts of them may not come back. This difference, many veterans maintain, is tied to ideological commitments to service, discipline, and sacrifice, and remains beyond the grasp of noncombatants and civilians. While experiences such as birth, accidents, and depression may be singular and traumatic, their sufferers do not assert their *incomparability, incommensurability,* or their *incomprehensibility* at anywhere near the levels that veterans do. Civilians, careful to show veterans respect, tend not to challenge such assertions and often collaborate in their reinforcement.

This chapter probes military representations and attitudes about civilians and "civvie" culture. We admittedly include some of the more critical, biting (often in the name of wit), and even angry elements of this discourse. Far from suggesting that outrightly contemptuous military attitudes towards civilians are pervasive or necessarily representative, we claim their significance comes in revealing the boundaries—albeit from the extremes—of deepening military-civilian cultural gaps under the post-9/11 all-volunteer, professionalized, and increasingly "standing" force. Whereas in chapter 1 ("PTSD=Pulling the Stigma Down") we explored how soldiers with PTSD suffer stigmatization, both within army units and out in civilian life, here we invert the lens, and consider ways in which military communities may stigmatize civilian-ness.[1] If "America is the land of the free *because* of the brave," as bumper stickers and banners around Colorado Springs proclaim, then for many military folks civilians become the un-brave, lazy couch potatoes, the feminized in need of protection. Military community members (for this often includes family members not themselves officially serving) may use their views about "the rest of America" to define themselves, and military culture (collective characteristics and values), by contrast. This othering of civilians, which can include outright stigmatization, is a vehicle through which service members and veterans voice an often despairing critique about the broader American society and culture.

Voices in this chapter include those of veterans remembering war, of soldiers transitioning back to civilian life, and of those who mediate between veterans and civilians. We ask what military personnel think civilians need to know and understand about their life and culture. The chapter concludes by considering an array of civilians who contradict the clueless stereotype, who become knowledgeable or intimate with the experiences of those who have gone to war. They, we argue, have each found ways of navigating the peripheries of war's labyrinth; many offer golden threads to bring the endangered—individuals, communities, nations—out, relatively intact.

## Comparisons, Comparisons

"She compared going into combat to putting on a show." Vietnam veteran Red Coughlin was having a beer with us one evening, a few days after one of the potluck gatherings for veterans and others involved with reintegration issues.

We remembered quite clearly the moment to which Red referred. Some 20 of us had filled our plates and sat down in the crowded living room of the music therapist who was hosting the potluck. We went around introducing ourselves, saying something about our involvement in the topic. Della Meyers, a performer who had been coming down from the Denver area to create short plays with veterans and students from military families at an elementary school on-post at Fort Carson, shared her experiences with us.

"One of the things we try to do is engage vets in their communities, and maybe show them that civilian life might offer other kinds of challenges, that something like putting on a show can have its own kind of stress," Della had reflected. The comment struck chords with both of us at the time, in a positive sense: she seemed to be inviting veterans to loosen their grip on the incomprehensibility, incomparability, and incommensurability of deployment by introducing a loose comparison to an intense experience in civilian life. She seemed to be asserting that life goes on, that our growth need not be unidirectional, but can flourish in many directions. The therapeutic and reintegrative potential of this invitation was obvious: how many times had we heard Iraq and Afghan veterans allude to their perceptions and fears about the boring, unchallenging, and trivial aspects of civilian life? Veterans and community members alike raise the issue of "adrenaline addiction" when discussing reintegration, especially in reference to outdoor recreation, motorcycle and car racing, and other vigorous, high-risk activities that expressly feed the adrenaline itch. Della made the point that worthy, stressful-but-growth-inducing challenges might exist beyond the battlefield. It was a theme we hoped to hear more about in community efforts to bring warriors back from war, as well as in creating varied forms of "intensity" which might also offer children alternatives to seeing military careers in their own futures as the only story worth writing.

In this light, it was distressing that our perceptive friend Red had found her comparison trivializing and offensive. She had sought to place art-making at home in a position, if not on a par with, then at least loosely comparable with, engaging in battle.

During the year Red spent in Vietnam, working as a medic, he experienced what he called in a piece aired on NPR "slices of brutality that I fear to this day will remain the eternal standard against which I will compare all other moments in my life." He spoke of losing his friend Trina, a nurse, in a "death so particularly pointless, so particularly cruel" that it caused his "light to go out," or what he also referred to as his "spiritual capitulation."

Red believed that the liberal arts education he received after the war "saved his life"; he reconciled his own survivor's guilt by making his juxtaposition of the horrors of combat and pleasant everyday experiences into a sacrament. He explained how he feels

> . . . blessed to be alive on this fine day, on this fine earth. Through letting go of anger and grief, I have seen that we can short-circuit the remorse of surviving our wars by purposefully sharing certain moments of our lives with the memory and spirit of those people we lost. As if they were still among us, I dial up each of my friends from time to time; this need to remember them is a good thing, and it doesn't happen on just Memorial Day. It usually comes upon me when I least expect it, but whenever it comes I surrender, right then and right there. And I crank up my senses for just one minute, for just one of them at a time. I will share certain moments or do certain things for them, and for me, together, and in those brief moments life is bigger, and louder, and so full of flavor. I've taken extra-long hot showers for them. I've gone to bed early for them. I've had hotdogs at hockey games, and an unbroken string of Christmas mornings with my beloved wife and my children, just for them. But I know I'll never stop grieving for my friends and my comrades, because they've earned to be grieved over forever.

Ultimately, Red's comparisons may have much in common with Della's: both find salve for war's emotional wounds through community building and connecting past to present, wartime to peacetime, exceptional—be it battle or performance—to mundane. So, it wasn't quite that combat experiences were strictly incomparable to others; rather, it mattered who was doing the comparing, and for what ends.

It is not difficult to find other assertions of the incomparability, incommensurability, and incomprehensibility of combat.[2] Just one example comes from Colorado Springs talk-show host Randy Roberts, who, in response to an indignant caller's comments on the embarrassing video of Marines urinating on three dead, allegedly Taliban Afghanis, said, "Well, I really hope we never discover the names of those Marines. I think they should be left alone: who are we to judge? Most people have *no idea* what these guys go through." Do not attempt evaluation or interpretation, he seems to say. You simply cannot understand. So common are admon-ishments warding civilians away from judgment that they may complicate civilians' efforts to actively engage the challenges of being at war.

At numerous events we attended for veterans, leaders offered strictures against comparisons. "Don't compare your story to anyone else's; it's only yours," one veterans' story-telling circle began. So frequently did we hear diverse versions of this advice that it soon became clear that rather than a rule that was followed, it served to try to mitigate comparativism that was rampant, and even potentially dangerous.

In fact, comparativism plays several distinctive roles in dynamics throughout military communities. As a near-total institution, the military is profoundly shaped by rank, and also by who is "squared away," deployable and/or dependable (and more about fit versus flabby in the next section), versus who is not. The most familiar, and tragic, comparisons between veterans are those that produce "survivor's guilt" and related struggles. When one has lost friends in battle but returned home alive and relatively whole oneself, or when one has killed and is plagued by the memory, it becomes difficult to feel deserving; the comparison can leach life from the present (Red's sanctification of the rituals of daily life offer one approach to reconciling that). Compared with ultimate sacrifices, one may feel one has given too little, and somehow feel insufficient and invalidated.

But comparisons between frontline soldiers, who "go on patrol," and "fobbits," those who remain "behind the wire" on FOBs, or forward operating bases,[3] also serve to lessen the authenticity or significance of the experiences of the majority. Yet another divide opens between never-deployed service members and those who have served in combat theater; hence, the public mystification about the one-third of soldier suicides that can be found within the ranks of those who never deployed.

JJ Thomas, the army wife we met in chapters 5 and 6 who excelled at the compartmentalization for coping with deployments, offers perspective on how comparisons may operate across deploying versus nondeploy-ing parents in a household. She reminds herself, "it's not about me. That's just how I feel. I'm fine up here. You know, I'm safe; nobody's shooting at me." Just as soldiers dedicate themselves to one another and ideally, something greater, spouses and family members participate by "bucking up," providing support, and resisting being overly self-involved. Lives become less "about me"; family members typically share with service members a strong collectivist mentality (tied to national identity, though in highly varied ways across the political spectrum)[4] often absent in the lives of civilians from nonmilitary families.

These sets of comparisons show how the enforced incomparability, incommensurability, and incomprehensibility so many veterans assert about the effects of combat do not happen in a vacuum. As communities we reproduce and reinforce the exceptionalism around combat across a graduated landscape of interactions: combat experience has no comparison, and if one has not been there, one simply cannot "get it." Paradoxically, soldiers with invisible wounds can use exceptionalism to assert simultaneous status as heroes and victims, often effectively checkmating civilians into limited positions as ignorant and unworthy.

## Fit and Focused versus Flabby and Frivolous

Living in Colorado Springs while working on this project, many of us found when we were trying to take breaks from research, we were inevitably presented with intimate fieldwork opportunities. Interns Hana and Joey went to a Couchsurfing dinner/mixer at a Thai restaurant where all the men happened to be military, for example, and an intense discussion about their deployments stretched late into the night. Or Jean, sitting in a local café having her morning coffee and overhearing the couple that sat down next to her, the man in uniform, planning their move to a new post when he returned from Afghanistan. Or there was the day Sarah realized all those people in street clothes hanging out in the lobby of her gym, many of whom were obviously military, were from the local psychiatric facility, which had a new program to use the gym as a place folks could get practice being in public.

A high school reunion was similar, when one of our former classmates had become a Marine colonel who was giving a session on "military-civilian relations." Eric Lansbury, crisp in his formal uniform for the Saturday morning session, began by raising the "current debate" about whether the all-volunteer force (AVF) was deepening a military-civilian cultural divide. Soon he was offering examples of mutual contempt between service members and civilians. "I am a US Marine, so if I am standing in the airport in uniform and I am 20 pounds overweight and sloppy, I am representing the country and it's a disgrace," he told the group. Upholding these ideals meant that "I looked at my civilian community with a degree of contempt," he admitted, especially in his early years in the Corps, before he married and had children. He found this contempt matched by civilians, particularly through pernicious stereotypes about those who enlist; many get reactions like "What, you couldn't find a real job?" making them feel undervalued and misunderstood.

Fatness, flabbiness, and lack of discipline together serve as a key countersymbol, signifying all that military members disparage and strive to not be. Examples can be found nearly anywhere: within the ranks, across military relationships, and especially in representations of civilians versus military members and their communities.

As we saw in chapter 6, fat could also serve as a symbol dividing service members from their spouses and other civilian family members. Another Corporal Lance cartoon is especially telling on this point; the "Dependapotamus's" flabbiness here simultaneously representing civilian wives' slothfulness, hyperdependency, and sense of entitlement to the fruits of service member labor (Figure 13).

**FIGURE 13.** Terminal Lance #56 (copyright Maximillian Uriarte 2010–2013).

No doubt it is to counteract such depictions that one essay giving advice to those entering into relationships with service members includes the following recommendation, as part of learning what "I Will Never Leave A Fallen Comrade" really means to a military team: "Learn how bad a 'charlie foxtrot' really is. Push your own physical limits by getting in phenomenal physical condition, so that you can appreciate the intensity and hard work that goes into the level of fitness required by the military."[5] For spouses and family members, adopting near-military levels of conditioning may count as acts of loyalty and solidarity; not to do so may engender scorn or shame, and even feelings of betrayal.

In the late 1990s, Pentagon correspondent Tom Ricks expressed concern about an all-volunteer military that "saw civilians as privileged and flabby" and "increasingly considered itself a breed apart, and held the public it served in contempt" (Astore 2011). Startled by how alienated a platoon of Marines he had followed through boot camp were from their old lives, he noted how they experienced "private loathing for public America," and were "repulsed by the physical unfitness of civilians, by the uncouth behavior they witnessed, and by what they saw as a pervasive selfishness and consumerism" (Ricks 1996:1), again tying fat with overconsumption-as-purchasing, as father Lionel's derisive comment regarding "going to the mall" indicates.

A 16 year-old who "cant wait to join the ARMY" asks an online, national guard forum, "Is it me, or after joining the military civilian life seems extremely annoying??" He continues, "Civilians are whinny annoying and flabby. And i look forward to putting my self in the status of the worlds best warriors and being something 1 in a 1000 would have the guts to be [sic].

GO ARMY AND HOOAH."[6] Here we have a civilian already repelled by his own civilian-ness and anxious to shed it, offering a window into the social reproduction of soldiering.

Others invoke fit-versus-fat as symbolically demarcating military and civilian boundaries. "The military creates a world in which people can be fit and focused on its mission, and then claims the fact that they are fit and focused as the basis of its moral superiority," writes Bruce Fleming in *Bridging the Military-Civilian Divide* (2010). He notes that this world depends on the availability of military spouses, overwhelmingly wives, to support the required regimens, and continues:

> *Of course, the average man or woman in the military is hard, and the average civilian is soft. . . . [I]t's understandable that a trip to the local mall is itself painful for many people in the military. They see malls as temples of consumption patronized by overweight people who recover from a grueling morning of shopping by scarfing down a Cinnabon or two. The official line is that the military exists to defend civilians. But why defend flabby, morally lazy consumers like these? The military, not unsurprisingly, concludes that it exists for itself—a view disseminated internally, if not to the outside. It makes those in the military seek out others in the military to befriend and connect with ex-military people in the world at large.* (2010:84)

Fleming calls for military recognition that it is not apart from the people it "outrightly despises," but instead is "drawn from it," again seeking to avert a cultural divergence he views as dangerous. Finally, he entreats fellow veterans to treat civilians sympathetically. After all, "[o]f course the military looks better. Of course it gets to do adult things that people who have to take care of babies can only dream of . . . " (Fleming 2010:88–9). Checking their sense of moral superiority over the citizens who pay for their on-the-clock physical training is the least they can offer in return for getting such adult- (versus "baby") oriented prerogatives.

### (Re)learning Civilian "Culture"

> *We are completely institutionalized. I hate that word, but it's true. We don't know how to make small talk or dress for a job interview—soldiers need a fashion show. We think sergeant is a first name! We've been told what to wear, what to do, what to think, every day for years. We need help coming back in.*

The speaker was a slender, pale soldier, one of six from the Warrior Transition Unit (WTU)[7] brought to give brief testimonials about their assignment to the new unit designed to help wounded soldiers prepare to process out of the army. He spoke to some 200 people; perhaps one in five wore the same green, camouflage-patterned ACUs (Army Combat Uniforms) of active-duty soldiers, from generals through privates.

The stories of the other soldiers from the WTU who spoke that morning traversed the by now all-too-familiar topics: addiction, relationship loss, interpersonal violence, depression and isolation, and suicidal thoughts. This was the first time we could remember, though, soldiers appealing to civilians for help becoming fluent in civilian life. Though all service members originate from "civilian" settings to some degree (though far less for those from military families, especially those who lived on installations or attended all-military schools), because of the young ages of those in the process of separating from the army (where the average age is 29 years[8]), many if not most would have in effect spent no time as adult civilians, and many had sustained contact with few civilian friends. We were struck by the candid vulnerability, and the recognition of civilian worlds as alien and challenging, conveyed in some of the soldiers' words that morning. Others expressed fear and despair at prospects of having to separate from the army. "I was so afraid the army was going to throw me away," one soldier said, and that he used this fear to focus on his recovery, and now has made enough progress that he might be able to stay in. Yet another WTU soldier intimated, "I hope that once I get out of the army it's not the end of the world—that there'll be a life after the army."

Hearing voices among this most vulnerable group of soldiers insist that military-civilian education needed to work in both directions was almost novel. Far more frequently, we would observe civilians being schooled in military ways. When the morning's presentations concluded and broke for lunch, we found ourselves chatting with two officers, the commander of the WTU and a psychiatric nurse, a captain, who had been integral to its creation. We asked about the soldier who was so afraid the "army was going to throw him away," and whether they thought that reintegration challenges were further complicated, in addition to the foreignness and newness of civilian culture mentioned by the soldier, by stigma attached to civilians as clueless, undisciplined couch potatoes with boring, meaningless lives.

The nurse, Captain Dawn Weaver (then retired, but still working at Fort Carson), chuckled and said "that's really dicey." Tellingly, she immediately inverted our question, reporting that she had given some dozen trainings for civilians on military culture, which she called "Military 101." She had distilled key nuggets into a list posted on the Internet.

## Ten Things You Should Know to Help
## Bring the OIF/OEF Veteran All the Way Home

By Dawn Weaver, RN, MS (Former Captain in the US Army Nurse Corps)

10. OIF stands for Operation Iraqi Freedom, also known as the Iraq War, and it began on March 20th, 2003. OEF stands for Operation Enduring Freedom and is a multinational military operation aimed at dismantling terrorist groups, mostly in Afghanistan. It officially commenced on Oct. 7, 2001, in response to the September 11th terrorist attacks;

9. Returning Service Members do not think of themselves as heroes, no matter how extraordinary their skills, courage, or actions may be. Their heroes are the ones still over there or coming home in flag-draped boxes;

8. Service Members are as varied in their political beliefs as everyone else in America. Some are adamantly against the war, others staunchly support it, and everyone else falls somewhere in between. Assuming that everyone who joins the military is a card-carrying right-winger will only make you look stupid;

7. No matter what his or her opinions about the war are, every Service Member of every branch of the military takes a solemn oath to support and follow our Commander In Chief, the President of the United States, and therefore cannot say anything derogatory about him;

6. No one can describe how hot it was while deployed in a war zone, so don't ask a returning Vet about the heat. Instead, imagine yourself putting on every piece of winter gear you own, in multiple layers, putting a metal bowl over your head, turning your oven on to 120 degrees, climbing inside, and living there for 6 months;

5. Worse still is asking any Veteran, "Did you kill anyone?" It is an unanswerable question. Perhaps she did and wished she hadn't. Perhaps he didn't and wished he had. Perhaps she did, but it wasn't fast enough to prevent a comrade's death. Perhaps it was accidental or perhaps it was so many instances of killing, he lost count. War requires things of us and taps into parts of us that are never otherwise touched—things most people need to work through or want to forget. US military personnel do not take killing lightly, and anyone who has not been there simply cannot discuss it with those who have, much less pass judgment. Listen quietly if they choose to talk about it, but otherwise, leave it alone:

4. OIF/OEF Veterans often want to go back to the war zone. Sometimes it's because they feel called to go in to finish the mission or support their buddies, sometimes it's because they feel they can no longer fit in to American society and its frivolous interests and fads. But regardless of reason, it is fairly common, so if they tell you they're planning on redeploying, please don't look at them as if they are insane;

3. They are exhausted when they get home—physically, psychologically, emotionally, and spiritually exhausted. They often do not have the energy or focus to talk for long periods of time. It will take some time for them to adjust, so follow their lead;

2. There is nothing black-and-white about what has happened to them. Almost always, there are good things that come from a deployment experience. Likewise, there are some pretty difficult things that they face once they are back home. Do not make any assumptions about their experiences:

And the # 1 thing you should know about OIF/OEF Veterans is . . .
1. They are not the same people they were before they deployed. But do not
assume that is a bad thing. The Service Member may come home more confident,
with better problem-solving skills. He may return with a deeper sense of gratitude
for the comforts that he used to take for granted or she may have found a greater
sense of purpose and direction than she ever had before. Yes, there may be many
unseen wounds of the soul and spirit. But there are tremendous resources to
help heal those wounds, both for the Service Member and the Service Member's
family, and an ever-growing number of people who truly care and want to help.
If every American understood these 10 important facts about our returning Veterans, life would be a lot easier for them. So pass it on.[9]

This tract pinpoints specific areas of difficulty in veteran-civilian relations,
both in the actual forms they take, and in the remedies the list proffers. Most
prominent is the conviction that civilians' lack of understanding of combat
experiences and military life makes the process of coming "all the way home"
more difficult. Civilians are taken to task for ignorance: for not knowing the
official name of the wars being fought in their names, for not understanding that warzones are unspeakably hot, or for stereotyping the military as
right-wingers. Civilians should bear in mind their frivolity before expecting
combat veterans not to want to return to theater, not ask about killing, and
not discuss politics bearing in mind that veterans are barred from doing so.

A more humorous, if still more revealing in its bellicosity, instruction
to civilians circulated widely on the Internet titled "Kick Ass Rules for the
Non-Military" is addressed to civilians "excited to join the military" but who
can't, and offers ways they can still "lend a hand." Whether one sees "adults
talking during the playing of the National Anthem," singing the anthem in
Spanish, disrespecting veterans, not standing for the American flag, or burning the flag in protest, the proscription is the same: **"kick their ass"** (bold in
original). Wearing military garb or using military "terms of endearment" (for
example, "grunt" for soldier, "Jarhead" for Marine)—even failing to forward
the Kick-Ass Rules—are all deserving of getting **"your ass kicked."** Most
meaningfully related to Weaver's list is rule #8:

8. *Don't try to discuss politics with a military member or veteran. We are
Americans, and we all bleed the same, regardless of our party affiliation.
Our Chain of Command is to include our Commander-In-Chief (CinC).
The President (for those who didn't know) is our CinC regardless of political party. We have no inside track on what happens inside those big important buildings where all those representatives meet. All we know is that
when those civilian representatives screw up the situation, they call upon
the military to go straighten it out. If you keep asking us the same stupid
questions repeatedly, you will get your ass kicked.*

The first time this was passed on to us, on paper, by a military acquaintance, number 8 was oddly missing, though we easily found it online. This may reflect the fact that, while many of our more critically thinking soldier acquaintances would consider the Kick-Ass Rules to be extremist, inflammatory jingoism, this same group would be the most likely to be disappointed by civilians who were *not* politically engaged, especially with regard to our wars. The resonance with Weaver's items about not politically stereotyping service members, and not criticizing the Commander in Chief, are directly parallel.

The Kick-Ass Rules appear in various versions across the Internet, many of which include flourishes such as being titled "Rules for the Non-Military, and all you America Haters." Nearly all end, though, with the quote (typically attributed "author unknown"):

'It's the Veteran, not the reporter, who has given us the freedom of the press.'

'It's the Veteran, not the poet, who has given us the freedom of speech.'

'It's the Veteran, not the community organizer, who gives us the freedom to demonstrate.'

'It's the Military who salutes the flag,

BECAUSE OF THE BRAVE!'[10]

Continuing the theme of invidious comparisons, it is the hierarchical arrangement of these comparisons, the imposition of an either/or dichotomy that establishes the primacy of veterans, and expressly *not* the civilian sector of American citizenry and democratic process, which stands out. These strictures to civilians, in concert, establish the primacy of veteran citizenship, based upon claims of their greater intimacy with what it means to be American, and their exponentially greater level of service and sacrifice for nation. All of this prefigures admonitions not to talk politics (in a society where many already consider talking politics unseemly) in important ways: if those primary citizens are effectively muzzled from talking politics, to do so with them or in their proximity inevitably undermines the legitimacy of anything a civilian might say in such contexts—civilian political engagement may be *a priori* rendered utterances of the ignorant and undeserving, where the knowing and truly loyal are obligated to maintain silence. The polite, respectful response for many civilians living closest to veterans is to voluntarily adopt the muzzle as well.

As with any generalization, this counts with innumerable exceptions and outright dissent. In our infantrymen interviews, for example, numerous soldiers mentioned that while antiwar propaganda or negative media reports on the war could be angering or upsetting, many qualified this with statements like "but it's their right," or "but I'll defend their right to say so." An officer disillusioned after an Iraq deployment told us, "I expect civilians to speak out about the war, because I'm not allowed to. They need to do it for us." Most, however, saw negative representations as biased and expressed simply "because they hate the war, and because they don't understand," as Stuart Gallup put it. He continued, "I hate certain people who think they know what they're talking about when they talk about the war, but they have no idea because they have never been. It bothers me a lot." The overriding message is unmistakable: only those who have gone can know, and since they cannot speak freely about it, others who can, but who inevitably speak in ignorance, should likewise refrain from comment.

We return to the issue of how the invalidation of civilian engagement shapes dialog across military and civilian lines in chapter 10.

### Civilians Coming Closer, Military Personnel Meeting Them Halfway

In an opinion piece in *Army Times*, Dawn Weaver expanded upon her view of the role of civilians, calling them to "step up and help combat veterans and their families in tangible ways" in view of the reality that "our military medical system is not equipped to provide all the physical and psychological care that returning veterans need." But significantly, she adds, "and we, as military personnel, need to accept their help."

*I know it's hard for warriors to accept help from anyone, much less a civilian or civilian group with little understanding of our world. But for this nation to remain strong, we must do everything we can to recover from wounds visible and invisible.*

*Like so much of America, many civilian health care professionals are disconnected from the impact the war is having on our combat vets. The bridge between the veteran and the civilian medical provider is in serious disrepair. Two things have to happen for that bridge to be rebuilt.*

*First, civilians need to come closer to our world. They need to read stories written by veterans who have been there and watch documentaries about the war. Civilians need to learn more about the heart and soul of a warrior. They need to stop asking, "What was the hardest part about being over there?" and start asking, "What's the hardest part about being home?" They need to start thinking about the reality of a seriously wounded vet and the impact those wounds have on each person in that veteran's life. But most of all, they need to find ways to reach out within their communities to embrace their returning service members and welcome them back. Military personnel must be willing to meet those civilians halfway.*

*We have to be willing to accept their help and teach them about our experiences.*[11]

Weaver's call is singular in its emphasis on reciprocity between civilians and military personnel. To be of relevance to veterans, civilians need to become better educated about their lives and experiences; in return, veterans need to be receptive to civilian engagement with them and with the nation's wider circumstances. In terms of this work, she might be saying that more civilians need to venture into the hazardous maze, despite its risks, because it is already there, and we are all responsible for finding safe and honorable exits.

### A Translator for Trauma

Despite the emphasis on military representations of civilian ignorance in this chapter, we would be remiss were we not to offer examples that contradict the stereotypes, for as with all overgeneralizations (as stereotypes must be), exceptions abound. We begin by looking still more closely at the life of Dawn Weaver, a narrative through which we can traverse the military-civilian boundaries and divides. Her story is an ultimate version of coming out of civilian cluelessness into specialized knowledge, because that knowledge came through "going native" and enlisting herself. Because she was a civilian until she was 45 years old, commissioned in 2004, and then separated from the military five years later, and since she also took to writing to civilians (mostly to prepare health care providers), she serves us as an apt translator.

But when Weaver told us, "I perceive myself as a translator," she was talking about translating something else entirely: trauma itself, and PTSD. The reason she became a psychiatric nurse specialized in combat-based PTSD was tied to giving birth: both she and her firstborn barely survived. Both have coped with symptoms of PTSD—hypervigilance, hyperactive startle responses, nightmares, and sleeplessness—to differing degrees ever since. Having had to build what she envisions as "bridges back" from her own trauma led her to believe she would be particularly able to help struggling soldiers.

She explains, "I can stand on that bridge, and I can go, 'Ok, follow my voice, try to stand up, come over here. You see me standing here now? Here's what you need to do to build your own bridge that looks just like this. Let me guide you through it.'"

Weaver deeply regretted that as a youth she had participated in being "silently disrespectful of Vietnam veterans" in a way that "was part of the culture at the time." She wanted to help prevent the same thing from happening to another generation of veterans. A year after the 9/11 attacks, Weaver experienced her "own personal September 11th" when the "wheels came off the wagon" of her 17-year marriage. Six months into the Iraq war, news reports about soldiers "not handling their experiences overseas well," and faring worse still upon returning to the United States, did not surprise her. "At that point in time, I literally got a flyer in the mail saying, 'We are looking for nurses in the US Army. If you are 46 and a half years old or younger, we are looking for you.' And I was 45 and a half."

Working as an emergency response psychiatric nurse in the emergency room taught Weaver things she believes too few people attempting to work with soldiers know or understand, like what she calls the "dirty little secrets" about soldiers discussed in chapter 2, that soldiers back from deployment always "pack" or run armed, that "crazy-making" rules of engagement had them "primed to kill," and that many "have had to kill children." But she had additional basic worries about clinicians "not getting it." For example: "When a guy comes to a therapist's office with a Monster (caffeine-based energy drink), a giant Monster in his hand, and his leg is jiggling, and he's talking about not being able to sleep," clinicians need to pick up the thread by asking, "How much caffeine are you drinking?"

In public settings speaking to therapists and other care providers, Weaver regularly tells a story of a soldier who, 12 years after the first Gulf War and before deploying to Afghanistan, finally sought help from a therapist. The clinician listened, then told the soldier, "Well, I'll try to help. But, I can't really get my head around the fact that you kill people for a living, so we'll have to see . . . ." The story epitomizes, for her, why so many soldiers can't trust therapists. When it comes to something profoundly disturbing, like killing children, therapists who will not leave politics at the door ensure that "the injury, therefore, never gets treated." She feared that her children would be in the places where untreated, sick, and suffering soldiers would erupt, something she saw as being just as inevitable as already-lit kegs of gunpowder.

In the face of soldiers' burdens, buying a veteran a drink, saying thank you for your service, or holding a welcome home ceremony doesn't do enough, Weaver argues. Soldiers need more from their communities.

*There is nobody there, there is no other warrior there, no other experienced warrior there with their arms open going, "You don't need to tell me what you've done. I've done it myself." You need to understand that there are two different worlds. The warrior world of heinous acts that happen when the primal brain gets tripped. And the world of the so-called civilized that will judge you harshly, and never forgive you for what you've done, if they knew about it.*

Vital to note is the confidence with which Weaver can call across this bridge with open, accepting arms, though she herself has never deployed, suggesting "warrior" here may not be limited to combatants.

The army nurse who beckoned to civilians to "coming closer to our world" as a soldier is now a civilian again, which allows her to speak frankly in ways soldiers cannot. While her expectations for civilian participation in bringing veterans "all the way home" might make some civilians uncomfortable, wary that serving veterans in this way becomes tantamount to becoming cheerleaders for the wars, Weaver's position on the politics of the wars might surprise many. "I think George W. Bush and Dick Cheney[12] should be brought up on war crimes," she told us some time after separating from the army. "I think they're despicable. They have created more evil, singlehandedly on this planet, than I will ever see in my lifetime before or since." She "never would have dreamed of saying that while active-duty, of course—it's really not that big of a deal to not voice your opinions," but her point once again sharply divides her commitment to injured soldiers from political or strategic perspectives.

## Civilians with a Clue (or Two)

While the acerbity of negative military representations of civilians is striking and important, it is by no means pervasive. Nic Gray, the soldier arrested after "clearing" his Colorado neighbor's house in flashback mode (chapter 7) and who now helps veterans become business owners, cites making civilian friends as a critical turning point in his recovery. "It was kind of part of the therapy—'make some friends'—so I did." He moved away from old friends and carefully chose "one individual" at first. Friendships with civilians ended up being key to learning to tune into civilians' lives more generally and become less judgmental which, alongside getting used to the lack of "order" and rank structure, he saw as most critical for reintegration. Where civilians might be "challenged or frustrated about the temperature or flavor of their coffee . . . in the military that's really the last thing you care about. It's living or dying. Keeping yourself alive, keeping your battle buddies alive." So, Gray says, "You have to go ahead and really try to understand, be able to relate to some degree to people in the civilian world . . . . That doesn't happen overnight. It takes—well, truly I don't think you ever get 100 percent back to that normalcy of being civilian. I don't think so, but it does get easier after a while."[13]

Civilian close friends and intimate partners surely form the inner circle of what Goffman called the "wise," people who are "normal but whose special situation has made them intimately privy to the secret life of the stigmatized individual and sympathetic with it, and who find themselves accorded a measure of acceptance" by the stigmatized (Goffman 1986 [1963]:28). Yet just as Goffman's presumption of a singular "normative" has been critiqued for situations that are bi- or multicultural (Kusow 2004), recall that in this chapter we are concerned with stigma inverted, or the in-group's (veteran's) stigmatizing of the out-group (civilians). Too, we repeat, veterans are singular in being simultaneously stigmatized and lionized in front of civilians, and service members have their own ways of both elevating "the home of the free" and depreciating how this may be taken for granted by complacent civilians. In seeking to understand civilian-military "cross-cultural" relations, then, we need to ask not only about how relatively "wise" civilians gain knowledge about veterans, but also what veterans can learn about how they fit into the world through the wise.

"Ultimate stories" like Dawn Weaver's, where the civilian joins up, are far from the sole way that civilians learn "secret handshakes" of in-group language, iconography, and classified information. Equally key are the emotional experiences civilians narrate about stepping into the labyrinth, or becoming intimate with being a nation at war. Colorado Springs offers literally hundreds of examples; chapter 7 portrayed working programs, networks, and treatment modalities that have grown up in the region, and chapter 10 addresses possibilities of reciprocal, public dialog. Here we will simply offer sketches of variously "wise" civilians from the community as they gathered for a panel discussion one particular November morning: the day after Veterans Day, in 2011.

In 2011, for the second year in a row, Vietnam veterans participating in this research enlisted us—Jean, Sarah, and students involved in the Deployment Stress project—in creating a multiple-day program surrounding Veterans Day. When activist John Champion (whom we met in chapter 8) saw the preliminary program, centered around veterans' story-telling circles, films, speakers, and panels, he emailed a group of fellow activists: "The CC [Colorado College] participation in war glorification takes a quantum leap forward this year and I thought last year was bad. What can we do?—John." Being who he is, he also emailed it to us directly, sharing his concern that the college, which he viewed as the sole liberal or progressive bastion in the city, appeared to him increasingly militarized and even militarizing.

Long discussions ensued, over coffee, tea, and email. John said, among other things: "I don't know how we get a realistic picture of the pain of war by focusing on those whom America dubs as heroes, while ignoring the much greater suffering of America's enemies." One response we made was to reframe the event as explicitly neither about military bolstering nor about protesting the wars; we attempted to establish as neutral a space as possible. A shared two minutes of silence "for all those touched by war" became the centerpiece of the event. These two minutes, held at 11 a.m. on the 11th day of the 11th month (and in 2011, the year as well), invoked the ceasefire commemorated as Armistice Day, as Veterans Day was called until 1954, originally marking the end of WWI. The events were held in Palmer Hall in the middle of campus, and attendance was modest—no more than 50 people at a session.

The first panel that morning was called "Reflections from the 'Homefront'—Military spouses, community organizers, writers, and artists." Following the double sessions of veterans sharing their stories the day before—billed as "'How to Tell a True War Story'[14]—All veterans are invited to share; all others bring receptive hearts and minds"—an emotional hangover lingered in the hall's ether. Not even our veteran collaborators managed to attend that morning. By the session's end, a single veteran, a retired colonel in full dress uniform who had driven three hours, took in the morning's discussion.

Sarah introduced the panel as a moment to shift the spotlight onto "supporting cast members" who live "very much in the trenches" with returning veterans. Acknowledging that some found holding Veterans Day events at a place like Colorado College itself problematic, she underlined that the worst way for a citizenry to be in relation with being at war was through silence, or lack of engagement. "We would rather see people arguing than being disengaged. This does, of course, raise important questions about how people can engage in ways that feel authentic."

Bruce Stone, the Downtown Mosaic artist we met in chapter 7, gave an overview of the community-building art projects with military circles, remembering moments where "it wasn't like military and community divided. It was this great united thing. And these guys, I learned so much more from that group of guys than they did from me. I said: I want to do more of this."

Bruce then introduced fellow artist Norah Brady. Norah had started a veterans' story-telling project through Downtown Mosaic, and confessed six months ago she "would have been intimidated to be on a panel about veterans," sure she had nothing to offer and "knew nothing about veterans." Through the story project, she quickly realized that claiming, "I know veterans" was as questionable as saying, "I know the human race" in the first place. "Each one is very, very different and each one has their own story to tell." She belatedly realized that she in fact came from a family of veterans (parents who hadn't seen war so she didn't think of them as such), and so began gathering stories with her family. From her mother joining the navy with the statement, "I'll do anything but work at a desk," and promptly being assigned to a desk job, to the father-in-law who survived on nothing but grass for 27 days on "Starvation Ridge" during WWII, where they found the nights "so still they shot at sound, whether it was a water buffalo or a child," Norah listened.

By the time she had moved beyond family and heard dozens of stories, she recognized a single, common refrain: "Afterward all of them said something like, 'I didn't know if I could do this. It brought up so much stuff.'"

Norah said, "What I've learned is that what matters is not veteran to civilian, but human being to human being. The audiences listened to stories they could identify with: laughing, being terrified . . . and their hearts went out. And these veterans felt that they were being heard and supported, often for the first time." For her, this listening dissolved a "gap between veteran and civilian." If more people grasped that, she thought, "All these chairs would be filled . . . ."

Kathleen Dougherty, married to a special operations service member, spoke next, and talked about weathering deployments from home. "It's hard to stay sane in the face of so much uncertainty and fear. It is really easy to move down the path of compulsive something: compulsive exercise, shopping, drinking, smoking. Anything you can do to kind of not be present with the terror." This led her to a "kind of spiritual crisis . . . and for me it ended up being this great opportunity to practice being in uncertainty and to practice coping with fear in a healthy way—to not do those compulsive things but to be willing to sit with this fear." Though a confirmed atheist, she read ancient religious texts and meditated. She also discovered that for her, there was no legitimate "division between the personal and the political. . . . Watching the news, and seeing an airstrike in Pakistan or something, I would just know that in some deep way that I was connected to that. Not to make myself more important than I was, but I just knew I was part of this web of things, that what was happening for me back home and what was happening there were deeply intertwined. And there was really nothing to do about that, except work through my own feelings of complicity." In the face of a "drive to be a flag-waving patriot, and to do all the right things and be this gung-ho military wife," she found that "I do feel those things, more deeply than I did before I met him, and at the same time just this deep ambivalence . . . that doesn't resolve."

The next panelist, Annie Jenkins, is executive director of an organization that gives assistance to active-duty personnel and increasingly, to veterans, had a few questions for the civilian community. She worried that, "as we well know," veteran's situations "are going to get worse," citing unemployment, homelessness, and facing health problems without benefits. Would "perceived drawdowns" mean that "our job is over with and we don't need support for our veterans and military? I think everyone knows that that's not true."

"My hope is for communication," Jenkins said, pausing. "My hope . . . . How can you heal your marriage, how can you heal your spirit, body, when you are worried about losing your home?"

Jenkins thought civilians needed to confront their "own biases about our military in our community," something she had found personally key in enabling her to do the work she does. "When I have someone pulling up in a far nicer vehicle than I've ever owned who can't pay rent, I ask: What's my bias? I have to stop and think that maybe this person can't make good judgments right now because they have a brain injury. Did I think about the fact that maybe while they were deployed one of their family members misspent all of their money [on such a vehicle]?" She had to learn about the impact of deployments: "I interviewed a veteran recently, his name's Stan; after I interviewed him, I saw him a week later and he didn't remember who I was . . . . It was kind of scary for me. It was beyond my comprehension that he didn't know who I was. And he has to manage in the day-to-day world and remember what needs to be paid and when and what's going on?" Stan told Annie about missing all of "the firsts" with his son, and how now he couldn't live with the son because he'd taken a swing at him during a night terror, and was homeless. "And he said to me," Jenkins remembered, "'Touch my feet because nightmares don't attack your feet.' What are our biases when we hear such things?"

Last to speak was Chase Fletcher, who has written two books on military procurement of hardware for communication and intelligence systems. "It all sounds very dehumanizing to look at the hardware aspect of things [war], but I've also worked with IVAW [Iraq Veterans against the War] and the Justice and Peace Commission on working with returning vets. Not only on health issues regarding PTSD but on some of the courts-martial on conscientious objection," he told the gathering.

For that morning, Fletcher had thought about where the civilian citizenry fit into these wars. "I noticed over time an odd change in the way veterans perceive the 'homefront' as we move from a drafted force to an all-volunteer force . . . and right now, as we are slowly but exhorbitantly moving towards an all-robotic force."

"There are perceptions regarding the veteran's place at the homefront and what is perceived as 'honor,'" he ventured, speaking carefully and adding, "When I say honor, I put quotations around it. Because in the 70 years since WWII there have only been a few isolated cases where we could see the deployments as clearly honorable." He recounts a few rescue missions— the first few months in Afghanistan prior to Tora Bora, the first few months of Korea prior to the Yalu River—where "in those, the honor was clear cut. Beyond that, we've had a lot of deployments involving a variety of counterinsurgency, police action, etc. where the soldier ends up slogging it out for goals that are not clear."

Chase asks the gathering: "The question is: 'Where is the blame placed?'" He observes that when there was a draft, he saw more questioning. Today, many perturbed veterans are gradually figuring out that "the people they've got to ask these questions to are the civilian leadership . . . . A veteran realizes *very* clearly that the responsibility lies 10 percent with the military leadership, and 90 percent with the civilian leadership." Concluding, Chase stressed, "If you're trying to get easy victory in a global situation that does not lend itself to easy victory, you're going to be falling into a mess that is going to impact a soldier," whether that individual is on the ground or piloting a drone. "Veterans," he repeated, "understand this very clearly."

That was the first hour. A painter in the audience spoke, then a teacher and administrator, a military grandmother. An army wife spoke about how much remains hidden from civilians that military families go through: evacuations, protests against them when stationed overseas. The level of disillusion she saw struck a counselor working on post: "More than anger. Disillusion."

The only apparent military member present that day, the retired colonel, stood and offered the last word. "I just want to say thank you to people taking time to travel to try learn about the 1 percent. I consider myself the 1 percent. I have a hard time relating to civilians that really don't care about their military." Looking back on his 28 years of service, he reflected, "War is not fun at times. But, at times, it is. It's like—can I say this here? We're all adults. It's like sex: it can be interesting or it cannot be interesting." The room releases into peals of laughter. "It can suck you in to where you live. When you do good things, you're happy about it. You know you're supporting something. In the long run, you're freeing the people. So soldiers today, in the short run, still won't see this, but in 30 or 40 years people might have democracy . . . . Again, thank you for trying taking time to try to learn about us."

We—Jean and Sarah—have understood ourselves to be as "clueless" as any other civilians venturing into the maze, and felt ourselves included in those the colonel addressed that morning. It was not clear, however, that the retired officer was convinced any of the civilians were "wise"; we were "trying." But civilians' own words that morning were clear: we had navigated our own paths into the labyrinth, becoming ensnared and caught unprepared, and also gaining small wisdoms through initial cluelessness. Not unlike soldiers, we discover new dimensions and layers to these wars, and to who we are in them. We discover it was always our own maze, too. Through listening and acting, faltering and learning from mistakes, we have seen walls dissolve between those deploying to wars and those trying to understand. As we come away from war, we pull one another from our labyrinthine hiding places, attempting to rebuild communal spaces where we can breathe, and hear one another. We continue studying attempts at military-civilian dialog in the chapter that follows.

## Chapter 10

# "Closing the Gaps":
# Seeking Military-Civilian Public Dialog

*In a world of deceptive and dissimulating doubles, the power of naming can drift into dangerous waters. We try to indicate, but our prattle makes what is not there.*

—Tom Matrullo, *Labyrinth of Prattle*

In this chapter we consider distinct kinds of public gatherings, all convened for purposes of accomplishing varied forms of military-civilian communication. Scenes from varied versions of "town hall" meetings, as well as a selection of interactions from more informal dialogs, illustrate efforts to promote veteran-civilian communication. The nature of the gatherings, some 20 of which we participated in, ranged from official to relatively informal, from rooms accommodating hundreds to more impromptu meetings of just a few participants. Immediate goals of the gatherings also varied: large-scale "town halls" were geared to prepare communities for a massive expansion of Fort Carson or reintegrating soldiers, where more informal events framed as "dialogs" were aimed at creating mutual exchanges between veterans (here including active-duty returned from theater) and civilians that could promote understanding and help close potentially problematic gaps in civil-military relations.

Why focus on dialog? Our premise is that meeting a range of challenges—from reintegration struggles all the way to ensuring competent civilian oversight of the military—requires far greater mutual knowledge. Previously, attention to a presumed cultural gap between civilian and military communities has focused on leadership and policy issues. Our ethnographic approach seeks to help understand the issue at levels of local community institutions and interpersonal interaction, based on the notion that it is in such contexts that veterans reintegrate and communities reckon with the effects of the post-9/11 wars.

The chapter asks a few questions: in what ways can such events be viewed as risky by organizers and participants? What kinds of measures do organizers take to contain risks, by carefully managing "scripts," directing interchanges, and trying to minimize ways in which dialogue can be threatening to veterans? We approach military-civilian dialog as fraught, potentially hazardous conversational territory for many, as starkly clashing views and experiences can be, and are, charged with feeling. We find this dynamic tension—between the impulse to take the risks of dialog on the one hand, and to control risk and maximize interests on the other—to enliven tense encounters in productive, albeit often uncomfortable, ways.

## Town Halls—Come One Come All

Organizers of a number of large-scale meetings between local military and civilians chose to call them "town halls." What does such a label mean for gatherings related to local military issues, convened in home communities during the post-9/11 wars? Scholars of the American town hall underscore that in its "proper" form it is strictly a New England convention, directly tied to self-governance, and epitomizing what Frank Bryan calls "real democracy."

> Real "democracy" (for good or ill) occurs only when all eligible citizens of a general-purpose government are legislators; that is, called to meet in a deliberative, face-to-face assembly and bind themselves under laws they fashion themselves. . . . It is better when attendance at meetings and participation in them are high and egalitarian. (Bryan 2004:3–4).

In the context of democracy's already inexpedient processes, town halls are notoriously messy, and have been described as "sprawling, sloppy, amateurish, hilarious, mawkish, and the best form of local government ever devised" (Raymond P. Clark, quoted in Zimmerman 1999:5). Effective town halls rely on citizens' buy-in to the notion that there are real stakes on the table that their participation can influence, and that governmental gatherings with constituents are not mere "performances," going through the motions of accountability and responsiveness to the citizenry, while actual decisions of governance are made elsewhere (Gans 1982 [1967]). In a setting where government is performed, public exchange is aimed at reducing uncertainty and getting things done; the kinds of "questions" admitted, for example, would be "softball" queries unlikely to broach deeper issues or revisit apparent "givens" or even screened ahead of time. In authentic town halls, by contrast, participation is ideally open, deliberative, and egalitarian. "As long as the rules remained in force," wrote Zimmerman, "proponents of the resolution could not be denied their right to a hearing" (1999:5; also Robinson 2011).

Town halls in southern Colorado, created to face challenges and explore opportunities connected to the large military presence, present immediate departures from this classic model. Instead of the strong local attachment to place of rural New Englanders, the individual representatives of the military rotate in and out of Colorado Springs and speak from national and international perspectives—about processes felt by most attendees to be far beyond their influence or control—as much as from local ones. There are no concrete decisions on the table or policies being formed. In fact, the format of these town halls was often indistinguishable from military "briefings," and in the case of some of them, they are named as such with the actual words placed alongside each other: "town hall briefing." Part of creating a convincing performance is creating the impression that mutual dialog, with results that are not completely predetermined, is possible.

### Dan Rather as Town Hall Moderator

The most unusual of the gatherings framed as "town halls" that we participated in was held when some of the battalions of the 4–4 (4th Brigade, 4th Infantry Division [ID]) had been back in Colorado for less than 24 hours, newly arrived from a 12-month deployment in Afghanistan. Journalist Dan Rather and his crew had spent time with the 4th Brigade, and the 2–12th Battalion in particular, in Afghanistan, and were doing a follow-up segment entitled "Return to Base." The event was held on-post, at the smart new 4th ID headquarters, and nearly all attendees appeared to be soldiers or spouses, in this case all wives. Apart from Rather and his crew, Sarah appeared to be the only non-spouse civilian present. Thus, the event was a "town hall" in the sense of these returning soldiers meeting and reporting to their public, responding to questions of public interest as posed by Dan Rather, through the vehicle of broadcasting. At the same time, the supreme irony of a national figure like Rather convening so localized an event as a "town hall," wherein one ethnographer represented townie civilian-ness singlehandedly, and which would then be televised and globally available on cyberspace, was so striking as to be humorous.

Sarah had almost crashed the event. When the brigade's Public Affairs Officer Major RJ Collins mentioned that Dan Rather was coming to Fort Carson in the first welcome-home emails they exchanged, she asked if she could sit in. RJ, who had a reputation for providing more journalistic (and anthropological) access than some PAOs thought prudent, responded by email: "Come at 1430 [2:30 p.m.]. Be low-key—as in don't say hi to anyone other than me. Sit and listen. If you can do that, then you can come . . . . Can you do that?"

On entering, Sarah quickly saw that the pants and button-down shirt she wore may have failed the "low key" requirement: everyone else was dressed either in uniform or, in the case of the assembled wives, in lovely, garden-party–styled summer dresses. Index cards had been distributed as invitees checked in for the audience question portion of the segment. Hoping she was not departing too much from RJ's directive to say hi to no one, after a time Sarah asked some of the wives seated near her if they would be submitting questions. They shook their heads, and one explained, "I don't want to throw our commanders off, because I love our commanders."

To begin, Dan Rather asked Colonel Holmes and his battalion commanders a basic question: "Did the mission succeed?"

"Our soldiers did an amazing job. We moved the ball farther down the field. But change is a long process," Holmes responded. He cited particular progress in connecting with the Afghan people, understanding how their challenges look from their own perspectives.

"Are American taxpayers getting value out of the costs of the wars?" Rather asked Colonel White, who had commanded the battalion placed under Canadian command. White explained their shift to smaller projects, away from building schools toward more modest things like constructing cement pads, meant that US taxpayers could rest assured that they were making more impact with smaller investments. Inevitably, Rather asked about the 4th Brigade becoming known as "the Murder Brigade" (see chapter 3) during their dwell time between Iraq and this last deployment. The commanders stressed the things they were doing to address behavioral health issues: better screening at recruitment so people who "didn't need to be soldiers" were not admitted in the first place, mobile behavioral health teams that responded immediately after incidents in theater, better screening upon returning home, and attempting to reduce stigma associated with struggles dealing with combat trauma.

It came time for the question and answer session. Sarah had not resisted the civically minded compulsion to submit a question. She had not expected, however, for hers to be the only one submitted.

"We have a question from . . . Sarah Hopslinger," Rather began, "who's an anthropologist. She wants to know, since this is the second and third deployment for many, what is being done that is new to help the families cope over multiple deployments." Colonel Holmes responded that working with the rear detachment, and asking for more community support, was helping families. The question did not appear to throw off this veteran commander of three deployments. We wondered, though, what kinds of questions some of the spouses might have asked, had they not been understandably sensitized to the purely performative fishbowl a Dan Rather broadcast could mean. What kinds of things might have "thrown off" the commanders they so loved, and what risks to the people living closest to America's wars did this pose?

This first encounter with a "town hall" sparked the question that drives our foray into town halls: who comprises the "town" in such exchanges, and what kinds of public interchange are organizers and participants seeking? As has been mentioned, we found that the army frequently invokes "town hall" alongside the term "briefing," as a time for a mostly one-way dissemination of information, as in the case of the heavy use of podcast town hall briefings between Colorado and Texas over the course of transferring a brigade from Fort Hood to Fort Carson.[1] Leaders sharing information, and then taking questions, was the basic format for all town halls we attended. Our focus turned to the question and answer sessions, where dialog might assume a relatively open form.

### "Uncontrolled Environment"—Creating Spaces for Dialog

By far the more common form of town hall in southern Colorado applies to a prominent series of events, billed as "Town Hall Meetings" (but also "Town Hall Forums and Briefings") convened between 2006 and 2011, with at least one per year. The city's local weekly newspaper, *The Independent*, initiated and cosponsored the first six of these, along with both garrison and 4th ID (4–4 ID) command from Fort Carson, the Pikes Peak Area Council of Governments (PPAGC), and 12 additional nonprofit, business, and higher-educational organizations. Despite difficult beginnings, the partnership between the scrappy, liberal-leaning paper and the ever-rotating host of Fort Carson commanders was surprisingly productive. "People really appreciated a chance to hear and listen to people directly," John Weiss, publisher of *The Independent*, told us. "You can't see the general most of the time." Relations between the newspaper and the PPACG's Military Impact Team members, whose jobs were integrally tied to the production of such events, were more tense. The strain eventually led to *The Independent* being "boxed out," according to Weiss. The most recent town hall meetings, with markedly smaller attendance, did not involve the paper (Weiss 2007).[2]

John Weiss came to his commitment to promoting civilian-military dialog in response to a crisis for his paper. In the hectic days just after September 11, 2001, his editor published an unscreened commentary stating that President George W. Bush was wrong in calling the people who hijacked planes to fly into buildings "cowards" when it was clearly a "ballsy act," no matter how heinous.

"She used the word 'ballsy,'" Weiss recalled. "She shouldn't have done that. She should have said 'zealots,'" which is what the subsequent clarification the paper published stated. The outcry from a local state senator and other prominent conservatives was immediate; some in the community attempted a boycott against the paper.

Before the boycott did much damage, and because they were disturbed by the allegations that they were not patriotic or civically minded, Weiss and his staff embarked upon a comprehensive program of community outreach, across the social and political chasms gaping between the paper and sizable sectors of the local population. They decided to reach out in three lines: to small, local nonprofits; to the evangelical community; and to the military. "We did the military outreach partly because this is a military town, and partly because we needed to be clear that we are not opposed to wars. We are opposed to *this* war. And, we support the troops. In fact, we actively want to keep them out of harm's way and being used efficiently."

Those became the precise words that Weiss offered as part of his introductory comments at the six town halls in which *The Independent* collaborated. There was a tacit ground rule that the meetings were not about the wars or associated politics, and Weiss no doubt meant for his comments to delineate just that: to invite even those who might have qualms about the war efforts to engage in supporting the soldiers and other service members who were also their neighbors. The commanding general who spoke at one of the same town halls surely intended something similar when he said, "You may have policy issues, but soldiers do what they're told to do, and we owe them absolute support."

This proposition may make for inclusive rhetoric, but many in the military do not find it to be so simple. Many soldiers shared the sentiments of one senior officer, who privately told us, "What is it they say, 'We support the troops; we just don't agree with the war.' It's like, 'Sorry guys, you can't have it both ways.' Ok, you're just not spitting on the guys, that's fine. And whether you believe in the war or not, that's irrelevant? That's kind of a dichotomy. That's hypocrisy. Support the troops, but don't believe in what they're doing?" A public affairs officer told us that for many stationed at Fort Carson, even venturing five miles north to downtown, where a number of the town hall meetings were held, already represented an unwelcome foray into hostile territory. "Anywhere north, well, of Southgate, really, has crossed a boundary already," he said, referring to a shopping center halfway between Fort Carson's northern boundary and downtown; he saw hopes of getting soldiers that far away from friendly territory as futile.

In the wars' early years, Fort Carson leadership did not easily warm to the town hall idea. "It was very difficult to do the first time," John Weiss remembered, "because we had strained relationships and Fort Carson had never done anything like this. And the idea of having an 'uncontrolled environment'—that was a quote they used—'This isn't what we do. All our events we like scripted.'" There was agreement that the meetings were not about the war or its politics, but focused on the impact that things like Fort

Carson's expansion would have on the area. Nonetheless, participants held different understandings about what this meant. "They mostly didn't want a protest," Weiss said. In that light, Weiss's ever-present introduction that *The Independent* was against the wars but supported the troops may have posed a problematic departure for some. Similarly, breakout group discussions about expanding the Piñon Canyon Maneuver Site were in keeping with the theme of regional impacts, but also inevitably somewhat political. Activist commanders like General Graham, determined to un-circle the wagons around Fort Carson, relished the exchanges, but from the mayor's office to the halls of the PPACG, others were less satisfied that benefits outweighed liabilities when the event became more uncontrolled and politicized, and tempers ran high. Ultimately, the "powers that be" wrested control over the events from *The Independent* to PPACG control, "[m]ostly because we were creating more work for them; they wanted an event that was controlled, that was less spontaneous," Weiss told us.

Commanders showed themselves to be realistic about the challenges of managing the coexistence of Fort Carson and the city to its north, along with their accountability to civil society. In chapter 8 we heard a 4–4 ID commander say at a town hall, "We are not a benign neighbor," and other Fort Carson commanders repeatedly emphasized, "We train soldiers to fight and kill the enemies of the United States of America." One town hall keynote speaker invited attendees to an open house at Fort Carson to view various military construction projects being built at a cost of more than two billion dollars. He wanted people to see what they were building, he said, "Because we're totally transparent. We are *your* Army. Soldiers are wonderful people because they're *your* sons and daughters."

Such statements convey desires for connection, to be understood by the wider community, and to account to taxpayers as their civil servants, especially in terms of managing tens of thousands of youth moving between combat theater and the bars, health care, educational, and other local institutions of Colorado Springs. "We live and shop among you, so you can get to know us," he continued. Efforts to connect and be understood also reveal concern about potential one-way *mis*understanding. But the emphasis on who needed to get to know whom was unidirectional, forgetting the voice of the soldier transitioning to civil society and begging for orientation we heard in the previous chapter. We also hear impulses to drum up the support, cooperation, and collaboration necessary to host a base with 26,000 soldiers.

### Shifting Concerns in Town Halls

The first town halls focused on the coming expansion of Fort Carson, and preparing for its impact on housing, education, health care, and social ser-

**FIGURE 14.** Town hall meeting in Colorado Springs with Fort Carson officers (photo by Samantha Koss).

vices (Figure 14). Between 2006 and 2012, the military went from being the biggest game in town to often being the only game in town, especially for construction and other infrastructure workers. From the beginning, growth and its attendant opportunities were the events' watchwords, and the earliest town halls were packed with realtors and other business people. Service providers and representatives of nonprofits aspiring to serve the military sector staffed informational tables with pamphlets and contact information. Some town meetings had breakout groups on housing demand, child- and after-school-care concerns, education, and employment. They also highlighted ways to "Get involved with Soldiers and Their Families," and "Citizen-Soldier Interaction, Communication and Community Building," such as through the organization Soldier-Citizen Connection, dedicated to "supporting our troops by bringing the military community and local community together in friendship."[3]

The clearest benefits from these gatherings included connecting people across institutional lines and social sectors. For example, each of the superintendents for the school districts with sizable military populations sat on a committee about military issues in the school, and most had a staffer assigned to this area; the town hall meetings were the first place these staffers met their counterparts from other districts. Another direct benefit of the town hall conversations, for example, was the implementation of a second "count day" for school enrollment numbers; critical for setting funding levels from the state, a single early count day had been a perennial problem for the military community, because their more transient patterns meant their enrollments were consistently undercounted.

By 2009, alongside the economy sliding into crippling recession, the community was absorbing the significance of the soldier-perpetrated homicides and other associated "behavioral health" issues with soldiers returning from overseas, discussed in earlier chapters. The town hall convened in November of that year, the last led by *The Independent*, introduced for the first time a breakout session on behavioral health issues and related initiatives, which attracted attendance that dwarfed the other breakout groups (save the group on housing). General Graham, the garrison commander who had lost both sons, escaped his own question-and-answer breakout session early, to join the behavioral health group. Toward the end of that session Sarah, who had been invited to speak on the behavioral health panel, ventured one of the questions typically omitted from the public exchanges:

"One thing we note with all the suffering related to combat trauma and PTSD is the absence of talking about primary prevention, or preventing these kinds of unseen wounds by avoiding going to war in the first place. Is this part of the behavioral health discussion?" General Graham took the question from where he sat in the audience.

"Well, there will always be the next war. The best we can do is prepare for it, and do everything in our power to take care of the troops and their families." Even in the rare instances when a question broaches issues of the ultimate costs of war, the script is quickly restored.

With the economic collapse beginning in 2008, subsequent town hall meetings shifted away from projecting new economic opportunities toward panic about absorbing losses. Of particular concern was the elimination of civilian jobs at Fort Carson and the area's air force installations. The town hall meeting convened in May 2011 was organized with just three sponsors (PPACG, the Colorado Springs Newspaper Group, and the local Fox News station) and generated such spare turnout that one of the PPACG organizers shared with us his disappointment (while many of the nonprofits later told us they were sorry not to have been invited and offered informational tables). All of the audience's questions concerned job loss as the Iraq war wound down and cuts by the Department of Defense appeared imminent. As in previous town halls, they were assured that Fort Carson units were "expected to stand" regardless of cuts, and that standard attrition could account for what reductions they would take. On civilian job loss, commanders acknowledged the 10,000 civilian jobs already lost nationally in the previous year affected southern Colorado, but assured that "as we right-size" they were committed to protecting jobs and to "nobody getting fired."

Then Colonel Jimmie Keenan, the career Army nurse now in command of Evans Hospital at Fort Carson, took the microphone to highlight that the behavioral health concerns provided a bright spot in the jobs outlook. "We are still hiring at Evans," she declared, with 60 new positions announced that week, mostly in areas of child psychology. The toll that the wars were taking on military families and children in particular made the hospital's work "a growth industry," news she offered as a break from the bad economic outlook overall.

By 2013, after the United States government "went over the fiscal cliff" into sequestration, or the forcing of sizable cuts across the board and especially in defense (by as much as 29% [Spring 2012]), assurances against job losses were long over, as civilian contractors were being let go at Fort Carson by the hundreds.[4]

## Breaks in Performance

If the purpose of the script is to contain emotion and control public conversation while maintaining the impression of participation and dialog, then deviations from the script, what Gans calls "breaks in performance," can open the event to genuine dialog and reveal underlying conflicts and contradictions.

From the perspective of some involved in producing the town halls, publisher John Weiss repeatedly stating he supported the troops but not "this war" serves as an example of a near-break in script; something admissible only when the paper controlled the program and, for some of his fellow organizers, unconstructive.

A clearer break in the script came in the question-and-answer period during the 2009 town hall, the first the PPACG oversaw. Questions were submitted in writing, and vetted by a Fox News anchorman who had moderated the panel. One man, who had clearly submitted a question, now moved to the front row in the aisle by the microphone in anticipation of making sure it would be addressed. He had eagle feathers tucked into his purple-and-white letterman sports jacket, and crimped black hair tied back in a ponytail. His overall appearance was a bit rough around the edges, as if perhaps he did not sleep in the same place every night. When the anchor announced there was time for just one more question, and flipped through the papers as if looking for a new submission, the man stood and spoke into the mike.

"If there's just one more question I don't think you'll get to mine," he began, intending to pose it verbally from the floor. It seemed to involve an objection to how Fort Carson was awarding contracts to minority-owned businesses. Before he got a sentence in he was cut off by the moderator, as a security-type in burgundy suit jacket rapidly approached. Many in the surrounding crowd snorted derisive laughs, and sneered or shook their heads, as he was chased out. A social worker we spoke with afterward said she wanted to call out, "Let him talk" early on, but did so only under her breath, when she saw there was no way he would be heard. As he shook off the guard and began to leave the hall on his own, he intoned in a loud voice to the large ballroom assembly, to the effect that the "same people—Native Americans, Blacks, Hispanics—were still being robbed by these people," and that he was "cheated out of $5 million in contracts . . . ." His voice trailed off into the hall as the door closed behind him.

Just before this, as Jean and Sarah entered the downtown conference hotel they greeted the protesters outside; Brigadier General Pettigrew (see chapter 8) had also stopped to talk with the activists. We had asked activist John Champion if any of them would be coming in for the meeting. "Oh, I went in already, and left a stack of these flyers on the table." He still had the bigger stack, not wanting to put them all down at once. The text read:

STOP

*The Stop the Whop Whop Campaign advocates that our community consider some alternatives to what is being promoted at today's debate. Bennet and Buck [then Democratic and Republican candidates for US Senate] are part of the movement that sees Fort Carson growing to at least 40,000 troops in the near future. Current levels are about 26,000. Right now this means 120 more helicopters and 2,400 more troops to support them. Internal documents show that this will add pressure for a huge land grab in Las Animas County. There is still time to stop this.*

*We say it is time to put on the brakes and start our city and state heading in a different direction. The world will be better off. The country will be better off. And we in Colorado Springs will be better off. We know it won't be easy. The military industrial complex has politicians from both major political parties under their control. Government, business, the political structures, almost all elements of our society have adopted a tunnel vision that sees the future as being more of the same. More troops, more wars, and more budget deficits. Enough is enough. We need some new thinking and planning. If you'd like to help, be in touch: [contact information].*

"I've been to these meetings and tried to participate," he went on. "I think I'll stay out here; probably do more good."

During the social hour after the question-and-answer period, we shared with Nathan Davidson of PPACG that another of the questions we knew was submitted also went unasked: "I saw Commission for Justice and Peace protesters outside. Are non-promilitary groups invited to this meeting? Should they be? Why or why not?" Nathan responded, "Oh, John Champion was in here earlier, and left his stupid little flyers that nobody reads," implying the forum was open, even to such irrelevant participation. Nathan said he wished Bill would have stayed and learned something, so he would stop citing such wildly incorrect numbers, such as having 40,000 new soldiers projected for Fort Carson.

Nathan didn't know, of course, that we had been the ones to leave, as a favor to the activists, a second stack of the same flyers on the table next to where we spoke. This table was now swept clean and left unused. For someone charged with managing the tables, the flyers had crossed a line, silently broken from the script.

Unvetted questions from the audience, like the eagle-feather–bedecked questioner mentioned here and unwanted "Stop the Whop Whop" flyers on tables, whose authors prefer to follow "counterperformance" scripts outside, present relatively innocuous departures from town halls as increasingly "controlled events." They do, however, help us define the imagined lines of control, outside of which behavior calls for being managed. These exchanges during town hall encounters evidence many of the "tactics of exclusion" discussed by Holland et al. (2007) for controlling public discourse: appealing to military credentials to confer authority, controlling the visibility of affairs "conducted for but not by members of the public," presetting agendas that do not include all citizens' concerns, "freezing out" participants who would redirect agendas away from planned topics, and physically removing those whose "participation is an inconvenience or challenge to those in authority" (Holland et al. 2007:182–84).[5] These tactics permit a degree of "controlled environment" that military command and governmental authorities find necessary to be willing to hazard the risks of public dialog on local military presence. In places where the "landscape of the state" is firmly shaped around military institutions, such tactics can make "[e]ffort[s] to imagine a new or expanded version of [the city's] future [seem] to be more chimerical . . . than in places organized around smaller, less powerful, or more local economic and cultural institutions" (Holland et al. 2007:29).[6]

## "Can You Tell Me Why Are We in Afghanistan?" as Performance Break

Performance breaks happen in more informal and intimate veteran-civilian public dialogs as well. While town halls are ostensibly concerned with at least performing democratic, participatory governance, an entirely distinct group of gatherings were aimed at community discussions to promote better understanding of veterans, and to provide opportunities for sharing across lines of military-civilian difference. Individual motivations for participation and the functions of such events grow more variable and diffuse; some relate to veterans having a "day in court" moment with their civilian communities, others are aimed at reducing public ignorance, others pursue such activities for therapeutic ends.

During events surrounding Veterans Day 2010, student researcher Joey Glick spoke on a panel with Jean and Sarah to a group of veterans. Our sharing about the then two-year history of our project came as a detour from the main program, framed as "Veterans Remember" and composed of various open mike or other storytelling events. The organizer, Vietnam veteran Joe Barrera, offered three explicit guidelines for all events sponsored by Veterans Remember (VR; an organization founded around open-mike story-sharing). Of primary importance was the exchange of stories between "older guys" and "younger guys." Second, there needed to be a "place of receptivity for the stories to be heard." Finally, Joe would emphasize "the importance of a nonjudgmental, civilian audience," which wouldn't politicize the sharing, but simply offer acceptance. We were mindful of the contradictory roles we were assigned as both presenters and, simultaneously, as accepting civilian witnesses.

Joey briefly described his study of the military chaplaincy and civilian churches' responses to soldiers' mental health problems. Halfway into his comments (on a single, animated slide), a soldier who came as part of a local PTSD support group from a mental health care unit raised his hand, interrupting the presentation. Quentin had recently returned from Afghanistan and was awaiting a medical discharge based on his TBI and PTSD. When Sarah, who moderated the session, nodded at him, he stood to speak.

"I have a question for you, but I'm not sure if you can answer it for me." He gestured up at Joey's slide, animated with different religious symbols standing for the faiths he'd investigated. "I'm listening to you say all this stuff about PTSD, and TBI, and the ABCs. But," Quentin looked from the screen to Joey, "can you tell me why we are in Afghanistan?" He looked around, then, at other faces, expectantly. A slightly uncomfortable pause followed. Joey later wrote,

> He was correct in expecting me to have difficulty responding to his question. I . . . have little confidence in my ability to give a meaningful response to such challenging questions of foreign relations. However, a more profound limitation stopped me from answering his question . . . . Throughout a summer's worth of fieldwork in Colorado Springs, I spoke with faith leaders ranging from pro-peace liberals to fundamentalist military chaplains. Of the people who regularly interacted with soldiers, none of my informants saw a reason to engage political or moral questions when counseling soldiers or their families. Instead, time and time again, informants talked

*about the importance of disconnecting the innocent soldier from the complex politics of American foreign policy. During the Veterans Day event, I could neither answer the soldier's question about Afghanistan from my own perspective as an ignorant civilian, nor could I give him an informed guess on how a pastor or chaplain might respond to his remark. This discourse simply did not exist in my research population.*

During the pause that followed Quentin's question, Jean and Sarah were also mentally reaching for answers, likely along the lines of "our job is to give voice to what different people in the community say and think about that." Responding in a public setting to such "ultimate" questions fell outside the role we saw ourselves as having signed up for in accepting Joe's invitation, and also been assigned, as still part of his "nonjudgmental civilian audience," even when we were presenting. This felt especially true on Veterans Day, when we had only reluctantly accepted the invitation to speak, to veterans about veterans, at all. We found this to be the most automatically political and most potentially volatile question. Thus we avoided and at least indirectly censured efforts at controlled civic exchanges.

The pause was just long enough, however, for Edward, a veteran in the first row, to stand up. "On September 11, 2001," he began, turning from where he stood in the front row to address the seated audience. What followed was the "master narrative" of the planes flying into the buildings and the United States of America's obligation to respond militarily to the unprecedented terrorist threat.

Edward had heard about our research, and introduced himself to us that morning by handing us a business card while saying, "Edward Tanner. A Tanner has fought in every war this country has waged, and I would like to place myself at your services." In the course of the day's storytelling, he had already shown himself to be the veteran in the room most anxious to step in and supplement, or correct, the record, furnishing historical details about weaponry or unit structure at will, regardless of speaker. He played a role we had come to recognize from other gatherings of civilians and military, where the turn-taking tended to lapse into question and answer with someone, typically a veteran, who "outranked" others and claimed authority to overspeak in the name of ensuring the record's facticity. Meanwhile, a veteran friend later told us that Edward was packing a gun that day; the friend had put his hand on the gun's butt a couple of times when Edward got heated, as if embracing him, worried he might reach for it.

Especially problematic, no doubt, in that particular moment, was the fact that we thought that in Quentin's inquiry an *ultimate* question—perhaps *the* ultimate question—had been broached, aimed straight at the war's purpose, and perhaps its worth. And, it had been asked *of* a civilian, a college student speaking at the bastion-of-liberalism college in a conservative, military city. Just as the town hall organizers "did not want a protest," civilians who politicized conversations at veterans' events were seen as disrespectful and even abusive. Edward's compulsion to wrestle the narrative away from the places he imagined it could go from there must have been particularly keen.

A fundamental ambiguity surrounded Quentin's question. If Edward heard Quentin as Joey, Jean, and Sarah did, as asking whether the war in Afghanistan was "worth it" and the wisdom in invading in the first place, he gave no indication. We later speculated that Edward heard Quentin's question quite differently, as in effect asking Joey, "So, you're concerned about the high costs of ministering to these wars' wounds, but do you know why they were rendered in the first place? Do you grasp how they were necessary, and that therefore costs cannot be weighed as too great?" If Edward heard the question this way, it would have been largely rhetorical, intended to underline the ignorance or naïveté of the civilian speakers. In this reading, it would still have been important to prevent the conversation from running off the rails by permitting relatively uninformed civilians the opportunity to authoritatively respond, especially if that response were to compound questions about the validity or worth of the campaign. In any case, consoling Quentin and shoring up his confidence in his own involvement was part of his urgency.

Sarah allowed him to go on at some length before interjecting, "Edward? Edward . . . *Edward*? I think some others would like to get in here." For the room had come alive, more than any moment that day, with people wanting to comment; we anthropologists on the panel were happy to shift from presentation into listening, fieldwork mode. The most vocal of the speakers to follow, like Edward, elaborated hawkish views of the threats to US security and the appropriateness of the US military response, alongside the indeterminacy of cost-benefit or moral clarity in war. Eventually, a civilian activist asked, from the back of the room, to return to our presentation. Time was short, and we hastily offered a concluding comment on the army's attempts to destigmatize PTSD and face reintegration challenges, calling for civilian engagement in facing formidable challenges over the coming years.

Event organizer Joe Barrera had also heard Quentin as asking about the futility of Afghanistan. "I kind of blame myself, too," he later told us. Just before the presentation, Joe and Quentin had walked back together from lighting candles at 11 a.m. at an Armistice Day monument. Quentin told Joe he'd thrown away his Purple Heart because he felt he didn't deserve it. "I'd said something about Vietnam being futile, and I think it really affected him."

As a result, Quentin faced at least some of us in the room with the most off-limits question: are service members' sacrifices, overall and at the end of the day, in vain? As Edward undoubtedly well knew, there are no simple yes or no answers to such questions. Wars come in infinite chapters and experiences, and parts will always be deemed utter lunacy by anyone up close.[7] Edward restored the performance script, though whether to console Quentin or to help ensure that the narration that unfolded that November afternoon did not descend into protest commentary is not clear.

In comparison to the town halls, here the script, nearly broken but rapidly restored, cleaves more closely to ritual in containing emotion and controlling its expression in ways that do not threaten the integrity of the social group. Joe Barrera's assigning civilians the role of "nonjudgmental audience" speaks to creating a public space of relative safety for veterans, setting up the day's event as a ritual that would contain the emotion of remembering the trauma of war and its meaning for veterans and community members.

### Posing Ultimate Questions: Who and How

As a still active-duty soldier and Afghanistan war veteran, Quentin can claim greater entitlement to pose what we have called an ultimate question in a public setting than can his civilian counterparts. In a similar, rare broaching of ultimate questions during a Veterans Remember session the following year, veterans themselves led the way. A crescent of easy chairs faced the rows of chairs for audience members, and the Vietnam veteran organizers had invited their fellow vets up in turn over the morning and afternoon to share stories. A veteran named John, who lived in Colorado Springs but represented Veterans for Peace in Pueblo, made an unusual appearance. When invited to speak, he referred back to the ritual of lighting candles and speaking the names of those lost in battle we had completed just moments before, at 11 a.m. on November 11, a practice commemorating the signing of the Armistice that ended WWI:

"When we did that moment of silence, a couple of my buddies I named . . . ." John paused before going on. "Well, it took me a long time to really settle my emotions. Has that changed for you guys? Is it easier to say some of those names and bring it back? My answer to that is: I talked about names that I thought [their deaths] were just total waste."

This opened up other stories of death assessed as ultimately wasteful. A vet remembered, "Ninety percent of the people [Iraqis], they didn't have weapons, but once again we were enforcing the curfew. And the utter waste of that." And another who had to kill elephants in Vietnam on the theory they were trained elephants used as scouts by the Viet Cong, but that he feared were wild: "Nothing haunts me more than that. I was probably more concerned about the elephants than the people that may have been down there. The waste of the whole thing. We need to find another way than resorting to this sort of thing—and start to use the mechanics of our government to make a rational decision about a declaration of war before we make the war."

These despairing comments seemed to set the stage for Keith, recently retired from special forces but working as a contractor, having just completed his 36th trip "between Afghanistan and Iraq." A veteran who had led counter-insurgency efforts in El Salvador asked him how the Iraq and Afghanistan wars were different from others the veterans present had helped wage.

"Well, I'll tell you if you really want to know." Keith paused before continuing.

*We are fighting a foe that is implacable—that cannot be mitigated, that cannot be appeased. And, they are rabid dogs. What do you do with a rabid dog? That sounds cold, calculated and very cruel, but it's the truth. They are the religious warrior. We don't like to frame it in that way in the discussion in this country, but they are in a religious war. It's not Islam against Christianity, etc. It's Islam against everybody. And we like to think, and we like to say, that it's only a small, small fraction of that religion that has that particular bent, but there are 1.2 billion Muslims on the face of the earth. My point is not castigating anyone's religion. My point is that even if five percent of that 1.2 billion population are radical jihadists—well, you do the math—that's a lot of folks. And it increases every day.*

Keith looked across at John from Veterans for Peace, addressing him directly: "So I understand your position, that war is wasteful. It *is* wasteful. But that doesn't engage in the fact that it is . . . inevitable."

Judging from the response these comments, and particularly the one about "rabid dogs," sparked in other veterans, some of whom began contentiously probing for what more appropriate policies might be, Keith had broken from script, disrupting the performance in a different direction. Just as, a year earlier, Edward sallied forth to restore a narrative that affirmed the US military's purpose and just cause, so had Keith, but in terms that seemed to make many of his fellow veterans decidedly uncomfortable. Moderator Joe Barrera interceded, redirecting by inviting another guest to comment, in another vein.

Merely broaching these kinds of ultimate, strategic, and moral questions, we repeat, was remarkably rare in such public settings. Veterans had earned the right to straddle the potentially treacherous ambiguities between political and personal, but for "nonjudgmental civilian audience" participants, introducing such turns would directly depart from the parameters proffered by organizers for safe, constructive, and nonpoliticized dialog.

## Spaces for "Staying with the Pain"

Every individual who takes the time to engage in public, face-to-face dialog about the effects of the current wars brings his or her own story, motivations, and objectives. Thus, dialog involves verbal and emotional exchanges across a sharply drawn border, which theorist Ron Arnett (1986) illustrates through the metaphor of a narrow ridge. A rocky spine, like the Continental Divide that cleaves across Colorado, is a vantage point from which widely discrepant views can be seen.[8] One cannot simultaneously "be" on both sides. While balancing on the ridge, looking left and right, we accept the ultimate impossibility of complete translation. As a result, genuine dialog requires that participants be aware of the stark otherness in their differences, even as they expand mutual understanding through taking in one another's views.[9]

Veteran John Walters explains why he seeks dialog with the civilian public in this way.

"As horrible as war is, many of us vets are not looking for pills, or sympathy, or money, or whatever. I believe most of us want the rest of America to know what we did, right or wrong, bad or good, and just be behind us, support our actions, and listen, truly listen, to what we have to say." Other veterans also expressed longing to be heard. An Iraq veteran spoke at a "Community conversation" following the presentation of a series of portrait paintings of veterans (BenAmots 2012). He cited the Zulu cultural practice of keeping warriors returned from battle outside the village, where they would "wash their spears" of their stains, sharing stories and grieving losses, preparing to re-enter the community. "I think I have washed my spear," he said, "but it's civilians who haven't." In a country at war, he suggested, we all carry spears, and the stains remain, for all of us, until they are consciously washed away. For many, and in particular those who question the validity of these wars, this may involve finding a delicate balance between suspending moral judgments in an immediate way, while also not abdicating the responsibility to discern and evaluate acts performed in the nation's name in more ultimate, political senses. That these are inherently contradictory and opposing practices, and that to do both is paradoxical, asks nothing more of civilians than to confront the dense complexities that service members face, at far closer range.

Another veteran spoke that night, saying that he served first in Kosovo, "where it felt so good to serve, and you saw the good we were doing." Later, in Iraq, he said, "We shot people. A lot of people. And, we could get really into it; it was exciting. A lot of the time, we *liked* it," he added.

A man from across the room interjected, "I just want you to know that your service, like what you did in Kosovo, is important. You served, and we honor your service. We can't forget to say thank you."

Later Jay Maloney, a veteran friend, reflected back on this exchange, offering us his interpretation and yet another metaphor. "When the guy thanked the young vet for Kosovo alone, he was saying, 'Put the mask back on.' He started to take off his mask when he was opening up about shooting people in Iraq. But that's the kind of thing people don't want to hear about. They want to pick and choose. So, he forced him back inside the mask."

What does it look like to create spaces where veterans can take off their masks? Author and minister Jan Christian asked this question in her message at a Unitarian Universalist service in Colorado Springs, in which she talked about her journey to reconcile the loss of her brother in Vietnam, and especially to grapple with that part of him who chose to be a Marine: "We are hungry, are we not? We are hungry for the spaces to speak from the heart, to share our hurts, and to listen to the hurts of one another. To find those things that connect us across political and religious differences across boundaries of race, gender, class, and age. Places where we do not rush to judge or fix."

Even as she remained a radical activist for peace, she sought relationships and dialog with veterans who served alongside the one she so missed. "I wonder," she asked,

> . . . if we might be more willing to set aside our need to be right, so that we can be in relationship. Not just with people like us, but with people not like us. I wonder if we can just learn to do a better job of being present to the suffering, which more than anything else connects the human family.[10]

Civilian engagement with that suffering, for her, was critical. "When we let those who are willing to serve be misused, we are the ones who are not holding up our end of the bargain. Not those who've agreed to serve." She embraced restorative justice as a framework for her engagement, asking "where are the hurts?" and stressing being willing to "stay with the pain" as critical points for doing this work.

Another champion of military-civilian dialog is Tamara Sherwood, founder of Military Matters and mother of a recent veteran Marine.[11] She brings her previous work with alternative dispute resolution to try to "close the gaps" of understanding between veterans and civilians, creating a "positive ripple effect" to facilitate reintegration through group dialog, mediation, and coaching services.

Veterans working through Military Matters decided to *create*—not *seek*—self-help through service. "We are trained to serve over there, and we should serve our own communities, *here*, as we do theirs there," as the young vet who emerged as the leader put it. An event we referred to as the Soldier-Santa giveaway, held a few weeks before Christmas, was a good example. The eight enlisted soldiers from Fort Carson who participated, seven men and one woman, had recently returned from tours. Most were processing out of the army and turning their sights toward "home"—southern Colorado—which was also a place most had never lived before.

The young veterans gathered dozens of presents donated from local businesses, which were wrapped and waiting under tables on the cold December morning outside of the public library downtown. The event was not merely a giveaway; the veterans also framed it as an opportunity to connect with community and share their stories. Each went to the mike and shared distressing homecoming-in-process stories: addiction, relationship loss, interpersonal violence, depression, and isolation—the now all-too-familiar stuff—as the kids stamped their feet for 90 minutes in the cold, eyeing the toys piled on and under tables in numbers far outnumbering the kids present.

"I'd just appreciate it if you'd come together and—I'm not talking about money or anything—but just support us. We need more programs like this," one told the spare crowd. Reframing reintegration away from therapy, and toward service, mitigated their resistance to being victims or asking for pity. It allowed them to summon the publics—real and imaginary—with whom they seemed to yearn to interact. Yet, standing in the cold that morning with the event's organizers, a few Vietnam vet activists and some two dozen underdressed children and families, most of them just shuttled over from local homeless shelters, we felt pained for the soldiers that their public had not quite shown up. While it was not clear exactly what "public" they were looking for, the audience of homeless adults and little children, restless in the cold, were hardly best positioned to provide the support and receptivity the soldiers sought. We recalled MacCannell's (1992) phrase "empty meeting grounds," used to capture the missing-each-other, lack of authentic interaction between locals and tourists. "Chief," a tall American Indian man who was among the homeless, won the grand prize girls' bike, then gave it to a little girl who was present, saying he was already happy because "now I have presents to send my own kids." This became a story retold at subsequent events, affirming the event's success.

In these informal attempts at dialog, creating spaces in which diverse concerns could be listened to, uncensored or "managed," turned out to be an area of considerable interest. Yet another dialog-staging group, One Freedom, began convening conversations in Colorado Springs in 2010.[12] They are the nonprofit complement, run by wife Elizabeth Hawkins, to husband Steven Robinson's Magis group, which provided the 4–4 Brigade's WAROPS program before their deployment to Afghanistan (chapters 1 and 5). Like Magis, One Freedom frames the domestic crisis as a "stress epidemic," both for deploying service members but also for family members and wider communities. The program emphasizes bringing "neurophysiology 101 to a basic audience" to teach how the body and brain respond to stress, and then provide tools for self-regulation, "with direct, beneficial effect on the body." These tools help relieve symptoms of overstress such as sleeplessness, irritability, anxiety, and depression. In their video, a woman speaks of having to "harden yourself" to bear the deployments. "One of the most important things I learned this week" she added, referring to a One Freedom retreat she attended, "is that it's important for the deploying spouse to recognize that the spouse at home is going through their own sort of trauma."

By talking about "stress" as the problem and offering a positive, adaptive outlook for coping, One Freedom creates a relatively neutralized space for veteran-civilian dialog. Framing a public dialog around the stress does not, of course, completely avert confrontations with the moral and political reality of war itself, as the words of one of One Freedom's planned speakers at a downtown Colorado Springs dialog circle illustrate. He introduced himself to the circle as CJ, a special forces veteran. He spoke about problems with his five "more liberal" siblings when he came back from Iraq. The "things I'd done [in Iraq] became a problem for us," he said. "I came home from freeing Iraqis to be a captive in my own mind, unable to solve conflict normally." Later in the discussion, CJ added that "if someone needs to pay in blood for the things we're doing, let it be one of us," referring to the three buddies he met with for nightly Bible study, "because we're okay with it." Imagining addressing his adversary, he later added, "Your life is hate and pain. It's 'We're gonna take you somewhere awesome,'" presumably meaning something like heaven, or hell.

In chapter 7 we found that, despite there being no shortage of need for services or those willing to provide them, finding effective ways to match those in need with providers was often fraught with difficulty. Mismatched expectations and motivations can equally be the case for those seeking connection through dialog. Military Matters has not yet succeeded in securing a sustaining source of funding, perhaps because its focus on "closing [cultural] gaps" is somewhat vague and also potentially volatile. By contrast, One Freedom, by narrowing the focus to a decontextualized and neutralized focus on stress management, appears to have secured more reliable support.

Not coincidentally, one could also view One Freedom's work as ultimately accommodationist—a "force multiplier"—in that one of their aims is to enable people to withstand the stresses of war and multiple deployments, while remaining silent about their root causes.

A central issue in "dialog" is, of course, that of mutuality: to what degree do members of the military come to public settings willing not only to share, but also to listen, to extend themselves, and to learn, even from civilians? Real connection and reconciliation, we submit, can only take place when the exchange is two-way, when veterans balance the sharing of their experiences with listening to responses. Just as service members might resist being reduced to medical diagnoses and positions as passive patients, civilians also have agendas that bring them to dialog, and which merit admission.

## Ethnographers as Citizens

Even in such complex and tense exchanges as those in this chapter, a careful choreography of what gets said, and by whom, remains. Again and again we hear careful admonishment to keep "politics" out of exchanges where non-judgmental empathy is key. One very clear reason that civilians expressing their views of the wars requires careful management is that veterans, their family members, and others frequently are barred from speaking openly.

Nevertheless, we recently have held high hopes for a newly emergent small group we've been part of, as a space welcoming candid civilian participation in dialog. We think of it as the "Golden Lotus Group" (after the restaurant where we first met). For us, this group represented a space where we were not first and foremost fieldworkers, but equally present as citizens looking for ways that civilians might support individual veterans' reintegration, while at the same time resisting being cast as cheerleaders for the wars or for veterans as super-citizens.

The men involved are nearly all vets, a mix from Vietnam, Iraq, and Afghanistan. And the women, so far, are all civilians drawn for motives of research, public art or art therapy, or restorative justice dialog. We began to meet to share our varied involvement related to reintegration for postdeployment Iraqi and Afghan vets. Thus far, Joe Barrera of Veterans Remember (VR) had led the meetings. He clearly viewed it as an outgrowth of VR, because he would reiterate VR's guidelines, including the participation of civilians as part of a "nonjudgmental, civilian audience." We, along with the other civilian women participants, were uncertain whether this newer group might afford opportunities to move beyond our prescribed role as purely receptive audience members. We were still trying to feel out what the guidelines, understandings, and expectations for these conversations would be.

A clear test of these boundaries came in response to a group email conversation. Joe, responding to a fellow Vietnam vet, wrote: "I've met many who opted out of Vietnam for various reasons, and they all have wanted to know 'what it was like.' That's code for 'I wish I had gone with you.'" We waited three weeks before responding. At the group's request, we scanned and circulated a chapter titled "The Enduring Appeals of War," from J. Glenn Gray's *The Warriors: Reflections on Men in Battle*, a book the older veterans revered and wanted the group to read.[13] This afforded us an opportunity to include a somewhat less glorifying, counterpoint reading, "Awakenings," from Matthew Gutmann and Catherine Lutz's book *Breaking Ranks* (2010), about six soldiers' epiphanies while serving in Iraq that turned them against the war. In explaining our selection, Sarah wrote to the group, "It's a stark reminder that not everyone deep down wishes they'd gone [to war], even as I am the first to embrace that one can easily be swept up in war's intensity and immediacy."

Sending this chapter was a risk: at minimum, it departed from the "audience" role prescribed by the parent group. We were not surprised that in the end at least one vet was disturbed by the suggestion. He later explained to us that his response was related to seeing Gutmann and Lutz exploiting veterans' accounts and perpetuating the "accusation" of soldiers being "the murder-rapist-genocidal 'baby killer' thing," which he viewed as "a cruel device that wounded many veterans permanently" after Vietnam. Here it seemed the "lessons learned" from Vietnam (about not vilifying soldiers) threatened to conspire with an all-volunteer, class-based military to effectively disallow genuine, face-to-face dialog about the current wars and their respective merits.

Though inserting this chapter made some uncomfortable, it did provoke searching conversations. Joe's email response, prior to the next gathering, read in part,

> *The Gutmann and Lutz reading holds up to the light the inherent difficulties of fighting so-called "asymmetrical" wars against insurgents in countries we have invaded and occupied, as we did in Vietnam and have done in Iraq and Afghanistan. We may have good reasons for these wars, but the moral and ethical lines quickly blur and become invisible. This means that for many soldiers the normal rules of war don't exist anymore. And bad things happen, like the killing of civilians or noncombatants who are not supposed to be targets. This creates huge guilt for many, leading to permanent moral dilemmas, bitterness, cynicism, complete disillusionment with patriotism and patriotic rhetoric, and then to PTSD and worse.*

Here Joe places the moral and emotional costs of war on the table for discussion. Continuing on, he pinpoints what he considers some of the stickiest issues in Iraq and Afghanistan.

> *Of course, there are no true noncombatants among the civilians in these wars. This is not because the enemy is hiding among the population. It is because the civilians are the enemy. They all want us out. That's enough to make all of them the enemy. In this kind of war in which we cannot distinguish between "good guys" and "bad guys," and we kill civilians out of frustration or simply because we don't know if they are the enemy masquerading as "friendlies," we fight at the peril of our own conscience.*
>
> *. . . This means that even if we went into these wars with the highest moral purposes—the desire to do good, to liberate people from despots and fanatics, to bring stability and democracy to benighted regions, to end terrorism—in the end we become tainted with the same crimes we fight against.*

Joe finished by asserting that, "[t]he practical matter at hand right now is how to take care of the returning soldiers." As a still-struggling veteran himself, being there for new veterans in ways no one was there for him provided a salve of sorts.

The stickier the exchanges, we found, the deeper goes the dialog, insofar as civility and mutual respect can be upheld. Public dialog that avoids zones of discomfort, given the spectrum of issues to face in the wake of more than a decade of controversial warfare, typically fails to meet the standard of mutual exchanges across difference that define dialog in the first place.

### Conclusion: Dialog and Civil-Military Relations

Town halls, Veterans Remember, and other civilian-military dialog-based events allow us to take in a spectrum of public interaction, from more official and formal to personal and casual. The objectives behind the town halls were largely practical. On the organizers side they served to report out, coordinate preparation, and to respond to public concerns; for many of the attendees, to network and problem-solve. In this context, desires for a "controlled environment" result in efforts at scripting the dialog; though never total, this scripting became more complete as the meetings shifted toward greater governmental control.

The objectives of both organizers and attendees at Veterans Remember and other informal dialogs are, by contrast, largely personal, motivated by the infinite ways military service in war affects lives of veterans and civilians alike. Even in these more informal gatherings participants are concerned with creating spaces ideally able to contain high emotions and protect the integrity of the group. In both settings, we find tension among ideals of openness, mutual receptiveness, and genuine dialog, yet it is precisely in the moments when scripts and performances fray, and where "ultimate questions" rear their heads, that we witness the beginnings of authentic dialog.

The field of civil-military relations has to date largely been concerned with the need for civilian oversight of the military. This prevents the emergence of militarism, memorably defined by Alfred Vagts as the condition of a society that "ranks military institutions and ways above the prevailing attitudes of civilian life and carries the military mentality into the civilian sphere" (1937:12). Disagreements arise as to whether a gap between military and civilian subcultures is problematic: is it merely to be controlled (Huntington 1957), or to be diminished (Feaver 2011; Janowitz 1960; Schiff 2008)? Effective dialog across the gap, Bacevich and Kohn (1997) assert, especially in the area of ethical decision-making, lessens the risk that the American military would lose the support of, or become antagonistic vis-à-vis, society and become problematically militaristic. These issues are sharpened from the vantage point of an all-volunteer force over a decade-plus of multiple deployments, and a growing divergence of intimate versus quite distant experiences of being a nation at war.

Civilian-military dialogs in community can then be viewed in part as spaces where military legitimacy is created and reproduced via civilian ratification. They also become, we submit, critical sites for the processes of negotiating public engagement with being at war, or resisting degrees of militarism and militarization. Eliot Cohen views military-civilian dialog as inherently "unequal" because civilian authority rightfully exercises ultimate authority power. He predicts that during wartime, the dialog becomes still more unequal and tense, with bounds of jurisdiction more blurred (Cohen 2001:433). Feaver (2011) distinguishes between "professional supremacism," which emphasizes the need for giving value to the military voice in the dialog, and "civilian supremacists" who maintain wariness about military voices getting too much deference and holding too much sway (see also Nielson 2012:376).

The finely grained interactions we examine here are less concerned with the policy and oversight that is the focus of most scholars of military-civilian relations. Of paramount interest here is the domestic cultural and relational climate to which veterans return. In these interactions we find ample support for the latter, "civilian supremacist" perspective. We underline ways in which the "culture of democracy" is constrained by militarist priorities

(Wolin 2008). Cornel West names the three basic commitments of democracy: to questioning, to justice, and a "tragicomic commitment to hope" (2004:19). In community settings, these become constrained and muffled under manifold projections of militarist power. While the draw to dialog is nonetheless strong for civilians, we demonstrate ethnographically that consistent practices of managing and of subtly shaping and censuring what can be said, particularly by civilians, hamper the mutuality of engagement. This undercuts how effectively dialog can serve reintegration, reconciliation, or preventive efforts. Ironically, we find that these dialogs serve such efforts best, and enact participatory democracy most meaningfully, precisely where they are messiest: where breaks in performance occur, where efforts to guide and control go awry and conversation ventures into tense and treacherous territory. Inconclusive though these early exchanges remain, they merit far more in their imperfect grappling than does the absence of dialog altogether.

# War and Collective Reckoning

*No one realized that the book and the labyrinth were one and the same.*
— Jorge Luis Borges, *The Garden of Forking Paths*

*The military doesn't reload bullets. They spend the bullet and the shell goes on the ground and it rusts. And it will be there for anthropologists to dig it up sometime in the future and they'll say, "Wow, that was a wartime period in history there; look at this."*

*But it's enlightening for everyone and I think that the only chance you have to evolve as a species away from war is if everyone is totally aware of the cost. If you hide any of it—if you hide flag-draped caskets, and you hide PTSD, and you hide slow alcoholism, suicide, and self-destructive behavior, and you hide and hide and hide and hide—then you sanitize it to the point of perpetuating it.*

— local activist Mark Lewis (quoting a Vietnam veteran friend)

This book raises more questions than it answers, points to more problems than it solves. Far from claiming to lead readers out of war's labyrinth, we hope these pages have beckoned many inside, or further inside. Perhaps they even have offered occasional navigational ideas or information to readers far more intimate with the shifting passageways of the maze than we could ever be.

Following a long career as a systems analyst, Donella Meadows concluded that the most effective way to intervene in a system comes from "the power to transcend paradigms" (1999:3).

Across the chapters of this book, we highlight potential paradigm shifts of various sorts: from conceptions of strength that stress physical might to those including psychological, social, and spiritual strength; from notions of security based upon national interests to human security, which stresses complex, interdependent wholes. From a reductive focus on PTSD as "the" unseen wound of war, we have asked, "What else do we also need to understand?" From versions of public engagement with war based on civilians-as-audience, whose job is merely to listen, we have called for reciprocal military-civilian interchange, and for civilians who shoulder responsibility.

Most important, we have suggested a shift in the way we narrate war for ourselves. Beyond war stories centered upon the individual, masculinized protagonist's journey, we offer a collective, mind-boggling labyrinth, a tangled plurality of many standpoints and stories both local and global, and lurking with variable, minotaur-like threats and fears. In so doing, we submit that coming back from war entails dismantling the compartmentalization that war creates, between "us" and our "enemies," between "here" and "over there," between soldier and civilian, between "their" war and "our" war. Meaning matters. Metaphors, relating something we know to something that is new or that we know differently, are one of the primary ways humans understand the world. War as labyrinth defies separation and insulation: it means that global echoes of war's violence reverberate and affect us all, and that they necessarily follow combatants home.

In dwelling considerably on PTSD even as we urge readers to also go beyond it, we argue the diagnosis means something distinct for afflicted soldiers and the clinicians who treat them from the meanings it takes on in wider public discourse. The unprecedented challenges presented by protracted wars and multiple deployments, and serviced through an all-volunteer force, create a circumstance in which what is good for treating individual bodies afflicted by PTSD—individualized, neutralizing medicalization—may be exactly the wrong prescription for the collective, social body, where nations and communities must reckon with war in all its components. Here, applying decontextualized, reductive assessments can be perilous, potentially consigning us to simply deepening the same trammeled routes through the maze, blinding us to alternatives.

In proffering the labyrinth, we raise the house lights to look around at the audience, the spouses and children, parents, and community members who also serve and also suffer. While we endorse a semirelativist perspective that honors multiple viewpoints and ways of being, we do not suggest that every way of managing terror culturally is equally constructive or morally sound. In fact, we entreat readers to attend to the moral dimensions of suffering, healing, and the divisions within and between communities accentuated by war. War is already so multifaceted, involving control over and access to resources, conflicting cultural values, biological drives, and environmental conditions. When we try to reduce it, to contain it, to suggest that we can predictably manage it to attain a favorable cost-benefit result, we are blindsided.

Stigma, the defining and labeling of difference as abnormal and undesirable, exists in varied forms. The stigma surrounding PTSD and physical disabilities resulting from the wounds of war differs from stigma associated with how military occupational specialties become ranked in ways that are gendered (and "classed," "raced," and so on). Stigma assigned to civilians as undisciplined, indulgent, and weak is something still again. Like most of the concepts we discuss, stigma is useful in describing social and institutional sources of tension and conflict and, with respect to PTSD, to explaining barriers to care. Many active-duty soldiers resist claiming the diagnosis of PTSD and seeking help because of its associated stigma as a mental disorder, as a sign of weakness, and as something that stands in the way of fulfilling their mission and their obligation to fellow soldiers. Yet it is never straight-forward. When soldiers leave the military, the stigma of PTSD may be trans-formed from a barrier to care to a socially legitimated need for care and compensation and a source of identity and solidarity with other veterans.

So we conclude that stigma in its myriad forms is better understood as one of many ways that humans manage terror. Terror is an existen-tial dilemma that we all face, on battlefields and in domestic life alike; it reminds us of our mortality and fragility, and that trauma is always, every-where, potentially just around the corner. Even at home, violence on a scale approaching what soldiers face in war plagues many communities. In war, violence takes on sharpened, particular forms. Terror, stress, and trauma punctuated by waiting and boredom become "normal" parts of life, no lon-ger buffered by the relative regularity of domestic culture. Millions of Iraqi and Afghan civilians have faced the acute terror of war daily for decades, compounded by economic insecurity and hardship. Life is intrinsically hard; where we have choices about the use of war and violence, it is best to con-sider carefully how we might avoid compounding the terror.

That we use culture to manage terror may be in part hard-wired, an aspect of our evolutionary adaptation for survival. But how we frame culture—our paradigms—are something we can and do change. On an individual and community level, the army's efforts to fight stigma associ-ated with war's invisible wounds so that soldiers and veterans seek help is an important step. Equally important are establishing effective, evidence-based clinical treatments complemented by a variety of community-based programs that reintegrate soldiers into civilian life and extend hands across the military-civilian divide. But by themselves they are inadequate. We must also ask ourselves: how will we manage terror culturally as a nation? If we condition a segment of our citizens, many already troubled by violence, declining economic opportunities, and poor education, to exercise lethal force, and repeatedly place them in embattled contexts where they become subject to and agents of violence, blow-back at home and abroad is inevi-table. The murders in Colorado Springs, Major Nidal Hasan gunning down

13 soldiers at Fort Hood, and Staff Sergeant Robert Bales killing 16 unarmed Afghan civilians were acts committed by individuals with unique histories and experiences. But at the societal level these were not isolated events; they form a pattern of violence spilling over from the sanctioned use of lethal force. Once again the labyrinth of war forces us to view these events as part of a global whole.

In considering the largely unpaid, undersung, and "voluntary" labor of military spouses and other community members, we note that they proudly prioritize this work even as it is undervalued. Social reproduction may be undervalued when war-work is prioritized and considered highly productive, yet we submit it may be the ultimate form of service.

We maintain that civilian disengagement with the plight of our service members and the campaigns they serve is dangerous. Checks and balances are an essential component of a vibrant democracy. In reaction to the power of standing armies in Europe, our country was founded on the idea of the citizen soldier who is willing and able to serve his or her country in time of need, but whose primary role is to pursue his or her own interests, to build the nation and community through agriculture, commerce, and civic organizations. To an extent this was a position of good fortune, of having less powerful neighbors to our north and south and oceans between us and Europe, Asia, and South America. But it allowed us to build national security and a powerful role in international affairs through peacetime pursuits: industry, technological innovation, and education. Soldiers frequently told us that they had been mistrained for what they were asked to do on deployments. Many soldiers, especially those in the junior enlisted ranks without a college education, find that military experience does not always translate into similarly well-paying jobs in the civilian workforce. At the national level, as we maintain a sizeable standing army (albeit much reduced from its greatest size in WWII), we must feed it, clothe it, equip it, and find things for it to do. This distracts attention and resources from honing other skills, maintaining infrastructure, investing in public education, and other national pursuits that have made us a strong nation. In a globalized world where national boundaries are increasingly porous, human security is essential in creating national security.

As civilians who have never served in the military and as academics whose previous areas of research did not focus on the military, we may be unlikely navigators for these landscapes of war come home. One reviewer of an early article we submitted was adamant that we were not the right people for this job. But we felt called—by people like Jody Newsome who was looking for ways to help soldiers feel comfortable seeking help, by living in a community surrounded by military installations where uniformed soldiers are a visible presence, by being citizens in a nation at war, and by being witness to the often unpublicized and under-acknowledged suffering of Iraqis and Afghans.

We are just now beginning to come to terms with the post-9/11 wars and their effects on soldiers, families, and communities across the nation. As we cast about for words to bring this book to a close, we recall words not of closure, but of invocation.

The chaplain welcomed those gathered in a vast hall on the morning of Veterans Day 2011. She said she hoped community members would find it "a place of hospitality," and specified why we gathered that day to listen to veterans' stories.

*As we gather today we do so not to glorify war or violence, or to focus on different ideologies or thoughts about peace or nonviolence. Those conversations are for another time. Rather, we gather mindful of experiences of women and men who have served our nation with, at times, great personal sacrifices. Who have given their lives in the service of this nation and to what they hold most dear about being American.*

Then, more formally, she invoked:

*So in gathering, may this space be a place of deep sharing. May all words be spoken with integrity. May all words be heard with compassion. May the experiences brought here be held without judgement and may the grace of this time help heal old wounds in our lives and in our community's life. And together, with the sacred, may we bless this time to come.*

Our hope for these pages is similar: that all the voices that speak through them bring us to mindfulness, enjoining us to share in the experiences, wounds, and sacrifices from the post-9/11 wars.

# Notes

## Introduction

Epigraph is from Solnit (200:70).

1 We sought no Department of Defense funding, and the institutional reviews of our research protocols with respect to the protection of human subjects (Institutional Review Boards) were through our academic institutions.

2 A month previously, following army protocol, we had notified Fort Carson's Public Affairs Office (PAO) of our research plan, and followed with calls, but had not heard back.

3 The US Field Army is organized hierarchically with the basic unit being the squad of four to ten soldiers, platoons of three to four squads (16–40 soldiers), companies of three to four platoons (100–200 soldiers), battalions of three to five companies (500–600 soldiers), brigades of three or more battalions (3,000–5,000 soldiers), divisions of three brigades (10,000–18,000 soldiers), and corps of two to five divisions. For details on how this relates to the command structure, see http://www.army.mil/info/organization/unitsandcommands/oud/ (accessed August 10, 2013).

4 *Anthropologists in the SecurityScape: Ethics, Practice, and Professional Identity* (Albro et al. 2012) presents anthropologists' experiences working in military- and security-related sectors.

5 To date, the RAND Corporation study (Tanielian and Jaycox 2008) gives the most definitive measure of the prevalence of PTSD, TBI, and depression in the US military. See also Hoge et al. (2004, 2006); Hosek et al. (2006); and Terrio et al. (2009). Use of different standardized measures, differences in study design, underreporting by military personnel, and changes in screening practices and collection of epidemiological data contribute to the lack of precision (Ramchand et al. 2010; Richardson et al. 2010).

6 For the full diagnostic criteria for PTSD, see APA (2013:309.81[F43.10]). The symptoms and behaviors are related to the traumatic event and cannot be explained by other medical conditions or effects of medications or alcohol or drugs.

7 On concepts of the body on soldiers and war-related injuries, see Carden-Coyne (2009). For historical and cultural analyses of the development of the diagnosis of PTSD, see Breslau (2004), McHugh and Treisman (2007), Summerfield (2001), and Young (1995). Fear et al. (2010) estimate the prevalence of PTSD among UK soldiers at 4 percent compared with 15 to 20 percent among US soldiers. For anthropological critiques of the universality of PTSD, see Bracken (2001), Bracken et al. (1995), Breslau (2004), and Hinton and Lewis-Fernández (2010).

8 On the role of trauma in contemporary discourse, see Fassin and Rechtman (2009). Mark Nichter (1981, 2010) proposed the concept of idiom of distress; Craig Janes (1999) elaborated the underlying power dynamics. Kilshaw (2009) studied Gulf War Syndrome.

9 Unemployment among teenagers is generally the highest of any age group, but following the economic downturn of 2008, unemployment among young people in this group constituted 45 percent of the unemployed workforce (Ruetschlin and Draut 2013). On characteristics of military recruits, see Elder et al. (2010) and Kelty et al. (2010). There are no accurate statistics on the percentage of veterans who graduate from higher-education programs, though some media accounts suggest that the dropout rate in the first year is very high. Student Veterans of America recently joined with the VA and National Student Clearinghouse to track student outcomes for GI bill recipients (Student Veterans of America 2013).

10 James Dao (2010) reported on changes in qualifications for disability. Karlin et al. (2010) discuss evidence-based therapies for PTSD and their dissemination in the Veterans Health Administration (VHA). Didier Fassin and Richard Rechtman (2009) explore the role of PTSD as "ending suspicion" of malingering though, based on our research, suspicion still exists among active duty military personnel and some therapists.

11 Colorado College. "Deployment Stress." http://www.coloradocollege.edu/offices/cce/community-based-research/military-engagement/Deployment-Stress/ (accessed August 30, 2013).

12 "Allies" has different implications for the two wars: the March 19, 2003, invasion of Afghanistan was led by North Atlantic Treaty Organization (NATO) forces, while that of Iraq was by a 48-member multinational force to which Great Britain, Australia, and Poland contributed troops and other countries later supplied with support troops after invasion.

13 As of April 15, 2012.

14 As of May 2011; Department of Defense and Veterans Administration. http://www.infoplease.com/ipa/A0004615.html (accessed August 30, 2013).

15 See Conarroe (2011) for Colorado Springs' specifics.

16 Female service members were officially exempt from serving in frontline combat roles until January 24, 2013, when Defense Secretary Leon Panetta lifted the ban under political pressure and in recognition that women were de facto already serving in frontline positions (Vanden Brook, 2013.

17 See also J. McGrath (2007) and Holmstedt (2007).

18 The first Persian Gulf War's duration ranged from 60 days to seven months.

19 U.S. Department of Defense. Secretary of Defense Robert M. Gates lecture at Duke University, September 29, 2010. http://www.defense.gov/speeches/speech.aspx?speechid=1508 (accessed August 10, 2013).

20 Catherine Lutz argues that the era between the end of the Cold War and the post-9/11 wars was not one of peace, but instead one of "Hot Peace: training other people's armies and police, drug interdiction, hurricane relief, hostage rescue, the quelling of civil disorder, and what it called nation-building assistance" (2001:217).

21 A study of UK soldiers shows that decreased dwell time is one of the few factors clearly associated with increased incidence of PTSD (Rona et al. 2007).

22 U.S. Department of Defense. Secretary of Defense Robert M. Gates lecture at Duke University, 2010.

23 The Ninth Quadrennial Review of Military Compensation published in 2004 found military compensation at the 60th percentile of civilian earnings. With the economic downturn of 2007 military compensation increased to the 70th percentile of civilian earnings (Warner 2012:89).

24 Recruiting officers find it easier to meet quotas during national economic recession (GAO 2006).

25 In 2007, only 70 percent of army recruits had high school diplomas. "Waivers for serious misdemeanors increased from 3,002 in 2005 to 8,259 in 2007," Inskeep and Bowman (2008).

26 Kelty et al. (2010) demonstrate that while both military men and women marry younger, rates are higher among men than women. Teachman and Tedrow (2007) studied age and marriage among enlisted men by race. Military service affected marriage more for white than for black men.

27 These three admittedly distinct images share, we submit, ubiquitous mythological bases. Ovid, in fact, is thought to have broken with Homer's earlier mention of a labyrinth as a dance for Ariadne, with a single path to the center and back out, in favor of something that is by definition closer to a maze, with twisting, interpenetrating passages, nearly impossible to navigate (Doob 1992). Conflating them, loosely, allows us to draw on elements of each.

28 Board Game Geek. Board Game: Labyrinth: The War on Terror, 2001-? http://www.boardgamegeek.com/forum/631159/labyrinth-the-war-on-terror-2001/reviews (accessed August 10, 2013).

29 This tack parallels Enloe's approach, asking "where are the women?" and using "a feminist curiosity" when thinking about war and militarization (2004; see also 2000, 2007, 2010).

## Chapter 1

Epigraph quotes are from Danielewski (2000:xi, 334).

1 US Army. "PTSD: Pulling The Stigma Down." youtube.com. www.youtube.com/watch?v =KlgR9N-EXng (accessed August 2, 2013).

2 The purpose is to identify people by their sex, which in our society we view as biological, fixed, and clearly defined, instead of their gender (men and women but also including transgender, gay, and lesbian), which is more self-identified, fluid, and ambiguous.

3 "The Army Values." Army.mil. http://www.army.mil/values/ (accessed August 2, 2013).

4 Army Strong. http://www.youtube.com/watch?v=YSbCnWe6e10 (accessed August 2, 2013); US Army Public Affairs (2006).

5 "The New US Army Strong Commercial." youtube.com. http://www.youtube.com/watch? v=cq-ZVIZJaI8&feature=related (accessed August 2, 2013). The warrior ethos can be found at http://www.army.mil/values/warrior.html (accessed August 2, 2013), and the Soldier's Creed at http://www.army.mil/values/soldiers.html (accessed August 2, 2013).

6 Veterans of many wars speak of the bond among soldiers as a motivation to fight and face death. See Dyer (2005), Gray (1998 [1959]), Grossman (2009 [1995]), and Remarque (1982 [1928]).

7 The relationship between PTSD and mild TBI is complex and clinicians disagree on this topic. Mild TBI and PTSD share symptoms such as fatigue, impaired memory and concentration, sleep disturbances and irritability (Elder and Cristian 2009). In one study, individuals who experienced mild TBI from blasts, with and without loss of consciousness, also reported high incidence of PTSD and depression (Hoge et al. 2008). At present the criteria set forth in the American Psychiatric Association's clinical definition is the definitive test for PTSD. There is no definitive biological test for either mild TBI or PTSD, though recent studies show promise for a magnetic resonance imaging (MRI) screening tool for PTSD (Georgopoulos et al. 2010).

8 A total of 34 of the 43 soldiers we interviewed made a clear distinction between TBI as a physical injury and PTSD as a mental condition.

9 Whereas Americans assume that "medicine" is culture-free and universal, medical anthropologists understand that medicine, like other medical systems (Ayurveda, Tibetan, Chinese) is based in the scientific, philosophical, cultural, and historical developments of European societies and elaborated and spread from Europe through its colonies from the Enlightenment to the present. Hence, they market medicine as biomedicine.

10 An exception is the popular image of the deranged veteran, highly masculinized and prone to violence.

11 *Breaking Ranks* is the title of Gutmann and Lutz's 2010 book; see also Cohn and Gilberd (2009) and Iraqi Veterans Against the War (IVAW) and Glantz (2009).

12 More recently, soldiers who chronically underperformed would likely have been chaptered out "other-than-honorably." See Dave Philipps's report on such discharges, many of whom have been diagnosed with PTSD and TBI (2009a, 2009b). See also readers' comments, which reflect the discourse surrounding these injuries (http://gazette.com/article/1500272 [accessed August 2, 2013]).

13 See Britt (2000), Gould et al. (2007), Greene-Shortridge et al. (2007), Hoge et al. (2004), and Milliken et al. (2007).

14 They could also answer that they had not received mental health services if those services were for marital, family, or grief-related issues, and they did not involve the soldier having used violence.

15 US Army Logistics Innovation Agency (USALIA) EPIC Policy Search Tool. "Use of Term 'Behavioral' Health in Lieu of 'Mental' Health"/MEDCOM Policy Memorandum 09-240 (accessed August 30, 2013).

## Chapter 2

Epigraph quote is from Plutarch (1967:29).

1 In 2012, the US Justice Department granted $111 million for its Community Oriented Policing Services (COPS) program. A majority (629) of the 800 new police jobs must go to veterans who served after 9/11 (Loria 2012). As a consequence, many of the police who responded to the bombing at the Boston Marathon in April 2013 were veterans trained in urban combat.

2 The public may not always see the work of police and firefighters as "disgusting or polluting or degrading," because they minimize these aspects of their work. For example, the majority of firefighters' emergency calls are not for fires, but to rouse unconscious drunks or respond to the indigent ill (Tracy and Scott 2006), and police officers routinely deal with corpses; abandoned, dirty buildings; and sex workers, drug dealers, and others that society views as "dirty" (Walker and Katz 2005).

3 In *The Spitting Image* (1998), Vietnam veteran and sociologist Jerry Lembcke argues that there is no factual evidence to support the stories of Vietnam veterans being spit upon, but he recognizes that these stories "continue to fill a need in American culture...through which many people remember the loss of the war, the centerpiece of a betrayal narrative that understands the war to have been lost because of treason on the home front" (Lembcke 2005). Lembcke attributes public reinvocation of the myth during the post-9/11 wars as a means of displacing attention from meaningful dialog about the wars to the "phony issue of who supports the troops" (Lembcke 2003).

4 Anthropologist Mary Douglas argues that while all societies define activities and areas of experience that are prohibited and considered contaminating or polluting if transgressed, even when that transgression is something necessary to its functioning, for example, tanning animal hides or burying the dead. But she notes that where those boundaries are drawn and what activities are defined as defiling varies cross-culturally, so we should not assume that handling dead bodies is polluting everywhere (Douglas 1966).

5 Thanks to Dr. Rhoda Singer for sharing this information.

6 In addition to the "secrets" discussed here, Tim O'Brien's classic title story for the collection *The Things They Carried* (1990; invoked in this section's subheader) stressed that soldiers shared the "common secret of cowardice" in the face of fear.

7 Rules of engagement are "Directives issued by competent military authority that delineate the circumstances and limitations under which United States forces will initiate and/or continue combat engagement with other forces encountered" (Department of Defense 2013).

8 For information on financial difficulties among US military personnel, see FINRA (2010).

9 Kriner and Shen define a casualty gap as "a systematic, significant difference in local casualty rates between communities that differ on a demographic dimension." They determine a community's socioeconomic status by the level of income and college education of its residents.

10 Veterans fare well in federal civil service jobs where their military service grants them points on the civil service exam (see "Veteran's Preference Points," at military.com; http://www.military.com/benefits/veteran-benefits/veterans-employment-preference-points.html [accessed August 27, 2013]).

11 "Friendly fire" refers to discharges from one's own side that threaten, injure, or kill one's own.

## Chapter 3

Epigraph is Abercrombie's (2006:11) rendering of Homer.

1 Team researcher Trevor Cobb reported this (see also Cobb 2010).

2 Names of individuals in this chapter not quoted from news media sources are pseudonyms.

3 Victor Turner (1967, 1972, 1974) and Van Gennep (1960) pioneered classic works on liminality in ritual.

4 See "IRR Reactivation" at the Iraq Veterans Against the War website (http://www.ivaw.org/resources/irr-reactivation [accessed August 14, 2013]).

5 For soldier's definition of "shit bag," see De Yoanna (2006). Philipps (2010) contrasts shit bags versus "squared away" soldiers throughout his text.

6 "Garrison" refers to an army post; a garrison commander oversees daily operations of the installation, but reports to the commanding general, who oversees the troops and, when at war, combat operations.

7 See the interview with Brigadier General Stephen Xenakis, M.D. (Ret.), at http://www.pbs.org/wgbh/pages/frontline/woundedplatoon/interviews/xenakis.html#ixzz1tvzUFfgQ (accessed August 14, 2013).

8 Additional coverage spanned the pages of the *Los Angeles Times* and *New York Times*, the *Colorado Springs Independent*, the *Rocky Mountain News* and the *Denver Post*, Denver's local weekly *Westword*, the *Army Times*, *The Nation*, and later of *Rolling Stone* and *Salon*. On television and online, the multipart PBS *Frontline* documentary (Edge 2010) was echoed by numerous segments on local and national news shows.

9 Ten days after the Army released the EPICON report about the 4th BCT, Colorado Springs' *Gazette* published a multiday investigative report that received a Pulitzer nomination. A year later, reporter Dave Philipps would deepen the account in the book *Lethal Warriors: When the New Band of Brothers Came Home—Uncovering the Tragic Reality of PTSD* (2010). The book argues that combat exposure resulted in PTSD that the Army neglected in its focus on preparing for the next deployment, and converted troubled combat veterans into threats unleashed onto the streets of Colorado Springs.

10 "Reflagging" units increased after World War II as the army placed more emphasis on retaining units with the most history and honors. See the entry on "Lineage" at http://www.globalsecurity.org/military/agency/army/lineage.htm (accessed August 14, 2013). See also US Army Center of Military History's online entry "Reflagging in the Army" at http://www.history.army.mil/books/Lineage/reflag/reflagarm.htm for an historical overview on reflagging. See also "4th Brigade Combat Team, 4th Infantry Division." http://www.globalsecurity.org/military/agency/army/4id-4bde.htm (accessed August 14, 2013).

11 Philipps quotes from Frontline interviews (Edge 2010); also see brigade "reset" at http://www.highbeam.com/doc/1P2-2773544.html (accessed March 6, 2012).

12 US Army Center of Military History, "Reflagging in the Army."

13 For more on 1-506th's history, see "2nd Stryker Brigade Combat Team. 2nd Infantry Division 'Strike Force'" at http://www.globalsecurity.org/military/agency/army/2id-2bde.htm (accessed August 14, 2013).

14 At the beginning of the Civil War, in October 1861 at Fort Hamilton, New York, the US Army reconstituted the 12th Infantry Regiment with the motto "Ducti Amore Patriae," "Having Been Led by Love of Country." The regiment lost half of its men as casualties in the Battle of Gaines Mill in 1862 (Department of the Army 2010). For more on 2–12th's history, see "12th Infantry Regiment (United States)" at http://en.wikipedia.org/wiki/12th_Infantry_Regiment_(United_States) (accessed August 14, 2013).

15 See "Ventura's Watershed with Paul Jenkins" at http://maverickmedia.wordpress.com/ (accessed August 14, 2013) for an extended, four-part film ("Smoked") and also a shorter, 40-minute version "Darkness in Al Doura"; the latter is also available at "On the Dark Side in Al Doura—A Soldier in the Shadows" (http://vimeo.com/33755968 [accessed August 14, 2013]).

16 Transcription from film "Smoked" (maverickmedia.wordpress.com).

17 For more of Michael De Yoanna's reporting on the Needham case, see De Yoanna (2012). For more on Andrew Pogany, see Philipps (2010:109–13, 233–34).

18 See the blog post "US Army Private John Needham's 'Notification of War Atrocities and Crimes' in Iraq," posted on November 28, 2011, at the Truthaholics website: http://truthaholics.wordpress.com/2011/11/28/us-army-private-john-needhams-notification-of-war-atrocities-and-crimes-in-iraq/ (accessed August 14, 2013).

19 During its 2009–2010 rotation in the Pech Valley, the 2nd Battalion saw heavy fighting throughout the area. A prominent feature of the 2–12th's tour was that it marked the first withdrawal of US forces from a key strategic valley—the Korengal Valley, known as a principal "rat line" or line for bringing supplies into Afghanistan from Pakistan to support the Taliban and other insurgent forces. Ironically, Sebastian Junger's film *Restrepo* and book *War*, both based on the fight for the Korengal two rotations before the 2–12th's arrival, celebrated the sacrifices made to gain that foothold.

20 "Videos of US Marines Urinating on Taliban Sparks Outrage." youtube.com. http://www.youtube.com/watch?v=SljHO-b4YEs (accessed August 14, 2013).

21 A "blue-on-green" attack is one in which coalition troops are attacked by people dressed in Afghan army or police uniforms. The Afghan army and police are the putative allies of the coalition forces.

22 Under the Geneva Conventions following WWII, military personnel who violated the conventions could be held individually responsible and tried for war crimes. "Crimes against international law are committed by men, not by abstract entities" (Heller 2011:3). Only rarely are national leaders tried for war crimes.

### Chapter 4

Epigraph are from Epstein (2013:SR8) and Homer (1996:78).

1 In 2007 the *Journal of Anxiety Disorders* devoted an entire issue to exploring the "challenges to PTSD construct" from the core assumptions underlying the diagnosis (Bodkin et al. 2007), to the evidence, based primarily on a large-scale national study of PTSD in Vietnam veterans (NVVRS) that had been used to assess its prevalence (McNally 2007), to issues of compensation and disability that complicate diagnosis and treatment (Jones and Wessely 2007).

2 Anthropologist Libbet Crandon-Malamud first asked this question in relationship to *susto*, a folk disease specific to Latin America. Instead of focusing on what *susto* is—its causes and symptoms—she argued that we should try to understand why specific groups of individuals were suffering from it at a given historical moment (Crandon-Malamud 1993). Nichter reinforced the need to ask why a particular diagnosis occurs in a given time and place in elaborating on his concept of "idioms of distress" (2010).

3 This process has been referred to as "looping," following philosopher of science Ian Hacking (1995); also see Young (2007).

4 The theory of traumatic memory is more complex than what we present here. Allan Young argues that its development says more about the social development of psychiatry than the nature of memory and its dynamics (2007).

5 For additional discussions of the history of PTSD as a medical diagnosis, see Breslau (2004), McHugh and Treisman (2007), and Summerfield (2001).

6 Many medical anthropologists view PTSD as a cultural syndrome specific to western societies, most specifically the United States. As a result, they object both to the western psychiatric view that PTSD is a universally applicable diagnostic category and to its active exportation to other societies through humanitarian relief efforts. For elaboration of the key arguments in the debate, see Breslau (2004) and de Jong (2004).

7 For the study of responses to 9/11, see Schuster et al. (2001). On bracket creep, see McNally (2006), and on the globalization of trauma care see Fassin and Rechtman (2009).

8 Also see The Headington Institute's discussion on "What is vicarious trauma?" (http://headington-institute.org/Default.aspx?tabid=2648 [accessed August 2, 2013]).

9 Here McNally cites the work of E. T. Dean (1997:209) and D. H. Marlowe (2001:73).

10 Moreover, Edward Tick, quoted in the subheading, finds PTSD cold and clinical, not reflecting the humanity and suffering soldiers face (2005:100).

11 Cognitive-behavioral therapy (CBT), prolonged exposure therapy (PE), and eye movement desensitization and reprocessing therapy (EMDR) are the three evidence-supported therapies (EST) recommended by the VA and Department of Defense. For a full description and evaluation of the protocols, see VA/Department of Defense (2010).

12 See Budden (2009), McNally (2003), and Young (1995) for excellent analyses of the relationship among shame, guilt, and anger in PTSD.

13 Cynthia Enloe's account of two women, one Iraqi (Nimo) and one US soldier (Emma), provides an important corrective to the homogenizing of women's experiences of the post-9/11 wars (Enloe 2010).

## Chapter 5

Epigraph is from Atwood (2005:88–89).

1 Fieldnotes by team member Hana Low contribute to this account.

2 Fort Carson Army Community Service. Reunion and Reintegration. DVD.

3 U.S. Army. "Basic Combat Training: The Ten-Week Journal from Civilian to Soldier." http://www.goarmy.com/soldier-life/becoming-a-soldier/basic-combat-training.html (accessed August 30, 2013).

4 "Marine Commercial." YouTube. http://www.youtube.com/watch?v=mplEt-7HNR8 (accessed August 30, 2013). For anthropological concepts of the rite of passage, see Van Gennep (1960) and Turner (1967, 1995 [1969]).

5 In a study of military reserve families, Faber et al. (2008) told the story of a veteran who struggled with readjusting to civilian life until he was placed in a job with more structure.

6 Goffman characterized the army as a total institution during basic training, and David Bayendor (2011), consultant to the project, argues that the military is a semi-total institution.

7 Kirmeyer, et al. (2007) presents current research.

8 Ready Army. "Comprehensive Soldier Fitness." http://www.acsim.army.mil/readyarmy/ra_csf.htm (accessed September 22, 2013).

9 For details on the CSF program, see Lester et al. (2011); for a critical view, see Eidelson (2011).

10 Since 1995, the percentage of married military personnel has declined. For officers, 72 percent were married in 1995 compared with 68 percent in 2006; for enlisted personnel, 57 percent were married in 1995 and 52 percent in 2006; for warrant officers, 85 percent were married in 1995 compared with 82 percent in 2006. Booth et al. (2007) suggest that this may reflect generational changes, at least among officers. See also *The Changing Profile of the Army* (Maxfield 2006) and Karney and Crown (2007).

11 Outserve-SLDN. "Family Benefits." http://www.sldn.org/pages/family-benefits (accessed August 30, 2013).

12 Service members make up 41 percent and family members make up 59 percent of the active component. In the reserve component, 58 percent are family members and 42 percent service members (Booth et al. 2007).

13 See also Hawkins (2001) on exaggerated surveillance over and demands placed on US military families living in Cold War Germany from 1986 to 1988.

14 National Military Family Assocation. "Military Culture." http://www.militaryfamily.org/get-info/new-to-military/military-culture/ (accessed August 30, 2013).

15 The AVF offers a route to US citizenship. Since 2002, active-duty military personnel could apply for citizenship regardless of time in the United States. In 2009, approximately 35,000 non-citizens were serving in the US military, many with spouses and children who did not speak English. Teresa Ibarra, whose center offers family counseling services to many military families in Colorado Springs's Latino community, told us that "the biggest problem isn't that the needs of the soldiers aren't getting met. It's the families of the soldiers. There's a real lack of communication. Somehow, Fort Carson doesn't have a program for the women and children...who are basically Spanish-speaking only and isolated."

16 Rates of marriage and dissolution of marriage (including annulment, separation, and divorce) rose and fell together, dropping to low levels from 1995 to 2001, then gradually rising back to 1995 levels by 2005. Karney and Crown (2007) conclude that high rates of marriage at younger ages explain more of the change in rates of marriage dissolution than do deployments.

17 Sheppard et al. (2010) proposes a model of the deployment process that includes five stages: (1) a pre-deployment stage of 3 to 6 months; (2) a deployment stage of 1 to 2 months; (3) a sustainment stage of 9 to 10 months; (4) a redeployment stage of 1 to 2 months; and (5) a postdeployment stage of 6 months. Stages 3 to 5 comprise the 12 months of a typical overseas deployment.

18 See Margaret Atwood's interpretive retelling *The Penelopiad* (2005).

19 In writing about military wives, we found ourselves deeply entangled in the gendered polarity of army life. Given the more intimate nature of our conversations and our shared gendered status as women, it felt strange to refer to them as "Neel" or "Harris," as we do with others, men and women, in these pages; hence, we call these spouses (and elsewhere, men with whom we were more familiar) by their first names here.

20 For studies of the relationship between parental coping and child mental health, see Amato (2001); Amato and Booth (2001); Booth and Amato (2001); and Ender (2005). For current research on the effects of multiple deployments on children of military personnel, see Chandra et al. (2009); Lester et al. (2010); Huebner and Mancini (2005); Richardson et al. (2011); Chartrand et al. (2008); and Price (2009).

21 Military personnel who have been away from their dependents for longer than 30 days under military orders are also eligible for a Family Separation Allowance of $100 to $250 per month (Powers 2003).

22 STS and STSD are not official diagnoses in the DSM-IV (APA 1994) and at this time will not be included in DSM-V (APA 2013).

23 Also see Allen et al. (2011); Finley (2011); Gimbel and Booth (1994); Karney and Crown (2007); Kessler (2000); Sherman et al. (2005); and Solomon et al. (2008).

### Chapter 6

Epigraph is from Atwood (2005:119).

1 Students Stephanie Tancer (2012) and Tara Milliken (2012) contributed invaluably to our FRG research.

2 "Army Wives" are a subset of "Military Spouses," the currently accepted official term in army usage; both are capitalized in army documents, as official titles. http://www.army.mil/women/today.html3/6/2013 (accessed July 30, 2012).

3 Army One Source. "Family Readiness Group." http://www.myarmyonesource.com/FamilyProgramsandServices/FamilyPrograms/FamilyReadinessGroup-FRG/Default.aspx (accessed July 31, 2013).

4 Capitalizing "Family" reflects its recognition as an official title; similarly, Senior Spouse bespeaks officialization-though-volunteer status.

5 "Don't refuse your rank W/My AUTHORITY!" http://www.youtube.com/watch?v=Kg3 TPNS-IeI (accessed August 22, 2013).

6 Citizen Soldier. "Afghanistan." http://www.citizen-soldier.org/ (accessed July 31, 2013).

7 Dual military where the wife leaves service and the husband stays is also a common pattern (Teplitzky et al. 1988; Westwood and Turner 1996).

8 On-post housing is organized into neighborhoods by the rank of personnel who occupy it. Since public schools on post are neighborhood schools, this means that officers' children and enlisted soldiers' children go to different schools.

9 See the official website for Fort Knox Kentucky at http://www.knox.army.mil/partners /4CAV1AE/frg.html (accessed July 30, 2012).

10 The Army Wife(dude) Blog. http://thearmywifedude.blogspot.com/ (accessed July 31, 2013).

11 As Henry Kissinger once commented on academia.

12 Although presumptions of private/public dichotomies as universal have been extensively critiqued, we maintain that in specific empirical cases, such as this, they retain emic relevance (Hautzinger 2007:138,140–2).

## Chapter 7

Epigraph is from Milton (1919).

1 Democracy Now! "Mind Zone": New Film Tracks Therapists Guiding Soldiers Through Traumas of Afghan War. http://www.democracynow.org/2012/3/16/mind_zone_new_film_tracks _therapists (accessed August 15, 2013).

2 These are teams of mental health professionals who provide early intervention to treat combat stress and prevent PTSD. See chapter 1 and Combat Stress Control. http://www.army-medicine.army.mil/about/tl/factscombatstresscontrol.html (accessed August 17, 2013).

3 Hasan was convicted and sentence to death in August 2013 (*Washington Post,* August 30, 2013).

4 Mount reports that the army has "123 of the 143 [psychiatrists] required" and employs or contracts an additional 204 civilian psychiatrists, some reservists or former military; nonetheless, a large proportion would lack the "tribal identification" West speaks of.

5 At that time soldiers stationed at Fort Carson were no more than 8.3 percent of the total city population, not counting those who are deployed (US Census State & County Quick Facts http://quickfacts.census.gov/qfd/states/08/0816000.html [accessed August 17, 2013]).

6 American Psychological Association. "The Critical Need for Mental Health Professionals Trained to Treat Post-Traumatic Stress Disorder and Traumatic Brain Injury." http://www.apa. org/about/gr/issues/military/critical-need.aspx (accessed August 30, 2013).

7 El Pomar, A Foundation for Colorado. "News from El Pomar." http://www.elpomar.org/ news/11 (accessed August 17, 2013). The El Pomar Foundation is the fifth-largest giving foundation based in Colorado, donating approximately $20 million annually to a range of nonprofit organizations in the state, and has a strong and visible presence in Colorado Springs. The Grantsmanship Center. "Top Giving Foundations, Colorado." http://www.tgci.com/funding/top.asp?st atename=Colorado&statecode=CO (accessed August 15, 2013).

8 "Fort Carson Hosts First Warrior Care Summit." http://www.army.mil/article/23821/ (accessed August 17, 2013).

9 Military and Family Life Consultant (MFLC) Program Summary www.mhngs.com/app/ resourcesfor/MFLC_Brochure.pdf (accessed August 15, 2013).

10 Contracts awarded to MHN Government Services for basic mental health services and mental health management/support from 2007 to April 5, 2012, total $961,488,812. (FPDS-NG ezSearch, https://www.fpds.gov/dbsight/fpdsportal?s=FPDS&indexName=awardfull&template Name=1.4&q=INN07PC10444+1406 [accessed August 17, 2013]).

11 See Forward Operating Base Colorado's website at http://fobsummitcountyco.org/ (accessed August 15, 2013).

12 See the Post-9/11 GI Bill at http://www.gibill.va.gov/benefits/post_911_gibill/index.html; Home Loans at http://www.benefits.va.gov/homeloans/ (accessed August 17, 2013).

13 On meaning and healing see Brody, cited in Hahn (1995) and Moerman (2002). On narrative and healing, see Becker (1997), Kleinman (1988), and Mattingly and Garro (2000).

14 Through years of doing community projects Woods found that people value programs to which they contribute something, so he often asks groups or organizations to contribute materials or refreshments to the project, but there is no fee or charge for individuals to participate.

15 The Foundation for Shamanism. http://www.shamanism.org/ (accessed August 17, 2013).

16 Rodgers does not specify if these are unduplicated visits, which would be important in assessing the magnitude of increasing demand for services.

17 In referring to "battle" as a trope, we look to trope theory for guidance in getting at what these appropriations of language may be expressing, and especially for entreating us to go "beyond metaphor." If, as "[m]etaphor is representational, metonymy is reductionist, synecdoche is integrative, and irony is negational" (with acknowledgment from Vicki Rea's website, "Metahistory," at http://www.lehigh.edu/~ineng/syll/syll-metahistory.html [accessed August 17, 2013]), considering how these different layers of tropes work in concert, as what Turner (1991) called a "polytrope," is useful. One could go much further in exploring to what degree our culture uses and identifies with militarist tropes more generally, from such team sports as football and soccer mimicking team defenses of territory alongside offensive attempts at penetrating the enemy's (and whereas baseball is structured more as the epic journey away from and returning to home [Shore 1996]), to the way video games shape military recruits' orientations to battle (Wright 2005).

18 Here Carrera was quoting the soldiers' wives, who told her there were "no" services. She clarified that in reality services did exist, the wives just didn't know about them.

19 DoD guidelines note that comparable effects have been achieved without the eye movement or body movement components, and concludes that "the mechanisms of effectiveness in EMDR have yet to be determined" (VA/DoD 2010:117).

## Chapter 8

Epigraph is from Green (2005:219).

1 Thanks to Katherine Um for sharing this expression.

2 "Fort Carson." http://www.carson.army.mil (accessed August 19, 2013).

3 "CPIS weekly peace bannering." youtube.com. http://www.youtube.com/watch?v=u-RqG-yAtmqc (accessed August 14, 2013).

4 "Space Symposium Protest 2013." youtube.com. http://www.youtube.com/watch?v= d7 QhmoUhXV4 (accessed August 14, 2013).

5 Costs of War (http://costsofwar.org/ [accessed August 14, 2013]) is a project dedicated to this question.

6 While the human security concept has been criticized as being overly ambiguous and inclusive, it has also been valued as an approach that "opens new lines of analysis, gives voice to new actors" (Fakuda-Parr and Messineo 2012:23).

7 Fittingly, a strong current of human security scholarship is feminist; see, for example, Marhia (2013), Hudson (2005, 2008), and Enloe (2000, 2010).

8 Army Ranges and Training Land Program. "Analysis of alternative study Piñon Canyon maneuver site, Colorado." http://www.leg.state.co.us/clics/clics2009/commsumm.nsf/b4a3962 433b52fa787256e5f00670a71/a247972c5df83dd88725758b006ef91b/$FILE/090401AttachI.pdf (accessed August 14, 2013).

9 The Vatic Project (http://vaticproject.blogspot.com/2011/10/stop-pentagons-51st-state.html [accessed August 14, 2013]), among others.

10 The PCEOC states that the report was leaked in 2005; "Response to the Army Report Required by the National Defense Authorization Act; Section 2831" http://www.Piñoncanyon. com/documents/PCEOC08NDAAComment.pdf (accessed August 19, 2013).

11 See Schiavitti et al. (2001) on the Late Ceramic, and Wright et al. (2006) on the approximately 5,000 archaeological sites, 500 of which have been determined eligible for listing on the National Register of Historic Places. On the army and environmental stewardship, see Not My Tribe, "Tom Warren—GreenGo pimp for the Pentagon." http://notmytribe.com/2007/tom-warren-greengo-whore-of-the-pentagon-82090.html (accessed August 14, 2013).

12 Conducted by PCOEC in conjunction with Colorado State University's Colorado National Heritage Program; http://www.cnhp.colostate.edu/download/documents/2008/2007-2008_annual_FINAL.pdf (accessed August 14, 2013).

13 Human terrain (cultural) specialists at PCMS would help prevent war crimes, as was the case for a unit of Marines being retrained at PCMS not to "start lazin' and blazin'," as they had done in the Haditha massacre of 2005 (they killed 24 unarmed men, women, and children) (Squires 2006).

14 CSAction, "CAB Landing Zones in Colorado." http://www.youtube.com/watch?v=0ErG 38A09jo (accessed August 19, 2013).

15 "Draft Environmental Assessment for the Establishment of Low Altitude Training for Cannon AFB, New Mexico." August 2011. http://www.cannon.af.mil/shared/media/document/AFD-110909-039.pdf (accessed August 14, 2013).

16 Ben Felson's fieldwork and thesis inform this chapter at various points; we are grateful for his cultural geography/ethnographic approach.

17 Pikes Peak United Way, Leadership Pikes Peak, and the Pikes Peak Library District led a team of volunteers to create the report, published annually since 2007. Acknowledging that measuring quality of life always involves subjective aspects, however, the group strives to create "an unbiased, objective compilation of facts and statistics" about the factors that "create the quality of life we enjoy in our community." See http://www.qlireport.org/leadership.html.

18 The Colorado Department of Health and the Environment performed a specialized analysis (PPQLI 2012:71).

19 "Military drain." Sept. 30, 2010. http://www.csindy.com/coloradosprings/letters/Content?oid=1863137 (accessed September 25, 2013).

20 The Encyclopedia of Domestic Violence cites that the rate of incidence is 25 per 1,000 among military personnel and three per 1,000 for the civilian population (Jackson 2007:487).

21 TESSA's Community Impact Year End Report 2011 http://www.tessacs.org/library/CommunityImpactReport2011.pdf (accessed May 20, 2013); the postdeployment figures come from TESSA staffers.

22 For more details on Colorado Springs economic and social indicators, see Pikes Peak Quality of Life (2011) and PPACG (2008).

23 Gallmeyer and Roberts report that 20 to 25 percent of the clientele of high-interest payday loan services are military, and 1 in 5 of such borrowers were active-duty military in 2004 (Gallmeyer and Roberts 2009:525; also Felson 2011:31–2). On soldier identity and tattooing in Colorado Springs, see Frecentese (2013).

24 Enlisted ranks go from E1 (private) to E9 (sergeant major).

25 Interview with Nic Gray conducted by Julia DeWitt (2010); also Warner (2010).

26 Critiques of problem-solving courts generally come from the theoretical perspective of Michel Foucault in which the state uses concepts of the self and illness to coerce its citizens to govern themselves (Lemke 2001; Nolan 1988, 2003). Mirchandani (2008) argues that we need to combine the Foucauldian view with an alternative view of the state based on the idea of deliberative democratic mechanisms of Jürgen Habermas (1996). For further discussion of these issues see also Berman and Feinblatt (2001); Hora (2002); Goldkamp et al. (2001); Wright (2008); and Wexler (1993).

27 See 719Moms. "Does Colorado Springs have post traumatic stress syndrome?" http://www. my719moms.com/news/does-colorado-springs-have-post-traumatic-stress-syndrome/ (accessed August 14, 2013).

### Chapter 9

Epigraph is from Summerscale (2009:68).

1 Goffman (1963) and others foresee this inversion, through which those in the stigmatized category stigmatize the "normals" (Becker 1983; Nettleton 2006; Smith 2012).

2 Exceptionalism, the idea that a group or institution is a special case, outside the norm, is found in places other than the military. Addicts, violence survivors, parents, and essentialist perspectives on gendered or sexual experiences are all examples; each amounts to an expression of singularity that also, to some degree, creates "otherness" and separation.

3 Readers may recognize the reference to J. R. R. Tolkien's "hobbits" (1937), who live in hobbit-holes and eschew adventure. See also how "tail" outweighs "teeth" in "Introduction."

4 Though service members do not distribute evenly across the political spectrum (Sattler 2013). See also Bacevich and Kohn (1997) and Desch (2001).

5 Hand 2 Hand Contact. "Welcome to Our Website." http://www.hand2handcontact.com/ default.asp (accessed July 31, 2013).

6 See the National Guard forums online at http://www.nationalguard.com/forums/show thread.php/19454-Is-it-me-or-after-joining-the-military-civilian-life-seems-extremely-annoying /page3 (accessed July 31, 2013).

7 Soon to become WTB—Warrior Transition Battalion—when it grew to battalion size.

8 The Defense Manpower Data Center (DMDC) produced a presentation called "Active Duty Demographic Profile, Assigned Strength, Gender, Race, Marital, Education and Age Profile of Active Duty Force" in 2008 (http://www.slideshare.net/pastinson/us-military-active-duty-demographic-profile-presentation [accessed August 29, 2013]).

9 Dawn Weaver's work can be found at Lighthall (n.d.a).

10 Patriot Unit. "Rules for the Non-Military, and all you America Haters." http://www.soda head.com/united-states/rules-for-the-non-military-and-all-you-america-haters/question-1842387/?page=4&link=ibaf&q=&esrc=s (accessed July 31, 2013).

11 Again, Dawn Weaver's work can be found at Lighthall (n.d.b).

12 The president and vice president, respectively, of the United States (2000–2008) at the outset of both campaigns.

13 Julia DeWitt's interview; see also DeWitt (2010).

14 Referencing O'Brien (1990).

### Chapter 10

Epigraph is from Matrullo (2011).

1 "Video: Fort Carson Town Hall Briefing, Part 3." Defense Video & Imagery Distribution System. http://www.dvidshub.net/video/49946/fort-carson-town-hall-briefing-part-3 (accessed July 31, 2013).

2 See also "Public Meeting Information and Materials" by the Pikes Peak Area Council of Governments at http://ppacg.org/military-impact/fort-carson-regional-growth-plan-intro/meetings/ town-halls (accessed July 9, 2012).

3 See the Citizen Soldier Connection website at http://www.citizensoldierconnection.org/ (accessed July 31, 2013).

4 Some 108,000 civilian jobs are projected to be cut in 2013 alone; see Koba (2013).

5 Schoch-Spana (2012) provides a public health perspective on military and public official attitudes about the general public and resultant policies.

6  This quote refers to Fayetteville, a counterpart to Colorado Springs as a distinctively military town; see also Lutz (2001).

7  See for example, O'Brien (1990); Gray (1998 [1959]); Heller (1961); and Vonnegut (1969).

8  Arnett develops an idea originally offered by Martin Buber (1970).

9  Anthropologists rejecting the analogical tradition, which assumes translatability is possible, follow in this line; for example, Clifford (1983:133) and Tedlock (1979:388).

10 See "Reflection: Always Faithful" at "Honoring Service: Worship with UUs in the Military," part of the Unitarian Universalist Association of Congregations' website (http://www.uua.org/ga/past/2011/worship/184981.shtml [accessed July 31, 2013]); see also Christian (2010).

11 "You're Invited to Network . . . Share Information. Ideas & Learn." Military Matters: Transforming the Ripple Effect. http://campaign.vpweb.com/618bfdc4-275d-44bf-9a18-83bfc6ccff4a/ (accessed July 9, 2012).

12 "Videos: ONE Freedom Promotional Video." One Freedom. http://www.onefreedom.org/videos (accessed July 31, 2013).

13 Gray, a veteran of the European theater in WWII, served as professor of philosophy at Colorado College in the decades following the war.

## Conclusion

Epigraph is from Borges (1962a:96).

# References

Ambercrombie, Joe. 2006. *The Blade Itself.* London: Orion Publishing Group.

Abrams, David. 2012. *Fobbit.* New York: Black Cat.

Albro, Robert, George Marcus, Laura A. McNamara, and Monica Schoch-Spana (eds.) 2012. *Anthropologists in the SecurityScape: Ethics, Practice, and Professional Identity.* Walnut Creek: Left Coast Press.

Allen, Elizabeth S., Galena K. Rhoades, Scott M. Stanley, and Howard J. Markman. 2011. "On the Home Front: Stress for Recently Deployed Army Couples." *Family Process* 50:235–47.

Amato, Paul R. 2001. "Children of Divorce in the 1990s: An Update of the Amato and Keith (1991) Meta-analysis." *Journal of Family Psychology* 15:355–370.

Amato, Paul R., and Alan Booth. 2001. "The Legacy of Parents' Marital Discord: Consequences for Children's Marital Quality." *Journal of Personality and Social Psychology* 81:627–38.

American Psychiatric Association (APA). 1980. *Diagnostic and Statistical Manual of Mental Disorders.* Arlington, VA: American Psychiatric Association.

_____. 1994. *Diagnostic and Statistical Manual of Mental Disorders.* 4th ed. Washington, DC: American Psychiatric Association.

_____. 2000. *Diagnostic and Statistical Manual of Mental Disorders: DSM-IV-TR.* 4th ed. Text revision. Washington, DC: American Psychiatric Association.

_____. 2013. *Diagnostic and Statistical Manual of Mental Disorders: DSM-5.* 5th ed. Arlington, VA: American Psychiatric Association. DOI: 10.1176/appi.books.9780890425596.991543 (Accessed September 15, 2013).

Arella, Lorinda, and Rebecca Rooney. 2011. "Post-Deployment Stress: Helping Veterans and Their Families." New York State Psychological Association. http://public.nyspa.org/index.php/articles/3-trauma-and-stress/13-post-deployment-stress-helping-veterans-and-their-families (accessed August 30, 2013).

Arnett, Ronald C. 1986. *Communication and Community.* Carbondale, IL: Southern Illinois University Press.

Ashforth, Blake E., and Glen E. Kreiner. 1999. "'How Can You Do It?': Dirty Work and the Challenge of Constructing a Positive Identity." *Academy of Management Review* 24(3):413-34.

Associated Press (AP). 2009. "Army: Violence by GIs at Home Tied to Combat." http://www.utvet.com/ViolenceTiedToCombat.html (accessed March 6, 2012).

Astore, William J. 2011. "How the Military and the Civilian Are Blurring in Washington." *Huffington Post*, June 14. http://www.huffingtonpost.com/william-j-astore/military-civilian-life_b_876908.html.

Atwood, Margaret. 2005. *The Penelopiad.* New York: Canongate.

Bacevich, Andrew J., and Richard H. Kohn. 1997. "Grand Army of the Republicans: Has the U.S. Military Become a Partisan Force?" *The New Republic* 217(Dec 23-8):22 ff.

Bailey, Amy Kate. 2011. "Race, Place, and Veteran Status: Migration among Black and White Men, 1940-2000." *Population Research and Policy Review* 30:701–28.

Balzer, Marjorie. 1996. "Shamanism." In *The Encyclopedia of Cultural Anthropology,* edited by David Levinson and Melvin Emberd, pp. 1182–6. New Haven, CT: Yale, HRAF.

Barnes, Patricia M., Barbara Bloom, and Richard L. Nahin. 2008. "Complementary and Alternative Medicine Use Among Adults and Children: United States." *National Health Statistics Reports* 12(Dec 10):1–24.

Barrett, Laura. 2011. "Repetition with a Difference: Representation and the Uncanny in House of Leaves." *Horror Studies* 2(2):247–64.

Bayendor, David. 2011. "Human Terrain Redux—A 'Halfie' Talks Anthropology and the Army." Paper presented at the annual meeting of the American Anthropological Association, Montreal, Canada, November 17.

BBC News. 2012. "Afghanistan massacre suspect named as Sgt. Robert Bales." BBC News US & Canada, March 17. http://www.bbc.co.uk/news/world-us-canada-17411009 (accessed August 14, 2013).

Becker, Ernest. 1973. *The Denial of Death.* New York: Free Press.

Becker, Gay. 1983. *Growing Old in Silence: Deaf People in Old Age.* Berkeley: University of California Press.

_____. 1997. *Disrupted Lives: How People Create Meaning in a Chaotic World.* Berkeley: University of California Press.

Bell, Nicole S, Thomas Harford, James E. McCarroll, and Laura Senier. 2004. "Drinking and Spouse Abuse among U.S. Army Soldiers." *Alcoholism: Clinical and Experimental Research* 28(12):1890–97.

Bemong, Nele. 2003. "Exploration #6: The Uncanny in Mark Z. Danielewski's House of Leaves." *Image [&] Narrative: Online Magazine of the Visual Narrative* 5.

BenAmots, Laura. 2012. "Lion & Lamb, Predator & Prey." In *Battle Portraits: Wounded Lions, Wounded Lambs,* by Laura BenAmots. Manitou Springs, CO: Art Book Publishing Project at the BAC.

Benson, Herbert. 1975. *The Relaxation Response.* New York: Morrow.

Benson, Herbert, with William Proctor. 1984. *Beyond the Relaxation Response: How to Harness the Healing Power of Your Personal Beliefs.* New York: Times Books.

Benzel, Lance. 2008. "Carson Soldier Admits He Killed Woman, Sheriff's Office Says." *The Gazette,* October 15. http://www.gazette.com/articles/old-41817-body-stage.html#ixzz1sDuxzcbg (accessed August 14, 2013).

Berman, Greg, and John Feinblatt. 2001. "Problem-Solving Courts: A Brief Primer." *Law & Policy* 23:123–40.

Biank, Tanya. 2006. *Army Wives.* New York: St. Martin's Griffin.

Bickford, Andrew. 2010. "*Shadow Elite:* Pat Tillman & Why Soldier Hero Worship Serves the Powerful . . . Not the Soldiers." *Huffington Post,* September 30. http://www.huffingtonpost.com/andrew-bickford/emshadow-eliteem-pat-till_b_744890.html (accessed September 20, 2013).

Binn, Brian. 2010. "Colorado's Valuable National Assets: A Brief Look at Colorado's Military." Colorado Springs: Greater Colorado Springs Chamber of Commerce. http://www.docstoc.com/docs/147466197/Colorado-s-Valuable-National-Assets—ColoradoSprings-Chamber (accessed November 2, 2013).

Blumenthal, Susan. 2012. "Stopping the Surge of Military Suicides: How to Win This Preventable War." *Huffington Post,* September 14. http://www.huffingtonpost.com/susan-blumenthal/military-suicide_b_1884083.html (accessed August 14, 2013).

Bodkin, J., Harrison G. Alexander, Michael J. Pope, Michael J. Detke, and James L. Hudson. 2007. "Is PTSD Caused by Traumatic Stress?" *Journal of Anxiety Disorders* 21:176–82.

Booth, Alan, and Paul R. Amato. 2001. "Parental Predivorce Relationships and Offspring Post-divorce Well-being." *Journal of Marriage and the Family* 63:197–212.

Booth, Bradford, Mady Wechsler Segal, and D. Bruce Bell. 2007. *What We Know About Army Families: 2007 Update.* Washington, DC: Caliber and US Army.

Borges, Jorge Luis. 1962a. "The Garden of Forking Paths." In *Ficciones,* translated by Helen Temple and Ruthven Todd, pp. 89–101. New York: Grove Press.

_____. 1962b. *Labyrinths.* New York: New Directions Publishing.

Bracken, Patrick J. 2001. "Post-modernity and Post-traumatic Stress Disorder." *Social Science & Medicine* 53(6):733–43.

_____. 2002. *Trauma: Culture, Meaning, and Philosophy*. London, Philadelphia: Whurr Publishers.

Bracken, Patrick J., Joan E. Giller, and Derek Summerfield. 1995. "Psychological Responses to War and Atrocity: The Limitations of Current Concepts." *Social Science & Medicine* 40(8):1073–82.

Brady, Kathleen T., Sudie E. Back, and Scott F. Coffey. 2004. "Substance Abuse and Posttraumatic Stress Disorder." *Current Directions in Psychological Science* 13(5):206–9.

Brandi, Giulio. 2012. *Alternative Counseling and PTSD: Cultural Frameworks and the Need for Narrative When Coping with Trauma*. Senior Paper, Department of Anthropology, Colorado College, Colorado Springs.

Bray, Robert M., Michael R. Pemberton, Marian E. Lane, Laurel L. Hourani, Mark J. Mattiko, and Lorraine A. Babeu. 2010. "Substance Use and Mental Health Trends Among U.S. Military Active Duty Personnel: Key Findings From the 2008 DoD Health Behavior Survey." *Military Medicine* 175(6):390–99.

Brenner, Lisa A., Brian J. Ivins, Karen Schwab, Deborah Warden, Lonnie A. Nelson, Michael Jaffee, and Heidi Terrio. 2010. "Traumatic Brain Injury, Posttraumatic Stress Disorder, and Postconcussive Symptom Reporting Among Troops Returning from Iraq." *Journal of Health Trauma Rehabilitation* 25(5):397–412.

Breslau, Joshua. 2004. "Cultures of Trauma: Anthropological Views of Posttraumatic Stress Disorder in International Health." *Culture, Medicine and Psychiatry* 28:113–26.

Britt, Thomas W. 2000. "The Stigma of Psychological Problems in a Work Environment: Evidence from the Screening of Service Members Returning from Bosnia." *Journal of Applied Social Psychology* 30(8):1599–618.

Bruno, James. 2009. "Military Police & Weapons: Support Troop to Combat Troop Ratios." *All Experts*, September 17. http://en.allexperts.com/q/Military-Policy-Weapons-346/2009/9/Support-Troop-Combat-Troop.htm (accessed August 10, 2013).

Bryan, Frank M. 2004. *Real Democracy: The New England Town Meeting and How It Works*. Chicago and London: University of Chicago Press.

Buber, Martin. 1970. *I and Thou: A New Translation with a Prologue "I and You" and Notes by Walter Kaufmann*. New York: Scribner.

Bucholtz, Mary, and Kira Hall. 2006. "Language and Identity." In *A Companion to Linguistic Anthropology*, edited by Allesandro Duranti, pp. 369–94. Malden, MA: Blackwell Publishing.

Budden, Ashwin. 2009. "The Role of Shame in Posttraumatic Stress Disorder: A Proposal for a Socio-Emotional Model for DSM-V." *Social Science & Medicine* 69:1032–39.

Campbell, Joseph. 2008 [1949]. *The Hero with a Thousand Faces*. 3rd ed. Novato, CA: New World Library.

Cancian, Mark F. 2011. "The All-Volunteer Force: After 10 Years of War, It's Time to Gather Lessons." *Armed Forces Journal* (October). http://armedforcesjournal.com/article/2011/10/7691489 (accessed August 30, 2013).

Carabajal, Shannon. 2011. "Army Expanding Successful Embedded Behavioral Health Program," November 17. http://www.army.mil/article/69479/ (accessed August 6, 2013).

Carden-Coyne, Ana. 2009. *Reconstructing the Body: Classicism, Modernism and the First World War*. Oxford: Oxford University Press.

Chandra, Anita, Sandraluz Lara-Cinisomo, Lisa H. Jaycox, Terri Tanielian, Rachel M. Burns, Teague Ruder, and Bing Han. 2009. "Children on the Homefront: The Experience of Children from Military Families." *Pediatrics* 125:16–25.

Chartrand, Molinda M., Deborah A. Frank, Laura F. White, and Timothy R. Shope. 2008. "Effect of Parents' Wartime Deployment on the Behavior of Young Children in Military Families." *Archives of Pediatrics & Adolescent Medicine* 162(11):1009–14.

Christian, Jan. 2010. *Leave No Brother Behind: A Sister's War Memoir.* Minneapolis: Mill City Press.

Clifford, James. 1983. "On Ethnographic Authority." *Representations* 2:118–46.

Cobb, Trevor S. 2010. *Multiple Deployments and Bringing Our Troops "All the Way Home": The Liminoid in Fort Carson Infantry.* Senior Paper, Department of Anthropology, Colorado College, Colorado Springs.

Cohen, Eliot A. 2001. "The Unequal Dialogue: The Civil-Military Gap and the Use of Force." In *Soldiers and Civilians: The Civil-Military Gap and American National Security,* edited by Peter D. Feaver and Richard H. Kohn, pp. 429–58. Cambridge, MA: MIT Press.

Cohn, Marjorie, and Kathleen Gilberd. 2009. *Rules of Disengagement: The Politics and Honor of Military Dissent.* Sausalito, CA: PoliPointPress.

*Colorado Observer.* 2013. "Piñon Canyon Concerns Hit Hagel Nomination." http://thecoloradoobserver.com/2013/02/pinon-canyon-concerns-hit-hagel-nomination/ (accessed September 25, 2013).

*Colorado Springs Independent.* 2008. "Army to Look into Murder Pattern." October 23. http:// www.csindy.com/colorado/army-to-look-into-murder-pattern/Content?oid=1145397 (accessed August 14, 2013).

Conarroe, Andrew. 2011. *The Culture of Substance Use in the Military: Contextualizing an Ongoing Problem.* Senior Paper, Department of Anthropology, Colorado College, Colorado Springs.

Cotter, Barbara. 2011. Winning the Battle against PTSD, Fighting a Battle for Legitimacy. *The Gazette,* August 5. http://www.gazette.com/articles/battle-122756-day-phobia.html (accessed August 17, 2013).

Cozza, Stephen J., Ryo S. Chun, and James A. Polo. 2005. "Military Families and Children during Operation Iraqi Freedom." *Psychiatric Quarterly* 76(4):371–78.

Crandon-Malamud, Libbet. 1993. *From the Fat of Our Souls: Social Change, Political Process, and Medical Pluralism in Bolivia.* Berkeley: University of California Press.

Crossley, Ann, and Carol A. Keller. 1993. *The Army Wife Handbook.* 2nd ed. Marietta, GA: ABI Press.

Da Costa, Jacob Mendes. 1871. "On Irritable Heart: A Clinical Study of a Form of Functional Cardiac Disorder and Its Consequences." *American Journal of Medical Science* 61:17–52.

Danielewski, Mark Z. 2000. *House of Leaves. Introduction and Notes Johnny Truant.* New York: Pantheon Books.

Dao, James. 2010. V.A. Is Easing Rules to Cover Stress Disorder. *New York Times,* July 7. http:// www.nytimes.com/2010/07/08/us/08vets.html?_r=0 (accessed September 24, 2013).

Dean, Eric T., Jr. 1997. *Shook over Hell: Post-traumatic Stress, Vietnam, and the Civil War.* Cambridge, MA: Harvard University Press.

de Jong, Joop T., and Ria Reis. 2010. "Kiyang-yang, a West African Postwar Idiom of Distress. *Culture, Medicine and Psychiatry* 34(2):301–21.

DeMott, Benjamin. 1990. *The Imperial Middle: Why Americans Can't Think Straight about Class.* New Haven, CT: Yale University Press.

Denver Channel. 2005. "Army: Back from Iraq, Colorado Soldier Shoots Himself, Wife." TheDenverChannel.com, August 4. http://www.thedenverchannel.com/news/4811407/ detail.html (accessed August 14, 2013).

Department of the Army. 2010. "Lineage and Honors: 2D Battalion, 12th Infantry Regiment." http://www.history.army.mil/html/forcestruc/lineages/branches/inf/0012in002bn.htm (accessed August 14, 2013).

Department of Defense. 2013. Department of Defense Dictionary of Military Terms http://www.dtic.mil/doctrine/dod_dictionary/ (accessed August 14, 2013).

Desch, Michael C. 2001. "Explaining the Gap: Vietnam, the Republicanization of the South, and the End of the Mass Army." In *Soldiers and Civilians*, edited by Peter D. Feaver and Richard H. Kohn, pp. 289–324. Cambridge, MA: MIT Press.

DeWitt, Julia Barefoot. 2010. "Supporting Our Troops": Combat-Related Posttraumatic Stress Disorder, Soldier Reintegration and The Soldiers Support Network in Colorado Springs, Colorado." Senior Paper, Department of Anthropology, Colorado College, Colorado Springs.

De Yoanna, Michael. 2006. "Pattern of Misconduct: Fort Carson Soldiers Allege Abuse and Intimidation." *Colorado Springs Independent*, July 13. http://www.csindy.com/colorado/pattern-of-misconduct/Content?oid=1134699 (accessed August 14, 2013).

_____. 2012. "Iraq Vets on the Road to Recovery." *Salon*, February 4. http://www.salon.com/writer/michael_de_yoanna/ (accessed August 14, 2013).

De Yoanna, Michael, and Mark Benjamin. 2009a. "That Young Man Never Should Have Come into the Army." *Salon*, February 13. http://www.salon.com/2009/02/13/coming_home_four/ (accessed August 14, 2013).

_____. 2009b. "The Army Denies That Combat Stress Causes Homicide." *Salon*, July 16. http://www.salon.com/2009/07/16/fort_carson_report/ (accessed August 14, 2013).

_____. 2009. Installation Mission Growth Community Profile. Office of Economic Adjustment. http://www.oea.gov/index.php/component/docman/doc_view/255-fort-carson-colorado?tmpl=component&format=raw.

_____. 2010. *Dictionary of Military and Associated Terms*. November 8 (amended through March 15 2012). Joint Publication 1-02. Washington, DC: Department of Defense.

_____. 2012. *Report of the 11th Quadrennial Review of Military Compensation, Main Report*. Washington, DC: Department of Defense.

Dick, Penny. 2005. "Dirty Work Designations: How Police Officers Account for Their Use of Coercive Force." *Human Relations* 58(11):1363–90.

Dobbs, David. 2009. "The Post-Traumatic Stress Trap." *Scientific American* (April):64–9.

Dohrenwend, Bruce P., J. Blake Turner, Nicholas A. Turse, Ben G. Adams, Karestan C. Koenen, and Randall Marshall. 2006. "The Psychological Risks of Vietnam for U.S. Veterans: A Revisit with New Data and Methods." *Science* 313:979–82.

Doob, Penelope Reed. 1992. "The Idea of the Labyrinth: From Classical Antiquity through the Middle Ages." *Comparative Literature Studies* 29:210–14.

Douglas, Mary. 1966. *Purity and Danger: An Analysis of Concepts of Pollution and Taboo*. London and New York: Routledge.

Douzinas, Costas. 2007. *Human Rights and Empire: The Political Philosophy of Cosmopolitanism*. New York: Routledge-Cavendish.

Doyle, Michael E., and Kris A. Peterson. 2005. "Re-entry and Reintegration: Returning Home after Combat." *Psychiatric Quarterly* 76(4):361–70.

Drescher, Kent D., David W. Foy, Caroline Kelly, Anna Leshner, Kerrie Schutz, and Brett Litz. 2011. "An Exploration of the Viability and Usefulness of the Construct of Moral Injury in War Veterans." *Traumatology* 17(1):8–13.

Durham, Susan W. 2010. "In Their Own Words: Staying Connected in a Combat Environment." *Military Medicine* 175(8):554–9.

Dyer, Gwynne. 2005. *War: The Lethal Custom*. Revised ed. New York: Carroll & Graf Publishers.

Eckhart, Jacey. 2005. *The Homefront Club: The Hardheaded Woman's Guide to Raising a Military Family*. Annapolis, MD: Naval Institute Press.

Edge, Dan. 2010. "The Wounded Platoon: Third Platoon's First Year in Iraq." *Frontline*. Public Broadcasting Station, May 18. http://www.pbs.org/wgbh/pages/frontline/woundedplatoon/view/?autoplay (accessed August 14, 2013).

Eidelson, Roy. 2011. "The Dark Side of 'Comprehensive Soldier Fitness." March 25. *Psychology Today* http://www.psychologytoday.com/blog/dangerous-ideas/201103/the-dark-side-comprehensive-soldier-fitness (accessed August 30, 2012).

Elder, Glen H., Lin Wang, Naomi J. Spence, Daniel E. Adkins, and Tyson H. Brown. 2010. "Pathways to the All-Volunteer Military." *Social Science Quarterly* 91(2):455–75.

Elder, Gregory A., and Adrian Cristian. 2009. "Blast-Related Mild Traumatic Brain Injury: Mechanisms of Injury and Impact on Clinical Care." *Mount Sinai Journal of Medicine* 76:111–18.

EMDR Institute, Inc. 2011. What is EMDR? http://www.emdr.com/general-information/what-is-emdr/what-is-emdr.html (accessed August 17, 2013).

Emert, Rick. 2010. "ACS Thanks Volunteers." *Fort Carson Mountaineer*, April 30, p. 1. http://csmng.com/wp-files/mountaineer-weekly-pdfs/mountaineer_2010-04-30.pdf (accessed August 15, 2013).

Ender, Morten G. 2005. "Divergences in Traditional and New Communication Media Use Among Army Families." In *New Directions in Military Sociology*, edited by Eric Ouellet, pp. 255–95. Whitby, ON: De Sitter Publications.

Engel, Charles C. 2004. "Post-War Syndromes: Illustrating the Impact of the Social Psyche on Notions of Risk, Responsibility, Reason, and Remedy." *The Journal of the American Academy of Psychoanalysis and Dynamic Psychiatry*. 32(2):321–34.

Enloe, Cynthia. 2000. *Maneuvers: The International Politics of Militarizing Women's Lives*. Berkeley: University of California Press.

_____. 2004. *The Curious Feminist: Searching for Women in a New Age of Empire*. Berkeley: University of California Press.

_____. 2007. *Globalization and Militarism: Feminists Make the Link*. Lanham, MD: Rowan and Littlefield.

_____. 2010. *Nimo's War, Emma's War*. Berkeley: University of California Press.

Enroth, Cindy, Dorothy Forbes, and Tina McFall. 2010. *U.S. Army FRG Leader's Handbook*, 4th ed. U.S. Army Family and Morale, Welfare and Recreation Command (FMWRC) and Cornell University, Department of Human Ecology, Family Life Development Center (FLDC).

EPICON. 2009. *Epidemiological Consultation No. 14-HK-OB1U-09, Investigation of Homicides at Fort Carson, Colorado November 2008-May 2009*. Aberdeen Proving Ground, MD: U.S. Army Center for Health Promotion and Preventive Medicine.

Epstein, Mark. 2013. "The Trauma of Being Alive." *New York Times, Sunday Review*, August 3. http://www.nytimes.com/2013/08/04/opinion/sunday/the-trauma-of-being-alive.html?pagewanted=all&_r=0 (accessed October 2, 2013).

Esquivel, Paloma, Christine Hanley, and Christopher Goffard. 2008. "Combat Follows Soldiers Home." *Los Angeles Times*, December 21. http://articles.latimes.com/2008/dec/21/local/me-battalion21 (accessed August 14, 2013).

Evans, Thomas W. 1993. "The All-Volunteer Army after Twenty Years: Recruiting in the Modern Era." *Army History: The Professional Bulletin of Army History* 27:40–6.

Faber, Anthony J., Elaine Willerton, Shelley R. Clymer, Shelley M. MacDermid, and Howard M. Weiss. 2008. "Ambiguous Absence, Ambiguous Presence: A Qualitative Study of Military Reserve Families in Wartime." *Journal of Family Psychology* 22(2):222–30.

Fakuda-Parr, Sakiko, and Carol Messineo. 2012. "Human Security." In *Elgar Companion to Civil War and Fragile States*, edited by Graham Brown and Arnim Langer, pp. 21–38. Northampton, MA: Edward Elgar Publishing.

Farmer, Ben, and Nick Allen. 2012. "Taliban Trophy Photographs 'Disgusting' Says Hamid Karzai." *The Telegraph*, June 29. http://www.telegraph.co.uk/news/worldnews/asia/afghanistan/9214238/Taliban-trophy-photographs-disgusting-says-Hamid-Karzai.html (accessed August 14, 2013).

Fassin, Didier, and Richard Rechtman. 2009. *The Empire of Trauma: An Inquiry into the Condition of Victimhood* [Rachel Gomme, translator]. Princeton, NJ, and Oxford: Princeton University Press.

Fata, Catherine. 2009. "PTSD: True Battle Scar? Do Mental Scars Deserve Military Decoration? Are These True Battle Scars?" *Psychology Today* (May 1, last reviewed July 1).

Faxon, Emily. 2013. *How Yoga Is Used to Treat Post-Traumatic Stress Disorder among Combat War Veterans*. Honors Thesis, Colorado College.

Fear, Nicola, Margaret Jones, Dominic Murphy, et al. 2010. "What are the Consequences of Deployment to Iraq and Afghanistan on the Mental Health of the UK Armed Forces? A Cohort Study. *The Lancet* 375:1783–97.

Feaver, Peter D. 2011. "The Right to be Right." International Security 35(4):93–4.

Felson, Benjamin A. 2011. "Camouflaged Costs: Military Influence on the Cultural Geography of Colorado Springs." Senior Paper, Department of Anthropology, Colorado College, Colorado Springs.

Ferguson, R. Brian. 2008. "Ten Points on War." *Social Analysis* 52(2):32–49.

Ferguson, R. Brian, and Neil L. Whitehead. 2000. Preface to the Second Printing. In *War in the Tribal Zone*, edited by R. Brian Ferguson and Neil L. Whitehead, pp. xi–xxxv. Santa Fe, NM: School of American Research.

Finkler, Kaja. 1994. "Sacred Healing and Biomedicine Compared." *Medical Anthropology Quarterly* 8(2):178–97.

Finley, Erin. 2010. "The Chaplain Turns to God: Negotiating Post-Traumatic Stress Disorder in the American Military." Unpublished draft received August 7, 2010.

_____. 2011. *Fields of Combat: Understanding PTSD among Veterans of Iraq and Afghanistan*. Ithaca, NY: Cornell University Press.

_____. 2012. "War and Dislocation: A Neuroanthropological Model of Trauma among American Veterans with Combat PTSD." In *The Encultured Brain: An Introduction to Neuroanthropology*, edited by Daniel H. Lende and Greg Downey, pp. 263–90. Cambridge, MA: MIT Press.

FINRA. 2010. *Financial Capability in the United States: Military Survey—Executive Summary*. Washington, DC: FINRA Investor Education Foundation. http://www.finra.org/web/groups/foundation/@foundation/documents/foundation/p122257.pdf (accessed August 30, 2013).

Fleck, Ludwik. 1979. *Genesis and Development of a Scientific Fact*. Chicago and London: University of Chicago Press.

Fleming, Bruce. 2010. *Bridging the Military-Civilian Divide: What Each Side Must Know About The Other—And About Itself*. Sterling, VA: Potomac Books.

Foucault, Michel. 1994 [1973]. *The Birth of the Clinic: An Archeology of Medical Perception*, translated by A. M. Sheridan Smith. New York: Vintage Books.

_____. 1995 [1977]. *Discipline and Punish: The Birth of the Prison*, translated by Allan Sheridan. New York: Vintage Books.

Frecentese, Victoria. 2013. *Tattooing Identity: An Analysis of Historical and Contemporary Tattooing Practices among Members of the Military Community*. Honors Thesis, Colorado College.

French, Lindsay. 2004. "Commentary." *Culture, Medicine and Psychiatry* 28:211–20.

Frosch, Dan. 2008. "3 Buddies Home from Iraq Charged with Murdering a 4th." *New York Times*, January 12. http://www.nytimes.com/2008/01/12/us/12soldier.html?pagewanted=all (accessed June 21, 2012).

Gans, Herbert. 1982 [1967]. *The Levittowners: Ways of Life and Politics in a Suburban Community.* New York: Columbia University Press.

GAO (U.S. Government Accountability Office). 2006. *Military Recruiting: DoD and Services Need Better Data to Enhance Visibility over Recruiter Irregularities.* GAO-06-846. Washington, D.C.: Government Accountability Office.

Gallmeyer, Alice, and Wade T. Roberts. 2009. "Payday Lenders and Economically Distressed Communities: A Spatial Analysis of Financial Predation." *Social Science Journal* 46(3):521–38.

Gallo, Robert C., and Luc Montagnier. 2003. "The Discovery of HIV as the Cause of AIDs." *The New England Journal of Medicine* 394:2283–85.

Garrison, Trey. 2009. "Not One More Acre!" *Reason* 40(10):38–45.

Gassmann, Jaime Nicole Noble. 2010. "Patrolling the Homefront: The Emotional Labor of Army Wives Volunteering in Family Readiness Groups." PhD dissertation, Department of American Studies, University of Kansas, Lawrence.

Gawande, Atul. 2004. "Casualties of War—Military Care for the Wounded from Iraq and Afghanistan." *New England Journal of Medicine* 351(24):2471–75.

Georgopoulos, A. P., H.-R. M. Tan, S. M. Lewis, A. C. Leuthold, A. M. Winskowski, J. K. Lynch, and B. Engdahl. 2010. "The Synchronous Neural Interactions Test as a Functional Neuromarker for Post-Traumatic Stress Disorder (PTSD): A Robust Classification Method Based on the Bootstrap." *Journal of Neural Engineering* 7(1):1–7.

Gillentine, Amy. 2012. "Chamber Report: Springs' Military Adds $5.93 Billion to Economy." *Colorado Springs Business Journal*, July 10. http://csbj.com/2012/07/10/chamber-report-springs-should-prepare-for-future-military-cuts/ (accessed August 19, 2013).

Gimbel, C., and Booth, A. 1994. "Why Does Military Combat Experience Adversely Affect Marital Relations?" *Journal of Marriage and the Family* 56:691–703.

Glantz, Aaron. 2008. "Wounded Vets Trade One Hell for Another." Antiwar.com, January 17. http://www.unz.org/Pub/Antiwar-2008jan-00045 (accessed July 23, 2013).

———. 2009. *The War Comes Home: Washington's Battle against America's Veterans.* Berkeley: University of California Press.

Glick, Joseph. 2011. "Spiritual Fitness and Compassion Fatigue: The Proliferation of Pro-Military Spirituality within the Army Chaplain Corps." Senior Paper, Department of Anthropology, Colorado College, Colorado Springs.

Goffman, Erving. 1961. *Asylums: Essays on the Social Situation of Mental Patients and Other Inmates.* New York: Anchor Books.

———. 1986 [1963]. *Stigma: Notes on the Management of Spoiled Identity.* Englewood Cliffs, NJ: Prentice-Hall.

Goldenberg, Jamie L., Tom Pyszczynski, Jeff Greenberg, and Sheldon Solomon. 2000. "Fleeing the Body: A Terror Management Perspective on the Problem of Human Corporeality." *Personality and Social Psychology Review* 4(3):200–18.

Goldkamp, John S., Michael D. White, and Jennifer B. Robinson. 2001. "Do Drug Courts Work? Getting inside the Drug Court Black Box." *Journal of Drug Issues* 31:27–72.

Goldman, Nancy L. 1976. "Trends in Family Patterns of U.S. Military Personnel During the 20th Century." In *The Social Psychology of Military Service*, edited by Nancy L. Goldman and David R. Segal, pp. 119–34. Beverly Hills, CA: Sage Publications.

González, Roberto. 2010. *Militarizing Culture: Essays on the Warfare State.* Walnut Creek, CA: Left Coast Press.

Gorman, Gregory H., Matilda Eide, and Elizabeth Hisle-Gorman. 2010. "Wartime Military Deployment and Increased Pediatric Mental and Behavioral Health Complaints." *Pediatrics* 126(6):1058–66.

Gould, Matthew, Neil Greenberg, and Jacquie Hetherton. 2007. "Stigma and the Military: Evaluation of a PTSD Psychoeducational Program." *Journal of Traumatic Stress* 20(4):505–15.

Gray, J. Glenn 1998 [1959]. *The Warriors: Reflections on Men in Battle.* New York: Harper & Row.

Green, Gill. 2009. *The End of Stigma: Changes in the Social Experience of Long-Term Illness.* London and New York: Routledge.

Green, John. 2005. *Looking for Alaska.* New York: Penguin.

Greene-Shortridge, Tiffany M., Thomas W. Britt, and Carl Andrew Castro. 2007. "The Stigma of Mental Health Problems in the Military." *Military Medicine* 172(2):157–61.

Greer, Paul Brian. 2009. "An Educational Methodology and Program for the Mitigation of Compassion Fatigue for Combat Deploying Chaplains." Thesis project for Doctor of Ministry, Liberty Baptist Theological Seminary, Lynchburg, VA.

Grossman, Dave. 2009 [1995]. *On Killing: The Psychological Cost of Learning to Kill in War and Society.* New York: Little, Brown and Company.

Gutmann, Matthew, and Catherine Lutz. 2010. *Breaking Ranks: Iraq Veterans Speak Out Against the War.* Berkeley: University of California Press.

Habermas, Jürgen. 1996. *Between Facts and Norms: Contributions to Discourse Theory of Law and Democracy.* Cambridge, MA: MIT Press.

Hacking, Ian. 1995. *Rewriting the Soul: Multiple Personalities and the Science of Memory.* Princeton, NJ: Princeton University Press.

Hahn, Robert A. 1995. *Sickness and Healing: An Anthropological Perspective.* New Haven, CT: Yale University Press.

Harrell, Margaret C. 2000. *Invisible Women: Junior Enlisted Army Wives.* Santa Monica: RAND.

_____. 2003. "Gender- and Class-Based Role Expectations for Army Spouses." In *Anthropology and the United States Military,* edited by Pamela R. Frese and Margaret C. Harrell, pp. 69–94. New York: Palgrave Macmillan.

Harvey, Paul. 2012. "Unnatural Disaster: When Conservative Theology and the Free Market Meet Wildfires." *Religion Dispatches,* July 10. http://www.religiondispatches.org/archive/atheologies/6143/unnatural_disaster:_when_conservative_theology_&_the_free_market_meet_wildfires_|_%28a%29theologies (accessed August 14, 2013).

Hautzinger, Sarah. 2007. *Violence in the City of Women: Police and Batterers in Bahia, Brazil.* Berkeley: University of California Press.

Havlick, David G. 2010. "Militarization, Conservation, and U.S. Base Transformations." In *Militarized Landscapes: From Gettysburg to Salisbury Plain,* edited by Chris J. Pearson, Peter Coates, and Tim Cole, pp. 113–33. New York: Continuum Press.

Hawkins, John P. 2001. *Army of Hope, Army of Alienation: Culture and Contradiction in the American Army Communities of Cold War Germany.* Westport, CT: Praeger.

Hedges, Chris. 2002. *War is a Force That Gives Us Meaning.* New York: Public Affairs.

Heller, Joseph. 1961. *Catch-22: A Novel.* New York: Simon and Schuster.

Heller, Kevin Jon. 2011. *The Nuremberg Military Tribunals and the Origins of International Criminal Law.* Oxford, UK: Oxford University Press.

Henning, Charles. 2009. "U.S. Military Stop Loss Program: Key Questions and Answers." http://www.fas.org/sgp/crs/natsec/R40121.pdf (accessed August 20, 2013).

Herbert, Melissa. 2000. *Camouflage Isn't Only for Combat: Gender, Sexuality, and Women in the Military.* New York: New York University Press.

Hesse, Amy R. 2002. "Secondary Trauma: How Working with Trauma Survivors Affects Therapists." *Clinical Social Work Journal* 30(3):293–309.

Hinton, Devon E., and Roberto Lewis-Fernández. 2010. "The Cross-Cultural Validity of Posttraumatic Stress Disorder: Implications for DSM-5." *Depression and Anxiety* 28(9):1–19.

Hochschild, Arlie Russell. 1979. "Emotion Work, Feeling Rules, and Social Structure." *American Journal of Sociology* 85(3):551–75.

_____. 2003. *The Managed Heart: Commercialization of Human Feeling.* Berkeley: University of California Press.

Hogan, Paul F., and Rita Furst Seifert. 2010. "Marriage and the Military: Evidence That Those Who Serve Marry Earlier and Divorce Earlier." *Armed Forces & Society* 36(3):420–38.

Hoge, Charles W., Jennifer L. Auchterlonie, and Charles S. Milliken. 2006. "Mental Health Problems, Use of Mental Health Services, and Attrition from Military Service after Returning from Deployment to Iraq or Afghanistan." *Journal of the American Medical Association* 295(9):1023–32.

Hoge, Charles W., Carl A. Castro, Stephen C. Messer, Dennis McGurk, Dave I. Cotting, and Robert L. Koffman. 2004. "Combat Duty in Iraq and Afghanistan, Mental Health Problems, and Barriers to Care." *New England Journal of Medicine* 351(1):13–22.

_____. 2008. "Combat Duty in Iraq and Afghanistan, Mental Health Problems and Barriers to Care." *U.S. Army Medical Department Journal* (July-September):7–17.

Hoge, Charles W., Dennis McGurk, J. Thomas, A. Cox, and Carl A. Castro. 2008. "Mild Traumatic Brain Injury in U.S. Soldiers Returning from Iraq." *New England Journal of Medicine* 358:453–463.

Holland, Dorothy, Donald M. Nonini, Catherine Lutz, Lesley Bartlett, Marla Frederick-McGlathery, Thaddeus C. Guldbrandsen, and Enrique G. Murillo Jr. 2007. *Local Democracy under Siege: Activism, Public Interest, and Private Politics.* New York: New York University Press.

Holmstedt, Kristen. 2007. *Band of Sisters: American Women at War in Iraq.* Mechanicsburg, PA: Stackpole Books.

Homer. 1996. *The Odyssey.* Translated by Robert Fagles. New York: Penguin Group.

Hora, Peggy Fulton. 2002. "A Dozen Years of Drug Treatment Courts: Uncovering the Theoretical Foundation and the Construction of a Mainstream Paradigm." *Substance Use & Misuse* 37(12&13):1469–88.

Hosek, James, Beth J. Asch, C. Christine Fair, Craig Martin, and Michael Mattock. 2002. *Married to the Military: The Employment and Earnings of Military Wives Compared with Those of Civilian Wives.* Santa Monica, CA: RAND National Defense Research Institute.

Hosek, James, Jennifer Kavanagh, and Laura Miller. 2006. *How Deployments Affect Service Members.* Santa Monica, CA: RAND Corporation.

Howell, Alison, and Zoë Wool. 2011. "The War Comes Home: The Toll of War and the Shifting Burden of Care." In *Costs of War Project Report.* Eisenhower Research Project at the Watson Institute for International Studies, Brown University, pp. 1–19. http://www.academia.edu/3363619/The_War_Comes_Home_The_Toll_of_War_and_the_Shifting_Burden_of_Care (accessed August 30, 2013).

Hudson, Heidi. 2005. "Doing Security As Though Humans Matter: A Feminist Perspective on Gender and the Politics of Human Security." *Security Dialogue* 36(2):155–75.

_____. 2008. "Feminist Analysis at the Intersection of Critical Security Studies and Peace Studies." *Conference Papers—International Studies Association* 1-21.

Huebner, Angela J., and Jay A. Mancini. 2005. "Adjustments among Adolescents in Military Families When a Parent Is Deployed." In *Final Report to the Military Family Research Institute and Department of Defense: Quality of Life Office.* Falls Church, VA: Virginia Tech, Department of Human Development.

Hughes, Everett C. 1951. "Work and the Self." In *Social Psychology at the Crossroads*, edited by John H. Rohrer and Muzafer Sherif, pp. 313–23. New York: Harper and Brothers.

Huntington, Samuel P. 1957. *The Soldier and the State; the Theory and Politics of Civil-Military Relations*. Cambridge: Belknap Press of Harvard University Press.

Inskeep, Steve, and Tom Bowman. 2008. Army Documents Show Lower Recruiting Standards. National Public Radio, April 17. http://www.npr.org/templates/story/story. php?storyId=89702118.

IOM (Institute of Medicine) and National Research Council. 2007. *PTSD Compensation and Military Service*. Washington, DC: National Academies Press.

Iraq Veterans against the War (IVAW) and Aaron Glantz. 2008. *Winter Soldier, Iraq and Afghanistan: Eyewitness Accounts of the Occupations*. Chicago: Haymarket Books.

Jackson, Nicky Ali. 2007. *Encyclopedia of Domestic Violence*. New York: Routledge.

Janes, Craig R. 1999. "Imagined Lives, Suffering, and the Work of Culture: The Embodied Discourses of Conflict in Modern Tibet." *Medical Anthropology Quarterly* 13(4):391–412.

Janofsky, B. J. 1989. "The Dual-Career Couple: Challenges and Satisfactions." In *The Organization Family: Work and Family Linkages in the U. S. Military*, edited by Gary L. Bowen and Dennis K. Orthner, pp. 97–115. New York: Praeger.

Janowitz, Morris. 1960. *The Professional Soldier: A Social and Political Portrait*. Glencoe, IL: Free Press.

Joffe-Walt, Chana. 2013. "We're Just Hiding You Guys." Part 2 of "Unfit for Work: The Startling Rise of Disability in America." National Public Radio, "Planet Money." http://apps.npr.org/ unfit-for-work/ (accessed August 8, 2013).

Johnson, Chalmers. 2004. "America's Empire of Bases." *Common Dreams*, January 15. http:// www.commondreams.org/views04/0115-08.htm (accessed August 30, 2013).

Jones, Edgar, and Simon Wesseley. 2007. "A Paradigm Shift in the Conceptualization of Psychological Trauma in the 20th Century." *Journal of Anxiety Disorders* 21:164–75.

Jordan, Brigitte with Robbie Davis-Floyd. 1992. *Birth in Four Cultures: A Crosscultural Investigation of Childbirth in Yucatan, Holland, Sweden, and the United States*. 4th ed. Prospect Heights, IL: Waveland Press.

Junger, Sebastian. 2010. *War*. New York: Twelve.

Kane, Muriel. 2012. "Record 45% of Iraq and Afghanistan vets have filed for disability." *The Raw Story*, May 27. http://www.rawstory.com/rs/2012/05/27/record-45-of-iraq-and-afghanistan -vets-have-filed-for-disability/ (accessed August 10, 2013).

Kane, Tim. 2005. *Who Bears the Burden? Demographic Characteristic of U.S. Military Recruits Before and After 9/11*. Washington, DC: The Heritage Center, Center for Data Analysis.

Kaplan, Fred. 2008. "The U.S. Army Lowers Recruitment Standards ... again." *Slate*, January 24. http://www.slate.com/articles/news_and_politics/war_stories/2008/01/dumb_and_dumb- er.single.html#pagebreak_anchor_2. (accessed September 24, 2013).

Karlin, Bradley E., Josef. I. Ruzek, Kathleen M. Chard, Afsoon Eftekhari, Candice M. Monson, Elizabeth A. Hembree, Patricia A. Resick, and Edna B. Foa. 2010. "Dissemination of Evidence-Based Psychological Treatments for Posttraumatic Stress Disorder in the Veterans Health Adminstration." *Journal of Traumatic Stress* 23(6):663–73.

Karney, Benjamin R., and John S. Crown. 2007. *Families under Stress: An Assessment of Data, Theory, and Research on Marriage and Divorce in the Military*. Santa Monica, CA: RAND Corporation.

Keller, Carol A. 2006 [1993]. "Prologue: Legacies." In *The Army Wife Handbook*, by Ann Crossley and Carol A. Keller. Marietta, Georgia: ABI Press.

Kelley, Michelle L., Lisa B. Finkel, and Jayne Ashby. 2003. "Geographic Mobility, Family, and Maternal Variables as Related to the Psychosocial Adjustment of Military Children." *Military Medicine* 168(12):1019–24.

Kelty, Ryan, Meredith Kleykamp, and David R. Segal. 2010. "The Military and the Transition to Adulthood." *The Future of Childhood* 20(1):181–207.

Kessler, R. C. 2000. "Posttraumatic Stress Disorder: The Burden to the Individual and to Society." *Journal of Clinical Psychiatry* 61(suppl.5):4–12.

Kilshaw, Susie. 2009. *Impotent Warriors: Gulf War Syndrome, Vulnerability and Masculinity.* New York: Bergahn Books.

Kimerling, Rachel, Amy E. Street, Joanne Pavao, Mark W. Smith, Ruth C. Cronkite, Tyson H. Holmes, and Susan M. Frayne. 2010. "Military-related Sexual Trauma among Veterans Health Administration Patients Returning from Afghanistan and Iraq." *American Journal of Public Health* 100(8):1409–12.

Kirmeyer, Laurence J., Robert Lemelson, and Mark Barad (eds.). 2007. *Understanding Trauma: Integrating Biological, Clinical, and Cultural Perspectives.* Cambridge, UK: Cambridge University Press.

Klein, Gary. 1995. "Naturalistic Decision Making and Wildland Firefighting." Findings from the Wildland Firefighters Human Factors Workshop Appendix D—Keynote Presentations. http://www.docstoc.com/docs/147466197/Colorado-s-Valuable-National-Assets—Colorado-Springs-Chamber (accessed November 2, 2013).

Kleinman, Arthur. 1980. *Patients and Healers in the Context of Culture: An Exploration of the Borderland between Anthropology, Medicine, and Psychiatry.* Berkeley: University of California Press.

———. 1988. *The Illness Narratives: Suffering, Healing & The Human Condition.* New York: Basic Books.

Koba, Mark. 2013. Sequestration: CNBC Explains. January 14. http://www.cnbc.com/id/100378424 (accessed July 31, 2013).

Krebs, Ronald R. 2009. "The Citizen-Soldier Tradition in the United States: Has Its Demise Been Greatly Exaggerated?" *Armed Forces and Society* 36(1):153–74.

Kriner, Douglas L., and Francis X. Shen. 2010. *The Casualty Gap: The Causes and Consequences of American Wartime Inequalities.* Oxford and New York: Oxford University Press.

Kristoff, Nicholas 2011. "Our Lefty Military." *New York Times,* June 16, p. A35.

Kusow, Abdi M. 2004. "Contesting Stigma: On Goffman's Assumptions of Normative Order." *Symbolic Interaction* 27(2):179–97.

Kusserow, Adrie. 2004. *American Individualisms: Child Rearing and Social Class in Three Neighborhoods.* New York: Palgrave Macmillan.

Lande, R. G., B. A. Marin, A. S. Chang, and G. R. Lande. 2008. "Survey of Alcohol Use in the Army." *Journal of Addictive Disorders* 27(3):115–21.

Lane, Anthony. 2009. "Little Kids, Big Problems." *Colorado Springs Independent* February 12. http://www.csindy.com/coloradosprings/little-kids-big-problems/Content?oid=1327878 (accessed August 30, 2013).

Lanier-Graham, Susan. 1993. *The Ecology of War: Environmental Impacts of Weaponry and Warfare.* New York: Walker.

Larson, Mary Jo, Nikki R. Wooten, Rachel Sayko Adams, and Elizabeth L. Merrick. 2012. "Military Combat Deployments and Substance Use: Review and Future Directions." *Journal of Social Work Practice in the Addictions* 12(1):6–27.

Lembcke, Jerry. 1998. *The Spitting Image: Myth, Memory, and the Legacy of Vietnam.* New York: New York University Press.

Lembcke, Jerry. 2003. "Spitting on the Troops: Old Myth, New Rumors." *The Veteran* 33(1):22.

_____. 2005. Debunking A Spitting Image. *The Boston Globe*, April 30. http://www.boston.com/news/globe/editorial_opinion/oped/articles/2005/04/30/debunking_a_spitting_image/ (accessed August 14, 2013).

Lemke, Thomas. 2001. "'The Birth of Bio-Politics': Michel Foucault's Lecture at the Collège de France on Neo-Liberal Governmentality." *Economy and Society* 30(2):190–207.

Lemmon, Megan, Mira Whyman, and Jay Teachman. 2009. "Active-duty Military Service in the United States: Cohabiting Unions and the Transition to Marriage." *Demographic Research* 20(10):195–208.

Lester, Patricia, Kris Peterson, James Reeves, Larry Knauss, Dorie Glover, Catherin Mogil, Naihua Duan, William Saltzman, Robert Pynoos, Katherine Wilt, and William Beardsless. 2010. "The Long War and Parental Combat Deployment: Effects on Military Children and At-Home Spouses." *Journal of the American Academy of Child and Adolescent Psychiatry* 49(4):310–20.

Lester, Paul B., P. D. Harms, Mitchel N. Herian, and Dina V Krasikova. 2011. "The Comprehensive Soldier Fitness Program Evaluation." In *Report #3: Longitudinal Analysis of the Impact of Master Resilience Training on Self-Reported Resilience and Psychological Health Data.* http://www.ppc.sas.upenn.edu/csftechreport3mrt.pdf (accessed August 30, 2013).

Lévi-Strauss, Claude. 1963. *Structural Anthropology*. New York: Basic Books.

Levine, Bruce. 2010. "Sharp Rise in U.S. Military Psychiatric Drug Use and Suicides." *Huffington Post*, April 1. http://www.huffingtonpost.com/bruce-e-levine/sharp-rise-in-us-military_b_521365.html.

Lighthall, Alison. n.d. "Ten Things You Should Know to Help Bring the OIF/OEF Veteran All the Way Home." http://sds.okstate.edu/index2.php?option=com_content&do_pdf=1&id=387 (accessed July 31, 2013).

_____. n.d.b. "U.S. Must Unite to Aid Vets." *Army Times* http://www.armytimes.com/community/opinion/airforce_backtalk_vets_071224/ (accessed July 25, 2012).

Litz, Brett T., Nathan Stein, Eileen Delaney, Leslie Lebowitz, William P. Nash, Caroline Silva, and Shira Maguen. 2009. "Moral Injury and Moral Repair in War Veterans: A Preliminary Model and Intervention Strategy." *Clinical Psychology* 29:695–706.

Loria, Kevin. 2012. "Military Veterans to Get Priority for Police Jobs under COPS Grant." *The Christian Science Monitor*, June 25. http://www.csmonitor.com/USA/2012/0625/Military-veterans-to-get-priority-for-police-jobs-under-COPS-grants.

Low, Hana. 2012. "A Possible Framework for Understanding the Intersection of Ethnicity and Mental Health within Army Communities." http://www.coloradocollege.edu/offices/cce/community-based-research/military-engagement/Deployment-Stress/theses-and-papers. dot (accessed August 30, 2013).

Lugo, Alejandro, and Bill Maurer. 2000. "The Legacy of Michelle Rosaldo." In *Gender Matters: Rereading Michelle Z. Rosaldo*, edited by Alejandro Lugo and Bill Maurer, pp. 16–34. Ann Arbor: University of Michigan Press.

Lundquist, Jennifer Hickes. 2007. "A Comparison of Civilian and Enlisted Divorce Rates During the Early all Volunteer Force Era." *Journal of Political and Military Sociology* 35(2):199–217.

Lundquist, Jennifer Hickes, and Herbert L. Smith. 2005. "Family Formation among Women in the U.S. Military: Evidence from the NLSY." *Journal of Marriage and Family* 67(1):1–13.

Lutz, Amy. 2008. "Who Joins the Military?: A Look at Race, Class, and Immigration Status." *Journal of Political and Military Sociology* 36(2):167–88.

Lutz, Catherine. 1990. *Doublespeak*. New York: Harper Collins.

_____. 2001. *Homefront: A Military City and the American Twentieth Century*. Boston: Beacon Press.

Lutz, Catherine. 2002. "Making War at Home in the United States: Militarization and the Current Crisis." *American Anthropologist* 104(3):723–35.

_____. 2009. *The Bases of Empire: The Global Struggle against U.S. Military Posts*. New York: New York University Press.

Lutz, Catherine, and Kathleen Millar. 2012. "War." In *A Companion to Moral Anthropology*, edited by Didier Fassin, pp. 482–99. Oxford, UK: Wiley-Blackwell.

MacCannell, D. 1992. *Empty Meeting Grounds: The Tourist Papers*. London and New York: Routledge.

MacFarlane, S. Neil, and Yuen Foong Khong. 2006. *Human Security and the UN: A Critical History*. Bloomington: Indiana University Press.

MacGregor, Morris J. 1981. *Integration of the Armed Forces, 1940–1965*. Washington, DC: Government Printing Office.

MacLean, Alistair, and Glen Elder. 2007. "Military Service in the Life Course." *Annual Review of Sociology* 33:175–96.

MacLeish, Kenneth. 2013. *Making War at Fort Hood*. Princeton, NJ: Princeton University Press.

MacManus, D., K. Dean, M. Al Bakir, A. C. Iversen, L. Hull, T. Fahy, S. Wessely, and N. T. Fear. 2012. "Violent Behaviour in UK Military Personnel Returning Home after Deployment." *Psychological Medicine* 42(8):1663–73.

Maguen, Shira, and Brett Litz. 2012. "Moral Injury in Veterans of War." *PTSD Research Quarterly* 23(1):1–6.

Mandel, Lee R. 2007. "Combat Fatigue from the Civil War to Desert Storm: An Overview." Paper presented at the Annual Meeting of the American Association of the History of Medicine, Montreal, Quebec, Canada, May 3–6.

Mansfield, A. J., J. S. Kaufman, S. W. Marshall, B. N. Gaynes, J. P. Morrissey, and C. C. Engel. 2010. "Deployment and the Use of Mental Health Services among U.S. Army Wives." *New England Journal of Medicine* 362(2):101–9.

Marhia, Natasha. 2013. "Some Humans are More Human than Others: Troubling the 'Human' in Human Security from a Critical Feminist Perspective." *Security Dialogue* 44(1):19–35.

Markusen, Ann, and Joel Yudken. 1992. *Dismantling the Cold War Economy*. New York: Basic Books.

Marlowe, David H. 2001. *Psychological and Psychosocial Consequences of Combat and Deployment with Special Emphasis on the Gulf War*. Santa Monica, CA: RAND.

Marshall, Burke. 1967. *In Pursuit of Equity: Who Serves When Not All Serve? Report of the National Advisory Commission on Selective Service*. Washington, DC: National Advisory Commission on Selective Service.

Martin, Emily. 1987. *The Woman in the Body: A Cultural Analysis of Reproduction*. Boston: Beacon Press.

_____. 1990. "Toward an Anthropology of Immunology: The Body as Nation State." *Medical Anthropology Quarterly* 4(4):410–26.

_____. 2004. *Flexible Bodies: Tracking Immunity in American Culture from the Days of Polio to the Age of AIDS*. Boston: Beacon Press.

Mastroianni, George R., and Wilbur J. Scott. 2008. "After Iraq: The Politics of Blame and Civilian-Military Relations." *Military Review* (July-August):54–60.

Matrullo, Tom. "Labyrinth of Prattle." *Metamorphoses: Reading Ovid in Sarasota*. http://ovids-metamorphoses.blogspot.com/2011/04/labyrinth-of-prattle.html (accessed October 3, 2013).

Matsakis, A. 1988. *Vietnam Wives: Facing the Challenges of Life with Veterans Suffering Post-Traumatic Stress*. 2nd ed. Baltimore, MD: Sidran Press.

Mattingly, Cheryl. 1998. *Healing Dramas and Clinical Plots: The Narrative Structure of Experience.* Cambridge, UK: Cambridge University Press.

Mattingly, Cheryl, and Linda C. Garro. 2000. *Narrative and the Cultural Construction of Illness and Healing.* Berkeley: University of California Press.

Maxfield, Betty D. 2006. *The Changing Profile of the Army.* Arlington, VA: Office of Army Demographics.

McGrath, Collicut J. 2007. *Ethical Practice in Brain Injury Rehabilitation.* Oxford, UK: Oxford University Press.

McHugh, Paul R., and Glenn Treisman. 2007. "PTSD: A Problematic Diagnostic Category." *Journal of Anxiety Disorders* 21:211–22.

McNally, Richard J. 2003. "Progress and Controversy in the Study of Posttraumatic Stress Disorder." *Annual Review of Psychology* 54:229–52.

_____. 2006. "The Expanding Empire of Posttraumatic Stress Disorder." *Medscape General Medicine* 8(2):9.

_____. 2007. "Can We Solve the Mysteries of the National Vietnam Veterans Readjustment Study?" *Journal of Anxiety Disorders* 21:192–200.

Meadows, Donella. 1999. *Leverage Points: Places to Intervene in a System.* Hartland, VT: Sustainability Institute. http://www.sustainer.org/pubs/Leverage_Points.pdf (accessed August 30, 2013).

Mershon, Sherie, and Steven Schlossman. 1998. *Foxholes and Colorlines: Desegregating the U.S. Armed Forces.* Baltimore, MD: The Johns Hopkins University Press.

MHAT (Mental Health Advisory Team). 2008. *Mental Health Advisory Team (MHAT) V: Operation Iraqi Freedom 06-08: Iraq, Operation Enduring Freedom 08: Afghanistan.* Washington, DC: Office of the Surgeon, Multi-National Force—Iraq and Office of the Command Surgeon and Office of the Surgeon General, United States Army Medical Command. http://www.armymedicine.army.mil/reports/mhat/mhat_v/Redacted1-MHATV-4-FEB-2008-Overview.pdf (accessed August 30, 2013).

MHN 2012. Military and Family Life Consultant (MFLC) Program Frequently Asked Questions. February 14. http://www.mhngs.com/app/resourcesfor/MFLC_FAQs.pdf (accessed August 15, 2013).

Milliken, Charles S., Jennifer L. Auchterlonie, and Charles W. Hoge. 2007. "Longitudinal Assessment of Mental Health Problems Among Active and Reserve Component Soldiers Returning from the Iraq War." *Journal of the American Medical Association* 298(18):2141–48.

Milliken, Tara. 2012. "Domination, Dependence, and Deviance: The Role and History of Family Readiness Groups and the Army Spouses of Which They Are Composed." Summer Internship Paper, Department of Anthropology, Colorado College, Colorado Springs.

Milton, John. 1919. "On His Blindness." In *The Oxford Book of English Verse: 1250–1900,* edited by Arthur Quiller-Couch. http://www.bartleby.com/101/318.html (accessed October 3, 2013).

Mirchandani, Rekha. 2008. "Beyond Therapy: Problem-Solving Courts and the Deliberative Democratic State." *Law and Social Inquiry* 33(4):853–93.

Mitchell, Carlyn. 2008. "2 Fort Carson Soldiers Arrested in Double Homicide." *The Gazette,* August 27. http://www.gazette.com/articles/fort-39881-soldiers-arrested.html# ixzz1rr GneXfr (accessed August 14, 2013).

Mitchell, Kirk. 2008. "Salazar: Review GI Violence." *The Denver Post,* October 19. http://www.denverpost.com/ci_10751096?source=rss (accessed August 14, 2013).

Moerman, Daniel. 2002. *Meaning, Medicine and the "Placebo Effect."* Cambridge, UK: Cambridge University Press.

Moghnieh, Lamia. 2011. "Humanitarian and Human Subjects in Lebanon: The Problem of Social Change." *Jadaliyya*, October 19. http://www.jadaliyya.com/pages/index/2903/ humanitarian-and-humane-s (accessed September 15, 2013).

Molinsky, Andrew. 2007. "Cross-Cultural Code-Switching: The Psychological Challenges of Adapting Behavior in Foreign Cultural Interactions." *Academy of Management Review* 32(2):622–40.

Moore, Bret A., and Greg M. Reger. 2007. "Historical and Contemporary Perspectives of Combat Stress and the Army Combat Stress Control Team." In *Combat Stress Injury: Theory, Research, and Management*, edited by Charles R. Figley and William P. Nash, pp. 161–82. New York and London: Routledge.

Moreau, Charles, and Sidney Zisook. 2002. "Rationale for a Posttraumatic Stress Spectrum Disorder." *Psychiatric Clinics of North America* 25:775–90.

Mount, Mike. 2009. "Shortage in Ranks Raises Questions about Hasan's Military Career." CNN, November 13. U.S. http://articles.cnn.com/2009-11-13/us/military.psychiatrists_1_ nidal-malik-hasan-army-documents-war-zones?_s=PM:US.

Murray, Janet. 2003. "Inventing the Medium." In *The New Media Reader*, edited by Noah Wardrip-Fruin and Nick Montfort, pp. 3–12. Boston: MIT Press.

Nash, William P. 2007a. "Combat/Operational Stress Adaptations and Injuries." In *Combat Stress Injury: Theory, Research, and Management*, edited by Charles R. Figley and William P. Nash, pp. 33–64. New York & London: Routledge.

_____. 2007b. "The Stressors of War." In *Combat Stress Injury: Theory, Research, and Management*, edited by Charles R. Figley and William P. Nash, pp. 11–32. New York & London: Routledge.

Nettleton, Sarah. 2006. *The Sociology of Health and Fitness.* Cambridge, UK: Polity Press.

Nichter, Mark. 1981. "Idioms of Distress: Alternatives in the Expression of Psychosocial Distress: A Case Study from South India." *Culture, Medicine and Psychiatry* 5(4):379–408.

_____. 2010. "Idioms of Distress Revisited." *Culture, Medicine and Psychiatry* 34(2):401–16.

Nielsen, Suzanne C. 2012. "American Civil-Military Relations Today: The Continuing Relevance of Samuel P. Huntington's *The Soldier and the State*." *International Affairs* 88(2):369–76.

Nocera, Joe. 2012. "The Cost of Football Glory." *New York Times.* February 3. http://www. nytimes.com/2012/02/04/opinion/nocera-the-cost-of-football-glory.html?_r=0.

Nolan, James. 1988. *The Therapeutic State: Justifying Government at Century's End.* New York: New York University Press.

_____. 2003. "Redefining Criminal Courts: Problem-Solving and the Meaning of Justice." *American Criminal Law Review* 40:1541–66.

Nordstrom, Carolyn. 1997. *A Different Kind of War Story (The Ethnography of Political Violence).* Philadelphia: University of Pennsylvania Press.

O'Brien, Tim. 1990. *The Things They Carried.* New York: Broadway Books.

O'Neil, Caitlin. 2010. "Changing of the Guard: A Look Back at 10 Years of War." Hidden Surge, February 14. http://hiddensurge.nationalsecurityzone.org/nsjihs_special_pages/changing-of-the-guard/ (accessed August 10, 2013.)

Operation Ready. 2010. *The Family Readiness Group Leader's Handbook.* 4th edition. https://www.armyfrg.org/skins/frg/display.aspx?ModuleID=2a285ab0-5db1-4f36-9b91-f2263c973c32&Action=display_user_category_objects&CategoryID=b1cf0310-be20-4e63-bd55-8c8c6f27c9b5 (accessed September 30, 2013).

Ortner, Sherry B. 2003. *New Jersey Dreaming: Capital, Culture, and the Class of '58.* Durham, NC, and London: Duke University Press.

Packer, George. 2011. "Coming Apart: After 9/11 Transfixed America, the Country's Problems Were Left to Rot." *The New Yorker*, September 12. http://www.newyorker.com/reporting /2011/09/12/110912fa_fact_packer (accessed October 5, 2013).

Pattison, E. Mansell. 1984. "War and Mental Health in Lebanon." *Journal of Operational Psychiatry* (15):31–38.

Paulsen, Daryl. 2005. *Walking the Point: Male Initiation and the Vietnam Experience*. 2nd ed. New York: Paraview Publishing.

Paulson, Daryl S., and Stanley Krippner. 2007. *Haunted by Combat: Understanding PTSD in War Veterans Including Women, Reservists, and Those Coming Back from Iraq*. Westport, CT: Praeger Security International.

Pew Research Center. 2011. *War and Sacrifice in the Post-9/11 Era: The Military-Civilian Gap*. Washington, DC: Pew Research Center.

Philipps, Dave. 2009a. "Casualties of War, Part 1: The Hell of War Comes Home." *The Gazette*, July 24. http://www.gazette.com/articles/iframe-59065-eastridge-audio.html (accessed August 14, 2013).

_____. 2009b. "Casualties of War, Part II: Warning Signs." *The Gazette*, July 24. http://www. gazette.com/articles/html-59091-http-gazette.html#ixzz1uEy8zvvk (accessed August 21, 2013).

_____. 2010. *Lethal Warriors: When the New Band of Brothers Came Home*. London: Palgrave MacMillan.

_____. 2013. Disposable: Surge in Discharges Includes Wounded Soldiers. *The Gazette*, http:// cdn.csgazette.biz/soldiers/day1.html (accessed August 19, 2013).

Phillips, Michael M. 2011. "Rx for Combat Stress: Comradeship." *Wall Street Journal*, April 2. http://online.wsj.com/article/SB10001424052748703362904576219184030233852.html.

Pikes Peak Area Council of Governments (PPACG). 2013 Fort Carson Regional Growth Plan Transition Report (Draft March 2013). http://www.ppacg.org/mip/fort-carson-regional-growth-plan/growth-plan-documents (accessed August 30, 2013).

_____. 2008. Fort Carson Growth Plan Phase Two Program Narrative and the Fort Carson Regional Growth Plan Phase Two Scope of Work at http://www.ppacg.org/cms/index. php?option=com_remository&Itemid=27&func=select&id=157 (accessed August 14, 2013).

Pikes Peak Quality of Life. 2010. Quality of Life Indicators Report 2010. http://issuu.com/pikespeakqli/docs/2010_qli_report (accessed August 25, 2013).

_____. 2011. Quality of Life Indicators Report 2011.http://www.qlireport.org (accessed August 30, 2013).

Pilkington, Ed. 2013. "US Military Struggling to Stop Suicide Epidemic among War Veterans." *The Guardian*, February 1. http://www.theguardian.com/world/2013/feb/01/us-military-suicide-epidemic-veteran (accessed August 14, 2013).

Plutarch. 1967. *Plutarch's Lives*. Vol. 1. Translated by Bernadette Perrin. Cambridge, MA. Harvard University Press.

Porter, Eduardo. 2013. "Inequality in America: The Data Is Sobering." *New York Times*. July 31, pp. B1, B9.

Powers, Rod. 2003. About.com US Military. "More Pay for Combat Zones." http://usmilitary. about.com/cs/moneymatters/a/combatzone.htm (accessed August 30, 2013).

Price, Jennifer L. 2009. "When a Child's Parent Has PTSD." National Center for PTSD. Washington, DC: United States Department of Veteran Affairs. http://www.ptsd.va.gov/professional/pages/pro_child_parent_ptsd.asp (accessed August 30, 2013).

Ramchand, Rajeev, Terry L. Schell, Benjamin R. Karney, Karen Chan Osilla, Rachel M. Burns, and Leah Barnes Caldarone. 2010. "Disparate Prevalence Estimates of PTSD among Service Members Who Served in Iraq and Afghanistan: Possible Explanations." *Journal of Traumatic Stress* 23(1):59–68.

RAND Corporation. 2009. "Assessing Combat Exposure and Post-Traumatic Stress Disorder in Troops And Estimating the Costs to Society." Santa Monica, CA: RAND Corporation.

Remarque, Erich Maria. 1982 [1928]. *All Quiet on the Western Front*. New York: Ballantine Books.

Renshaw, Keith D., Galena K. Rhoades, Elizabeth S. Allen, and Rebecca K. Blais. 2011. "Distress in Spouses of Service Members with Symptoms of Combat-Related PTSD: Secondary Traumatic Stress or General Psychological Distress?" *Journal of Family Psychology* 25(4):461–69.

Riccio, Gary, Randall Sullivan, Gerald Klein, Margaret Salter, and Henry Kinnison. 2004. *Warrior Ethos: Analysis of the Concept and Initial Development of Applications*. Arlington, VA: U.S. Army Research Institute for the Behavioral and Social Sciences.

Rich, Tracey R. 2011. "Life, Death and Mourning." *Judaism 101*. http://www.jewfaq.org/death.htm (accessed August 14, 2013).

Richardson, Amy, Anita Chandra, Laurie T. Martin, Claude Messan Setodji, Bryan W. Hallmark, Nancy F. Campbell, Stacy Ann Hawkins, and Patrick Grady. 2011. *Effects of Soldiers' Deployment on Children's Academic Performance and Behavioral Health*. Santa Monica, CA: RAND Corporation.

Richardson, Lisa K., B. Christopher Frueh, and Ronald Acierno. 2010. "Prevalence Estimates of Combat-related Post-traumatic Stress Disorder: Critical Review." *Australian and New Zealand Journal of Psychiatry* 44:4–19.

Ricks, Thomas E. 1996. *On American Soil: The Widening Gap between the U.S. Military and U.S. Society*. John M. Olin Institute for Strategic Studies, Harvard University. http://www.wcfia.harvard.edu/olin/publications/workingpapers/civil_military/no3.htm (accessed November 12, 2012).

Robinson, Donald. 2011. *Town Meeting: Practicing Democracy in Rural New England*. Amherst, MA: University of Massachusetts Press.

Rodgers, Jakob. 2012. "Fort Carson Officials Explain Rise in Behavioral Health Visits." *The Gazette*, April 26. http://www.gazette.com/articles/health-137628-visits-behavioral.html (accessed August 30, 2013).

Roeder, Tom. 2008a. "Fellow Soldiers Surprised by 2 Men's Arrests." *The Gazette*, August 30. http://www.gazette.com/articles/soldiers-40006-battalion-falu.html (accessed August 14, 2013).

_____. 2008b. "Homicide Gives Reason to Review Standards." *The Gazette*, October 17. http://www.gazette.com/articles/army-42037-iraq-mental.html.

_____. 2011. "Top Sergeant Praised for Turnaround of Once-Troubled Unit." *The Gazette*, October 23. http://www.gazette.com/articles/troubled-127185-sasser-ago.html#ixzz1sKDmqs6r (accessed August 14, 2013).

_____. 2013. "Iraq: Ten Years Later." *The Gazette*, March 15. http://gazette.com/article/152318 (accessed August 30, 2013).

Rogers, Reginald P. 2004. "New Values Cards, Warrior Ethos 'Dogtags' Available to Army Units." TRADOC News Service, September 24. http://www.tradoc.army.mil/pao/tnsar-chives/september04/092304.htm (accessed August 2, 2013).

Rona, R., N. Fear, L. Hull, N. Greenberg, M. Earnshaw, M. Hotopf, and S. Wessely. 2007. "The Mental Health Consequences of "Overstretch" in the UK Armed Forces." *British Medical Journal* 335:603–7.

Rona, Roberto J., Richard Hooper, Margaret Jones, Amy C. Iversen, Lisa Hull, Dominic Murphy, Matthew Hotopf, and Simon Wessely. 2009. "The Contribution of Prior Psychological Symptoms and Combat Exposure to Post Iraq Deployment Mental Health in the UK Military." *Journal of Traumatic Stress* 22(1):11–19.

Rosaldo, Michelle Zimbalist. 1980. "The Use and Abuse of Anthropology: Reflections on Feminism and Cross-Cultural Understanding." *Signs* 5(3):389–417.

Rosaldo, Michelle Zimbalist, and Louise Lamphere. 1974. "Women, Culture and Society: A Theoretical Overview." In *Women, Culture and Society*, edited by Michelle Zimbalist Rosaldo and Louise Lamphere, pp. 17–42. Stanford, CA: Stanford University Press.

Rosen, Gerald M., and B. Christopher Frueh. 2006. "Challenges to the PTSD Construct and Its Database: The Importance of Scientific Debate." *Journal of Anxiety Disorders* 21:161–63.

Rostker, Barnard D. 2006. *I Want You! The Evolution of the All-Volunteer Force*. Santa Monica, CA: RAND Corporation.

Rousseau, Cécile, and Toby Measham. 2007. "Posttraumatic Suffering as a Source of Transformation: A Clinical Perspective." In *Understanding Trauma: Integrating Biological, Clinical and Cultural Perspective*, edited by Laurence J. Kirmayer, Robert Lemelson, and Mark Barad, pp. 275–94. Cambridge, UK: Cambridge University Press.

Routon, Ralph. 2010. "Stop the Local Self-pity." *Colorado Springs Independent*, September 23. http://www.csindy.com/coloradosprings/stop-the-local-self-pity/Content?oid=1854891 (accessed August 14, 2013).

Ruetschlin, Catherine, and Tamara Draut. 2013. "Stuck: Young America's Persistent Jobs Crisis." New York: Demos. April 4. http://www.demos.org/publication/stuck-young-americas-persistent-jobs-crisis.

Satel, Sally L., and B. Christopher Frueh. 2009. "Sociopolitical Aspects of Psychiatry: Posttraumatic Stress Disorder." In *Comprehensive Textbook of Psychiatry*, 9th ed., edited by Benjamin J. Sadock, Virginia A. Sadock, and Pedro Ruiz, pp. 728–33. Baltimore, MD: Lippincott, Williams, & Wilkins.

Sattler, Joseph. 2013. "Only 43.8 Percent of Military Identify as Republican, Down from 56 Percent in 2005 versus 9.3 Percent Identifying as Democrat in 2013." *The National Memo*, March 28. http://www.nationalmemo.com/only-43-8-percent-of-military-identify-as-republican-down-from-56-percent-in-2005/ (accessed August 19, 2013).

Scandlyn, Jean S. 1993. "When the Social Contract Fails: Intergenerational and Interethnic Conflict in an American Suburban School District." PhD Dissertation, Department of Anthropology, Columbia University, New York.

_____. 2009. "Local Conflicts, Global Forces: Fighting for Public Education in a New York Suburb." In *Border Crossings: Transnational Americanist Anthropology*, edited by Kathleen Fine-Dare and Stephen Rubenstein, pp. 171–210. Lincoln: University of Nebraska Press.

Scandlyn, Jean, and Sarah Hautzinger. 2013. "Playing Set® to Discover Qualitative Data Analysis." *The Qualitative Report* 18, Article T&L 4:1–13. http://www.nova.edu/ssss/QR/QR18/Scandlyn4.pdf.

Scarry, Elaine. 1985. *The Body in Pain: The Making and Unmaking of the World*. New York: Oxford.

Schechner, Richard. 1985. *Between Theater and Anthropology*. Philadelphia: University of Pennsylvania Press.

_____. 1993. *The Future of Ritual: Writings on Culture and Performance*. New York: New York University Press.

Schiavitti, Vincent W., Lawrence L. Loendorf, and Erica Hill. 2001. "Archaeological Investigations at Eleven Sites of Welsh Canyon in the Piñon Canyon Maneuver Site, Las Animas County, Colorado." Fort Carson Cultural Resource Management Series Contribution Number 8.

Schiff, Rebecca L. 2008. *The Military and Domestic Politics: A Concordance Theory of Civil-Military Relations*. New York: Routledge.

Schlosser, Eric. 2003. *Fast Food Nation: The Dark Side of the All-American Meal*. New York: Houghton Mifflin.

Schoch-Spana, Monica. 2012. "Standing at the Crossroads of Anthropology, Public Health, and National Security 101." In *Anthropologists in the SecurityScape: Ethics, Practice, and Professional Identity*, edited by Robert Albro, George Marcus, Laura A. McNamara, and Monica Schoch-Spana, pp. 101–14. Walnut Creek, CA: Left Coast Press.

Schogol, Jeff. 2009. "Pentagon: No Purple Heart for PTSD." *Stars and Stripes*, January 6. http://www.stripes.com/news/pentagon-no-purple-heart-for-ptsd-1.86761 (accessed August 30, 2013).

Schroeder, Pat. 2010. "The Adversarial Legal System: Is Justice Served?" *The Law Insider*, September 3. http://www.thelawinsider.com/insider-news/the-adversarial-legal-system-is-justice-served/ (accessed August 19, 2013).

Schulz, Priscilla. 2011. "Meaning-making, PTSD, and Combat Experiences." The Center for Deployment Psychology. http://old.deploymentpsych.org/topics-disorders/ptsd (accessed August 30, 2013).

Schuster, Mark A., Bradley D. Stein, Lisa H. Jaycox, Rebecca L. Collins, Grant N. Marshall, Marc N. Elliott, Annie J. Zhou, David E. Kanouse, Janina L. Morrison, and Sandra H. Barry. 2001. "A National Survey of Stress Reactions after the September 11, 2001 Terrorist Attacks." *New England Journal of Medicine* 345(20):1507–12.

Scurfield, Raymond Monsour. 2006. *War Trauma: Lessons Unlearned, from Vietnam to Iraq.* Vol. 3. New York: Algora Publishing.

Segal, David R., and Mady Wechsler Segal. 2004. "America's Military Population." *Population Bulletin* 59(4):3–40.

Segal, Mady Wechsler. 1986. "The Military and the Family as Greedy Institutions." *Armed Forces & Society* 13(1):9–38.

Selby, Edward A., Michael D. Anestis, Theodore W. Bender, Jessica D. Ribeiro, Matthew K. Nock, M. David Rudd, Craig J. Bryan, Ingrid C. Lim, Monty T. Baker, Peter M. Gutierrez, and Thomas E. Joiner. 2010. "Overcoming the Fear of Lethal Injury: Evaluating Suicidal Behavior in the Military through the Lens of the Interpersonal-Psychological Theory of Suicide." *Clinical Psychology Review* 30:298–307.

Senior, Jennifer. 2011. "The Prozac, Paxil, Zoloft, Wellbutrin, Celexa, Effexor, Valium, Klonopin, Ativan, Restoril, Xanax, Adderall, Ritalin, Haldol, Risperdal, Seroquel, Ambien, Lunesta, Elavil, Trazodone War." *New York Magazine*, February 6. http://nymag.com/news/features /71277/.

Sennett, Richard, and Jonathan Cobb. 1973. *The Hidden Injuries of Class.* New York: Vintage Books.

Shah, Amir. 2012. "Afghanistan Attacks: Gunman in Afghan Army Uniform Opens Fire on NATO Troops, Kills One." *Huffington Post*, May 11. http://www.huffingtonpost.com/2012/ 05/11/afghanistan-attacks-gunman-nato-troops_n_1508743.html (accessed August 14, 2013).

Shalev, Arieh Y. 2007. "PTSD: A Disorder of Recovery?" In *Understanding Trauma: Integrating Biological, Clinical, and Cultural Perspectives*, edited by Laurence J. Kirmayer, Robert Lemelson, and Mark Barad, pp. 207–23. Cambridge, UK: Cambridge University Press.

Shay, Jonathan. 2002. *Odysseus in America: Combat Trauma and the Trials of Homecoming.* New York: Scribner.

Shea, Neil. 2012. "Afghanistan: A Gathering Menace." *The American Scholar*, Spring. http:// theamericanscholar.org/a-gathering-menace/ (accessed August 30, 2013).

Sheppard, S. C., Malatras, J. W., and Israel, A. C. 2010. "The Impact of Deployment on U.S. Military Families." *American Psychologist* 65(6):599–609.

Sherman, M. D., D. K. Zanotti, and D. E. Jones. 2005. "Key Elements in Couples Therapy with Veterans with Combat-related Posttraumatic Stress Disorder." *Professional Psychology: Research and Practice* 36(6):626–33.

Sherman, Michelle, and Ursula Bowling. 2011. "Challenges and Opportunities for Intervening with Couples in the Aftermath of the Global War on Terrorism." *Journal of Contemporary Psychotherapy* 41(4):209–17.

Shore, Bradd. 1996. *Culture of Mind.* Oxford: Oxford University Press.

Singer, Merrill, and Hans Baer. 2007. *Introducing Medical Anthropology: A Discipline in Action.* Lanham, MD: AltaMira Press.

Singer, P. W. 2007. "Can't Win With 'Em, Can't Go to War Without 'Em: Private Military Contractors and Counterinsurgency." Foreign Policy at Brookings. Policy Paper No. 4 (September):iii–21. http://www.pwsinger.com/pdf/FPS_paper_4_revise.pdf (accessed August 30, 2013).

Smiley, Sarah. 2005. *Going Overboard: The Misadventures of a Military Wife.* New York: New American Library.

_____. 2008 *I'm Just Saying . . . A Collection of Essays.* Pensacola, FL: Ballinger Publishing.

Smith, L. Christopher. 2009. "The Fort Carson Murder Spree." *Rolling Stone* 1091:52–86.

Smith, Rachel A. 2012. "Segmenting an Audience into the Own, the Wise, and Normals: A Latent Class Analysis of Stigma-Related Categories." *Communication Research Reports* 29(4):257–65.

Snyder, Douglas K., Molly F. Gasbarrini, Brian D. Doss, and David M. Schneider. 2011. "Intervening with Military Couples Struggling with Issues of Sexual Infidelity." *Journal of Contemporary Psychotherapy* 41(4):201–8.

Solnit, Rebecca. 2000. *Wanderlust: A History of Walking.* New York: Penguin Books.

Solomon Z, Dekel R, Mikulincer M. 2008. "Complex Trauma of War Captivity: A Prospective Study of Attachment and Post-traumatic Stress Disorder." *Psychological Medicine* 7:1–8.

Spitzer, Robert L., Michael B. First, and Jerome C. Wakefield. 2007. "Saving PTSD from Itself in DSM-V." *Journal of Anxiety Disorders* 21:233–41.

Spring, Baker. 2012. "Fiscal Cliff Danger: More Budget Cuts to Come." *The Foundry,* December 20. http://blog.heritage.org/2012/12/20/fiscal-cliff-danger-more-defense-budget-cuts-to-come/ (accessed July 31, 2013).

Squires, Chase. 2006. "New War Demands New Training for Troops." *The Washington Post,* June 26. http://www.washingtonpost.com/wp-dyn/content/article/2006/06/25/AR2006062500269_pf.html (accessed August 14, 2013).

Stahre, Mandy A., Robert D. Brewer, Vincent P. Fonseca, and Timothy S. Naimi. 2009. "Binge Drinking among U.S. Active-duty Military Personnel." *American Journal of Preventive Medicine* 36(3):208–17.

Stein, Dan J., Soraya Seedot, Amy Iversen, and Simon Wessely. 2007. "Post-traumatic Stress Disorder: Medicine and Politics." *The Lancet* 369:139–44.

St. Louis-Sanchez, Maria, and Dave Philipps. 2009a. "Carson GI Troubled Unit Arrested in Woman's Death." *The Denver Post,* May 11. http://www.denverpost.com/breakingnews/ci_12342622?source=rss (accessed August 14, 2013).

_____. 2009b. "Soldier Arrested in Shooting Death of 19-Year-Old"; *The Gazette,* May 11. http://www.gazette.com/articles/old-53558-today-police.html (accessed August 14, 2013).

Storti, Craig. 2001a. *The Art of Coming Home.* Yarmouth, ME: Intercultural Press.

_____. 2001b. *The Art of Crossing Cultures.* Yarmouth, ME: Intercultural Press.

Strine, Tara W., and Jennifer M. Hootman. 2007. "US National Prevalence and Correlates of Low Back and Neck Pain among Adults." *Arthritis Care & Research* 5(4):656–65.

Summerfield, Derek. 2001. "The Invention of Post-Traumatic Stress Disorder and the Social Usefulness of a Psychiatric Category." *British Medical Journal* 322:95–98.

Summerscale, Kate. 2008. *The Suspicions of Mr. Whicher.* New York: Walker Publishing Company.

Sussman, Nan M. 2000. "The Dynamic Nature of Cultural Identity Throughout Cultural Transitions: Why Home Is Not So Sweet." *Personality and Social Psychology Review* 4(4):355–73.

Szakolczai, A. 2009. "Liminality and Experience: Structuring Transitory Situations and Transformative Events." *International Political Anthropology* 2(1):141–72.

Student Veterans of America. 2013. "Majority of Student Veterans Graduate." March 4. http://studentveterans.org/index.php/media-news/80-majority-of-student-veterans-graduate.html (accessed July 20, 2013).

Tancer, Stephanie. 2012. "The Militarization of Families: Exploring the Gender Dynamic of the Army Wife in the United States." Honors Thesis, Department of Anthropology, Colorado College, Colorado Springs.

Tanielian, Terri, and Lisa H. Jaycox (eds.). 2008. *Invisible Wounds of War: Psychological and Cognitive Injuries, Their Consequences, and Services to Assist Recovery.* Santa Monica, CA: RAND Corporation.

Tarantino, Tom. 2013. "The Ground Truth on Veterans' Unemployment." *Time,* March 22. http://nation.time.com/2013/03/22/the-ground-truth-about-veterans-unemployment (accessed August 14, 2013).

Teachman, Jay, and Lucky Tedrow. 2007. "Joining Up: Did Military Service in the Early All Volunteer Era Affect Subsequent Civilian Income?" *Social Science Research* 36:1447–74.

Tedlock, Dennis. 1979. "The Analogic Tradition and the Emergence of a Dialogic Anthropology." *Journal of Anthropological Research* 35:387–400.

Teplitzky, M. L., S. A. Thomas, and G. Y. Nogami. 1988. "Dual Army Career Officers: Job Attitudes and Career Intentions of Male and Female Officers." ARI Technical Report 805. Alexandria, VA: U.S. Army Research Institute for the Behavioral and Social Sciences (AD A199 071).

Terrio, Heidi, et al. 2009. "Traumatic Brain Injury Screening: Preliminary Findings in a US Army Brigade Combat Team." *Journal of Head Trauma Rehabilitation* 24(1):14–23.

Thomas, Kathleen C., Alan R. Ellis, Thomas R. Konrad, Charles E. Holzer, and Joseph P. Morrissey. 2009. "County-Level Estimates of Mental Health Professional Shortage in the United States." *Psychiatric Services* 60(10):1323–28.

Tick, Edward. 2005. *War and the Soul: Healing Our Nation's Veterans from Post-Traumatic Stress Disorder.* Wheaton, IL: Quest Books.

Tolkien, J. R. R. 1937. *The Hobbit, or There and Back Again.* London: Allen and Unwin.

Tracy, Sarah J., and Clifton Scott. 2006. "Sexuality, Masculinity, and Taint Management among Firefighters and Correctional Officers: Getting Down and Dirty with 'America's Heroes' and the 'Scum of Law Enforcement.'" *Management Communication Quarterly* 20:6–38.

Turner, Terence. 1991. "'We Are Parrots,' 'Twins Are Birds': Play of Tropes as Operational Structure." In *Beyond Metaphor: The Theory of Tropes in Anthropology,* edited by James W. Fernandez, pp. 121–58. Stanford, CA: Stanford University Press.

Turner, Victor. 1967. "Betwixt and Between: The Liminal Period in Rites de Passage." In *The Forest of Symbols.* Ithaca, NY: Cornell University Press.

_____. 1972. "Comments and Conclusions." In *The Reversible World: Symbolic Inversion in Art and Society,* edited by Barbara A. Babcock, pp. 276–96. Ithaca, NY: Cornell University Press.

_____. 1974. "Liminal to Liminoid in Play, Flow, and Ritual: An Essay in Comparative Symbology." *Rice University Studies* 60(3):53–92.

_____. 1995 [1969]. *The Ritual Process: Structure and Anti-Structure.* New York: Aldine de Gruyter.

US Army. n.d. "Changing Profile of the Army." Office of Army Demographics.

_____. 2006a. "The Real Warriors Campaign: An Overview." Washington, DC: Department of Defense. http://www.realwarriors.net (accessed August 30, 2013).

_____. 2006b. *Family Readiness Group Leader's Handbook.* Alexandria, VA: Department of the Army.

_____. 2009. "Epidemiological Consultation No. 14-HK-OB1U-09 Investigation of Homicides at Fort Carson, Colorado November 2008-May 2009." Aberdeen Proving Ground, MD: U.S. Army Center for Health Promotion and Preventive Medicine.

_____. 2010. *Health Promotion, Risk Reduction, and Suicide Prevention Report.* Washington, DC: Department of the Army. http://csf2.army.mil/downloads/HP-RR-SPReport2010.pdf (accessed August 30, 2013).

US Army Public Affairs. 2006. "Army Strong Campaign Announced." October 27. http://www.mccoy.army.mil/vtriad_online/10272006/Army_Strong_Campaign_10-27-06.htm (accessed August 2, 2013).

US Army War College. 2011. *Battle Book IV: A Guide for Spouses in Leadership Roles.* Carlisle Barracks, PA: U.S. Army War College. http://www.carlisle.army.mil/usawc/mfp/battlebook/default.cfm (accessed August 30, 2013).

US Marine Corps. 2000. *Combat Stress.* PCN 144 000083 00. Washington, DC: Department of the Navy.

VA/DoD (Veterans Administration/Department of Defense). 2010. *VA/DoD Clinical Practice Guideline for Management of Post-Traumatic Stress.* Washington, DC: Veterans Administration/Department of Defense.

Vagts, Alfred. 1937. *A History of Militarism: Civilian and Military.* New York: W.W. Norton & Company.

Van Gennep, Arnold. 1960. *The Rites of Passage.* Chicago: University of Chicago Press.

Vanden Brook, Tom. 2013. "Pentagon Makes Women in Combat Rule Change Official." *USA Today,* January 24. http://www.usatoday.com/story/news/nation/2013/01/24/women-combat-change-panetta/1861995/ (accessed August 10, 2013).

Varga, Somogy. 2011. "Defining Mental Disorder: Exploring the 'Natural Function' Approach." *Philosophy, Ethics, and Humanities in Medicine* 6(1):1–10.

Vedantam, Shankar. 2005. A Political Debate on Stress Disorder. *The Washington Post,* December 27. http://www.washingtonpost.com/wp-dyn/content/article/2005/12/26/AR2005122600792.html (accessed August 2, 2013).

VHA (Veterans Health Administration). 2012. *Review of Veterans' Access to Mental Health Care.* Document #12-00900-168. Washington, DC: VA Office of Inspector General.

Vonnegut, Kurt. 1969. *Slaughterhouse-Five, or, The Children's Crusade, A Duty-dance with Death.* New York: Dell.

Vrecko, Scott. 2006. "Folk Neurology and the Remaking of Identity." *Molecular Interventions* 6(6):300–3.

Walker, Samuel, and Charles M. Katz. 2005. *The Police in America: An Introduction.* 5th ed. New York: McGraw Hill.

Walsh, David. 2009. "Iraq Veterans Charged with Murders and Other Crimes." World Socialist Web Site, July 28. http://www.wsws.org/articles/2009/jul2009/colo-j28.shtml (accessed August 14, 2013).

Warner, Joel. 2010. "Can a Veterans Court Help Former GIs Find Justice Here at Home?" Westword, February 4. http://www.westword.com/content/printVersion/1392890/ (accessed May 20, 2013).

Warner, John T. 2012. "The Effect of the Civilian Economy on Recruiting and Retention." In *The Eleventh Quadrennial Review of Military Compensation*, pp. 71–91. Washington, DC: Department of Defense. http://militarypay.defense.gov/reports/qrmc/11th_QRMC_Main_Report_(290pp)_Linked.pdf (accessed October 5, 2013).

Watanabe, Henry K., and Peter S. Jensen. 2000. "Young Children's Adaptation to a Military Lifestyle." In *The Military Family: A Practice Guide for Service Providers*, edited by James A. Martin, Leora N. Rosen, and Linette R. Sparacino, pp. 209–23. Westport, CT: Praeger.

Weiss, John. 2007. "Fort Carson Expansion Affects Pueblo As Well." *Colorado Springs Independent*, April 12. http://www.csindy.com/colorado/fort-carson-expansion-affects-pueblo-as-well/Content?oid=1138101 (accessed July 31, 2013).

West, Cornel. 2004. *Democracy Matters: Winning the Fight against Imperialism*. New York: Penguin.

Westwood, J., and H. Turner. 1996. *Marriage and Children as Impediments to Career Progression of Active Duty Career Women Army Officers*. Carlisle Barracks, PA: Army War College (AD A311 198).

Wexler, David B. 1993. "Therapeutic Jurisprudence and the Criminal Courts." *William and Mary Law Review* 35(1):279–99.

Wolin, Sheldon. 2008. *Democracy Incorporated: Managed Democracy and the Specter of Inverted Totalitarianism*. Princeton, NJ: Princeton University Press.

Woock, Randy. 2011. "Army Completes New Piñon Canyon Environmental Assessment." *Trinidad Times*, January 28. http://trinidad-times.com/army-completes-new-pion-canyon-enviromental-accessment-p1457-1.htm (accessed August 14, 2013).

Woolard, Kathryn A. 2006. "Codeswitching." In *A Companion to Linguistic Anthropology*, edited by Alessandro Duranti, pp. 73–94. Malden, MA: Blackwell Publishing.

Wright, Evan. 2005. *Generation Kill*. New York: Berkeley Publishing Group.

Wright, K. Dean, John Gust, and Kelli E. Barnes. 2006. "The Impact of GIS Technology During the 2002-2006 Site Reevaluations at PCMS." Fort Carson, CO: Directorate of Environmental Compliance and Management (DECAM).

Wright, Katie. 2008. "Theorizing Therapeutic Culture: Past Influences, Future Directions." *Journal of Sociology* 44(4):321–36.

Yingling, Paul. 2010. "Breaking Ranks?" *Small Wars Journal*, September 30. http://smallwarsjournal.com/jrnl/art/breaking-ranks (accessed August 30, 2013).

Young, Allan. 1995. *The Harmony of Illusions: Inventing Post-Traumatic Stress Disorder*. Princeton, NJ: Princeton University Press.

_____. 2007. "Bruno and the Holy Fool: Myth, Mimesis, and the Transmission of Traumatic Memories." In *Understanding Trauma: Integrating Biological, Clinical and Cultural Perspectives*, edited by Laurence J. Kirmayer, Robert Lemelson, and Mark Barad, pp. 339–62. Cambridge, UK: Cambridge University Press.

Young, Allan, and Naomi Breslau. 2007. "Troublesome Memories: Reflections on the Future." *Journal of Anxiety Disorders* 21:230–2.

Zimmerman, Joseph Francis. 1999. *The New England Town Meeting: Democracy in Action*. Westport, CT: Praeger.

# Index

Note: Italicized page numbers indicate photographs or figures.

# about the authors

**Sarah Hautzinger** earned her doctorate in anthropology at the Johns Hopkins University and is associate professor of anthropology at Colorado College. A political anthropologist, Hautzinger's research emphasizes the institutional processes related to interpersonal, state, and transnational levels of violent conflict. She has published *Violence in the City of Women: Police and Batterers in Bahia, Brazil* (University of California Press, 2007) about the creation of all-women police stations in a newly democratizing Brazil, and in addition to her work on the post-9/11 wars with Jean Scandlyn, she has published on tourist economies, research methods, and international community-based learning.

**Jean Scandlyn** worked as a registered nurse in a variety of clinical settings prior to earning her doctorate in anthropology at Columbia University. She is currently a research associate professor of health and behavioral sciences and anthropology at the University of Colorado Denver. A medical anthropologist, Scandlyn's research focuses on the transition from adolescence to adulthood, health care delivery to underserved populations, and global health. Along with her research work on the post-9/11 wars with Sarah Hautzinger, she has published on conflicts over spending for public education, homeless and runaway youth, child labor, ethnographic field schools, and teaching qualitative research methods.